CHARLES EVANS HUGHES

THE MACMILLAN COMPANY
NEW YORK · BOSTON · CHICAGO
DALLAS · ATLANTA · SAN FRANCISCO

MACMILLAN AND CO., LIMITED
LONDON · BOMBAY · CALCUTTA
MADRAS · MELBOURNE

**THE MACMILLAN COMPANY
OF CANADA, LIMITED**
TORONTO

BY MERLO J. PUSEY

Charles Evans Hughes

IN TWO VOLUMES

Volume Two

THE MACMILLAN COMPANY

New York · 1951

COPYRIGHT, 1951, BY MERLO J. PUSEY

First Printing

PRINTED IN THE UNITED STATES OF AMERICA

CONTENTS

Volume Two

ILLUSTRATIONS

Volume Two

CHARLES EVANS HUGHES

Chapter 39

SECRETARY OF STATE

PROBABLY no Secretary of State has ever faced a more chaotic and perplexing situation than Hughes inherited from the Wilson régime. "The murk of the Paris peace settlement," as the London *Times* remarked, "lay over international relations." [1] Nearly two and a half years after the fighting had ceased the United States was still technically at war. Relations with Mexico were immersed in confusion and bitterness. Yankee imperialism in Santo Domingo, Nicaragua, and Haiti cast a shadow over our relations with Latin America. In the Far East suspicion and distrust were rampant. "There is hardly a phase of our foreign policy," observed *Current Opinion*, "that is not hanging in mid-air." [2]

In the face of this spreading demoralization, the State Department, as Root said, was "in a condition of virtual coma." [3] For months it had been feebly putting aside international problems against the day when a new hand could take over the helm. The United States' prestige abroad was in a state of eclipse. The big, sprawling democracy that had mustered so much power in wartime had lapsed into disorder and impotence—a fact that contributed greatly to the malaise afflicting the postwar world.

When the transition came, it was like a sudden passing out of fog into light. Moving with speed almost unknown in diplomatic circles, Hughes inaugurated firm, clear, simple, and straightforward policies in each area needing attention. Without forsaking idealism, he was realistic enough to talk about interests, islands, ships, and national rights when more lofty projects were unattainable. "Our foreign relations," as one commentator remarked, "had been the subject of passion. Mr. Hughes made them the subject of reason."

On his very first day in office the affirmative character of his policy was in evidence. Costa Rica and Panama were exchanging hot lead on top of hot words across their controversial boundary. Their dispute had been arbitrated years before by President Loubet of France and later by Chief Justice White of the United States, but Panama had reneged after the second award was made, and Costa Rica had resorted to force to take the territory that had been awarded to her. Hughes had begun probing into the controversy on inaugura-

[1] March 3, 1921.   [2] April, 1921, p. 442.
[3] Speech, Nov. 10, 1925; Hughes Papers.

tion day even before he had been sworn in. The next day he conferred with Undersecretary Davis and Sumner Welles, chief of the Latin American Division, and got approval of his plans from the White House. Before nightfall, pointed notes had gone out to the two little Central American countries, telling them to stop fighting, and two warships had been dispatched to protect United States interests.

Costa Rica obediently withdrew her troops. Panama too ceased firing but stubbornly rejected the White award. Hughes sternly called upon Panama to live up to her solemn agreement. When the Panamanian National Assembly again turned down the award in secret session, Hughes threatened to take such steps as might be necessary to establish the line where the arbitrators placed it.[4] He felt that our protégé Panama simply could not be permitted to flout an arbitration award that she had pledged herself to accept. The United States had guaranteed the independence of Panama. In order to fulfill its obligations, the Secretary said, it would have to know where the Panama boundary lay. Moreover, a naked question of international justice had been raised—a question arousing the interest of all Latin America. On August 18 he informed Panama that the "reasonable time" allowed her to withdraw from the Coto region had expired and that Costa Rica would be justified in taking jurisdiction over it. United States marines were sent to the Canal Zone. A few days later Panama evacuated the disputed district, and the White award became effective.

Hughes' handling of the case was typical. His policy was to be underscored by prompt and vigorous action, an alert sense of justice, and firm insistence upon the recognition of rights and obligations.

The Secretary lost no time in gathering the numerous reins controlling foreign policy into his own hands. Even before he was sworn in he observed that Colby was preparing to make about twenty-five shifts in the diplomatic service and sent word to the retiring Secretary that he would prefer to make those changes himself. Colby acquiesced cheerfully.

Within the department Hughes had a free hand in shaping his organization and made the most of it to assemble a staff of career men. His first Undersecretary, Henry P. Fletcher, was a personal friend of President Harding's, but Hughes selected him. Fletcher was an able and experienced diplomat who had served in the United States legations in Cuba and China and had been ambassador to Chile and Mexico. Organization of the department became his special assignment while the Secretary gave most of his time to major questions of policy. Although Fletcher was devoted to his chief, he gladly left the department in 1922 to become ambassador to Belgium. The Undersecretaryship had proved to be a little dull because most of the work was done by the Secretary himself.

[4] *Foreign Relations of the United States, 1921,* I, 212.

William Phillips, another career man, then minister to the Netherlands, was brought in to take Fletcher's place. Hughes' third Undersecretary was Joseph C. Grew, who had made a brilliant record in Egypt, Mexico, Russia, Germany, the State Department, and the secretariat at the Paris Peace Conference, in addition to having been minister to Denmark and to Switzerland. The Secretary made a routine practice of bringing men home from foreign posts so as to enrich the department by contact with diplomats experienced in the field. At the same time he sent men from the department to foreign posts to broaden their outlook and give our diplomats abroad a better understanding of the policies taking shape in Washington.

Not a single expert in the department was ousted to create a vacancy for any deserving politician. Hughes leaned backward, as he had done at Albany, to avoid any suspicion that he might be building up any personal organization. He even retained Colby's secretary, William H. Beck, in the same capacity. Appointments were made on merit, and promotions went to the men who demonstrated the greatest capacity for advancement in the service. Some of the President's senatorial friends put him under pressure to set up in the State Department a sort of watchdog to look out for their political interests, but Hughes would have none of it, and Harding did not press his request. "I am the only politician in the department," the Secretary used to say.

He assembled a distinguished roster of Assistant Secretaries who have since served in American embassies and legations. Among them were Fred Morris Dearing, later ambassador to Peru; Leland Harrison, later minister to Sweden, Uruguay, Rumania, and Switzerland; Robert Woods Bliss, later minister to Sweden and ambassador to Argentina; Wilbur J. Carr, later minister to Czechoslovakia; John V. A. MacMurray, who became minister to China, Estonia, Latvia, and Lithuania as well as ambassador to Turkey; J. Butler Wright, who presided over our legations in Hungary, Uruguay, and Czechoslovakia and our embassy in Cuba.

Men of training and ability were either retained or brought in to head the various divisions in the department. Sumner Welles remained head of the Latin American Division until 1922, when he was succeeded by Francis White, later minister to Czechoslovakia. William R. Castle, Jr., in charge of Western European Affairs, was later to become Undersecretary in the Hoover régime. Allen W. Dulles was chief of Near Eastern Affairs; John V. A. MacMurray, of Far Eastern Affairs (before his appointment as Assistant Secretary); and De Witt C. Poole, of Russian Affairs. Charles Cheney Hyde, later Hamilton Fish professor of international law and diplomacy at Columbia University, came in as solicitor in 1923.

Hughes' door was always open to these men. He dealt with them in the utmost frankness and exercised a profound influence over them. His manner, his integrity, his industry, and a sort of intellectual aura that characterized the man seemed to inspire his associates with his own zeal.

While he won the unbounded esteem of the men around him, some of them discovered that he had a temper. A piece of incompetent work would strike fire in his eye. With a few knife-edged words he could strip a blunder to appalling nakedness. Yet his indignation seemed always to have an inner lining of good humor. One day a document prepared by Undersecretary Grew brought a flare-up. "You've missed the whole point," Hughes impatiently complained. Grew was making an inconspicuous exit when the Secretary looked up at him and beamed, "Nothing personal, you know." [5]

Castle smelled trouble one morning when his buzzer sounded and he heard a sharp, "Come down." "How do you suppose I can do my work," the Secretary challenged as soon as Castle entered the room, "if you send me an idiotic paper like this?" [6] Castle murmured something about having honestly expressed his views and went back to his office thinking that the end of his career in the State Department was at hand. Hughes soon buzzed again and, instead of firing Castle, he apologized. His explosion had come after he had read only two pages of Castle's memorandum. Having now finished the document, he said he agreed with the conclusion but thought some of the reasoning was faulty.

A spirited encounter between the Secretary and Solicitor Hyde followed the accidental transfer of a carelessly drafted note to the President's office. As soon as the mistake was discovered, Hyde completely redrafted the note and sent it to the Secretary for a final check. Weary from overwork, Hughes sent for Hyde and irritably cross-examined him. [7]

"Look at this first sentence," he commanded. "What does it mean?" The solicitor explained. "And this third paragraph!" Again Hyde defended his product with facts and logic. "And what about this last sentence?" the Secretary finally challenged. As the solicitor finished his last explanation, a sudden flash of sunshine completely obliterated the scowl on the Secretary's face. "Hyde," he exclaimed, "you're all right." These two men came to understand each other so well that they sometimes conversed in racy, half-finished sentences.

The swiftness with which Hughes' mood could change from stern determination to affability is legendary among his associates. Butler Wright asked the Secretary if he would greet the students of a girls' school who were to visit the department. "You know I have no time for that sort of thing," was the testy reply. "You see them." When the young ladies arrived several days later, however, Wright tried again.

[5] Author's interview with Mr. Grew, March 4, 1949.
[6] Author's interview with Mr. Castle, March 31, 1949.
[7] Author's interview with Professor Hyde, Oct. 1, 1947.

"The young ladies are here," he said, peering into the Secretary's office.

"What young ladies?" Hughes demanded.

Wright repeated his previous explanation and urged the Secretary not to disappoint a group of young women who were eager to get a glimpse of him. Hughes resisted stubbornly.

"Couldn't you just take the bull by the horns and get it over with?" Wright pleaded.

"Don't you think you have your metaphor a little mixed, Mr. Wright?" the Secretary retorted, his whiskers suddenly dancing with merriment. "Show the young ladies in."

No one in the department cared to challenge Hughes. His prodigious industry made him master of every subject that was likely to come under discussion, and his keen mind cut through sham, sophistry, and superficiality with equal ease. "He has an amazing mind," Castle wrote in his diary, "but demands terrifyingly quick reactions from his subordinates. I should hate to be his undersecretary unless I had a mind which worked like lightning." [8] Yet Hughes was no intellectual tyrant. He highly respected a subordinate who could hold his ground with the support of facts and reason. None of his associates had cause to complain of unfairness, and he stood by the men under him with the same fidelity that he expected of them.

Solicitor Hyde was troubled by a summons from the House Committee on Foreign Affairs to testify on the constitutionality of the liquor-traffic treaty that the department had negotiated with Great Britain. "Don't you go," Hughes told him. "The House has no right to inquire into a treaty that requires ratification by the Senate only. You refuse, and if they put you in jail, I'll get you out." [9]

Hugh R. Wilson took over the Division of Current Information with some trepidation because of reports he had heard of Hughes' severity. "I soon found, however," he tells us, "that the inspiration and joy of working with him far outweighed any apprehension that might have come from his occasional caustic manner. . . . At times his booming laugh would burst forth, at times he would enter into reminiscence, and on those occasions no character could have been more interesting and more fascinating. Even after months of experience with him one was startled at the breadth of his knowledge, at the penetration of his intellect, at his ability to thrust unerringly and swiftly to the heart of any matter." [10]

Sumner Welles was especially impressed by the Secretary's generous recognition of the work done for him. "No chief," he said, "could better inspire his subordinates to the best that was in them. Those of us who served under him

[8] Castle's diary, 1924, I, 57.
[9] Author's interview with Professor Hyde, Oct. 1, 1947.
[10] *Diplomat Between Wars* (New York, Longmans, 1941), pp. 162f.

will always regard that experience as beyond price." [11] The personal loyalty and devotion that Hughes inspired in amazing degree was to survive as long as his associates lived.

In spite of his belief in experts, Hughes virtually acted as his own secretary, entering his office appointments in a desk diary and his social engagements in a little pocket diary. His secretary, William H. Beck, became his personal stenographer. Beck's ability to write shorthand at more than two hundred words a minute made it possible for Hughes to dictate at top speed. Beck would then read back his notes, with Hughes rapidly inserting punctuations, corrections, and additions. By this means the letter or statement would be whipped into final form before being typed, and no rewriting would be necessary. Often Beck would fill half a shorthand book at a sitting and then have to redictate part of it to two other stenographers. So devoted was he to his boss that he "gladly gave up social and other engagements" in the evening and on Sundays to take dictation.

In keeping his fingers on every major activity of the department, Hughes made a practice of calling in the experts and specialists as well as the division chiefs and Assistant Secretaries. Any one of them might be asked to perform a miracle on short notice. Late one afternoon Hughes handed Solicitor Fred K. Nielsen a stack of documents a foot high and asked for a report the next morning. Nielsen had to work most of the night. Incidents of this sort ruffled the department's customary placidity, however routine they might be to the Secretary himself.

His office hours usually stretched from 9:00 A.M. to 7:00 P.M. He used to say that he distrusted his judgment after five o'clock but had to use it anyway. Reports from the various divisions and dispatches from the embassies invariably accumulated on his desk near the end of the day. Nearly every night he took a pile of these home with him, and on Saturday night he always cleared his desk by taking home a suitcase or two full of papers for Sunday reading. The next morning he would dispose of these items with the dispatch of a naval captain giving orders from the bridge. At fifty-nine he had the energy and exuberance of a man of forty.

The Secretary frequently went home at noon to lunch with Mrs. Hughes. Walking briskly both ways and eating lightly, with no cigar to linger over, he would return promptly, swallow a dyspepsia tablet, and wonder why the department was almost deserted. His buzzer would buzz in vain, with consequent embarrassment to "the boys" of the department when they did return. The example of his industry had far more effect upon the department than did its leisurely customs upon him. "It is amazing," Castle wrote in his diary, "how the Department machine limps when Mr. Hughes' hand is removed."

[11] *Washington Post*, Sept. 7, 1948.

A page from the yearbook in which his engagements are listed will give an idea of the pressure he was under:

9:30 Senator Lodge.
10:45 House Foreign Affairs Committee.
12:00 General George W. Wingate.
12:15 White House to see the President.
12:45 Mr. Emery.
3:00 Mr. H. G. Chilton.
3:15 Minister Hugh Gibson.
3:45 Senator McCormick.
4:00 M. Francisco Peynado.
5:00 Ambassador Houghton.
5:15 Secretary Mellon.
8:00 Representative and Mrs. Ernest R. Ackerman—dinner in honor of Ambassador Houghton.

Hughes' freedom in managing the department did not extend to the selection of ambassadors and ministers. The President had incurred political debts, and in some instances he had made specific promises as to the pay-off. To be sure, the Secretary was able to get a good many careerists and outside men of distinction into diplomatic posts. Myron T. Herrick, former Governor of Ohio, became ambassador to France for the second time. Alanson B. Houghton left a seat in Congress for the ambassadorship at Berlin. Hughes' old friend Jacob Gould Schurman went to China as minister after twenty-eight years as president of Cornell University. But campaign contributors and misfits were chosen often enough to irk so ardent an apostle of merit appointments as Hughes. As he grew impatient of trying to work with some of the men that were sent to foreign capitals, his only consolation was that "his was the common lot of all Secretaries since John Quincy Adams."

Sometimes Hughes was able to scotch these raids, for Harding was reluctant to override the Secretary's judgment. One day he called Hughes on the telephone and said that he wished to give a specified diplomatic post to an individual he must have known to be unqualified. Hughes vigorously protested.

"But I want to appoint him," the President said; "I want to appoint him."

"Of course you are at liberty to do so," the Secretary retorted, "if that is your decision."

The appointment was not made.

Nothing could dissuade the President, however, from carrying through his most notorious pay-off. George Harvey, editor of the *North American Review*, had lived with Harding during much of the campaign and poured his fluency into many a Harding speech. Now he coveted the position of ambassador to the Court of St. James's. Harvey had broken with Wilson to support Hughes in 1916; there was no bad blood between him and Hughes. The Secretary recognized Harvey's ability and his journalistic knack for picking up information. But he also saw that Harvey's cocky manner and his "one notorious failing" (addiction to alcohol) would make him a liability to the diplomatic service. One night at a private dinner Hughes noted that the arrogant editor was intoxicated, that he talked recklessly and scarcely knew what he was saying. In trying to convince the President that Harvey was not the man for the embassy in London, Hughes made use of this incident. At the time Harding seemed to agree that the appointment should not be made.

But Harvey knew the President's weakness. When Harding taxed him with irresponsible conduct, the "passionate patriot" burst into tears and promised to give up drinking. That settled it. The President concluded that, in view of Harvey's great service in the campaign and his promise to reform, he would have to make good his pledge. For Hughes this meant repeated embarrassment. According to many reports reaching the department, Harvey did not keep his pledge to the President and at times became quite unreliable.[12] By nature he was always presumptuous, and on two occasions he went so far as to dispute the veracity of Lord Curzon, the British Foreign Minister. His speeches were often at variance with State Department policy. As if to add insult to injury, he appears to have inspired rumors that he was to become Secretary of State in Hughes' place.

On January 21, 1923, the *World* and several other newspapers published stories of sharp differences between Harding and Hughes, with Harvey on the side of the President, and indicated on the authority of "an informed and dependable administration source" that the Secretary was about to return to the practice of law. Hughes publicly denied the report and in private called it a "stupid lie." [13] In a tart radiogram telling Harvey, "you are reported to have given expression to this antagonism during your recent visit here," he asked the ambassador to help "squelch" the rumor by a statement if he approved of that course. Harvey sent a message to the *North American Review* saying that the statements attributed to him were "absolutely false" and that he was in complete accord with Secretary Hughes. Nothing could wipe out the friction between them, however, so long as Harvey remained in London.

Early in his régime Hughes reorganized the department and began a systematic campaign to improve the Foreign Service. Under the impact of war the department had undergone a sudden growth without much order or pattern. Hughes recast the department with special emphasis upon regional divisions devoted to distinct geographical areas, which greatly enhanced its capacity to deal with foreign affairs on a global scale.

In seeking reorganization of the Foreign Service by law, the Secretary out-

[12] CEH, Notes, p. 357.   [13] CEH to Theodore T. Joslin, Feb. 6, 1923.

lined three major objectives. The first was to obtain men of special aptitude and training. He was full of sympathy for the practice of going outside the service for men of wide experience, sagacity, and ability to fill important diplomatic posts. Such men could reinvigorate diplomacy. Yet they would be helpless without the backing of trained staffs. The bulk of the work would necessarily have to be carried on by career officials, and the ablest young men simply would not be available for this work unless the service could offer them fair opportunities to become heads of missions.

With isolationism rampant, some extremists in Congress were saying that communications had improved so much that it was no longer necessary for the United States to have ambassadors in other countries. "An hour of direct intercourse between responsible ministers," Hughes pointedly replied, "is often worth months of written communications . . . it is a poor patriot who would scrap both his ships and his diplomats at the same time. . . . Every American should feel ashamed that any country in the world should have a better diplomatic organization than the United States. This is not a matter simply of national pride; it is a matter of national security." [14]

The second focal point of his attack was the salary scale that made the diplomatic service "a rich man's club." Budding young diplomats were hired at $2,500 a year and advanced to a maximum of only $4,000. "The salaries are so low in the classified Diplomatic Service," Hughes complained, "that the choice of candidates is largely restricted to young men of wealthy families who are able and willing to a considerable extent to pay their own way. It is a most serious thing to be compelled to say that a young man without means, who desires to marry and bring up a family after the American tradition, cannot be encouraged to enter upon one of the most important careers that the country has to offer. I say bluntly that no American can face the facts without a sense of humiliation, and he is compelled to qualify his boasting of our intelligence and civilization so long as this condition continues."

Hughes' third objective was to merge the Diplomatic and Consular services. The Diplomatic Service could not confine its work wholly to political interests; nor could the Consular Service devote itself wholly to commercial interests. By bringing the two units together into a single Foreign Service, the Secretary insisted, better use could be made of special aptitudes and talents and a wider range of opportunity would be opened to men interested in representing their country abroad.

These far-reaching reforms were finally achieved in the Rogers Act of 1924. Wilbur Carr worked out the technique of the measure in collaboration with Representative John Jacob Rogers of Massachusetts, but the inspiration for its enactment came largely from Secretary Hughes. The Act lifted the

[14] Speech to U.S. Chamber of Commerce, May 18, 1922.

upper limit on Foreign Service salaries from $4,000 to $10,000 and granted allowances for rent, light, and exchange-rate adjustments. It made all appointments and promotions in the Foreign Service contingent upon personal merit rather than upon politics. A contributory pensions system enabled aged employees to retire. The consular and diplomatic branches were consolidated, and the new Foreign Service at last emerged as a genuine career service.

Probably the most notable result of these changes was the democratization of the Foreign Service in the following decades. Men already representing the United States abroad also saw in the Act new incentives for exerting their best efforts. A "vastly superior organization" began to take shape.[15] The Rogers Act came to be recognized as "the great basic charter of the modern diplomatic service." [16] Not until 1946 was the Foreign Service extensively reorganized again and the Act of that year was essentially a refinement and extension of the principles that Hughes helped to shape in 1924.

In the social aspects of his assignment Hughes was no less wholehearted than in his official duties. While neither he nor Mrs. Hughes had any hankering for social life, they entered upon a program of entertainment as ambitious as any ever undertaken by a Secretary of State. Nor were they long-faced about it. At one of the gatherings of the State Department Club, composed of officers and personnel of the department, he gaily announced that he and Undersecretary Phillips were prepared "to dine for our country."

The Secretary could always be relied upon to attend any celebration at an embassy or legation, whether it was the wedding of a diplomat's daughter, the observance of a king's birthday, or a reception for a visiting dignitary. In addition, the Hugheses dined once a year with the heads of every diplomatic mission in Washington and entertained every chief of mission in their own home.

Mrs. Hughes brought to this task the same natural charm and grace that had previously distinguished her as a hostess. Her table was always beautifully arranged. Some thought that she went to extraordinary efforts to make up for the lack of alcoholic beverages at their dinners and receptions. The Hugheses served no intoxicants during the prohibition era, although the Secretary never hesitated to take a cocktail at the embassies or elsewhere beyond the reach of the "noble experiment."

Even if a diplomatic dinner were "deadly," it might yield dividends of intelligence. "I seldom went to a dinner party," Hughes said, "without gaining some information which helped me in my work. And many highly prized

[15] Hugh R. Wilson, *Diplomat Between Wars* (New York, Longmans, 1941), p. 167.
[16] Bertram D. Hulen, *Inside the Department of State* (New York, Whittlesey House, 1939), p. 89. Copyright, 1939, by Bertram D. Hulen.

friendships resulted from these meetings." [17] His extraordinary grasp on the forces and trends that were shaping the world had a direct relationship to his personal contacts with the diplomatic corps.

The diplomats learned that they could rely upon anything Hughes told them and that he always respected their confidence. He spoke to them with disarming candor and for the most part got candor in return. Sometimes his directness shocked the professionals in the department. In the traditional sense of the word, his approach was lacking in diplomacy, but that was because he believed sincerity, frankness, and a free meeting of minds were more important than any conventional jargon invented to conceal thought. Hating pomposity and duplicity, he was likely to be severe in dealing with either. When the Iranian minister called a third time in connection with his country's attempt to avoid payment of indemnity for an American who had been stoned to death in Iran, Hughes cut him off and gave his own review of the unsavory facts and ended by saying, "Good day, Mr. Minister." The chargé d'affaires of another country who had been given an appointment with the Secretary became so fearful that he could not answer Hughes' questions that he called to have his appointment shifted to someone else in the department. But if Hughes unceremoniously cut through pretense, he never took unfair advantage of a diplomat.

His method was open diplomacy, but he well understood that diplomacy must be secret in process if it is to be open in result. He had little patience with those who seemed to think that differences between sovereign governments could be settled in a sort of town meeting. Negotiators for each country had to be free to make tentative suggestions and later withdraw them without embarrassment—to make concessions without losing face before their own people. "Even the most democratic governments must desire to succeed in their negotiations," Hughes said, "and there is no reason why democracy should turn upon itself and deprive its agents of its essential means of defense." [18] Yet secrecy in negotiations was only a means of attaining relations between peoples that would be open, candid, and direct.

Hughes brought into our foreign relations a concept that was the reverse of diplomatic intrigue. What he asked of other nations was simply good faith, respect for American rights, equal opportunities, and honesty and fairness in the settlement of any differences that might arise. Anything smacking of deception or hidden purposes was beneath the dignity of a democratic power. Those were the tools of despotism. The United States had a mission to stand out in all its dealings with other countries as an exemplar of the justice that it sought to attain between man and man within its own jurisdiction. "The first

[17] CEH, Notes, p. 360.   [18] Address at University of Michigan, June 19, 1922.

requirement of those who demand justice and security," he said, "is to give justice and security." [19]

Under his guidance, therefore, the department did not take up the fight of any American interest abroad simply because it was American. In each case he asked, not what American power might command, but where the equities lay. At no time, his associates say,[20] did he sponsor any unfair cause. His aim was to place international relations on a basis of high principle without departing from any legitimate national interest. "All things are possible," he said, "if nations are willing to be just to each other."

This pursuit of justice on a global scale was an expression of Hughes' deep interest in the welfare of mankind. He refused to fall in with any of the petty jealousies of nations or their short-sighted scrambling for power. Repeatedly he identified American interests with the peace, prosperity, and well-being of peoples in other parts of the world.

The legalism that sometimes pursues lawyers when they operate in other fields is noticeably absent from his conduct as Secretary of State. Indeed, he often irritated other lawyers in the department by subordinating law to common sense. After Congress passed the Immigration Act of 1921, William Roy Vallance of the Legal Division sought to have the department recognize boundary changes resulting from the war and its aftermath so as to facilitate the application of the new quotas. Castle and Dulles resisted on the ground that boundaries were then too fluid to be given formal approval. Vallance argued that the department should not recognize Rumanian visas for immigrants coming from Bessarabia unless it also recognized the transfer of Bessarabia from Russia to Rumania. Political refugees were coming to America from Bessarabia in large numbers, however, and Hughes declined to exclude them on a legal technicality.

"Vallance," he said, with a good-natured smile that seemed to take any sting out of his words, "you have made your record perfectly clear as a lawyer. As you say, your plan is legally simple. You can remain legally simple by remaining tightly shut in a hermetically sealed compartment. But I cannot afford to make this Government ridiculous. I must face facts and surmount difficulties arising from those facts. I have respect for the law but I am not willing to be a damn fool." [21]

The Secretary expressed this same guiding principle in more compact form when he addressed the Brazilian Bar Association in Rio de Janeiro on September 12, 1922. "I have great respect for the appropriate technique which is essential to correct administration," he said, "but I have no sympathy with those who lose the spirit of the law in the worship of its garments."

[19] Speech to Pan American Conference of Women, April 28, 1922.
[20] Sumner Welles, Charles Cheney Hyde, J. V. A. MacMurray, and others.
[21] Castle's Diary, 1923, p. 80.

Having a completely open policy, Hughes went to extraordinary effort to let the people know about it. "I always felt," he said, "that I should be greatly relieved if I could shout from the housetops every morning everything I had done or proposed to do." [22] That was not always possible, but Hughes' consistent effort was to see how much he could disclose and not how much he could withhold. He felt a special responsibility to educate the people in foreign affairs; for Americans were only beginning to think internationally at a time when the fate of the world truly hung on the decisions they would make.

Another factor counted heavily in determining his attitude. "A public officer has always got to remind himself," he told the press, "and he ought to say every morning as he approaches his task: 'I am a servant and it is my business to see what I can do for the American people. I am not a boss, and my little authority or great authority that I happen to have for a day, is not a personal perquisite.' " [23]

In spite of this attitude, his first brush with the press as Secretary of State brought sparks of friction. His notes in the flare-up between Panama and Costa Rica had been published by the newspapers without authorization before they could reach the recipient governments. Hughes expressed his displeasure and asked that all news concerning the activities of the department be funneled through himself or other high officials. Fearful of being "gagged," the press reacted with typical vehemence. But its complaint was soon forgotten because of the unprecedented flow of news that came from the Secretary himself.

Sweeping away the timorousness and taboos that had prevailed under his predecessor, Hughes became a bubbling fountain of information. He held two press conferences daily, with Henry Fletcher sometimes taking over one of them. The stilted and ponderous verbiage of the old school gave way to direct, lucid, and succinct answers to reporters' questions. In ten minutes he would range from Mexico to Yap, from China to Mesopotamia, with candor that sometimes brought applause from the blasé men of the press. "The lucidity and frankness of his press conferences," Sumner Welles was to write a quarter of a century later, "are a Washington tradition." [24]

Much of what he had to say to the press was "not for quotation." He spoke for enlightenment of the public and not to get his name in the newspapers. He gave the press the background facts of every situation affecting our foreign relations, in so far as the facts could be disclosed without jeopardizing negotiations that might be under way. In addition to his press conferences, his door was always open to reporters. "I wish every man in the newspaper work to feel that if there is anything that he wants to know, he can come to me at any time and ask," Hughes said. "If I can't tell him, I will say so, but there

[22] CEH, Notes, p. 358.
[23] The Pathway of Peace (New York, Harper, 1925), p. 247.
[24] Washington Post, Sept. 7, 1948.

is no reason why anyone should set afloat a doubtful report because he hasn't the opportunity at least to ask the Secretary whether his information is accurate or not." [25]

The Secretary further clinched his favorable standing with the press by strict adherence to two cardinal rules. The first was: Never lie to a newspaperman. Deceptive propaganda might appear to be useful in some instances, but it was a perilous indulgence. Hughes' experience had taught him that newspaper confidence in his integrity was the first essential to a successful public career, and he instinctively avoided anything that might cast a shadow upon that confidence. His second rule was to treat all newspapermen alike. No one of them could be favored without antagonizing all the others. It was only the experienced journalists in Washington to whom he spoke freely, however. Repeated misquotation had left him ultracautious about giving interviews during his travels to reporters he did not know.

Lighter touches often enlivened his press conferences. It was not unusual for Hughes to roar with laughter or banter the journalists about their inaccurate use of words. When classical-minded Matthew Tighe wrote Hughes a note in Latin to ask the substance of his conference with Ambassador Harvey, the Secretary replied to his "learned friend"—also in Latin. To a reporter who asked if "certain deductions" could not be drawn from the Secretary's silence on a subject about which he had been questioned, he laughingly said that the usual "deductions" of the press reminded him of a definition of oratory: "Unhampered by facts, unrestrained by circumstance, unlimited by time."

The newspapers and magazines broke out with a rash of exuberance over the Hughes policy of talking to the country through their columns. Day-to-day news of foreign affairs began to rival local murders and the Stillman divorce case for front-page space. The leading correspondents in Washington, in addition to the regular reporters covering the State Department, thronged the Secretary's conferences as they have never done since. In his relations with the press, wrote Arthur Wallace Dunn, Secretary Hughes is "the equal, if not the superior, of all his predecessors."

At the end of Hughes' first year in the State Department the Washington correspondents, whom Matthew Tighe had dubbed the Independent Order of Ungodly Intellectuals, presented him with a pair of golden shears in token of their "gratitude" for his "kindly assistance to them in their work." To this formal inscription on the shears Tighe added an expression of the correspondents' "personal esteem, regard and affection." Responding with a twinkle in his eye, Hughes said that he would use the gift, not to cut the Gordian knots of international diplomacy, as Tighe had suggested, but to clip from the news-

[25] *The Pathway of Peace,* p. 249.

papers the voluminous accounts of his activities so as to keep himself "duly humble" and avoid any "lack of understanding on my part of my duty." [26]

A wholly unpremeditated demonstration of the Secretary's mental endowments set tongues wagging in the press room. As he left his desk to hold his press conference, an official handed him a three-page memorandum that was ready for public announcement. While walking to the conference room, he focused his photographic mind on the three pages, then thrust them into an inside pocket and made the announcement from memory. Reporters later compared the stenographic record of the conference with the memorandum and found that Hughes had recited its content with the change of only one unimportant word.[27]

More astonishing to the press than Hughes' intellectual feats was his cordiality. While he had been in private life, his reputation as a "human icicle" had been refurbished. Such a man, the press had assumed, would direct our foreign relations with cold and unrelenting formality. Instead the correspondents found the new Secretary to be "a veritable spring of geniality."

So striking was the contrast between the austerity of his reputation and the good humor of his day-to-day performance that many journalists rushed into print with their "discovery." "The new Hughes" became the theme of a monotonous plethora of feature stories and articles. He was portrayed as being in his "second youth," as always smiling and radiating abundant energy, and as fast becoming "one of the most popular men in public life." A wit struck close to the truth when he said, "Mr. Hughes never lets his dignity get thawed or his geniality get frozen."

Hughes' close friends and some of the older correspondents who had known him at Albany smiled knowingly at these "discoveries." No doubt he had mellowed as most men do at the approach of sixty. But the only significant changes were in the nature of his work and his accessibility to the press. In the sense of controlling his appetites, of avoiding loose gossip and questionable conduct, of adhering steadfastly to his purposes, and of mastering each task with the utmost seriousness, he was as austere as he had ever been. What the news writers had really discovered was that the pressure under which he worked and his "moral unapproachableness," as William Hard called it, did not cloud his sense of humor or dull his enjoyment of living. Hughes could relish laughter, join wholeheartedly in funmaking, and sound the depths of emotion without wavering one iota from the path that his towering intellect marked out for him. In this we have perhaps the most striking aspect of his character.

[26] *Ibid.*, p. 248.   [27] Hulen, *op. cit.*, p. 50.

Chapter 40

THE HARDING CABINET

PRESIDENT HARDING called his Cabinet together for the first time on March 8, 1921. For two hours the new presidential advisers sat around the big mahogany table in the White House Cabinet room discussing the responsibilities they had taken over and sizing up one another and their new chief. The Cabinet was a symbol of the changed order that had been established in Washington, but a many-sided symbol as diverse and complex as the character of Warren Harding himself.

On the President's left was a wizened and taciturn but shrewd and fabulously wealthy little man who was holding public office for the first time— Andrew W. Mellon, Secretary of the Treasury. Mellon seldom spoke, but when questioned about any business, economic, or financial matter he seemed always to know the answer. Beside him sat the smooth and sinister Harry M. Daugherty, whom Harding had rewarded with the Attorney Generalship over many vehement protests. The large, good-natured fellow of limited capacity sitting next in line was Edwin Denby, Secretary of the Navy. Then came short, thick-set Henry C. Wallace, publisher of an Iowa farm journal and now Secretary of Agriculture, and James J. (Puddler Jim) Davis, the Secretary of Labor.

At the far end of the table sat the "calm little Yankee," Vice President Calvin Coolidge, looking very much the fifth wheel that he was. Harding always gave the canny New Englander a chance to speak after members of the Cabinet had had their say. "Well," was Coolidge's typical remark, "I don't see anything we can do about the railroad situation." [1] But Coolidge let nothing escape him.

At the President's right was Hughes, looking the acme of dignity in his gray striped trousers, white-trimmed vest, and morning coat. Next to him was John W. Weeks of Massachusetts, engineer, banker, former Representative and Senator, and now Secretary of War. Trim and alert Will Hays, who had so ably conducted the Harding campaign and was now Postmaster General, sat between Weeks and Albert B. Fall, Secretary of the Interior. At the end of the row was Herbert Hoover, Secretary of Commerce, who was hated by the Old Guard and who, next to Hughes, held the distinction of having the best mind in the Cabinet.

[1] Author's interview with CEH, Nov. 19, 1946.

Shaggy, mustachioed Fall held a special distinction of a different sort. He was the most garrulous member of the Cabinet. Ranging over a wide field, he would chatter about anything outside the scope of his own department. Secretary Hughes summarized his impression of the New Mexican windbag in words much sharper than he was wont to use: "He would discourse at length on foreign affairs, showing neither acumen, discretion, nor accurate knowledge. But he thought he was an authority. His flow of words without wisdom was very boring to me at least, and I think to others. I had little to do with him, but I did not suspect him of anything worse than vanity and mental indigestion." [2]

Hughes assumed that the Cabinet would function as a team of presidential advisers. When the President called on him at the first meeting, he described rather fully the important business on which the State Department was currently working. Some others followed this example. The warp of administration and the woof of policy-making were thus woven together at the highest level of government.

This cooperative spirit quickly wilted, however, in the aftermath of the first Cabinet meeting. On Hughes' suggestion Harding had bound his advisers to secrecy as to Cabinet discussions. But full accounts of what happened at the meeting were on the front pages of the newspapers the next morning. On several other occasions confidential data that Hughes disclosed only to the Cabinet "leaked" to the newspapers. [3] Some member was obviously currying favor with the press by violating his pledge to the President. Concluding that the Cabinet was not a safe place to talk of anything confidential, Hughes soon confined his remarks there to matters that were ready for public announcement. "I have nothing to say now," he would respond to the President's invitation to speak, "but I should like to see you after the meeting."

Similarly embarrassed by "leaks," other Cabinet members began going to the President individually. Each member became wrapped up in the affairs of his own department and probably felt, as Hughes did, that he was scarcely in a position to offer useful comment on policy outside his own bailiwick. The Cabinet meetings thus came to be brief and not very helpful, the talk running to generalities and politics. [4]

Hoover, Hays, and Weeks were the only members of the Cabinet Hughes had known before his appointment. Mutual admiration as well as mutual interest in foreign commerce brought Hughes and Hoover frequently together. The long-existing conflicts between the State and Commerce departments concerning foreign representation in commercial matters quickly subsided under their cooperative techniques. In less than ten minutes they agreed that information on business and economic conditions abroad could best be gathered

[2] CEH, Notes, p. 253d.   [3] Ibid., p. 253a.   [4] Ibid., p. 253d.

by Department of Commerce men reporting to the American ambassador in each foreign capital.[5]

A "delightful friendship" sprang up between Hughes and the Secretary of Agriculture. Wallace was a man of character, strength, and common sense, with an earthy quality about him that appealed to the city-bred lawyer in Hughes. Early summer mornings often found them playing golf together at the Chevy Chase Club. During the summers of 1921 and 1922, when the Hughes family occupied Greystone on the edge of Rock Creek Park, Mrs. Hughes sometimes accompanied the two men around the course, although she no longer dabbled in golf. "Look at him," Hughes said to her, as Wallace followed a ball he had driven down the fairway. "He is the picture of health; he'll live forever." Within two years, however, Wallace was dead.

The President's manner of addressing the men in his Cabinet roughly divided them into two categories. Those who had been chosen for their ability or special knowledge were always Mister Hughes, Mister Hoover, Mister Mellon, or, more simply, Mister Secretary. The presidential cronies were called by their first names. Harding in turn was "Warren" to his personal friends, even "Wernie" to some, but Hughes always adhered to the formal "Mr. President." Their relations were close on an official plane but never intimate in the personal sense. Hughes himself is the best witness on this point:

> President Harding was a most kindly man,—always eager to please his old friends and to make new ones. He found it difficult to say No. To me, he was a most agreeable Chief, always accessible, anxious fully to understand each problem as it arose. I soon came to understand the limitations which were imposed upon him by the situation which had developed in the Senate in consequence of the wrangle over the Treaty of Versailles, and I sought to avoid embarrassing him by stirring up futile conflicts. I realized that I must take a full measure of responsibility when I felt definite action should be taken. I did not go to him with a statement of difficulties and ask him what should be done, but supplemented my statements of the facts in particular cases by concrete proposals upon which he could act at once, and to which he almost invariably gave his approval. Our relations were of the happiest sort. Engrossed as I was, night and day, in the work of the Department of State, I knew nothing of his intimacies with those who later abused his trust and brought his administration into disrepute.[6]

While Hughes kept the reins of foreign policy securely in his own hands, he never took advantage of the President. Going to the White House almost every day, he kept Harding thoroughly informed on everything of importance that the department proposed or had ascertained. The effect was to confirm the President's trust and bolster his willingness to follow Hughes' lead in any and all dealings with other countries. According to James Grafton Rogers,

[5] Herbert Hoover to author, March 14, 1949.
[6] CEH, Notes, p. 253a.

Hughes was allowed perhaps the widest range of discretion ever permitted an American Cabinet officer in this field.[7]

As a frequent visitor at the Executive Office, Hughes got a close-up view of the President's troubles. The waiting room was usually filled with people seeking access to the President's ear, and Harding's ambition to become the best-loved President seemed to make him available to all of them. When a White House aide would slip Hughes into the presidential office ahead of the other visitors, Harding would often put his arm across the Secretary's shoulders and exclaim, "Hughes, this is the damnedest job!" [8]

The President sought relief through golf in the afternoon and poker and parties at night. Secretary Hughes was frequently pressed to join in the golf, and occasionally he did so. During the Washington Conference, Harding, Hughes, and Arthur Balfour played eighteen holes at the Chevy Chase Club in the rain. For the most part, however, the Secretary of State found it impossible to squeeze an afternoon of golf into his busy schedule even at the request of the President.

Some of the politicians who had opposed Hughes' nomination claimed to have assurance that he would be shifted to the Supreme Court as soon as Chief Justice White had been given a graceful opportunity to retire.[9] Secretary Fall, the rumor ran, would then be elevated to the State Department. In spite of his great affection for the Supreme Court, Hughes found these rumors very irritating.

The venerable Chief Justice had clung grimly to his office even though his sight was virtually gone and he had been told that an operation was urgent—even though his intention to retire had been communicated to Justice Hughes back in 1916. White had later told Taft that he was holding the office open for him and that he would give it back to a Republican administration.[10] Whether this reflected only gratitude to Taft for his appointment of White or involved also some resentment against Wilson because of the 1916 incident may never be known. The Chief Justice's last opportunity to carry out any pledge was cut off on May 19, 1921, by his death from the operation that he had long postponed.

"William H. Taft, Charles E. Hughes and George Sutherland," said the *Washington Post* the next morning, "were the names most prominently mentioned . . . as possible successors of Edward Douglas White. . . ." At the State Department Undersecretary Fletcher carried the paper into Hughes' office.

"I hope this isn't true, so far as you are concerned," Fletcher said. "No," Hughes replied with typical finality. "If the President should offer me the

[7] *American Bar Association Journal*, July, 1941, p. 411.
[8] CEH, Notes, p. 253b.   [9] New York *Call*, Feb. 27, 1921.
[10] Henry Pringle, *The Life and Times of William Howard Taft*, p. 955.

Chief Justiceship, I would not accept it and I would resign as Secretary of State." [11]

Hughes had no idea that the President was thinking of him for the Chief Justiceship. But, with the Irreconcilables still gunning for him, he wanted it clearly understood that he would regard any proposed shift as an indication of no confidence in what he had been doing at the State Department.

"I'm going to play golf with the President this afternoon," Fletcher volunteered. "Do you want me to tell him what you have just said?"

"Yes," was the clipped reply.

Out on the golf course Fletcher repeated the conversation. The President put his arm around Fletcher's shoulders and reassured him in typical off-the-record verbiage:

"No, I'm not going to disturb the 'old chief.' [Harding himself was only two years younger than Hughes.] I'm going to appoint old man Taft to the court."

The incident may well have strengthened Hughes' high standing with the President. It was a new application of the Hughesian principle that to be fit for high office a man must be willing to leave it at any time. Harding respected this attitude, and, since he was loath to lose the greatest asset of his Administration, he permitted nothing to come between them. The President's own attitude was reflected in a half-gay, half-rueful remark to the Reverend Mr. William F. McDowell, in praising Hughes' achievements. "The truth is," he said, "he ought to be President and then I would not have to be." [12] It is almost needless to say that Hughes had no such idea. He was wholly absorbed in the fascinating business of being Secretary of State and was happy to serve such an agreeable President as Harding always proved to be.

[11] Author's interview with Henry Fletcher, Aug. 10, 1946.
[12] McDowell to CEH, Sept. 3, 1923.

Chapter 41

POLICY OF THE FREE HAND

TO JOIN or not to join the League of Nations was the first great question that arose to bedevil the Harding Administration. Having straddled the League issue in the campaign, Harding came to Washington free from entangling commitments, let alone convictions. The one thing certain about his attitude was that he was willing to be led, and his selection of Charles Evans Hughes to be Secretary of State indicated that he was not averse to being led toward the League.

Hughes' convictions had never been in doubt since his speech of March 26, 1919. Indeed, he had actively campaigned for American participation in an international organization to keep the peace when he ran for the Presidency in 1916. While he had fought for "mild reservations" to the Covenant that Wilson brought back from Paris, it was a forward-looking fight designed to improve and not to scuttle the League.

Harding was well aware of these facts when he gave Hughes a free hand in directing the nation's foreign affairs. In their conference at Marion, moreover, he had seemed to acquiesce in Hughes' candidly expressed desire to see the United States join the peace-enforcing organization.[1] His idea was that they could analyze the Versailles Treaty and decide what should be accepted and what rejected, and that the Senate would then consent to ratification of the treaty with the suggested reservations. The Secretary-designate went into office prepared to follow that course.

In Washington, however, it quickly became evident that sentiment against the League had hardened. Cox had made the League the "paramount issue," and the people had buried him under the Harding landslide—16,152,000 votes to 9,147,353. To be sure, Harding had the support of many pro-League Republicans, but the sweeping nature of his victory had sapped their influence. The strength of the Irreconcilables had been enhanced. Of the twelve Republican bitter-enders who had voted against the League in March, 1920, ten were still in the Senate and two had been replaced by other Republicans. Most of the Democrats who had voted against the treaty were also still there. It was clear to anyone who surveyed the outlook that the "little group of willful men" held the balance of power more securely than before the election.

[1] CEH, Notes, p. 258.

431

Their mood had been reflected in their stiff opposition to Hughes' appointment as Secretary of State. On that point their case was weak; but the two-thirds rule gave them the whip hand in respect of treaty ratification, and they were determined to use it. Hughes got a foretaste of what was to come when Senator Frank B. Brandegee went to the State Department to offer his advice. The Senator was blunt and blustering. Hughes replied in his most incisive and devastating manner. Waggling with excitement, Brandegee dashed back to the Capitol and told his colleagues they could expect the Versailles Treaty by the next White House messenger; that "whiskered" Secretary of State would soon have the country in the League of Nations.

There were many other conferences in which discussion waxed warm and intense. When Hughes continued to press for early consideration of the Covenant with reservations, Brandegee, Johnson, Borah, and others openly threatened, by way of retaliation, to block everything the Administration might attempt to do.[2]

Hughes went over the situation with Harding many times. Every exploration led back to the same stone wall of Senate opposition. Senator Frank B. Kellogg and other pro-League men in the Senate reviewed the situation with Hughes but could offer no hope of getting a two-thirds majority for the Covenant at that late date. A renewal of the struggle could result only in disaster for the Harding Administration without taking the United States any closer to the League.

Hughes concluded that he had no right to drag the Administration into the maelstrom that had engulfed Wilson. That decision not only blighted fond hopes; it also left him in the awkward position of failing to carry out the policy to which he had committed himself. "The Republican Party is bound by every consideration of good faith," the statement of the Thirty-One had said, "to pursue such a course [ratification of the Covenant with reservations] until the declared object is attained." The pro-League forces were counting heavily on Hughes to make this pledge effective. He could not forsake the League without subjecting himself to charges of breaking faith.

The situation was less embarrassing for Harding because he had never been a warm supporter of the League anyway. He announced his surrender to the Irreconcilables on April 12, 1921, in his message to Congress: ". . . there will be no betrayal of the deliberate expression of the American people in the recent election . . . the League Covenant can have no sanction by us."[3] In less than six weeks the new Administration had completely abandoned the chief objective of the foreign policy it had intended to pursue.

Having bowed to the inevitable, Hughes then had to decide whether to pro-

[2] Author's interview with CEH, Nov. 26, 1946.
[3] *Congressional Record*, 67th Cong., 1st session, Vol. 61, p. 172.

Antoinette Hughes at home, about 1915
". . . a perfect companion . . ."

A strange sort of austerity—at Rangeley Lake, 1915

Three generations of Charles Evans Hugheses

ceed along other lines or to resign. His resignation so soon after taking office would have penalized Harding for not doing what Hughes knew he could not do.[4] It would also have deprived Hughes of the opportunity of carrying out other important policies that had begun to take shape and would probably have brought into power an anti-League Secretary of State. Pondering deeply on his predicament, Hughes decided that to resign would be a futile gesture unworthy of himself and unfair to the Administration. He had accepted office to do the best he could for the country in whatever circumstances might arise and he held on to his office for the same purpose.

That he made the best of a bad situation is scarcely open to question. His decision involved no sacrifice of integrity. While the Thirty-One had candidly voiced their hopes and convictions, they had not assumed the position of guarantors of American entry into the League. The inescapable fact was that the voters had made it impossible for the Administration to carry out the policy to which the Thirty-One had tried to commit it. The worst that can be said of Secretary Hughes in connection with this incident, therefore, is that he bowed to the will of the people and the Senate without an open fight.

Some of his friends concluded that he had lost his crusading zeal. In Albany when the bosses thwarted him he had gone straight to the people with his reforms. Could he not now similarly whip the Senate into line? Those who urged him to do so overlooked two compelling facts. In New York he had come into power as the head of a great popular movement that was demanding a housecleaning. As Secretary of State, he was an appointed official responsible to the President. No fight was possible without the President behind him, and in this matter the President was not behind him. In New York, legions of outraged voters had been eager to swoop down upon the hapless legislators who stood against his progressive measures. But in 1921 public opinion was running strongly against his plans for American adherence to the League.

Only a one-track mind would have carried over the Albany technique into these totally different circumstances. Hughes was not one to think in grooves, nor would he bankrupt statesmanship by clinging to the carcass of a dead policy. His willingness to be guided by facts and conditions beyond his control indicated a flexibility of mind and an attention to realities which are the beginning of wisdom in the conduct of foreign policy.

Repeatedly he was asked to explain the discrepancy between the pledge of the Thirty-One and his conduct as Secretary of State. Hamilton Holt, president of the Woodrow Wilson Democracy, wrote an open letter to the Thirty-One expressing the suspicion that they had been "betrayed and repudiated." [5] The World pointedly asked why a man who "is believed to represent the highest order of integrity in our public life" felt free to disregard his pledge and act

[4] CEH, to Edwin Gay, Aug. 1, 1922, p. 10.   [5] Independent, Aug. 6, 1921.

contrary to it.[6] One of Thirty-One signers (Wickersham) indignantly accused the Secretary of being unfaithful to his trust. Discretion forbade Hughes to reveal the fight he had made for the League within the Administration, but he went as far as he could in defense of his position in a confidential letter to Wickersham:

The plain fact is that President Harding, if he had undertaken to bring about our entry into the League, even upon the basis of reservations or a modified agreement, would have precipitated a controversy of the most serious character, but he could not have achieved the result. The opposition was too determined and resourceful. They had decided that there should be no participation in the League on any terms. No matter what Mr. Harding had said as a candidate, or the Thirty-One had said, the President was required as a statesman to take account of this condition. He would have been unworthy of his place had he not made the best appraisement possible . . . if he had proposed entry into the League with reservations, or modification of the Covenant, he would have wrecked the Administration by involving it in a most bitter fight and he would not have succeeded.[7]

Meanwhile the United States' strained relationship toward the League was a source of befuddlement abroad as well as controversy at home. Following the Senate's rejection of the Treaty of Versailles and Harding's election, the Wilson Administration had withdrawn from all contact with the League as if it had become contaminated. Communications from the League had been left unanswered. American officials had been instructed to go no more to the Council of Ambassadors. Even the "unofficial representative" on the Reparation Commission had been compelled to retire.[8] After March 4, Hughes tried to shake off this extremism so far as it was feasible. Ambassador Harvey was instructed to act as the President's representative in the Supreme Council, Ambassador Wallace in Paris to resume his status as "unofficial American observer" in the Conference of Ambassadors, and Roland W. Boyden to sit once more, unofficially, on the Reparation Commission. But a few months later the Senate attempted to slam the door upon any sort of American participation in League activities. Its consent to the peace treaty with Germany was given subject to the understanding "that the United States shall not be represented or participate in any body, agency or commission . . . unless and until an Act of the Congress of the United States shall provide for such representation." [9] The President accepted this probably unconstitutional invasion of the executive power as part of the instrument ratifying the treaty.

In these circumstances it was utterly impossible for Hughes to cooperate with the political agencies of the League, but he refused to close his eyes or stop his ears to what was going on in the world. By a liberal interpretation of the Senate's prohibition, he made increasing use of "unofficial observers"

---

[6] July 21, 1922.   [7] CEH to Wickersham, March 28, 1923.
[8] *Foreign Relations, 1921*, I, 2–6.   [9] *Ibid.*, II, 33.

in League agencies that were dealing with humanitarian problems or other issues in which the United States had a special interest. These "unofficial observers" became the butt of much ridicule in the United States and other countries. They sat in numerous League meetings without authority to join in the debate or to influence decisions. To be sure, they officially represented the United States in the only role it could play at Geneva. Still, they were merely outsiders listening in. The greatest power in the world was pretending to withdraw from world councils and then creeping back to learn what was happening.

While Hughes chafed under the limitations that had been laid upon him, he made no apology for doing the best he could in the circumstances. ". . . there is nothing obscure or reprehensible, nothing derogatory to our influence, dignity, or prestige, in the form of our cooperation," he said. "It is simply adjusted to an inescapable fact. Of course, as the United States has decided not to become a member of the League of Nations, this Government cannot act as though it were a member." [10]

While he was careful to avoid ventures that would be certain to start a cyclone of protest, the Secretary considered each separate proposal for joint efforts with the League on its merits. If it appeared that American interests were directly involved or that the general welfare of humanity would be promoted by an international undertaking, he went as far as he could in cooperating with the League. The United States named representatives to work with League committees in relation to opium, anthrax, public health, antitoxin serums, traffic in women and children, relief work, customs formalities, and the control of traffic in arms.

Some of the pro-League men expected Hughes to sponsor a new League as an alternative to securing ratification of the Versailles Treaty. The President had hinted that new "covenanted relationships" might be sought. Hughes explored the possibilities. He was convinced that Wilson had blundered in making this association for the promotion of peace an enforcing agency for the victors of the war. At one time he tentatively suggested that the League might be left to its task of "enforcing agency" and that "a new association on an acceptable basis not directly connected with the Peace Treaty might be formed for the broader purposes in view." Nothing came of it. Earlier he had put out a feeler that the League itself might become an acceptable peace agency if divorced from its enforcement function under the Versailles Treaty, but Ambassador Jusserand scotched the idea with a sharp declaration that it would never win approval in France.

Wickersham, Lowell, and others persistently clung to the fanciful hope of a new phoenix rising out of the supposed ruin of the League. But any Ameri-

[10] Speech to New York Republican State Convention, April 15, 1924.

can suggestion of a new peace organization just after this country had abandoned the existing League fathered by an American President would have been laughed to scorn in Europe. And it would have been little more acceptable to the Senate than was the experiment at Geneva. Hughes advised Lowell in July, 1922, that any further reference by the President to an association of nations would call for a more or less definite plan and that general conditions were such that it would be "impracticable to suggest a plan at this time." He added:

We have been dealing with matters in a practical way and have accomplished a great deal. If there are those who think that they should renew a barren controversy, that is their right. Nothing good will come of it, and very likely it will stand in the way of much that might otherwise be accomplished.[11]

In the heat of the 1924 presidential campaign, Raymond B. Fosdick, former Undersecretary General of the League, fired a broadside of charges that were reechoed by disgruntled pro-League forces. The Secretary of State, he said, had slighted the League by failing to reply to many of its communications. He had snubbed the Barcelona Conference, put "wooden images" on League committees, and stooped to "indirection, deliberate obstruction and bad manners" in dealing with the League.[12]

The practice of ignoring League communications had begun, as previously noted, in the Wilson Administration. Of thirty-three notices, requests, and invitations from the Geneva organization, the department had replied to only fifteen when Hughes came in. For the next two and a half months a bungling career officer who remained in charge of the "desk" where League communications were received continued to file them in a sort of dead-letter drawer. As soon as the Secretary learned this, he angrily ordered the League communications to be answered and banished the hapless young man to the American Legation in Cairo. Whether or not we are in the League, he told his associates, we can at least be courteous.

As for the Conference on Communications and Transit held at Barcelona in the spring of 1921, Hughes was content to send no representative because of its preoccupation with European problems. But the invitation to attend it had been declined by his predecessor, Secretary Colby, in deference to the Senate's isolationism.

Another source of complaint was the State Department's brush-off of the League in connection with the arms-traffic convention. The Secretary General, Sir Eric Drummond, inquired on March 8, 1921, and again on November 21 whether the United States would ratify the Convention of Saint Germain. Hughes discussed the arms-traffic problem with the British at the Washington Conference, with Secretaries Denby and Weeks and President Harding. It was

[11] CEH to A. Lawrence Lowell, July 20, 1922.   [12] *New York Times*, Oct. 19, 1924.

July 28, 1922, however, before he got around to informing Drummond that the United States did not approve the convention. Even then he communicated his reasons for disapproval only to the British Government, which had also been urging the United States to accept the convention. It was scarcely considerate treatment of the League.

Hughes declined to submit the convention to the Senate chiefly because it would have prevented the United States from supplying arms to many Latin American countries that were not signatories and because its provisions were so closely "intertwined" with the League. In 1924 he authorized Grew, then minister to Switzerland, to sit with the Temporary Mixed Commission, which was trying to work out a new agreement on control of the arms traffic. But, as the new draft treaty was drawn to buttress the League system of collective security, the State Department washed its hands of the whole business.

In seeking international control of narcotic drugs, the United States took the lead. The 1924 opium conference at Geneva was under the direction of a League committee, but the driving force behind the whole project was largely American. The comprehensive plan that Hughes cabled to Edwin L. Neville, the American representative on the preparatory committee, called for rigid control over production of the opium poppy and the coca-leaf plant in addition to control over transportation and manufacture of narcotic drugs. That plan was later embodied in a draft convention submitted by the American delegation to the conference. No real progress toward limiting the production of raw opium to the medicinal and scientific needs of the world could be made, however, and after two months of futile negotiations Hughes authorized the American delegation to withdraw.

The fiercely pro-League Americans often proved to be the League's worst enemies in its relations with the United States. If the State Department failed to do something that the League requested, they complained of "discourtesy." And when the department cooperated with the League, they shouted aloud that the United States was about to join, thus arousing a new wave of suspicion on Capitol Hill. Hughes had no sympathy with these short-sighted maneuvers. Yet he was often as irritated as the League enthusiasts by the handicaps under which he worked. Never was he free from petty obstruction. It is against this background that his work must be judged. If he "betrayed" the internationalists, it was only, as William Hard said, "in order to outwit and outflank the isolationists for the benefit of internationalism and international law and order." [13] Certainly his achievements would have to be sketched on a broader canvas if he had been Secretary of State when full cooperation with the world community was possible.

The chief difference between Hughes and the more passionate Leaguers

[13] New York *Herald Tribune*, Sept. 2, 1928.

was over the latter's faith in mere organization. Many Americans came to believe that our adherence would in itself make the League an effective organization and that peace would then be assured. Hughes never had any such illusions. "Had we entered the League," he said, "our cooperation would have been facilitated and our representatives would have taken an appropriate part in various discussions. This would have afforded a valuable training in participation in an international organization. Most likely it would have eliminated some of the fears, as well as dashed some of the hopes, created by the prospect of that participation. I question whether, with respect to important matters especially in relation to distinctly European questions, the actual results would have been different." [14]

As he watched the League struggle ineffectively with the postwar problems of Europe, Hughes asked himself philosophically what the United States might have done as a member to change the outlook. The League Council was impotent in all matters of larger importance because the great powers of Europe who were its chief members could not agree among themselves. They could not agree because their interests were diverse. The presence of an American representative on the Council would not have changed these basic facts. Nor would public sentiment have permitted the use of American arms abroad if League policies had called for such measures.

When the League buckled under the pressure of events that led to World War II, Hughes felt there was no justification for attributing its weakness to the continued absence of the United States. Secretary Stimson had seized the initiative in trying to curb Japan's aggression in Manchuria in 1931. He had worked openly with the League, in some instances spurring it into action and consistently demonstrating greater boldness than was evident at either London or Geneva.[15] "Certainly . . . there is no basis for saying that this result would have been altered by our membership in the League." [16]

Hughes was equally certain that our presence at Geneva would not have stopped Mussolini's imperialistic adventure in Ethiopia in 1935, or the "undeclared war" of Japan against China in 1937, or the rearming of Germany that led to Hitler's aggressive sprees. His reasoning is convincing:

Hitler rearmed in violation of [the] treaty and in the presence of Europe. There was no real secret about it. His development of Germany's air power was his boast and was well known. The European Powers could easily have stopped him but they did not. Even when he sent troops into the Rhineland, they did not oppose him. Why? I suppose that the controlling thought in Great Britain was that Germany had been harshly treated and that if she were permitted to regain her prestige and take her place again as a Great Power, she could be dealt with satisfactorily by

[14] CEH, Notes, p. 261.
[15] A. Whitney Griswold, The Far Eastern Policy of the United States, pp. 417–418.
[16] CEH, Notes, p. 262.

diplomatic methods and war would be prevented. Neither Great Britain nor France wished war. And there was always the supposition that at the worst there was adequate protection in the redoubtable French Army.

Can any well-informed person, who looks at the matter realistically, believe that we should have taken a different view and as a member of the League would have thrown our weight against the policy of Great Britain and France, insisting on military action? They were immediately concerned and they, not we, had the military power to hold Hitler in check before it was too late. But they did not desire to use that power. It was in the absence of the exercise of that power that Hitler continued his aggressions and mocked at the efforts of appeasement; and when after overrunning Austria, Denmark, Norway, The Netherlands and Belgium, he invaded France, her great Army crumbled. It is vain to suppose that these tragic events would have been prevented if our Government had been a member of the League! [17]

To the end of his days Hughes' faith in international organization to keep the peace remained steadfast, and his thinking was to be reflected in the United Nations. But he never permitted idealism to blind him to the nature of national power. ". . . the experience of the League of Nations teaches," he wrote in his Notes, "that, despite international organization, when it comes to the use of force, the Great Powers who have the force and upon whose willingness to use it reliance must be placed will act or fail to act according to the policy which they believe to be dictated by their respective essential interests at the time. Formal international organization will provide a useful mechanism to facilitate united action in the interest of peace but will not insure that action."

This seasoned view was not entirely garnered, however, out of the League's failure. It is a reflection of the realism that Hughes consistently preached and practiced as Secretary of State. In a striking address to the Canadian Bar Association at Montreal on September 4, 1923, under the title "The Pathway of Peace," he exploded the idea that councils, rules, and formulas alone can insure peace.

"War should be made a crime," he said, "and those who instigate it should be punished as criminals." But, with the outlawing of war, he reasoned, other means of redress for injuries will have to be provided; and, since there is no lawgiver for independent states, the discipline essential to peace will have to come from self-imposed restraints. War can be abandoned, therefore, only by common willingness to let international law take the place of force. "As the restraint is self-imposed," Hughes emphasized, "it will prove to be of avail only while there is a will to peace.

"All contrivances for maintaining peace by economic pressure, as well as by military force, depend upon the sentiment which will apply the pressure and direct the force when the test comes. . . . There is no path to peace except as the will of peoples may open it. . . ." [18]

[17] *Ibid.*, pp. 263–264.   [18] *The Pathway of Peace*, pp. 7–8.

Chapter 42

THE PEACE TREATIES

HOPE OF saving some portions of the Treaty of Versailles lingered for several months after the Harding Administration had turned its back upon the League of Nations. The two were not inseparable. And some means of ending the state of war between the United States and Germany had to be found. Secretary Hughes reasoned that the best way of safeguarding American rights as one of the victorious powers was to ratify the pertinent sections of the Treaty of Versailles, excluding the League Covenant.

It was vital, he thought, to protect American interests in Germany's overseas possessions. These had been ceded, not to the League, but to the five Principal Allied and Associated Powers, including the United States. We did not demand any of the former German territories for ourselves, but Hughes was determined that these colonies should not be disposed of without our consent. The much maligned treaty also provided that Germany should pay the costs of the armies of occupation. Without a treaty, these payments would be in jeopardy. Finally, the treaty set up an elaborate system of tribunals for the settlement of the claims of private citizens against Germany. Hughes thought it would be absurd to give up such obvious advantages merely because an emotional bias had come to be associated with the name "Versailles Treaty."

Sharply different views prevailed on Capitol Hill. On July 2, 1921, Congress passed a joint resolution declaring the war with Germany to be at an end and laying legislative claim to "all rights, privileges, indemnities, reparations, or advantages" to which the United States or its nationals had become entitled under the armistice and the Treaty of Versailles. But the rights to which the Government laid claim would still be insecure until directly confirmed in a treaty with Germany. Ratification of the pertinent sections of the Versailles Treaty, Hughes said, was still the best means of accomplishing this end.

The Secretary's earnest arguments won Harding to this point of view. When the President ran into senatorial hostility, he called a conference at the White House. About fifteen Senators attended. There was no roof-raising, but Hughes employed all his powers for logical, clear, and forceful exposition in an effort to make the Senators see the benefits that the United States would derive from ratification of the treaty. To give up this means of getting recognition for the very rights that the Senate had claimed in its resolution of July 2, he said, would be an act of incredible folly.[1]

The voice of reason beat in vain against the wall of passion which the Irreconcilables had put up. Some of them said bluntly that submission of the treaty to the Senate would provoke the same kind of futile struggle that the League Covenant had done, with a harvest of nothing but bitterness and trouble for the Harding Administration. Several mild Reservationists agreed that the outlook for approval of the treaty was hopeless.

Hughes saw that to proceed as he had planned would indefinitely delay the establishment of peace. That would be detrimental to American interests in addition to prolonging uncertainty and hampering economic recovery in Europe. Reluctantly he accepted another behind-the-scenes defeat, and began to rack his brain for ways and means of getting a new treaty with Germany that would satisfy the Senate.

The baffling nature of his task is apparent. He would have to draft a treaty that would look new to the Senate and old to Germany. The Treaty of Versailles was voluminous and complex. It seemed impossible to redraft its intricate provisions affecting American interests in a form that would be acceptable to Germany. New text covering the same ground as the text already in effect as between Germany and the Allies might plunge the peace settlements into an abyss of conflicting interpretations. Hughes shuddered as he thought of the Allies traveling one road with their treaty and the United States traveling another road with a separate treaty.

Of course, the new treaty would have to include all the rights and privileges reserved by the congressional resolution declaring the war at an end. If its language could be deemed to have a different significance from that contemplated in the joint resolution, the bitter-enders would tear it to pieces. Congress appeared to have given the Secretary a riddle impossible of solution.

One morning after Hughes had been mulling over his dilemma, he awoke with a brilliant idea that seemed to have taken shape while he slept. He could probably satisfy the Senate and avoid interminable negotiations with the Germans by incorporating into a treaty the specific language of the congressional resolution along with those parts of the Treaty of Versailles which stipulated rights and privileges for the benefit of the United States. In this way he could avoid redrafting either the treaty or the resolution.[2] Germany would have to accept such a treaty because the rights for which the United States would be asking had already been granted at Versailles. The Senate would have to accept it because it would be a verbatim compliance with congressional demands.

The Secretary went to his office that morning tingling with eagerness to get the job started. What had seemed hopelessly complex was now reduced to

[1] Author's interview with CEH, Nov. 26, 1946.   [2] CEH, Notes, p. 273.

simplicity. He wondered why he had not thought of this solution before. Calling in Fred K. Nielsen, he told him precisely what the treaty should contain and asked the solicitor to draft it promptly. Before an hour had elapsed, he telephoned Nielsen to ask what progress had been made. His inquiry was repeated several times during the day, and, as Nielsen had still made no progress, Hughes threatened to take over the drafting himself.

The treaty finally took shape as he had visualized it. An extraordinary document it was, giving the United States all the benefits accruing to any power under the Treaty of Versailles and imposing none of the responsibilities assumed by the other victors. The United States could participate in the Reparation Commission or remain aloof at its discretion. Similarly, it could take advantage of the Mixed Arbitral Tribunal or work out a different arrangement for the settlement of claims. "This gives us a footing that is practically unassailable," Hughes wrote to his son on August 27, "and while it may be swallowed with a wry face, it is privately recognized by all those who have sense enough to appreciate the facts that it is the best that could be done."

In spite of the absence of American obligations, Germany accepted the treaty. It was signed in Berlin on August 25, 1921, and Hughes made his first appearance before the Senate Foreign Relations Committee to request its approval. "Never before had we met a Secretary of State," said one Democratic member of the committee, "who so thoroughly understood his subject and so clearly explained every phase of it." The Senate consented to ratification of the treaty the following October. Diplomatic relations with Germany were resumed a few weeks later, and similar treaties were negotiated with Austria and Hungary.

These separate peace settlements were criticized by the same groups that were hounding the Administration on the League issue. Hamilton Holt flatly charged Hughes with having abandoned the Allies. "The separate peace with Germany was concluded," Hughes replied, "for the sufficient reason that it became perfectly clear, after the most careful consideration, that the re-submission of the Treaty of Versailles with suggested reservations would have no other result than the renewal of the former controversy and its continuance for an indefinite period." [3]

Hughes had sought no special favors from Germany. He had merely refused to give up rights to which the United States was entitled, and he had recognized the practical necessity of restoring peaceful relations outside the Treaty of Versailles. The policy of "going it alone" was almost as disturbing to him as it was to his critics, but he was pragmatist enough to concentrate on what was possible instead of sighing over what might have been.

In the creation of claims machinery Secretary Hughes again ran head-on

[3] CEH to Holt, July 13, 1922.

into Senate opposition. His plan was to adhere to the Versailles pattern. In the Treaty of Berlin, as the separate peace settlement came to be known, he had made a special point of establishing the right of the United States to use the claims machinery that the Allies had already set up. But the prospect of battle with the Senate, when he had no legions at his command, caused him to change his mind and negotiate a separate claims agreement with Germany. It must be remembered that the Senate had attached to the Treaty of Berlin a reservation to the effect that the United States should not be represented on any body, agency, or commission without specific authorization from Congress.

Hughes began discussions with the German Foreign Office, through Ambassador Houghton, in the spring of 1922. His plan was to refer the claims of American nationals against Germany to a "mixed commission" on which Germany as well as the United States would be represented. While negotiations were going forward, Senator Oscar Underwood introduced a bill for settlement of these claims through a commission composed entirely of Americans. Claims thus approved would have been satisfied from German property in the United States which had been seized during the war under the Trading with the Enemy Act.

Chairman Knute Nelson of the Senate Judiciary Committee sent a copy of the bill to Hughes, and he tagged it a confiscation measure. Enactment of the bill, he wrote, would be "embarrassing to the Executive" and would make it necessary to abandon the plans under way to set up a mixed claims commission. The governments which would be asked to pay these claims, he argued, certainly ought to be represented on the commission that would fix the amounts. The fact that the United States held property from which claims might be satisfied made it the more important to avoid any unfairness. "I should hope," he declared, "that in any case no measure of confiscation would be adopted until there had been a failure, after reasonable opportunity, to provide for the satisfaction of the claims of American citizens, duly ascertained." [4]

Let us be just, his restrained language said in effect, even to our former enemies.

Hughes was fearful that the Senate would pass the Underwood bill in spite of his protests. Even if it did not, the bill would be a hazard to any treaty on German claims that he might submit to the Senate. Under this stimulus, he looked for other means of accomplishing his aim and hit upon the idea of setting up a claims commission by executive agreement without the advice or consent of the Senate.

Never a man to cut corners, Hughes carefully checked the authorities and found ample justification for what he wished to do. Settlement of the claims of nationals solely by executive action was an old practice going back to Jeffer-

[4] *Foreign Relations, 1922,* II, 252–255.

son's day. When he was ready to spring his surprise on the Senate, however, he asked the President to bring in Senator Borah for an interview. The Secretary poured out his abhorrence of confiscation and told the Lion of Idaho that the best way to avoid it was to set up an American-German claims commission by executive agreement. Borah asked for the authorities supporting this course of action, and when Hughes gave him the citations the Senator said he would raise no objection. The Secretary then wired Ambassador Houghton to close the agreement, and it was signed on August 10, 1922. In an exchange of notes the United States promised Germany not to press any claims of American nationals for pensions to disabled soldiers or "separate allowances" to their dependents, although claims of that sort were allowed under those sections of the Treaty of Versailles which had been incorporated in the Treaty of Berlin.

These American strokes for fair treatment of a defeated country were matched by a unique gesture on the part of Germany. The agreement called for an umpire on the mixed claims commission whose judgment would be decisive in case of disagreement between the American and German representatives in allowing claims and fixing their amount. The German Government suggested that a prominent American citizen be named by the President of the United States to act as umpire. It was a striking tribute to the sense of justice that characterized American foreign policy under Secretary Hughes.

Responding in the same spirit, the Secretary suggested that Justice Day of the Supreme Court be named as umpire. Day was acceptable to the German Government as well as to President Harding, but failing health compelled him to withdraw shortly after his appointment. Harding then named Edwin B. Parker of Texas. The commissioners were Chandler P. Anderson for the United States and Dr. Wilhelm Kiesselbach for Germany. Congress recognized the commission by appropriating its share of that body's operating funds, and a large part of the American claims against Germany was to be settled before Hughes left office.

Chapter 43

OPENING THE MANDATED ISLANDS

No ASPECT of the peace settlement was more enmeshed in confusion in March, 1921, than Japan's mandate in the Pacific. Washington and Tokyo were exchanging heated notes over the Island of Yap. Great Britain was supporting the Japanese. The controversy was inflamed by conflicting reports as to what had happened in the Council of Four on May 7, 1919, when Japan had been awarded a class "C" mandate over the German islands in the Pacific north of the Equator. Suspicion and distrust were fast creeping in where understanding had vanished.

Yap is relatively a pin point in the Pacific 700 miles from the Philippines. But it happened to be the cable center for the German-Netherlands Telegraph Company from which cables ran to Shanghai, Manado (Dutch East Indies), and Guam, the latter cable making connections with lines to the United States, Japan, and the Philippines. Control of Yap meant mastery over the communications system of the Pacific. Wilson had insisted at Paris that Yap be internationalized so that all nations could be assured of equal access to its cable facilities. In the May 6 meeting of the Council of Four the President had agreed in principle that Japan should have a mandate over "certain islands" taken from Germany, believing that his prior objection to the inclusion of Yap would stand. The following day this decision had been formalized without further discussion. No reference to Yap had been recorded in the minutes of either day's proceedings.

This muddled situation made a perfect background for a battle of words. The British Foreign Office declared flatly that all the former German islands in the Pacific north of the Equator had been included in the mandate given to Japan. President Wilson had been present on that occasion and had offered no objection. "It does not appear to be open to His Majesty's Government," the note concluded, "to regard the decision of May 7, 1919, as other than definitive." [1]

Japan almost shrieked her arguments. If a decision to exclude Yap had been made at the May 7 meeting, at which no Japanese representative was present, said an arrogant note from Tokyo, "it could not but have been regarded as an

[1] *Foreign Relations, 1921,* II, 264.

act of entirely bad faith." [2] As to Wilson's prior reservations on Yap, Japan insisted that they amounted to only meaningless "preliminary conversations."

The United States informed the League of Nations that mandates could not be allotted without its consent, but the League Council replied that allocation of the mandates was the function of the Supreme Council, and that body had assigned the German islands to Japan in spite of Wilson's protests. Clearly the United States was losing its fight for a voice in the granting of mandates.

One of Wilson's last official acts was to send to the State Department on March 3, 1921, a communication as to his handling of the problem of Yap. Reviewing his efforts to have the island internationalized for cable purposes, he concluded:

I never abandoned or modified this position in respect to the Island of Yap, and I did not agree on May 7, 1919, or at any other time, that the Island of Yap should be included in the assignment of mandates to Japan.

As a matter of fact, all agreements arrived at regarding the assignment of mandates were conditional upon a subsequent agreement being reached as to the specific terms of the mandates, and further, upon their acceptance by each of the Principal Allied and Associated Powers. The consent of the United States is essential both as to assignments of mandates and the terms and provisions of the mandates, after agreement as to their assignment or allocation.

The consent of the United States, as you know, has never been given on either point, as to the Island of Yap.[3]

When Hughes surveyed the situation, he encountered equally emphatic British and Japanese assertions that Wilson had given his consent. The great issue of the United States' relation to these strategic islands in the Pacific had boiled down to a contest in veracity between the former President and foreign chancelleries over the disposition of a single atoll. The larger American interests in the mandated territories seemed to be entirely forgotten. The nation which had turned the tide of victory had been reduced to squabbling for a crumb from the peace table.

Secretary Hughes' first conclusion was that the demands of the United States would have to be shifted to new ground. Important though it was, Yap was not the sum of our interests. Japan's acquisition of the Marshall, Mariana, and Caroline islands directly athwart the sea lanes from Pearl Harbor to the Philippines had a bearing of the utmost importance upon American security in the Pacific. Of course, there was no possibility at that late date of upsetting the mandate that had been given to Japan. Even at the peace conference Wilson had encountered a virtual *fait accompli*, as Hughes was soon to learn. But the United States could protect its rights in the islands, including the right to keep them demilitarized, and the Secretary decided that any lesser course would be a craven surrender of our basic national interests.

[2] *Ibid.*, p. 274.   [3] *Ibid.*, p. 281.

It is not to be supposed that Hughes looked across two decades and foresaw the Japanese attack on Pearl Harbor that plunged the United States into World War II. But he did see that the mandated islands were potential strongholds for conquest in the Pacific. This was enough to convince him that the United States must have free access to the islands and equal rights with the League to see that no fortifications were built there. The absence of the United States from the League of Nations did not mean that we could safely draw into our shell or forsake rights that might prove to be vital.

In working out his new approach, Hughes pointed out that the right to dispose of Germany's overseas possessions had been acquired only through the victory of the Allied and Associated Powers. Consequently, that right was shared by the United States; there could be no valid disposition of German territories without the assent of the United States. The Supreme Council could not bind the American Government. Indeed, the rights accruing to this country by reason of the common victory could be ceded to Japan only by treaty, and no such treaty had been made.

Nor could the failure of the United States to ratify the Treaty of Versailles detract from the rights it had acquired. No country could be bound by a treaty to which it was not a party. It made no difference, then, what the Supreme Council had decided on May 7, 1919. It made no difference whether President Wilson had reiterated his reservations as to Yap. Under no circumstances would the allocation of the Pacific islands to Japan be final until confirmed by a treaty with the United States.[4]

Identic notes setting forth these views went out to Tokyo, London, Paris, and Rome on April 2, 1921. Since the Supreme Council had attempted to put into effect a mandate "purporting to be made in the name of the United States, but without the assent of the United States," Hughes expressed his trust that this action, presumably taken under "a misapprehension," would be reconsidered. What had appeared to be a humiliating rout for the United States was suddenly reversed with a stunning blow to Japanese hopes and British arguments.

At his press conference the Secretary insisted that his notes were not "sharp." The correspondents took him at his word and called them "blunt." The language he used was restrained enough, but his logic was devastating. It cut beneath all the petty squabbling and the contest in veracity; with typical Hughesian incisiveness it went straight to the fundamental issue. There was no valid argument left.

The Republican leaders in Washington, who had been watching Hughes with a fishy eye, hailed this stroke with unbounded enthusiasm. "Unambiguous," "masterly," and "unassailable" were the adjectives most frequently heard

[4] CEH, Notes, p. 269; *Foreign Relations, 1921,* II, 279–282.

in their comments. The Senate seemed especially delighted by this evidence that the Secretary's interest in international cooperation took no edge off his skill in upholding American rights.

France and Italy swung over to support of the American position. The British Ambassador, Sir Auckland Geddes, called on the Secretary to say, as an individual, that his government was bound by its agreement with Japan in 1916 to favor the awarding of the North Pacific islands to Japan. Hughes asked if President Wilson had been familiar with this agreement, and Geddes said that Mr. Balfour had given the President a copy of it when he was in Washington. Had Balfour called Wilson's attention to the document? the Secretary asked. Geddes did not know, but he was certain that Wilson knew of the secret deal when he reached Paris.[5]

Hughes talked earnestly to Geddes about the effect of the British position on American public opinion. Cooperation between Great Britain and the United States, he implied, could give the world stability. But little progress could be made in this direction if the American people should get the idea that Britain was making a secret engagement with Japan before this country entered the war the basis for resisting the very modest demands of the United States for equal rights in the mandated territories. Geddes replied that the British would have to stand by their agreement.

When the Japanese Foreign Office finally replied to Hughes' note, late in May, its tone was courteous and the door was left open to further discussion. Baron Shidehara, the Japanese ambassador, followed up with a call at the Secretary's office on June 3. He thought that an agreement might be reached on the division of the German cables and internationalization of Yap for cable purposes. Hughes replied that it was not merely a question of cables but of all means of communication. If Yap was useful for any other purpose, the United States should have a share in that use. Did Japan desire to fortify the island? he asked. Shidehara denied any such intention.[6]

Through a long period of negotiations the differences between the two governments were narrowed to the question of free access and equal opportunity. Japan complained on October 17 that acceptance of Hughes' open-door proposals would "virtually imply that foreign nationals and vessels shall have access, on the same terms as Japanese, to the territories and territorial waters committed to Japan's charge." This principle would be acceptable only if it were applied to territories held by other powers under class "C" mandates.

Once more Hughes interposed an unanswerable argument. The United States, he said, was not trying to force upon Japan the general principle of equality of opportunity. What he wished to emphasize was that the United States was one of the powers granting Japan the right to administer these islands as an integral

[5] Foreign Relations, 1921, II, 284.   [6] Ibid., p. 289.

part of its territory. If Japan had acquired the islands outright without our aid, they would have been open to American commerce under existing treaties. Obviously the United States could not yield its interest in the islands to Japan under a less favorable arrangement.[7]

The negotiations were still dragging on when the Washington Conference met in November, 1921. In the atmosphere of good will that pervaded the conference, Hughes finally induced the Japanese to accept his terms. The heads of the other Allied delegations acquiesced, and Hughes and Shidehara signed the treaty on February 11, 1922. The Senate voted its approval in less than three weeks.

The Secretary's persistence and skill had won for the United States every substantial advantage for which he had contended. As to Yap, free access was given for the operation of cables and radiotelegraphic service. The rights of residence and acquisition of property were guaranteed against restriction. Cable messages were to be free from censorship; persons and property were to have free entry and exit; they were to be free from taxes, landing charges or exactions, and discriminatory police regulations.

Agreement on the disposition of the Pacific cables came more easily. The cable from Yap to Guam was allocated to the United States; the cable from Yap to Shanghai and the Japanese mainland, to Japan; the cable from Yap to Manado, to the Netherlands. Mr. Balfour and M. Sarraut readily accepted the arrangement for Great Britain and France, and after Hughes repulsed a maneuver by Ambassador Ricci to hold up the Pacific agreement as a means of buttressing Italy's demands for cable facilities in the Atlantic the six-power treaty for allocation of the Pacific cables was eventually signed and ratified.

In later years Hughes negotiated treaties with France to protect American rights in several mandated territories: the Cameroons and Togoland in 1923, Syria and Lebanon in 1924. Belgium signed a similar treaty dealing with East Africa in 1923. The British put up much stiffer resistance, but finally signed treaties guaranteeing American rights in Transjordan and Palestine in 1924. The treaty as to Iraq was not concluded until 1930.

The mandate treaties would now be a comparatively minor item in Hughes' Secretaryship, except for Japan's notorious violation of her pledge not to fortify the islands entrusted to her. The failure of the ban on fortifications is a tragic chapter in the history of World War II and demands special attention.

As to all the islands mandated to Japan, Hughes' treaty provided for freedom of religion and protection of vested American property rights. It also extended to the mandated islands the Treaty of Commerce and Navigation of 1911 giving citizens of both countries the right "freely to come with their ships and cargoes to all places, ports and rivers in the territories of the other which

[7] *Ibid.*, p. 303.

are or may be opened to foreign commerce." Japan gave us a specific pledge
not to establish any military or naval bases or fortifications in the mandated
territories.[8] She even consented to send the United States a duplicate of her
annual report to the League Council on the administration of the Pacific
mandate.

Another of Hughes' suggestions ripened in an exchange of notes at the time
the treaty was signed. The note of the Japanese ambassador, reaffirming the
right of American nationals and vessels to visit the mandated islands, was as
follows:

Japanese Embassy, Washington, February 11, 1922.

Sir:

In proceeding this day to the signature of the Convention between Japan and
the United States with respect to the islands, under Japan's Mandate, situated in
the Pacific Ocean and lying north of the Equator, I have the honor to assure you,
under authorization of my Government, that the usual comity will be extended
to nationals and vessels of the United States in visiting the harbors and waters of
those islands.

Accept, Sir, the renewed assurances of my highest consideration.

K. SHIDEHARA

Honorable Charles E. Hughes,
Secretary of State.[9]

"Usual comity" means the courtesy which is normally accorded by one
country to the nationals and vessels of another. Here was ample authority for
the United States to keep watch over what Japan was doing in the mandated
islands and to revoke our assent to the mandate if the treaty should be violated.

In spite of these thoughtful precautions, the islands became advance bases
in Japan's war against the United States. Construction of the first naval base
on the Island of Truk apparently began in 1930.[10] Reports that the islands
were being fortified were numerous in 1932, and the State Department certainly knew of the violations as early as 1933. "As for Japan's action in fortifying Yap and the other mandated islands in contravention to express treaty
stipulations," Ambassador Grew wrote into his diary in Tokyo on March 27
of that year, ". . . we have abundant firsthand evidence." [11]

Tokyo's reports to the League and the United States on administration of
the Pacific mandate were masterpieces of evasion. Westerners were seldom
allowed to visit the islands, and then under Japanese chaperonage.[12] In 1936
Secretary of State Cordell Hull was concerned about "a strong undercurrent of

[8] *Foreign Relations, 1922*, II, 601.
[9] *United States Statutes*, Vol. 42, Pt. 2, pp. 2149–2152.
[10] Navy's report to author, April 21, 1949.
[11] Joseph C. Grew, *Ten Years in Japan* (New York, Simon and Schuster, 1944), pp. 84f.
Copyright, 1944, by Joseph C. Grew.
[12] Huntington Gilchrist in *Foreign Affairs*, July, 1944, p. 639.

suspicion and conjecture" as to fortification of the mandated islands and sought permission for the American destroyer *Alden* to visit the islands' unopen ports. As a means of allaying suspicions, the United States had consistently admitted Japanese vessels to harbors in Alaska and the Aleutian Islands not ordinarily open to foreign commerce. Hull cabled to Grew, ". . . it is unfortunate that the Government of Japan so far has not adopted an attitude similarly liberal in the face of allegations that in the Japanese mandated islands of the Pacific improvements are being carried out which are irreconcilable with Japan's treaty obligations not to fortify those islands." [13] Tokyo would not budge, and nothing was done.

In 1939 Secretary Hull admitted to the Senate Committee on Naval Affairs that the Japanese authorities had denied every request (four in number) that the department had made for the privilege of visiting harbors and waters of the mandated islands. At the same time he asked the committee to keep this information secret.[14] Under hush-hush precautions, the State Department replied to another query from the committee:

With regard to the questions whether the terms of the treaty have been violated by Japan . . . the Government of the United States has at no time raised any question with the Japanese Government in regard to the obligations of Japan to the United States with respect to the Japanese mandated islands.[15]

The rights that Hughes had so carefully safeguarded were thus surrendered by subsequent régimes without raising a finger. The grave impairment of our security in the Pacific resulting from this course was then concealed from the public in an effort to avoid criticism and postpone a showdown with Japan. The effect was to encourage Tokyo in the belief that American rights could be flouted with impunity and to leave our own people asleep as to the perils mounting in the Pacific.

The Army's Pearl Harbor Board linked the disaster of December 7, 1941, directly to "our failure to have a showdown with Japan on her fortifications of the mandated islands." The board's report continued:

Had the United States successfully insisted upon Japan living up to those treaty stipulations, the entire naval and military structure in the key Pacific islands erected by the Japanese might have been made impossible. Japan, without authority of international law and in violation of the treaties and mandates above referred to, for nearly twenty years successfully and completely excluded other nationals from the mandated territories, and during this time built up army, navy and air installations of tremendous strategical value.

As a consequence of the foregoing, Japan gained the enormous advantage of a string of naval and air and army bases across our lifeline to the Philippines and

---

[13] *Foreign Relations—Japan, 1931–1941*, I, 307f.
[14] Sen. Doc. No. 202, 78th Congress, 2d session, pp. 8f.   [15] *Id.*

rendered futile and impotent any fortification of our own islands, such as Guam, Midway, Christmas, Palmyra, etc. It also placed the dagger's point at the heart of the Hawaiian Islands because such a base at Jaluit in the mandated islands was a thousand miles closer to Hawaii than to the homeland of Japan.

Our policy through the successive years appears to have been based upon a combination of fear of the Japanese and of an obsession not to give offense to the Japanese; a policy which because of their temperamental characteristics, proved to be one of weakness rather than of strength.[16]

Nothing is to be gained by speculating as to what Hughes might have done if he had been Secretary of State in the thirties. But it is worthy of note that the price of his good will was honest fulfillment by every nation of its obligations to the United States. His technique was to offer each country friendship and just treatment while demanding, without fear of the consequences, that our rights be respected. Subsequent history has at least proved that relinquishment of rights and winking at treaty violations will buy neither friendship nor peace.

[16] *New York Times*, Aug. 30, 1945.

Chapter 44

THE WASHINGTON CONFERENCE

LESS than three years after the delirium of the Armistice, the ugliest word in the language—"war"—was creeping back into the headlines. Germany was crushed and Austria-Hungary dismembered, but new suspicions were clouding the relations of the victors. Especially in the Pacific, the march of events was in the direction of war.

Stimulating these postwar antagonisms was a naval armament race of proportions never before experienced. The United States had set out to build the largest battle fleet in the world. When the war ended, our Navy had under construction or authorized enough dreadnoughts and battle cruisers to add nearly 750,000 tons and 152 sixteen-inch guns to the American battle line.[1] Work on that program had begun in 1916. In December, 1918, the Wilson Administration had laid before Congress a request for 156 additional ships, including ten battleships, a duplication in all essential particulars of the 1916 program.

This gigantic paper fleet was the club with which Wilson had hoped to force the victorious powers to accept a league of nations, disarmament, and freedom of the seas. Fearing loss of her naval supremacy, Great Britain had come to an agreement with Wilson under which the proposed building program of 1919 was withdrawn. Then Wilson had offered the League to the American people as the only alternative to resumption of naval construction on a gigantic scale. When the League was rejected, the idea of building the largest navy in the world had naturally come to the fore again.

In this atmosphere the ultranationalistic press had whipped up a good deal of British-American discord. Some had gone so far as to visualize an Anglo-American war for commercial supremacy. Ill feeling had been accentuated by the Anglo-Japanese Alliance in spite of protestations that it would never be invoked against America. In March, 1921, London announced plans to resume the building of fighting ships on a scale that would keep His Majesty's fleet equal to, or superior to, any other navy. A futile and possibly ruinous struggle for supremacy on the sea was in the making. The two great English-speaking nations were unmistakably drifting apart.

[1] Harold and Margaret Sprout, *Toward a New Order of Sea Power* (Princeton, Princeton University Press, 1940), p. 53. Copyright, 1940, by the Princeton University Press.

In the Pacific, Japan was straining her resources to match the United States' expanding naval strength. Her substantial building program of 1917 had been stepped up in each of the following three years. In 1920 the Diet had approved plans designed to give Japan twenty-five capital ships by 1927, including eight new superdreadnoughts and eight giant battle cruisers. Japan had had her own way in Asia during the war. Now she seemed to be girding for further expansion. This menace to American insular possessions in the Pacific, to the open door in China, and to the peace and stability of the Orient was an ever-increasing source of apprehension.

Japan was equally alarmed by the sudden burgeoning of American sea power. Our Navy had established a separate fleet in the Pacific. Admirals were talking about a "strongly fortified naval base" on Guam and an improved secondary base in the Philippines. The Japanese interpreted this sudden rise of American navalism as a threat to the very existence of their empire. Relations were further strained, as we have seen, by the dispute over Yap. Washington and Tokyo were deadlocked at every point.

In each of the three leading sea powers, however, public sentiment was rising against the new navalism. Japan was spending nearly half its governmental revenue on its armed forces. Business groups, the press, and even politicians were beginning to cry out against the cost of meeting the American naval challenge. To the statesmen of Great Britain some means of curbing the naval race seemed imperative. While they had resumed naval construction, Britain's war-strained economy was in no condition to withstand an unrestrained shipbuilding race.

Men who have forgotten the spirit of the twenties sometimes assume that the Harding Administration thus had a golden opportunity to attain supremacy on the seas and enforce an era of peace. Actually, the revolt against navalism was running stronger here than in any of the other major powers. Many newspapers took up the cause, and the big-navy men encountered a veritable cyclone of opposition in Congress.

Late in 1920 Senator Borah introduced a resolution requesting the President to seek an understanding with Great Britain and Japan for curtailment of naval building by 50 per cent over the next five years. The movement won powerful support. General Pershing was among those who aroused the public with his plea for armament limitation to prevent us from plunging "headlong down through destructive war to darkness and barbarism." [2] The House slashed away almost half of the appropriation requested by the Navy Department, and Borah's filibuster when a more generous appropriation was sought in the Senate led to expiration of the Sixty-sixth Congress without any provision for support of the Navy having been made.

[2] *New York Times,* Dec. 30, 1920.

The Harding Administration was thus confronted, even before it took office, with a powerful demand for easing the burden of armaments. That was not disturbing, for both the President and Secretary Hughes were thinking favorably of an arms-limitation conference. Harding had expressed his willingness to cooperate with other powers for "approximate disarmament," but in their early discussions the first suggestion that it would be advisable to call an arms conference came from Hughes.[3] The President readily assented and said the conference could be called whenever Hughes thought the time was ripe for it.

In the first months of the new Administration the time was not ripe. The Secretary of State was immersed in the business of unscrambling the postwar chaos. He was also eager to avoid any positive commitment until the outlook for success of the conference was auspicious. At the same time he was aware of the danger of waiting too long. Determined that the conference should be held before the eyes of the American people, and that the initiative should remain in his own hands, he kept a hawklike watch over the situation to make certain that when the time came for issuing invitations they would go out from Washington rather than from any other capital.

Meanwhile the fight to reduce naval expenditures went forward in the extraordinary session of Congress which Harding had assembled. Senator Borah introduced a new resolution calling for negotiations among Great Britain, Japan, and the United States to halt the naval race. Similar proposals were made in the House. Harding attacked the Borah resolution and warned Congress to cease its efforts "to force the hand of the Executive" in this matter.[4] Ignoring the Borah resolution, big-navy Republicans in the Senate added $100,000,000 to the Navy supply bill for warship construction. But the foes of navalism redoubled their efforts. Pleas for disarmament rang from hundreds of pulpits as well as from the press and civic gatherings. The Administration promptly retreated, and Congress overwhelmingly adopted the Borah resolution as part of a sharply reduced naval appropriation bill.

Hughes had closely watched these events without being a direct participant. Now he would have to act with reasonable promptness. The people and the Congress had rebelled against further participation in the naval race. Only an international agreement could save the United States from being dangerously worsted in the armament competition that it had begun.

As the drama in Congress approached its climax, Hughes was besieged on July 7 by reporters who said that the British Government was about to call a conference on Far Eastern problems. Questioned on this subject in the House of Commons, Lloyd George had replied that he hoped to be able to make a statement on the following Monday if replies were received from the United States, Japan, and China. The Foreign Office hastened to explain that no

[3] Beerits' Memorandum X, 4.   [4] *New York Times*, May 4, 1921.

"reply" was expected from the United States because there was nothing to reply to. But rumors of a forthcoming conference filled the air, and Washington reporters were indignant because they suspected Hughes of trying to keep it a secret.

While no inkling of these events in London had come through diplomatic channels, the press reports convinced Hughes that he would have to act immediately. Rushing to the White House, he told the President that "if the British got ahead of us in calling any kind of conference our show would amount to little." [5] Harding agreed. At four o'clock on Friday afternoon, July 8, the same day that the House and Senate conferees abandoned Harding's naval program, cables went out to four American ambassadors instructing them to inquire whether Great Britain, Japan, France, and Italy would agree to participate in a conference on limitation of armament to be held in Washington at a mutually convenient time.

A few hours after his instruction had gone out, Hughes received a long cablegram from Ambassador Harvey in London. Britain and the overseas Dominions were holding in London a conference on foreign policy and problems of the empire. Out of it had come a hot debate over Lloyd George's proposal to renew the Anglo-Japanese Alliance.[6] That bond between the British and Japanese empires was as obnoxious to Canada as it was to the United States. The cogent arguments of the Canadian Prime Minister, Arthur Meighen— added to Secretary Hughes' previous confidential and informal protests against the alliance—had finally convinced British statesmen that it should not be renewed in its then existing form. But something else would have to be put in its place. Britain would not suddenly abandon her ally of twenty years. As soon as plans for renewal of the alliance had run aground, therefore, the British Foreign Minister, Lord Curzon, had asked Harvey to propose to his government that the President invite the powers directly concerned to a conference on Far Eastern and Pacific questions, including the peaceful settlement of disputes and the elimination of naval warfare.

Curzon's request had been made on Tuesday evening, three days before Hughes sent out his proposal for an arms conference in Washington. Thinking there was no urgency about it, Harvey had delayed sending his message until Friday night, after Lloyd George had been questioned in Commons. Even then Curzon had had to prod Harvey into action. Laxity of this sort was always irritating to the Secretary, but in this instance it worked to his advantage. The two cablegrams proposing different kinds of conferences crossed in mid-ocean. Hughes insisted that his proposal would have to stand, as it had gone also to Tokyo, Paris, and Rome. "Limitation of armament question is vital here and

[5] Diary of William R. Castle, Jr., 1922, p. 182.
[6] A. Whitney Griswold, *The Far Eastern Policy of the United States*, p. 287.

is not confined to the Pacific," he cabled back to Harvey.[7] But as the Far Eastern questions in which London was primarily interested were related to the limitation of arms, he instructed Harvey to "ascertain and cable immediately" whether Britain would agree to enlargement of the American proposal so as to include all Far Eastern problems, with China as an additional participant.

While waiting for a reply on a hot July day, Hughes drafted informal invitations to be sent to the powers and a statement to be issued by the President. Harding's approval of both was obtained before he left on Saturday for a cruise down the Potomac. On Sunday afternoon Harvey showed Lloyd George a copy of the proposed statement, and the Prime Minister praised it as "admirable." [8] Harvey's report of this visit reached Hughes the same day at Greystone. He telephoned his assistants who were waiting at the State Department to cable the invitations and release the statement to the press. On Monday morning the whole world knew that the United States had invited Great Britain, Japan, France, Italy, and China to a momentous conference in Washington. "President Harding has taken a step," said the London *Evening Standard*, "which, whatever its results, must affect profoundly the history of the world." [9]

Although the British were delighted to have the United States take the initiative in calling the conference, they still expected to shape it to their own ends. Curzon immediately pressed for a preliminary meeting on Far Eastern and Pacific problems to be held in London for the convenience of the Dominion Premiers, who were still there. The disarmament section of the conference could then follow, he said, at Washington.

Hughes' ideas ran in a very different channel. A preliminary conference devoted to the Pacific would have the appearance of sidetracking the limitation of armament. It would give the British and probably the Japanese a chance to present their demands and to take positions that could scarcely be abandoned in Washington. France and Italy, left out in the cold, would certainly resent any preliminary understanding that might be reached. Concluding that Curzon's scheme would wreck the conference, Hughes firmly rejected it. Between the lines of his reply it is easy to read the prevalent American distrust of European diplomacy. The Secretary was determined that this conference should remain under American leadership.

Ambassador Geddes came in two weeks later, however, with a long telegram in which the British Foreign Office took the preliminary conference for granted. According to Geddes, Harvey had "warmly approved the idea" when he showed the President's statement to Lloyd George at Chequers on July 10 and had subsequently suggested to Curzon that a preliminary conference be

[7] *Foreign Relations, 1921,* I, 23. [8] *Ibid.,* p. 25.
[9] *Evening Standard,* July 11, 1921.

held at London or Havana.[10] Harvey hotly denied it by cable. Reading the cablegram aloud, Hughes slammed it down on his desk and exclaimed, "Who is the liar?" [11]

Curzon tried another tack. As the door had been closed to a preliminary parley in London, he sent word that Lloyd George and himself and the Dominion Premiers were ready to sail for Bar Harbor on August 12 if that would be acceptable to the United States. Hughes stood his ground. In a long cablegram for Curzon's attention he pointed out that he had taken pains to get British approval of the statement summoning the conference before it was released to the press. While he had later agreed to "consultations to facilitate preparation for conference," he had at the same time positively rejected anything that might be considered a preliminary conference. The meeting of top officials of several countries would be a conference regardless of what name might be given to it. The President could not possibly call such a gathering on American soil just after he had invited a larger group of nations to a conference on the same subjects.

Failing to get what they wanted, the British cooled toward the entire undertaking. Geddes said solemnly that his government would drop the idea of a preliminary meeting and "desired the United States to take full responsibility for arrangements in order to avoid possibility of further misunderstanding." [12] The implication of hand-washing was unmistakable, but this gave Hughes precisely what he wanted—the opportunity of planning the conference in his own way.

Apparently Lloyd George declined to attend the conference because he feared that Hughes would be "extremely *difficile*," somewhat dogmatic, and "not easily swerved" from a position he had taken.[13] The coolness between London and Washington was further emphasized when the British attempted to bring the question of Panama Canal tolls into the conference. Hughes' cutting reply to Geddes was that "the time had come when the constant sentiments and cordial expressions which were made at dinners and on various occasions with respect to the friendly cooperation between the two Governments should be translated into something definite." [14]

France and Italy had promptly accepted the conference invitation. Japan was skeptical. She wished to avoid scrutiny of her occupation of Chinese and Russian territory, but she could not afford to give up the Anglo-Japanese Alliance without getting something else in its place. While willing to discuss the limitation of arms, she wished to know the "nature and scope" of the Pacific and Far Eastern problems that would be taken up before making any commitment to attend.

10 Memorandum of interview, July 30, 1921, Hughes Papers.
11 Castle Diary, 1922, p. 183. 12 *Foreign Relations, 1921*, I, 50.
13 Harvey to CEH, Sept. 28, 1921. 14 *Foreign Relations, 1921*, I, 73.

Hughes thought the agenda should be broad enough to embrace the open door, equality of commercial opportunity, the integrity of China and Russia, the status of the former German possessions in the Pacific, cable and radio communications, narcotic traffic, and other Far Eastern questions. Before replying to the Japanese, however, he asked the British view. Curzon sounded out the Japanese, and, finding them reticent, he urged that opium traffic, immigration, the mandated islands, and the integrity of Russia be excluded. Hughes had already excluded immigration as a domestic issue, and he agreed with Curzon as to opium traffic. Beyond that, however, he would not compromise.

Having been advised by the American chargé d'affaires in Tokyo that Japan would doubtless accept the invitation, the Secretary stood firm against the Japanese effort to restrict the scope of the conference. Any agreement of that sort as the price of Japan's participation, he said, might gravely minimize the usefulness of the gathering and "produce an unpleasant reaction." After two weeks of stalling, Japan yielded with a statement that Far Eastern questions should come into the conference only as a sideline to the limitation of armaments.

Long before the conference assembled, therefore, Hughes had clearly demonstrated that the reins were in his hands. Both the British and the Japanese were on notice that this was to be an American "show" and that its success or failure would depend largely upon the initiative of the Secretary of State.

Belgium, the Netherlands, and Portugal were belatedly invited to send delegates because of their interests in the Far East. The Secretary advised that all delegations be kept small so as to facilitate agreement. He also urged, much to the irritation of the armed services, that delegations be composed of civilians, with representatives of the Army, Navy, finance, and labor confined to advisory groups. All the principal powers except Japan followed this suggestion.

It was taken for granted from the beginning that Hughes would head the American delegation, and his high standing with the President enabled him to choose his own associates. Harding readily agreed that two of the four American delegates should be members of the Senate. There would be no repetition of Wilson's mistake at Paris. With his eye upon ratification of the treaties that would come out of the conference, Hughes selected Senator Lodge, chairman of the Foreign Relations Committee, and Oscar W. Underwood, the Democratic leader of the Senate.

The Secretary was well aware of the risk he would run in choosing a strong delegation. Three men of independent minds could take the conference out of his hands. That risk might have caused a less courageous man to take one of his own trusted followers for the fourth delegate. Instead, Hughes singled out the great elder statesman who had been Secretary of War as well as Secretary of State and Senator from New York and who was credited with more experience and wisdom in international affairs than any other living American—Elihu Root. Harding was lukewarm toward this selection because Root had antagonized the Irreconcilables, but Hughes was insistent, and the President yielded after conferring with Root.

With the conference now an approaching reality, the Hardings became apprehensive. Failure of this venture might be a fatal blow to the Administration. Mrs. Harding asked the Secretary one day how he was going to handle all the top-ranking statesmen who would descend upon Washington. "You've got to see this thing through," was the President's comment.[15] It was one thing, he seemed to imply, to call a conference and quite another to make it a success.

Preparations for the conference began on an elaborate scale. Hughes reviewed past efforts in disarmament and then turned to mountains of data related to the naval requirements of the three chief participants. His survey ranged also over the broad fields of Far Eastern policy, the Allies' venture in Siberia, the economic problems of China, the Shantung question, Japan's twenty-one demands on China, Japanese propaganda, American interests in the Far East, fortifications in the Pacific, gas warfare, submarines, and a host of other subjects. Days given to conferences, interviews, reports, and discussions were followed by nights of reading and deliberation.

From the beginning Hughes worked closely with the Navy, largely through its Assistant Secretary, Theodore Roosevelt, Jr.; the Chief of Operations, Admiral Robert E. Coontz; and Coontz' assistant, Captain (soon to be Rear Admiral) W. V. Pratt. Later on he used former Senator George Sutherland as liaison with the Navy. Hughes was scrupulous in exploring the Navy's point of view while insisting that civilian statesmanship rather than naval strategy should guide the conference.

Nothing in the voluminous data that came to him seemed to offer any plan, device, or theory by which naval strength could actually be limited. The Navy talked in terms of national needs. The admirals said they should have enough ships and men to protect all American territory, guard our commercial sea lanes, and defend the rights of citizens anywhere they might be menaced. In more specific terms this meant parity with Great Britain and twice the naval strength of Japan. "If the Anglo-Japanese Alliance is to be continued," the General Board added, "the minimum strength that the United States can safely accept for its navy is equality with . . . the two nations combined." [16] Similar elaboration of national needs was heard in other countries. On this basis every nation could make a convincing case for strengthening instead of limiting its fighting power on the high seas. There was scant hope of reconciling these claims. If the conference were to become entangled in controversy over relative

---

[15] Author's interview with CEH, Nov. 26, 1946.
[16] Report of General Board of Navy, Sept. 30, 1921.

naval needs, the result would probably be intensified competition and enormous expenditures, with no gain in security for any power. Hughes decided that some other formula would have to be found.

The Navy's first concrete proposal was that the United States insist on completing all the fifteen battleships and battle cruisers for which keels had been laid. Older ships would then be scrapped so as to fix the American and British capital-ship quotas at approximately one million tons. Against the world-wide outcry for reduction of armaments, such a proposal would have been farcical. Hughes discarded it at once. The General Board then suggested that four or five of the ships under construction might be scrapped. It was not enough. Roosevelt, Coontz, and Pratt worked up a third plan to scrap eight of the uncompleted ships,[17] but this too was to be discarded.

Pondering over the problem from every angle, Hughes was driven to the conclusion that the one hope of ending naval competition was to induce the powers to stop where they were.[18] No power could seriously object to a quota that would preserve its relative strength at the time the conference began. Only by this means, he reasoned, could the quandary of conflicting national needs be avoided. About October 1 he sent J. Reuben Clark, Jr., former State Department solicitor (later to become Ambassador to Mexico), to the Navy Department to find out what action on the part of Great Britain and Japan would be equivalent to the scrapping of all the American ships under construction.

This method of operation was to be followed consistently. While Hughes and his delegation fixed guiding principles, the Navy was always asked to fill in the technical details. On the basis of Clark's oral requests, the Navy prepared a chart showing what vessels Great Britain and Japan should scrap to maintain their relative standing if (a) the United States should give up all capital ships then being built and (b) if the United States should scrap its ships less than 60 per cent completed.

With these data, Hughes went to the White House and converted the President to the "stop now" formula. It was then presented to other members of the American delegation. Working independently, Root too had concluded that maintenance of relative existing strength was the only basis on which an agreement was likely to be reached.[19] The two Senators readily concurred. Underwood was especially enthusiastic in his approval.

The next question was how the relative strength of the existing navies should be measured. As this was a technical matter, Hughes relied wholly upon the Navy's contention that displacement tonnage of capital ships (battleships and battle cruisers) was the best yardstick. But what ships should be included? The American delegation took the position that paper programs should not be

[17] Colonel Roosevelt's diary, Oct. 24, 1921.
[18] CEH, Notes, p. 282. [19] Philip Jessup, *Elihu Root*, II, 448.

counted, but only ships laid down or upon which money had been spent. At the same time there was general agreement that ships under construction should be counted to the extent that construction had progressed at the opening of the conference.[20]

Using capital ships as an index to naval power and making allowance for ships under construction as well as the age, speed, gun power, and armor of ships then in service, the Navy calculated the existing relative strength of the British, American, and Japanese fleets at approximately the ratio of 5:5:3. With that ratio agreed upon as the basis of the American proposal, the logic of Hughes' drastic curtailment plan was obvious; for, if Congress intended to trim the American Navy anyway, our security would be promoted by a proportionate trimming of other navies by agreement.

Following this reasoning, the American delegation rejected the proposal fixing an upper limit of approximately 600,000 tons for the British and American navies and saving the ships that were more than 60 per cent completed. On October 25 Hughes formally asked the Secretary of the Navy what ships the British and Japanese ought to scrap to match a possible abandonment of "our entire building program for capital ships." [21] The next day the General Board of the Navy came back with a stern warning that such a proposition would be fraught with danger because Japan respected only force. "Our superiority today lies in these ships . . . ," the Navy's statement said. "If these fifteen ships be stricken from the Navy list, our task [in the western Pacific] may not be hopeless; but the temptation of Japan to take a chance becomes very great." [22] Denby sent the protest to Hughes. On October 30 the delegation decided, in spite of the admirals, to call for a naval holiday and the scrapping of all ships under construction.

The wisdom of this decision has often been challenged—more so in recent years since the facts before the conference have been forgotten. While conclusions must be left to a later chapter, it may be noted in passing that the problems which the Washington Conference faced were not those of 1937 or 1941. It had been assembled to meet an irresistible demand for curtailment of naval expenditures. Naval officers could close their ears to public opinion, but Hughes felt that he could not. His task was to safeguard American security and bid for peace and stability on the basis of irrefragable facts. The facts supplied to him by the Navy showed that, in spite of a strong drive for American superiority on the sea, Congress had trimmed appropriations for the Navy by $332,000,000 in the last year. Japan in the same period had increased her naval outlays by $61,000,000—in four years by $177,000,000. She was determined to go ahead, as events subsequently showed. The United States was not.

[20] CEH, Notes, p. 283.   [21] CEH to Secretary Denby, Oct. 25, 1921.
[22] General Board to the Secretary of the Navy, Oct. 26, 1921.

Hughes had taken pains to inquire what would be the result of letting the naval programs then under way run their course. A Navy report to the American delegation indicated that, with the completion of the three shipbuilding programs (about 1928), the relative standing of the navies would be: United States, 100; Great Britain, 106; Japan, 87.[23] Under the Hughes proposal, of course, the ratio would remain: United States, 100; Great Britain, 100; Japan, 60—an enormous relative gain for the United States.

Great importance was attached to the unwillingness of Congress to vote funds for completion of the American ships. Root asked at one of the first preliminary meetings of the American delegation whether there was any likelihood that Congress would vote funds to continue the naval program and fortify the Philippines in accord with the policy the Navy then favored. Lodge, who had the reputation of being a big-Navy leader in the Senate, replied that there was no possibility of obtaining the necessary appropriations. Underwood supported that statement, and the President came to the same conclusion.[24] The unfinished ships were "frozen assets." Only one of the ten battleships authorized in 1916 had been completed. Three more were well along, but six were less than 20 per cent finished in January, 1921, and none of the battle cruisers was more than 11 per cent complete. Congress was abandoning the ships without any agreement.

It was perfectly clear, therefore, "that unless we could obtain an agreement for a limitation of naval armament, we were headed for a disastrous competition." [25] Distrust arising out of the naval race might have stimulated building in America, but in that event Great Britain and Japan were determined to launch still larger programs. The choice was between "wasteful and senseless" rivalry, in which the United States was virtually certain to be outclassed, and an agreement that would bite deeply into existing naval tonnage. Before the conference opened, the naval chiefs seemed to be reconciled to the "stop now" formula and prepared a memorandum showing why it was fair to each of the naval powers. Rear Admiral Pratt consistently stood by this far-sighted conclusion.

In twelve lengthy sessions the American delegates reached a complete understanding both as to strategy and as to the principles on which they would stand. There was no lack of teamwork among them, but the program that emerged had a very positive Hughesian cast; for the chairman followed his customary practice of presenting not merely problems but also solutions bearing evidence of long and careful deliberation.

As the opening date approached, a new danger loomed up. If the customary method of having each delegation present its demands behind closed doors

[23] *Book of Recommendations of the General Board of the Navy,* p. 196, Hughes Papers.
[24] CEH, Notes, p. 278.   [25] *Ibid.,* p. 279.

should be followed, the conference might be embroiled in controversy before world opinion could be focused upon the American proposal. Clashing national interests would get the emphasis instead of the world-wide desire for relief from the armament burden. That danger might be minimized by a bold statement at the outset of what the United States was willing to do, but such an offer by itself would undermine our bargaining position. Weighing every element of strategy, Hughes finally decided to surprise the conference with a sweeping proposal that would slash into the British and Japanese navies as well as into our own. That technique involved some risk, but it seemed to offer the only hope of getting a fair hearing for genuine reduction of armaments.

Realizing the great importance of the surprise element in his strategy, Hughes guarded his secret with the utmost care. Only nine men, including the President, were permitted to share in the final consultations. So confidential was the American proposal that the final draft was mimeographed by an admiral, and all the copies were locked up in the Navy Department. No attempt was made to print copies until the morning the conference opened. The one copy of Hughes' speech was similarly under lock and key in his office.

It has sometimes been assumed that Hughes whispered his secret to Balfour when the chief of the British delegation called at the State Department on the afternoon of November 11. During the interview Balfour did make every gentlemanly effort to worm from his host the substance of the arms-limitation proposal he intended to make, but on this subject he found Hughes utterly uncommunicative.

"I am going to have the pleasure of nominating you as chairman of the conference," Balfour said as he was about to depart.

Thanking him, Hughes replied, "I have said nothing to you about what is in the speech I am going to make, and when you hear it I am sure that you will understand why." [26] There was no implication that Balfour could not keep a secret. Hughes was determined, however, to avoid any possible impression that the United States and Great Britain had entered into a deal which they wished to impose on the conference.

Most of Hughes' speech had been written on the train as he returned to Washington after spending election day in New York. As soon as he had finished it he called the American delegates together and got their approval. There had been no opportunity to show it to the President. Harding himself was to open the conference with a welcoming address on Saturday, November 12, following the dedication of the tomb of the Unknown Soldier on Armistice Day. Hughes' speech outlining the American proposal was to be reserved for the second plenary session on Monday or Tuesday.

On Thursday night before the opening, however, the Secretary became

[26] Author's interview with CEH, Nov. 26, 1946.

*The Secretary of State found
some moments for relaxation*

On the porch at "Greystone," 1922

Time out from the Washington Conference

Left to right: Prince Tokugawa of Japan, Arthur James Balfour of the British Empire, Secretary Hughes, Premier Briand of France, Baron de Cartier of Belgium, Senator

worried over the possibility that news of his thunderbolt might leak out in the press over the week end. There was the additional danger that Borah might muddy the waters with a proposal of his own in the Senate. The tantalizing thought that months of careful preparation might be upset by some misstep drove Hughes to the telephone.

"I had not planned to make our proposal on the opening day," he explained to the President, "but I am so afraid that a leak or some other development might spoil its effect that I think I should get it off right away."

"Oh, that's all right," replied the agreeable Mr. Harding. "Go ahead." [27]

This timing was notably to enhance the explosive power of Hughes' message that was to be heard round the world.

[27] *Id.*

Chapter 45

INSPIRED HOUR

THE GREAT day dawned chill and blustery. Tension, excitement, and expectation were in the air. Traffic whisked through streets lined with thousands of spectators craning their necks to catch a glimpse of the eminent statesmen from many lands who were converging on Continental Hall. Swarms of newspapermen heightened the awareness of history in the making. For the first time Washington had become the center of the world stage.

In this Conference on the Limitation of Armament the hope of humanity was centered. Yet it was a tenuous and evanescent hope. No general disarmament conference had ever been successful. The conclave which the Czar of Russia had assembled at The Hague in 1899 had gone no further than the adoption of a resolution expressing the desirability of reducing the burden of armaments. Again in 1907 the powers had succeeded only in reiterating this futile gesture. Every country was eager to disarm its neighbors but not itself.

Fear that the great undertaking in Washington would simmer down to pious mouthings signifying nothing was dominant in the comment as the conference assembled. "The Washington Conference will be as useless as all those which have preceded it," forecast Maurice Maeterlinck. The Socialist *Daily Herald* of London said flatly that, so far as disarmament is concerned, "the conference will fail." [1] The British were especially dubious. They had had a surfeit of American idealism and were puzzled by Hughes' refusal to enter a preliminary conference. Pessimism from many sources underscored the forebodings of war that were rising out of the Pacific.

Nor was there anything in the public record since the President had summoned the conference in July to offset the prevailing skepticism. Even young America seemed to be infused with anxiety as the statesmen, diplomats, legislators, experts, distinguished guests, and journalists filed into the marble hall on Seventeeth Street. The major participants in the drama were observed to be "intensely nervous." Seldom if ever had American officials faced a greater challenge.

Official and social Washington thronged the conference chamber. Vice President Coolidge sat beside Mrs. Harding in a box. Near by were Mrs. Hughes, the wives of other delegates and Cabinet members, and Mrs. Longworth, the

[1] *Literary Digest,* Nov. 12, 1921.

daughter of Theodore Roosevelt. Among those in the section reserved for the Supreme Court were Chief Justice and Mrs. Taft and Justices Holmes and Brandeis. William Jennings Bryan, entering in his silk hat and old-fashioned cape, lent a touch of showmanship, but later, when the crowd called for "Briand"—the French premier, whose name they mispronounced—and Bryan arose to take a bow, his dignity was badly ruffled.

The delegates were seated at a specially constructed walnut table in the shape of a huge block U. Hughes, as chairman, occupied the key position at the bottom of the U, with Lodge, Root, and Underwood at his right. At his left was Arthur James Balfour, the tall, white-haired philosopher-statesman who headed the British delegation. At the left leg of the U sat the Italians headed by Carlo Schanzer, whom Root later described as "a German Jew, born in Vienna, speaking for Italy in French, to an audience that can understand only English." On the right leg were the French and the Japanese. Japan had sent, as window dressing, her Prince Tokugawa, descendant of the first ruling Shogun, and, as chief negotiator, her shrewd, impassive Minister of the Navy, Admiral Baron Tomosaburo Kato.

Under the alphabetical seating arrangement that had been copied from the Paris peace conference, the American and British delegates occupied all the places at the strategic end of the table. It happened that the French Premier, M. Aristide Briand, distinguished looking in spite of his short neck and drooping mustache, was just around the corner to the right. Briand was indignant and let it be known that he considered himself entitled to a seat at the "table d'honneur." Hughes said there was no "table d'honneur," but he diplomatically requested all the delegates to shift one chair to the left so that France's eloquent apostle of peace and European unity could face in the same direction as the Americans. That move averted what had threatened to be the first unpleasant incident of the conference.

Pent-up emotions broke loose in applause when the President, "groomed within an inch of his life," entered and took a seat next to Hughes. At 10:30 A.M. the chairman rapped for order, and a Baptist minister offered an uplifting prayer. Then came the President's speech, resonant in its fervor and spiritual overtones. "How can humanity justify or God forgive?" he asked in reference to the horrors that the world had recently witnessed. "Our hundred millions frankly want less of armament and none of war." [2]

While the European delegates were registering shocked surprise at the undiplomatic cheering started by the Senators at the close of Harding's remarks, Hughes grasped his chief's hand. Briand, Balfour, Viviani, and others followed suit. Soon the hubbub subsided and an easier atmosphere prevailed. English and French were announced as the official languages of the conference.

[2] *Conference on the Limitation of Armament*, p. 48.

Balfour arose to express what he believed to be the unanimous wish of the delegates—that Mr. Hughes should act as chairman throughout the conference. Responding gracefully, Hughes spoke with an easy mastery that belied the excitement boiling within him. It was his great hour.

> Born for success he seemed,
> With grace to win, with heart to hold,
> With shining gifts that took all eyes.

At first he dwelt upon the opportunities that the conference opened to the delegates sitting before him. The words rolled pleasantly off his tongue; he seemed to be inviting his listeners to relax. After a few minutes of this came a natural climax to his introductory remarks: "The world looks to this conference to relieve humanity of the crushing burden created by competition in armament, and it is the view of the American Government that we should meet that expectation without any unnecessary delay." [3] The audience applauded. Some thought he was finishing on a note of high-sounding generalities.

Instead of quitting, however, Hughes went on to review the "futile suggestions" that had come out of previous attempts to reduce the burden of arms by international agreement. Apparently he was enjoying this diversionary maneuver. Newspaper men dropped their alertness and began to whisper among themselves. In the galleries people were "looking about the room, recognizing acquaintances, and nodding to them." [4] The first session was proving to be a humdrum affair. Then all of a sudden the speaker assumed a commanding manner. His face, a mirror of health and good will, glowed with a kind of spiritual exaltation that gave tone and timbre to his voice. [5] As he turned from the past to the pulsating present, his words rang with sincerity and conviction stripped clean of sentimentality.

"We not only have the lessons of the past to guide us, not only do we have the reaction from the disillusioning experiences of war, but we must meet the challenge of imperative economic demands. What was convenient or highly desirable before is now a matter of vital necessity. If there is to be economic rehabilitation, if the longings for reasonable progress are not to be denied, if we are to be spared the uprisings of peoples made desperate in the desire to shake off burdens no longer endurable, competition in armament must stop."

The plaudits signified that the audience was now alert. Hughes followed up his advantage by increasing his tempo and driving home point after point. The

---

[3] *Ibid*, p. 52.
[4] Mark Sullivan, *The Great Adventure at Washington* (New York, Doubleday, 1922), pp. 19f. Copyright, 1922, by Doubleday, Page & Co.
[5] William Allen White, *Autobiography* (New York, Macmillan, 1946), p. 600. Copyright, 1946, by The Macmillan Company.

hour of great opportunity for the "liberty-loving and peace-preserving democracies" had come. "We can no longer content ourselves with investigations, with statistics, with reports, with the circumlocution of inquiry. . . . Power and responsibility are here and the world awaits a practicable program which shall at once be put into execution."

The immediate difficulty was the naval arms race. "Competition will not be remedied," he said, "by resolves with respect to the method of its continuance. One program inevitably leads to another, and if competition continues, its regulation is impracticable. There is only one adequate way out and that is to end it now.

"It is apparent that this cannot be accomplished without serious sacrifices. Enormous sums have been expended upon ships under construction and building programs which are now under way cannot be given up without heavy loss." Yet the nations would have to face these sacrifices, he declared with typical Hughesian candor, or yield their purpose.

"It is also clear," he continued, "that no one of the naval Powers should be expected to make these sacrifices alone. The only hope of limitation of naval armament is by agreement among the nations concerned, and this agreement should be entirely fair and reasonable in the extent of the sacrifices required of each of the Powers." In other words, navies should be trimmed so as to maintain their existing relative strength.

Now it was evident that Hughes was moving toward some momentous proposal. Each new sentence seemed to split the electric atmosphere with greater impact than the last.

"It would also seem to be a vital part of a plan for the limitation of naval armament that there should be a naval holiday. It is proposed that for a period of not less than ten years there should be no further construction of capital ships.

"I am happy to say that I am at liberty to go beyond these general propositions and, on behalf of the American delegation acting under the instructions of the President of the United States, to submit to you a concrete proposition for an agreement for the limitation of naval armament."

Men came forward in their seats. Looks of amazement were hastily exchanged, and ears were strained to catch every word of what this whiskered enigma was saying. While the import of a ten-year naval holiday was sinking in, Hughes explained that his immediate proposal concerned only the British Empire, Japan, and the United States, leaving the navies of France and Italy for later discussion. Then came his neat and precise "four general principles," hitting naval competition broadside with the impact of four sixteen-inch shells:

(1) That all capital shipbuilding programs, either actual or projected, should be abandoned;

(2) That further reduction should be made through the scrapping of certain of the older ships;

(3) That in general regard should be had to the existing naval strength of the Powers concerned;

(4) That the capital ship tonnage should be used as the measurement of strength for navies and a proportionate allowance of auxiliary combatant craft prescribed.

Delegates caught their breath and moistened hot lips as Hughes went on to detail the sacrifice that the United States was prepared to make. Only one of the ten battleships in our 1916 program had been completed. On the remaining nine battleships and six battle cruisers the nation had spent more than $330,000,000. "Still," the speaker's voice rang out, "the United States is willing in the interest of an immediate limitation of naval armament to scrap all these ships." Nor was this all. To the fifteen uncompleted ships to be scrapped the United States would add fifteen old battleships, making a total of thirty capital ships with an aggregate of 845,740 tons.

No nation had ever before made such an offer to reduce its own arms. For a moment the boldness of the American example seemed overpowering. The tumult that broke loose was more than applause. It was an outburst of joyous acclaim. Those foreign delegates who could believe their own ears were "resonant with enthusiasm." Even the British journalists, who had been exuding gloom ever since their arrival in America, were shocked out of their pessimism. Everyone seemed to take it for granted that the session would end with this glorious gesture in the hope that other delegations would prepare to match the American offer. The clamor in the hall seemed to be "an immense and burning ceremonial for the close of a day that had made unprecedented history." [6]

But as soon as the noise subsided, Hughes turned his devastating logic upon the other big navies. "The plan contemplates that Great Britain and Japan shall take action which is fairly commensurate with this action on the part of the United States." For Britain this would mean giving up "the 4 new *Hoods* . . . not laid down but upon which money has been spent" and the scrapping of nineteen first- and second-line battleships—an over-all total of 583,375 tons.

Balfour scribbled notes on an envelope without changing his expression while consternation spread over the faces of England's hard-bitten men of the sea. Admiral Chatfield "turned red and then white, and sat immovable." Lord Lee of Fareham, civilian head of the Admiralty, "half rose and whispered to Balfour." Admiral Beatty, First Sea Lord and the living embodiment of the idea that Britannia rules the waves, leaned forward with the belligerent expres-

[6] Sullivan, *op. cit.*, pp. 23f.

sion of a waking bulldog that had been "poked in the stomach by the impudent foot of an itinerant soap-canvasser." [7] But the general atmosphere was one of deep silence while Hughes sank more British battleships than "all the admirals of the world had destroyed in a cycle of centuries." [8]

Leaving his listeners no time to recover from this shock, Hughes turned to the Japanese, who were grinning over the idea of so many American and British ships going under. Smiles turned to stolidity or sagging gestures as the chairman named the ships Japan should scrap, including the giant *Mutsu,* pride of the empire. Four battleships and four battle cruisers not yet laid down should be abandoned. Three capital ships and four battle cruisers under construction should go, in addition to ten older ships, a total loss of 448,928 tons.

"Thus, under this plan," he summed up, "there would be immediately destroyed, of the navies of the three Powers, 66 capital fighting ships, built and building, with a total tonnage of 1,878,043."

After the ten-year holiday capital ships could be replaced at the age of twenty years; no single ship could exceed 35,000 tons; and the maximum tonnage of capital ships for the three powers during the life of the agreement would be:

United States .... 500,000 tons
Great Britain .... 500,000 tons
Japan .... 300,000 tons

"With the acceptance of this plan," Hughes concluded, "the burden of meeting the demands of competition in naval armament will be lifted. Enormous sums will be released to aid the progress of civilization. At the same time the proper demands of national defense will be adequately met and the nations will have ample opportunity during the naval holiday of ten years to consider their future course. Preparation for offensive naval war will stop now."

The conference went wild in its sudden release of emotion. From the galleries came a "tornado of cheering" initiated by Senators and Representatives. Exuberant democracy trampled down the rules of diplomacy. "Hats waved, handkerchiefs fluttered, men shook one another's hands, hugged one another, slapped one another, exhibited every kind of animal delight of which human beings are capable in their high moments." [9] Correspondent William Jennings Bryan looked on with tears streaming down his face. No such wave of exultation had ever swept an international conference within the memory of man.

[7] *Ibid.,* p. 26.
[8] H. W. Nevinson, *Manchester Guardian Weekly,* Nov. 18, 1921, p. 384.
[9] White, *loc. cit.*

Cries for Briand brought a warm but noncommittal statement from the alert little Frenchman, and various other delegation heads responded with brief tributes to American leadership. Then the conference adjourned until Tuesday, in accord with a prearranged plan, so that Hughes' words might echo around the globe and people everywhere might let the delegates know their wishes before those delegates would have a chance to make official responses.

Hughes had expected his speech to create a sensation, but he had no idea that it would loose such an avalanche of praise as now descended upon him. Members of Congress could scarcely contain their enthusiasm. A canvass revealed that a treaty embodying the Hughes plan would be approved by the Senate almost without dissent. Borah referred to the speech as "the first great triumph of open diplomacy."

The kind of stories that reporters wrote may be indicated by the fact that, almost to a man, they rushed into press headquarters "bubbling with happiness." Editors the nation over brought out their most scintillating adjectives. Hughes' proposal was a "master stroke"; "a most astounding and stupendous move"; an experiment in "practical idealism"; a "drastic but workable" plan. Like Napoleon, he was said to have stunned the enemy by a sudden, decisive, offensive blow.

"Yesterday Charles Evans Hughes was a big man in the United States," wrote one Democratic editor, "today he is one of the biggest men in the world." [10] "I'm going home," declared Ring Lardner. "This is going to be a bum show. They've let the hero kill the villain in the first act." [11] "It was probably the most wonderful and sensational thing that ever occurred in an international conference," observed Rollo Ogden, soon to be editor of the *New York Times*. "But it was entirely characteristic of the Hughes we have long known." [12] "Of all human conclaves I have ever witnessed," William Allen White was to write nearly a quarter-century after the event, "the gathering of the Disarmament Conference in Washington furnished the most intensely dramatic moment I have ever witnessed." [13]

The clergy was almost ecstatic. There was much repetition of Bishop William T. Manning's declaration from the pulpit of the Cathedral of St. John in New York that the Hughes speech was "one of the greatest events in history." Almost the sole discordant note came from the Communist American Labor Alliance, which ridiculed the idea of disarmament until the workers of the world had control of the armies and navies.

Touching compliments from old friends swelled the Secretary's mail. Among them was this note:

[10] Martin H. Glynn in the Albany *Times-Union*, Nov. 14, 1921.
[11] Mark Sullivan in New York *Evening Post*, Jan. 28, 1922.
[12] Ogden to H. H. Kohlsaat, Nov. 13, 1921.
[13] White, *op. cit.*, p. 598.

DEAR HUGHES

No answer—

This is simply to say that I was proud of your dignity and thrilled by what you said yesterday.

Your affectionate old colleague,

O. W. HOLMES

"It has given us more than we ever have dared to hope," wrote Judge Learned Hand; "it covers our country with glory more than ten victories. . . ." A note from Theodore Roosevelt, Jr., said, ". . . in my opinion, your speech is one of the great documents of American history." So it went. If Hughes had been a vain man, his head would certainly have been turned by the stream of unrestrained laudation that flowed into his office.

News pouring out of Washington choked the cables both to Europe and to Asia. Tokyo correspondents put the entire speech on the wire at $1.50 a word. The Japanese registered deep surprise, and many were critical. *Kokumin* saw it as a "plot" to place Japan at the mercy of Britain and America. *Nichi Nichi* said it was a hostile scheme by powers bent on humiliating Japan. But the keynote of the comment, according to Associated Press reports, was "keen satisfaction and admiration." France registered "almost unreserved approval." In London "nothing else was talked about." Winston Churchill told Harvey that "he could not find words to express his rejoicing as an Englishman and his pride in his American ancestry. His hat was not only off but as high as he could throw it." [14]

Balfour referred to the Hughes proposal as "one of the most remarkable utterances which has ever been made by any statesman under any circumstances. . . . I don't know," he added, "whether Mr. Hughes was conscious that he was at that moment not merely a great statesman but a great artist. But, to speak perfectly impartially, I say that he was both." [15]

At the end of the conference Balfour also acknowledged that "it was the inspired moment of November 12th on which all the greatness of this great transaction really depends." [16] Hughes had chosen the only technique that was likely to force a sweeping reduction of naval strength and create an atmosphere in which major causes of conflict could be removed. And he had carried out his plan with consummate skill. His tour de force gave him overnight the moral leadership of the world and brought the United States once more into an influential role in shaping the future. It commands a high place among the great gestures of men in behalf of world peace.

[14] Harvey to CEH, Nov. 14, 1921.
[15] *Current Opinion*, January, 1922, p. 36.
[16] *Conference*, p. 368.

Chapter 46

NEGOTIATING THE NAVAL TREATY

THE FEELING that it was a "time for greatness" carried over into the second plenary session on Tuesday, November 15. The delegates had worked feverishly since Saturday combing over the details of the "great American scheme" and getting instructions from their governments. Everyone seemed to come to the same conclusion. In the face of the almost universal acclaim, there could be no open rejection of the Hughes proposal.

"I count myself among the fortunate of the earth," Balfour told the conference, "in that I was present, and to that extent had a share in the proceedings of last Saturday . . . we felt that a new chapter in the history of world reconstruction had been worthily opened. . . . the United States have shown . . . that there is a way by which wars can really be diminished, by which the burdens of peace, almost as intolerable as the burdens of war, can really be lightened for the populations of the world. And in doing that . . . they have, believe me, made the first and opening day of this Congress one of the landmarks in human civilization." [1] Before he sat down, Balfour had accepted the Hughes plan "in spirit and in principle," with a few vague exceptions.

Baron Kato, in his solemn and matter-of-fact way, also accepted the Hughes principles subject to "a few modifications." "Mr. Hughes has quite rightly made it plain," said Briand, "that the duty before us is to find the straight path and to enter upon it at once; and he has set the example." At the end of the day one enthusiastic journalist wrote, "What was an impossibility is now a fact." [2] While this appraisal ignored the subtle reservations that had crept into the speeches, it was none the less clear that Hughes had the statesmen assembled in Washington coming his way.

The organization of the conference also made certain that it would operate with Hughesian efficiency. The heads of delegations constituted an unofficial steering committee. The detailed work of the conference was assigned to a Committee on Limitation of Armament representing five powers and a Committee on Pacific and Far Eastern Questions representing nine countries. In each of these fields there was also a committee on program and procedure and numerous working subcommittees. Hughes, Balfour, and Kato became a sort

---

[1] *Conference on the Limitation of Armament*, pp. 96, 98, 104.
[2] Edwin L. James in *New York Times*, Nov. 16, 1921.

of inner steering committee in working out the naval agreement. As soon as they could bring their respective governments into accord, they would meet with the heads of the French and Italian delegations. The conclusions of those five would be taken to the Subcommittee of Fifteen on Naval Limitation. At this stage the naval experts who were included among the fifteen had a chance to check and recheck the agreement. Then it would go to a drafting subcommittee to be put into treaty form and to a committee of legal advisers for further checking. At last the finished product would go to the Committee on Limitation of Armament and then to a plenary session of the conference itself for formal approval and signature.

As chairman of the conference, Hughes was also chairman of all its committees. Carefully budgeting his time, he attended more committee meetings than seemed possible for one individual. Nearly every morning he met the American delegates in his office, and he reported to the President every day. Before taking any step, he made certain that he had the approval both of the President and of the delegation.

Each afternoon Hughes held a press conference, with about 250 reporters from many different countries attending. The foreign reporters were admitted because the chairman of the conference was eager to have the whole world informed of what it was doing. Public opinion in Great Britain, Japan, and France was especially vital to achievement of his aim. Yet he felt that he could not talk to the reporters from all countries in the same confidential manner that marked his regular press conferences. In the words of one journalist, Hughes was "terribly outleaked." Lord Riddell, a brilliant newspaper man who was in the confidence of the British delegation, repeatedly divulged what had taken place behind closed doors. Even when Riddell did not know the facts, he was clever enough to put two and two together and accurately forecast what the conference would do. Reporters besieged Hughes for similar inside information without success.

Some of the world's most famous journalists were covering the conference. Among them were H. Wickham Steed, editor of the *Times* of London, H. W. Nevinson of the *Manchester Guardian,* "Pertinax" (André Géraud) of the *Echo de Paris,* H. G. Wells, William Allen White, Frank H. Simonds, Mark Sullivan, and many others. Keenly aware of the danger of antagonizing these molders of public opinion, the Secretary nevertheless held fast to his policy of not divulging confidential data. Being chairman of the conference, he knew everything that was going on. He could not speak freely without risking disruption of the negotiations. Neither the roasting that he got in the press nor his own distress over what Riddell was doing could induce him to incur the distrust of the delegates by forecasting unfinished agreements.

Hughes and Balfour ironed out the differences between their countries in a spirit of full cooperation. The obstacle to prompt agreement was Japan. In spite of their acceptance of the Hughes proposal "in principle," the Japanese brought in demands for a 10:10:7 ratio, parity with Britain and the United States in aircraft carriers, and retention of their new battleship, the *Mutsu,* on the ground that it was already completed. Anything less than 70 per cent of the tonnage allotted to the larger powers, the Japanese insisted, would undermine their national security. The argument was once more back on the basis of national needs. To buttress this demand, however, the Japanese asserted that the United States had miscalculated the relative strength of their navy. Giving no weight to American ships not yet completed, the Nipponese experts claimed that the ratio between the two fleets was somewhere between 69 and 86 to 100.

Tokyo's demands could not have been granted without upsetting the basic principle on which the American proposal rested and destroying the existing balance of power in the Pacific. Hughes held doggedly to his original stand. For several weeks this deadlock darkened the outlook for an agreement.

On December 1, Kato, who was affiliated with liberal elements in Japan and was genuinely eager to reach an agreement, came up with the suggestion of preventing new fortifications in the Pacific. He first presented the idea to Balfour, and Balfour passed it along to Hughes when they conferred at the Pan American Building later in the day. The Secretary's first reaction was that naval and military opinion would strongly oppose the proposal and that the American people probably would not wish to fetter themselves by giving up the right to fortify their own possessions.[3] His own idea was that the United States and Japan could agree that if either one or the other should wish to build fortifications in the Pacific it should give notice of its desire, and the opposite party would then have the right to terminate the whole naval agreement. Under these circumstances bases would probably never be built, he said. But he dropped the suggestion in deference to Balfour's fears that it would detract from the stability of the arms treaty.

Other members of the American delegation saw no objection to granting Japan's request when Hughes laid it before them. He especially questioned Lodge and Underwood on what the attitude of Congress would be. "There should be no hesitation in making the agreement," the Senators replied, "since Congress would never consent to spend the vast sums required in adequately fortifying these islands."[4] Root took the same view. Since Lodge had for a quarter of a century advocated a strong American policy in the Far East, his assurance on this point was especially impressive. "You're not giving up anything," he told the Secretary. When the fortifications agreement later was attacked in the Senate, Lodge became its foremost defender.

[3] *Foreign Relations, 1922,* I, 74.   [4] CEH, Notes, p. 286.

Admiral Coontz complained some years later that, to the best of his knowledge, neither the Navy nor the General Board was consulted about giving up the right to fortify our Pacific islands.[5] The implication seems to be that the delegation acted without technical advice. But the General Board's report to Hughes on October 14, 1921, amply covered the subject. That report vigorously opposed any agreement to dismantle fortifications and insisted that the security of American possessions in the Pacific was "dependent upon proper development and defense of Oahu, Guam, and Manila Bay." [6]

The Secretary also had the whole subject of Pacific bases investigated by Dr. George H. Blakeslee before the conference began. The Blakeslee report took note of the desire of the armed services for strongly fortified bases in Hawaii and Guam. So Hughes was well advised as to the views of the strategists. Confronted by the Japanese request, moreover, he discussed it with the Assistant Secretary of the Navy, assuming that Roosevelt would in turn consult the admirals.

In the end the Navy was overruled. The conference was, as Root said, "the complete negation of naval policy." Hughes was pursuing, not the chimera of an impregnable navy, but a policy of live and let live. His expert, Dr. Blakeslee, had pointed out that fortification of Guam, while it would assure earlier success of American naval operations in the western Pacific, was not essential to our national security or to the maintenance of American policy in the Far East. On the other hand, it would be an obvious menace to the security of Japan, which would doubtless prevent her from reducing her naval forces. The gain from fortifying Guam, he concluded, would not equal the loss resulting from failure of the conference and increased friction with Japan.[7] This reasoning harmonized with Hughes' keen desire to make offensive war more difficult while safeguarding defenses. And if bases would never be built in Guam and the Philippines anyway, maintenance of that sterile right at the cost of continuing the naval race would be a colossal blunder.

When the Big Three met again on December 2, after the failure of the technical experts to break the deadlock, Kato again defended his claim for a 10:10:7 ratio and retention of the *Mutsu*. Instead of being 98 per cent complete, as the American proposal indicated, the *Mutsu* was finished and had 500 miles of sea travel behind her. If he were to give up the pride of the Japanese Navy and accept the 60 per cent ratio, how could he justify it to the Japanese people? Certainly it would be of great assistance in getting agreement on the lower ratio, Kato said, if the United States would consent not to increase its fortifications at Guam, the Philippines, and Hawaii. Japan in turn

[5] *Hearings on the London Naval Treaty* (of 1930), p. 436.
[6] Copy of report is in the Hughes Papers; see p. 10.
[7] "The Existing Strategic Situation in the Pacific in Relation to Limitation of Armament," Hughes Papers.

would agree not to fortify Formosa, the Pescadores, and Oshima. Incidentally, Kato had admitted to Balfour that Japan was planning to fortify these islands.

Hughes began by saying that Japan was in the fortunate position of having no great naval power as a neighbor. The 10:10:6 ratio was entirely fair to Japan because it represented her own estimate of her national needs. To be sure, Japan could reject an agreement and build more ships, but that would be futile because the United States would build, too. In spite of his qualms about getting money from Congress, Hughes insisted that the ratio would be maintained as it was in any event.

To another of Kato's arguments, Hughes replied that American ships under construction must be counted as part of our naval strength. A warship 90 per cent complete would be an enormous asset in case of emergency. "Similarly," he added, "in the case of a ship 70 per cent or 50 per cent or other per cent completed, the work done was so much naval strength in hand . . . the American people would never consent to scrap the ships in course of construction, on which they had spent $330,000,000, and at the same time not count what they actually had in course of construction as a part of their naval strength." [8] Japan's naval experts were permitted to examine the pertinent Navy records to remove all doubt as to the work done on the unfinished ships. Under the pounding of Hughes' logic, Kato retreated from his contention that a ship was not a ship unless it was ready to fight.

Turning to the *Mutsu*, Hughes said that if Kato wished to know how he could justify this sacrifice to the Japanese people, "surely his best line of argument was to explain the sacrifices which America was making. She was not giving up merely one ship but three ships that were very little behind the *Mutsu*, and no less than fifteen capital ships which were under construction."

As to Kato's proposal to "freeze the Pacific" in regard to fortifications, Hughes said that the American delegation might be willing to consider it but only as part of a general agreement that would embrace the proposed four-power pact and the American plan for reduction of naval armament. And in no event could Hawaii, which was solely a defensive base, be included in any such agreement. The conference broke up with the understanding that Kato would seek further instructions from Tokyo. Because of the congestion of the cables, ten days elapsed before he was ready to talk again.

When the Big Three met in Hughes' office on December 12, Kato definitely offered to accept the 10:10:6 ratio in return for maintenance of the status quo as to fortifications and naval bases in the Pacific. The two proposals were inseparable in the Japanese mind. Kato said frankly that if naval bases were to be developed in the Philippines or Guam, "the better tendency in relations between the two countries which had lately been observable would be changed

[8] *Foreign Relations, 1922*, I, 75–82.

to hostility." [9] Hughes gave his blessing to the arrangement, again exempting Hawaii, and stating his assumption that Japan would refrain from fortifying her outlying islands and that existing fortifications would be left intact. Balfour likewise acquiesced.

The *Mutsu,* however, appeared more than ever to be a sacred cow. School children had contributed pennies to help finance her. She was now fully manned, Kato said, and could not be destroyed without striking a disastrous blow to Japanese morale. Kato offered to sink the old *Settsu* instead.

Both Hughes and Balfour argued powerfully against this course. Retention of the *Mutsu* would upset the carefully devised ratio of the American proposal. Japan could not camouflage that fact by offering to scrap an older vessel in place of her giant, modern man-of-war. Kato tried to squeeze out of the tight place he was in by saying that the 10:10:6 ratio was to apply at the end and not the beginning of the ten-year naval holiday. Hughes replied pointedly that he had always understood the ratio to be immediately applicable as a means of measuring what each country had to sacrifice. If Japan insisted on retaining the *Mutsu,* Great Britain would have to build and the United States would have to finish the construction of equivalent ships. Kato was sorry, but in any event the *Mutsu* had to be saved.

The Secretary was keenly disappointed over this defeat. All he could do, however, was to insist that the list of doomed ships be altered so as to maintain the 10:10:6 ratio with the *Mutsu* spared. Having consulted his naval advisers, he informed the Japanese the next day that the United States would have to complete the *Washington* [10] and the *Colorado,* the two ships farthest advanced, while scrapping the *Delaware* and the *North Dakota,* to match Japan's departure from the original plan. The result would be to give the United States roughly 525,000 tons of capital ships and Japan 315,000 tons instead of the 500,000-ton and 300,000-ton limits originally proposed.

Japan's intransigence convinced the British that they would have to build two of the enormous super-*Hoods* that were under contract. Unless building went forward, Britain would have no ships designed after the Battle of Jutland, except the *Hood,* which had been somewhat altered after Jutland. Britain was loath to spend money on new ships, but all agreed that it would be the only fair and feasible thing to do if the *Mutsu* were to be kept.

This raised a new difficulty, for the super-*Hoods* would far exceed the 35,000-ton limit that Hughes had proposed for all battleships. He strenuously objected to any further breach in the original plan. Neither Japan nor the United States would have a ship larger than 35,000 tons, he said. Could not Britain reduce the size of her ships and thus avoid excessive scrapping of

[9] *Ibid.,* p. 91.
[10] The Navy later decided to complete the *West Virginia* instead of the *Washington.*

existing vessels to keep within the maximum tonnage allowance? Balfour said that large sums had been spent in designing the super-*Hoods*. It would take a year to change the designs. Meanwhile Britain would be in a position of serious inferiority. The argument waxed warm for several days.

Two sessions were held on December 14, the final one at Secretary Hughes' home that evening. There was much talk about a plan under which Britain would build two 35,000-ton battleships and scrap four in the *King George V* class. The British experts and delegates strongly favored, however, the alternative plan of building two super-*Hoods* which would necessitate the scrapping of five older ships. Balfour begged Hughes not to ask the British to sacrifice the size and weight that would be necessary to give their ships adequate protection against submarines and airplanes. But Hughes was not convinced. By way of emphasis he questioned Balfour on what size the super-*Hoods* would attain.

"Would those ships displace more than 35,000 tons?"

Balfour said they would.

"As much as 40,000 tons?"

Again Balfour answered affirmatively.

"As much as 45,000 tons?" Hughes then asked with pointed emphasis on the figure.

"Yes," Balfour admitted, "the plans call for ships that would displace nearly 50,000 tons."

Kato agreeably consented to the British plan, but Hughes became increasingly alarmed over the prospect. The more he thought about it, the more indefensible it seemed for an arms limitation conference to put its stamp of approval on 49,000-ton battleships. When the Big Three met in his office on the morning of December 15, he launched a final assault on Britain's sea monsters. If we agree to this, he said, the British can go home from the conference and start building battleships of a magnitude never before seen on the oceans. Her example would quicken the desires of other countries for larger ships. Instead of encouraging peace and ending naval rivalry, the conference would thus be undercutting its own handiwork.

"How could we possibly defend such a decision before our peoples?" Hughes asked. "They are looking to us to curtail naval strength. We cannot be content with agreement upon mathematical formulas. No matter how we might try to justify the building of warships of such colossal size, most of the moral and psychological impact of the conference would be lost." [11]

Balfour was visibly shaken in his position. Excusing himself, he went across the hall to consult Admiral Chatfield. On his return he said frankly that the Admiralty would not agree to any reduction in the size of the super-*Hoods*. "But I think," he said dramatically, turning to Secretary Hughes, "that you

[11] Author's interview with CEH, Nov. 19, 1946; *Foreign Relations, 1922*, I, 125.

are right. I do not like to act without consulting my government, but what you have proposed is so manifestly just, and I am so impressed with the importance of avoiding further delay, that I will take the responsibility of accepting the scheme under which Great Britain would have the right to build two new ships of not more than 35,000 British tons." [12]

It was the most intense moment in all the negotiations of the conference. No other delegate could have taken so much upon himself. The courage and statesmanlike attitude of Balfour won Hughes' unbounded admiration, and it goes a long way toward explaining their close teamwork through the remainder of the conference. The French got little sympathy from Hughes when they later clashed with the British. "I can't go back on Mr. Balfour," he told Castle, "nor would you if you could have seen him day after day sitting beside me in this office and backing up all I had to say on the subject of destruction of capital ships, to the great amazement of Baron Kato, who had expected the British to support some, at least, of the Japanese claims." [13] Balfour's comment was that the three months he and Hughes spent together represented "the perfect ideal of that which international negotiations ought always to possess, but which too often are absent." [14]

Prior to Balfour's dramatic concession, Hughes had agreed to a second minor breach in his plan—that the limit of 35,000 tons placed on the two British battleships should be deemed to mean British tons, thus raising the limit to about 37,000 American tons. Except for this and the upward revision of the tonnage cuttings because of the *Mutsu,* the Hughes plan had come through the negotiations intact. On December 15 the Big Three announced their agreement to the world. They had accepted (1) the 10:10:6 ratio; (2) a ten-year naval holiday, except for two American and two British ships to offset Japan's retention of the *Mutsu;* and (3) maintenance of the status quo as to fortifications and naval bases "in the region of the Pacific." It was a notable victory for the patient and unrelenting statesman who had summoned the conference, fixed the scope of its undertakings, and nursed it through several crises.

A sea of trouble lay ahead, however, for this accord was contingent upon a satisfactory agreement with France and Italy. Those two countries had not been invited to the discussions of the Big Three because Hughes wished to avoid the intrusion of relatively minor issues into the major problem of arresting the Anglo-American-Japanese naval race. That was certainly the best strategy for hastening the major accord, but it aroused suspicions among the French and doubtless stiffened their demands. M. Briand had come to Washington without any program, hoping to play the role of mediator between the United States and Great Britain. No such opportunity arose. The weak bargaining

[12] *Id.*   [13] Castle's diary, 1922, p. 29.
[14] Address to Pilgrims, London, July 21, 1924.

position of the French was further accentuated because the war had forced them to neglect naval building. As the conference seemed to move along without them, they felt frustrated and unhappy.

Sensing this restiveness among the French delegates, Hughes asked Theodore Roosevelt, Jr., to see Admiral de Bon and find out what total tonnage the French expected. The admiral declined to commit himself. Roosevelt and his naval experts concluded that France and Italy should agree to a replacement limit of 175,000 tons while retaining all the warships they then possessed. Hughes agreed that the proposal was reasonable. It asked nothing of France to match the 40 per cent reduction proposed for the British and American fleets.

Ambassador Jusserand attempted to sound out Hughes as to what he had in mind for France as the two climbed the stair at the Pan American building one day. Finding that Jusserand had no suggestion to offer, Hughes asked, "Would 175,000 tons be satisfactory?" Jusserand made no definite reply.[15]

It is not clear whether Jusserand passed along this suggestion to Premier Briand. The Premier returned home late in November before there was any opportunity for the French to enter the negotiations on naval limitation. He had, however, come to a friendly understanding with Hughes as to general policies. Just before Briand left Washington, he visited the Secretary at his home and they chatted amiably together without the aid of an interpreter, Briand speaking French, which Hughes understood, and Hughes speaking English, which Briand largely understood. The Premier said in no uncertain terms that he was in sympathy with what Hughes was doing, that although he was leaving he would still be head of the French delegation, and that if at any time during the conference he could be helpful the Secretary should call on him.

This offer assumed major significance when the French delegates in Washington demanded a quota of no less than 350,000 tons of capital ships. The Secretary had called in Albert Sarraut and Jusserand to tell them of the accord he had reached with Great Britain and Japan. In spite of previous indications of French pique, he was shocked by the unreasonableness of their stand. Sarraut was claiming the right to build a navy more than twice the size of France's existing fleet.

Seeing the great achievement for which he had labored so indefatigably slipping from his grasp, Hughes addressed the French delegates with bluntness approaching severity. France's economic position, he said, would not permit her to build so many ships. "Why," he undiplomatically exclaimed, with obvious reference to France's unpaid war debt to the United States, "you can't even pay your debts."

[15] *Foreign Relations, 1922,* I, 134.

"We are as proud of our debts," Jusserand came back, with a stiffening gesture, "as we are of our wounds." [16]

Hughes begged the French delegates not to announce their demand publicly. It would cause a revulsion of feeling throughout America. The numerous efforts of the American people to extend financial aid to the French would be left virtually without support. France, he said, would scarcely have a friend left in the United States. The irritable and quarrelsome Sarraut indicated that he would fight publicly for the 350,000-ton quota. He did so and brought a storm of indignation upon his head.

Rent by feuds among themselves and plagued by the incompetence of René Viviani and Sarraut, the French delegates were in a state of acute agitation. Hughes' proposal to limit their fleet to 175,000 tons was denounced as an affront to the honor and dignity of France. It was "unspeakable." Bristling with anger, Admiral de Bon declared that the French Admiralty was planning to build twelve capital ships and could not accept a holiday until 1931.

Hughes called in Jusserand the next day and told him, as ambassador, of Briand's friendly offer before he had left. "Although I dislike going over M. Sarraut's head," he said, "I feel that it is imperative to communicate with the Premier." Jusserand merely remarked that that would be quite within the Secretary's rights. The "personal message" which Hughes dictated was put into Briand's hands just as he was leaving Paris for London.

Success or failure of the conference hung on the word of France, Hughes told the Premier. If France were to make the same sacrifices that the other powers were making, her tonnage of battleships would be reduced to 102,000. "We do not ask this," Hughes hastened to add. His plan for France would allow her to keep all her 164,000 tons of dreadnoughts and even increase her quota to 175,000 tons. Likewise her pre-dreadnoughts could be saved, although all other countries were scrapping theirs.

"If it be said that France desires a greater relative strength," he argued, "the obvious answer is that this would be impossible of attainment." [17] The result would be no agreement; then the United States and Britain would shortly have navies, not of three to one in relation to France, but of six to one. "The proposed agreement," he drove home to Briand, "really doubles the relative strength of the French Navy." Should France insist on a quota of more than 300,000 tons, he concluded, she would wreck the conference and blight the hope of the world for relief from the burden of excessive armaments.

Unquestionably the French had padded their demand for capital ships in the hope of winning favorable concessions as to smaller craft and submarines.

[16] Author's interview with J. Reuben Clark, Jr., Dec. 12, 1948.
[17] *Foreign Relations, 1922,* I, 130ff.

When confronted with the risk of defeating all agreement, Briand cabled to Hughes: "With regard to the tonnage of capital ships—that is to say, ships of offense, which are the most costly—I have instructed our delegates in the sense you desire." [18] However, it would be impossible, he insisted, for France to accept corresponding reductions as to light cruisers, torpedo boats, and submarines.

Hughes thought this response ended the controversy so far as capital ships were concerned. But Sarraut, Jusserand, and Admiral de Bon insisted that Briand's acceptance of Hughes' proposal as to capital ships was conditional on the granting of France's desires as to light cruisers, flotilla leaders, destroyers, and submarines. Saying that he would resort to the language of the street, Sarraut ranted about France being "blotted out of the surface of the sea" and "cut into shreds and done away with piecemeal." [19] He read "confidential instructions" from his government to the effect that France must have an irreducible minimum of 330,000 tons of light cruisers, torpedo boats, and so forth, and 90,000 tons of submarines. Referring to Secretary Hughes' success in bringing the British and Japanese around to his point of view, Sarraut asked pointedly for a guarantee that, in return for France's acceptance of the capital-ship limit of 175,000 tons, France's other demands would be met.

Hughes rejected this fantastic high-pressure scheme, but the exorbitant French demand for auxiliary craft was untouchable. Once more he appealed to Briand for some indication, to be given in confidence, as to his minimum figures for the so-called "defensive" ships. The Premier promised to comply while he was still in London, but, back in Paris, where he was having trouble holding the confidence of Parliament, he dropped the idea. Eventually the French accepted the 175,000-ton limit on capital ships, but refused to go an inch beyond it.

This attitude spelled the doom of Hughes' hope for proportionate reductions in auxiliary craft. The United States had originally suggested a 90,000-ton limit on submarines for itself and Great Britain and a 54,000-ton limit for Japan. A later American plan called for 60,000 tons of submarines for the two largest naval powers, with Japan, France, and Italy keeping what they then had. Both France and Japan objected, and apparently nothing would induce the French to lower their demand for 90,000 tons, although their existing fleet of submarines was little more than one-third that size. The British had urged complete abolition of submarines, and in view of the fabulous French demand in this category Balfour was unwilling to accept any limit on destroyers or other small craft used to combat submarines. Both the British and Italians hinted at aggressive intentions behind the French demands, and this led to the bitterest row of the conference.[20] Since M. Briand had realistically

[18] *Ibid.*, p. 135.   [19] *Ibid.*, p. 137ff.   [20] *Conference*, pp. 574ff.

closed the door to any reduction of land armaments until the security of France could be guaranteed by other means, the French took the chief blame for limiting the achievements of the conference.

Feeling the necessity of getting some action as to submarines, the American delegation, with Root taking the lead, put through a treaty stating the rules of international law as to submarines and attempting to prohibit their use as commerce destroyers.[21] Any submarine commander violating the rules was declared to be subject to punishment, "as if for an act of piracy," by the military or civil authorities of any country. The same treaty undertook to prohibit the use of poisonous gases and chemicals in warfare. It was ratified by the United States, Great Britain, Italy, and Japan, but France held out until the treaty was superseded by a milder agreement at the London Naval Conference of 1930.

To prevent the building of larger cruisers to take the place of capital ships, the conference limited the individual size of auxiliary craft to 10,000 tons and the caliber of their guns to eight inches. Aircraft carriers were limited both as to the over-all tonnage each power might have and as to individual size. The American delegation at first proposed a limit of 27,000 tons displacement for aircraft carriers, but the Navy, fearing it would never get money out of Congress for carriers, conceived the idea of converting the battle cruisers *Lexington* and *Saratoga* into carriers. These vessels, designed to displace 43,500 tons, could not be stripped as carriers to less than 33,000 tons. So the treaty was written to retain the 27,000-ton limit, with an exception that any of the powers might convert into carriers two of their ships that would otherwise be scrapped, and these might be of a tonnage up to 33,000.

Taking advantage of this idea while the treaty was still in the drafting stage, the British inserted clauses permitting doomed ships to be converted to commercial or harbor use. Hughes raised a furor. "It is of vital importance," he said, "that nothing be done which would tend to impair the moral value of the *whole* treaty. No petty economies or fancied saving would compensate the destruction of the moral value. . . . Sincerity of purpose is the thing the treaty will be judged by." The world was looking for something comparable to the destruction of the German fleet at Scapa Flow and "would brook nothing which enabled these ships to be kept alive." Permit them to be converted to commercial and harbor use and they would all remain available in case of war. The average man would say "the treaty was a sham." [22]

Admitting the possibility of misunderstanding, Balfour asked if it was not difficult to defend conversion of the *Lexington*s into aircraft carriers if the British were not allowed to economize by converting their old warships for

[21] *Report of the American Delegation*, pp. 36f.
[22] *Foreign Relations, 1922*, I, 189–192.

harbor service. Hughes could not see the comparison. A warm argument ensued. The American delegation was opposed, the chairman said, to having the treaty say one thing when meaning another. If necessary to avoid that blunder, he personally would eliminate the provision as to the two aircraft carriers. "I will not for the sake of ten or twenty millions of dollars," he declared, "spoil this treaty."

A strenuous discussion followed within the American delegation, with Hughes disposed to strike out the concession on aircraft carriers and Root and Underwood agreeing. Roosevelt saved the carriers by arguing that Congress might continue spending money on two ships under construction but probably would not appropriate for entirely new ships. Hughes went back to the committee of chief delegates and won his point without sacrificing the carriers. That was the logical outcome, for there was really no relation between converting battle cruisers into carriers, which the United States had a right to build in any event, and saving warships in excess of quotas by devoting them to civilian uses.

The American draft of the treaty was accepted largely because Hughes had had the foresight to put a group of experts to work on it shortly after the conference assembled. He personally scrutinized each new draft the experts produced, penciling in additions and corrections and clarifying the language. By January 4 the American draft had been approved by the committee of legal experts with only minor changes.

Fresh difficulties arose, however, as to the status quo agreement on fortifications and naval bases in the Pacific. The experts asked what should be the boundaries of the "Pacific region" in which no bulwarks should be built. The statement of December 15 said only that the region included Hong Kong and did not include the Hawaiian Islands, Australia, New Zealand, the islands composing Japan proper, and the coasts of the United States and Canada. That left many questions unanswered. What would be the status of the Aleutians? What of the British naval base at Singapore? What islands constitute "Japan proper"?

The British evolved a clever scheme based on a parallelogram bounded on the east by the International Date Line, on the north by the thirtieth degree of latitude, on the west by the 110th meridian and on the south by the Equator.[23] All the islands inside the parallelogram, including most of the American and Japanese islands, were not to be fortified. All the islands outside, including most of Great Britain's, would be unrestricted. Meanwhile the Japanese had put in a claim for exclusion of the Bonins and other islands several hundred miles distant from the Japanese coast.

[23] Harold and Margaret Sprout, *Toward a New Order of Sea Power*, pp. 244f.

Kato visited Hughes informally on January 16 and said that the nonfortifications agreement had been transformed into a political issue in Japan. Tokyo would not accept the British proposal. Apparently some of Kato's enemies at home were using the agreement to embarrass him. He asked the Secretary to give him a few days to see if he could work the problem out quietly without having to face the Naval Committee.

On January 22 Kato reported that acceptance of the British proposal would cause the Japanese Cabinet to fall and no treaty could then be ratified. Against the background of that ominous forecast, he offered a concrete proposal of his own. He would leave the United States free to fortify the Hawaiian Islands and islands adjacent to the mainland. Britain could fortify islands adjacent to Canada, Australia, and New Zealand; Japan could fortify any of her islands, except Amami-Oshima, the Bonin Islands, Formosa, and the Pescadores. Balfour immediately called for exemption of Singapore. After consultation with the Navy Department, Hughes wished to exempt, in addition to the Hawaiian Islands, the islands adjacent to "the coast of the United States, including Alaska and the Panama Canal Zone." He added to Kato's list of Japanese islands to remain unfortified Okinawa-Oshima and "any insular possessions in the Pacific Ocean which Japan may hereafter acquire."

Kato objected because this reference to Alaska would permit fortification of the Aleutian Islands, which extend in the direction of Japan. We cannot give up our right to fortify the Aleutians, Hughes replied, unless Japan, in return, will give up her right to fortify the Kurile Islands, which stretch out toward Alaska, and the Loochoo Islands, which point toward the Philippines. After cabling his government, Kato proposed that the Aleutians, the Kuriles, and the Loochoos be brought into the status-quo agreement and that Okinawa-Oshima be left out. This proposal was finally adopted.

The fortifications agreement, Colonel Roosevelt wrote in his diary, "leaves us, in my opinion, in a slightly better position than Japan. We trade certain fortifications which we would never have completed, for fortifications which they [the Japanese] would have unquestionably completed. We retain one outpost in the Pacific of great importance and they give up all but their mainland." [24]

Three days after Kato got his final instructions from Tokyo the naval treaty was completed. Secretary Hughes had compromised with the Japanese on fortifications and on the *Mutsu,* and the French had blocked agreement as to auxiliary craft. With these exceptions, he had won every major controversy with every delegation, and all the principles laid down in his initial speech were safely embedded in the text of the treaty. From beginning to end it had

[24] Jan. 29, 30, 1922. Quoted by Sprout, *op. cit.,* p. 251.

been Hughes' conference. "A powerful locomotive pulling a great express train gives a slight idea of the force and the speed of the Chairman of the conference," wrote one of the experts of the American delegation.[25]

Even in his hour of triumph, however, the Secretary was bedeviled by a minor irritation. Plans had been laid for printing the treaties with the equally authentic French and English texts in parallel columns. Hughes advanced the idea that, since the conference had been held in the United States, with English dominant in the discussions, the English text should have the more conspicuous place in the left-hand column. Jusserand was horrified. Sarraut is said to have threatened to withhold France's approval of the treaties unless the French text were given the "place d'honneur." [26] The vehemence of this demand, added to the arbitrary conduct of the French in the naval-treaty negotiations, aroused Hughes' Welsh-Irish ire.

After a spirited debate with Jusserand over the telephone, Hughes was discussing the controversy with Solicitor Fred K. Nielsen when Senator Lodge dropped in. "Mr. Secretary," the Senator remarked in his squeaky voice, "what's the difference?" [27] A smile of acquiescence crept over Hughes' face. While he had been human enough to haggle over a petty matter as the greatest drama in his career approached a finale, he was quick to recognize that his own precept of not letting insignificant details stand in the way of great achievements had been effectively turned against him.

The proud moment for presentation of the Naval Armaments Treaty to the conference came on February 1. Again Continental Hall was filled to capacity by a distinguished audience. But the tension of November 12 had given way to a quiet feeling of satisfaction and renewed faith in peace. With no manuscript before him, Secretary Hughes reported the details of the treaty, the ships to be scrapped and their tonnage, the deviations from the original American plan, the agreement as to fortifications, the miscellaneous provisions, and the processes of reasoning that led to agreement on each point. Nothing was missing. His associates shook their heads over this feat of memory as Hughes summed up:

May I say that no more extraordinary or significant Treaty has ever been made. It is extraordinary because we no longer merely talk of the desirability of diminishing the burdens of naval armaments, but we actually limit them. (*Applause.*) . . .

This Treaty ends, absolutely ends, the race in competition in naval armament. (*Applause.*) At the same time it leaves the relative security of the great naval Powers unimpaired.

[25] George H. Blakeslee, *The Recent Foreign Policy of the United States* (New York, Abingdon Press, 1925), pp. 236f. Copyright, 1925, by George H. Blakeslee.
[26] Chandler P. Anderson's diary, Feb. 6, 1922.
[27] Author's interview with Mr. Nielsen, July 21, 1949.

By Larry Keys in the *Columbus Citizen*, February 7, 1922.

PROOF OF THE PUDDING IS IN RATIFICATION

The significance of the Treaty is far more than that. In this Treaty we are talking of arms in the language of peace. The best thing about the engagement is the spirit which has been manifested throughout our negotiations and to which is due our ability to reach this fortunate conclusion. In other words, we are taking perhaps the greatest forward step in history to establish the reign of peace. (*Applause.*) [28]

[28] *Conference,* p. 248.

Chapter 47

THE FOUR-POWER PACT

THE destruction of weapons, standing by itself, is a negative achievement. It becomes positive in effect only when it is supplemented by better means of keeping the peace. The Washington Conference courageously attacked both problems. Much of its time was given to removing sources of friction, defining rights, and creating obligations that would eliminate any necessity for appeal to the arbitrament of arms.

Secretary Hughes concluded that four sources of unrest in the Pacific would have to be dealt with if the experiment in arms limitation were to have a fair chance of success: first, the Anglo-Japanese Alliance; second, Japanese imperialism on the continent of Asia; third, the Shantung controversy that was keeping Japan and China at daggers' points; fourth, the controversy over the mandated islands which had strained relations between the United States and Japan. If these sore spots could be healed and the naval race ended, the drift toward war could be arrested and future aggression would be made more difficult.

The exertion of pressure for modification of the Anglo-Japanese Alliance had started in the Wilson Administration. Secretary Hughes put increased vigor behind that policy. American public opinion was deeply hostile toward the alliance, for it legally bound Great Britain to go to war with the United States if Japan should do so. The British had attempted to strip the alliance of this obligation when it was renewed in 1911 by including a provision that it should not operate against a third power with which either ally might conclude a treaty of general arbitration. But the Senate had rejected the Anglo-American arbitration treaty. When the postwar tension between the United States and Japan reached its height in 1920 and 1921 and renewal of the Anglo-Japanese Alliance was under consideration, both Japanese and British spokesmen denied that it was a menace to the United States. Nevertheless, it was a fertile source of unrest in the United States, Britain, and Canada.

An inaccurate press report in June, 1921, gave Hughes the opportunity he had been seeking to voice his antagonism toward the alliance. "It is understood," said a dispatch dealing with the London Imperial Conference, "that the State Department has been kept fully informed of the plans of the British Government, and that it has been given assurances that in the renewal of the treaty every precaution will be taken to guard against the inclusion of anything inimical to American rights." [1] Hughes publicly denied that he was being kept informed and said that he had received no assurances; he did not wish the public to get "a false impression." The following day Ambassador Geddes hastened to the Secretary's office to ask if he wished to say anything in regard to the proposed renewal of the alliance.

Hughes replied that, since the defeat of Germany and the collapse of Russia had removed the original cause for entering into the alliance, the American people would regard its continuance as an alliance against them.[2] His chief emphasis, however, was upon the unfortunate encouragement the alliance gave to Japanese imperialism. There were no questions between the United States and Japan that could not be solved, he said. But the American Government had some very clear policies in the Far East, including the Open Door, the integrity of China, and now, in view of existing conditions, those policies embraced the integrity of Russia. If he could "speak freely in an informal and confidential way," the Secretary said, "he felt that if Great Britain and Japan had any arrangement by which Great Britain was to support the special interests of Japan, the latter might be likely, at the instance of the militaristic party . . . to take positions which would call forth protests from this Government . . . leading to a state of irritation among the people in both countries; that such a condition of affairs would be fraught with mischief; that if it were true that the policies of Great Britain in the Far East were like our own there should be cooperation between Great Britain and the United States, and it should be possible for the United States to find complete support on the part of Great Britain in their maintenance and execution. . . ." [3]

Geddes wondered whether it would not be possible "to have cooperation with Japan,—that is, on the part of the three nations." It was a bid for the United States to come into the alliance. Hughes made it plain that the United States would not accept such an arrangement. What he had in mind was pursuit of common policies. But he approved Geddes' suggestion for a common declaration of Far Eastern policies if it could be made to square with the principles he was trying to uphold.

Seizing every argument to impress upon the British the desirability of working closely with the United States, Hughes then told Geddes that a resolution for recognition of the Irish Republic would be introduced in Congress. In his opinion it would not pass, but in the debate the enemies of Great Britain would take full advantage of any relation between Great Britain and Japan indicating disregard for American interests. On the contrary, British action

[1] *Foreign Relations, 1921*, II, 313.   [2] Author's interview with CEH, Nov. 26, 1946.
[3] *Foreign Relations, 1921*, II, 314f.

indicating a desire to support the Far Eastern policies to which the United States was committed "would give great aid and comfort to those who were opposing such a resolution."

By this combination of persuasion and pressure Hughes sought to shift British influence from the Japanese side of the Far Eastern equation to the American side. The effect of the alliance had been to shield Japanese imperialism in China and Russia. Japan had interpreted it as a sort of hunting license on the continent of Asia, with her ally maintaining a benevolent hands-off attitude. The Japanese thus laid great store upon renewal of the alliance, and Hughes was equally determined, if at all possible, to bring the British into a tacit partnership for the purposes of holding the Japanese in check.

For a time the issue was clouded by another dispute about Ambassador Harvey's veracity. Geddes returned to the department on July 6 to confirm his understanding that the Secretary had informally said the United States would regret the renewal of the alliance. Hughes assured him that his understanding was correct. Sir Aukland then said that Harvey had given exactly the opposite impression in London.[4] In talking with Lord Curzon, Harvey had said that whether or not Great Britain renewed the alliance or made a special arrangement with Japan was of no concern to the United States. No such statement had been authorized, Hughes replied, and it did not represent the opinion of the Administration.

The Secretary cabled Harvey for an explanation, and pointedly reminded him that he was expected to "await instructions before expressing opinions as to policy." Harvey read part of the cablegram to Curzon and quoted the Foreign Minister as saying: "That is simply monstrous. Of course you never said anything of that kind and I never said you did."[5] According to Harvey, Curzon had asked him if he could give a hint as to his government's attitude toward renewal of the alliance, and he had replied that he could not but would be glad to submit any question Curzon might wish to ask. To another question he had replied that he personally thought the American people would look upon renewal of the alliance with disfavor and mistrust. Harvey had not bothered to pass along Curzon's query to the Secretary of State. Final responsibility for the conflicting assertions was never fixed.

By the time the Washington Conference assembled, the British appeared not only willing but also eager to modify their alliance with Japan. Curzon, Lloyd George, and even King George himself had confided to Harvey their desire to get rid of that bond.[6] Balfour came to Washington, therefore, with the problem of the Anglo-Japanese Alliance uppermost in his mind. Calling on Hughes the day before the conference opened, he spoke of the danger of

[4] CEH to Harvey, July 6, 1921.   [5] Harvey to Hughes, July 8, 1921.
[6] Willis F. Johnson, *George Harvey: "A Passionate Patriot,"* pp. 322f.

wounding Japan's sensibilities, and of the need for control over Japanese action and for safeguarding the Dominions. The situation was very delicate. If the alliance were not to be continued, what could be substituted for it? Answering his own question, Balfour said he had sketched two memoranda of possible agreements.

Hughes assured Balfour that the United States was friendly to Japan and would not oppose natural and legitimate economic opportunities for the Japanese. Their need was not political expansion, he said, but economic opportunity. Balfour ultimately came back to his drafts. Hughes asked time to consider them, and reiterated that the United States would not enter an alliance. Remembering the Senate, he was even averse to the word "treaty" and preferred to talk of "a definitive statement of principles and policies" that would take the place not only of the Anglo-Japanese Alliance but also the Root-Takahira and the Lansing-Ishii notes. Especially the Root-Takahira agreement was "a coin to be reissued." Balfour then substituted "arrangement" for "treaty" and "alliance" wherever they appeared in his drafts and penciled a note to the effect that "arrangement" as used was "deliberatively vague." [7]

The Secretary scrutinized Balfour's proposed "arrangements" and decided that neither was acceptable. One contained the germ of what was later to become the Nine-Power Treaty, but only the germ. The other was little more than the old Anglo-Japanese Alliance rewritten to include the United States. Each of the trio would agree to respect the rights of the others in the islands of the Pacific and bordering territories and to consult together if any one of them thought its rights to be imperiled. If threatened, any two of the signatories would be at liberty "to protect themselves by entering into a military alliance provided (*a*) this alliance is purely defensive in character and (*b*) that it is communicated to the other High Contracting Party."

Hughes' high opinion of Balfour must have sagged as he analyzed this scheme. It offered the United States the shell of a tripartite agreement and allowed Great Britain and Japan to keep the nut of their military obligations in case of trouble. Any war threat in the Pacific could transform the "arrangement" overnight into the old alliance. Indeed, the alliance was not even specifically cancelled by the Balfour proposal.

Hughes concluded, moreover, that no three-party agreement would protect American interests. If we should join with two countries that had been allies for twenty years, he said, the American people would feel that their government had put its head into a noose. The only way to avoid the risks of a two-to-one combination, with the United States in the minority, he decided, was to bring in France. When Hughes broached this idea to Balfour in one of their

[7] Papers on the Four-Power Treaty, Hughes Papers.

early interviews, the latter not only welcomed it but also agreed to seek the consent of Japan.

"It was Hughes' idea to bring in the French," Balfour wrote to a friend, "in order to soothe their somewhat ruffled pride." [8] That motive undoubtedly entered into the decision, but it was incidental to his feeling that a four-power agreement was necessary to shake off the odium of the old alliance and remove the danger that "England and Japan might combine against us." If France were brought in and the old alliance were abandoned in favor of a mere consultation treaty, the Secretary thought he might be able to get it approved by the Senate.

On November 26 Shidehara brought in a tripartite proposal similar to Balfour's. The British and Japanese had frequently consulted together. Hughes thus found himself a minority of one, as he feared his country might if it entered the Anglo-Japanese scheme. Nevertheless, he clung doggedly to his own ideas, and a series of meetings won the British and Japanese delegations to his point of view.

There was much delay, however, in getting final instructions from Tokyo. Not a word had been said to the French delegation about the proposed quadruple agreement because of the delicate situation that would arise if Tokyo should object to the inclusion of France. Meanwhile the restive French delegates were a source of increasing apprehension. At the meeting of the Big Three on naval limitation on December 2 Hughes asked Kato if he could say anything as to Japan's attitude on the proposed four-power agreement. Kato replied that he had had no response to his cable. Foreseeing no objection, he thought it would be reasonably safe to approach the French, but Hughes was reluctant to take such a chance, and Kato promised to cable a request that his government expedite its reply.

Finally the word came that Tokyo would accept a quadruple agreement. Thinking he had to have something definite to show the French, Hughes went to work immediately to draft the treaty. A preliminary American draft prepared by Chandler P. Anderson, with an alternative preamble by James Brown Scott, both legal advisers to the American delegation, had been handed to Hughes a fortnight earlier. With all the previous drafts before him, Hughes wrote an entirely new document that was to become the Four-Power Treaty.[9]

The first article pledged each of the four powers to respect the rights of the others to their insular possessions and dominions in the Pacific, and in case of controversy between any two of the four powers "likely to affect the relations of harmonious accord now happily subsisting between them," they were to invite the other powers to a conference in which "the whole subject" could be

[8] A. Whitney Griswold, *The Far Eastern Policy of the United States* (New York, Harcourt, Brace, 1938), p. 310. Copyright, 1938, by Harcourt, Brace & Co.

[9] CEH to Underwood, March 11, 1922.

"considered and adjusted." [10] Article II was a pledge that, in case of an aggressive threat from the outside, the four powers would "communicate with one another fully and frankly in order to arrive at an understanding as to the most efficient measures to be taken, jointly or separately, to meet the exigencies of the particular situation." It was a reissuance of the Root-Takahira "coin." The agreement would remain in effect for ten years, and then might be terminated by any party on six months' notice. As soon as it was ratified, the Anglo-Japanese Alliance would be terminated.

Root and Lodge were the first to see the draft and they unhesitatingly approved it. After making a few verbal changes, Hughes showed it to Balfour and Shidehara and won their consent. Determined to put the French in a happier mood, he invited M. Viviani to his home on the evening of December 7. When he sprang his surprise offer to the French, giving them an advantage they had not even sought, Viviani rushed up to the Secretary and kissed him on both whiskered cheeks.

In a conference with Balfour, Viviani, Jusserand, Kato, and Shidehara, Hughes made skillful use of the Four-Power Pact as a prod to hasten settlement of the mandates controversy. Since the mandates treaty with Japan was not yet signed and negotiations with Great Britain as to islands south of the Equator had not even begun, he inserted a clause in the Four-Power Pact to the effect that it should "not be deemed as an assent" on the part of the United States to the mandates.

Shidehara, at this same session, handed around copies of a new draft of the proposed treaty. It provided that if a dispute arose in the Pacific, the two parties, "in mutual agreement with each other," should invite the other powers to a conference. That would give Japan a chance to prevent a conference from being called if her imperialistic policies should be challenged. Shidehara said, however, that the chief reason for his draft was to break up Hughes' first article into two parts since it contained two ideas. The group agreed to divide the article into two sentences, but rejected the Japanese joker.

Shidehara asked if the agreement extended only to insular possessions and dominions. Hughes replied with pointed candor that it was so limited, and the reason was "to avoid the difficulties connected with the mainland, especially as to China." There are matters, he said, which "still required adjustment." [11] Both the Balfour and Shidehara drafts had dealt with rights and interests in eastern Asia as well as the Pacific islands, but Hughes was not willing to give any suggestion of countenance to Japan's imperialism in Shantung or elsewhere in China. By the astute means of narrowing the geographical scope of the agreement, as Harold and Margaret Sprout point out, Hughes had transformed the project, in practical effect, "from an American recognition of

[10] *Foreign Relations, 1922*, I, 7, 8.   [11] *Ibid.*, p. 14.

Japan's conquests in Asia, into a Japanese pledge to respect United States sovereignty over the Philippines." [12]

The most embarrassing mix-up of the conference came over the question of whether the Four-Power Pact included the main islands of Japan. Shidehara first raised the question at the December 8 meeting. Hughes said that, being both "islands" and "possessions," they would be included in the language of the treaty. Balfour agreed. Since the mainland of no other party to the agreement was included, Shidehara said he would like to have the main islands of Japan excluded. Balfour at once declared that he could not admit that Australia and New Zealand, which were definitely in the treaty, were less important than any other part of the British Empire. A spirited discussion ensued in which Hughes expressed his willingness to meet Japan's wishes in the matter, and Balfour remained skeptical. Shidehara then attempted to bring in all the regions bordering on the Pacific Ocean. Both Hughes and Balfour resisted this. Finally, the meeting broke up with the understanding that the Japanese delegates would further consider an exchange of notes stating that the agreement did not apply to domestic issues and did not cover the main islands of Japan.

When the same group met the next morning at Hughes' home, Shidehara completely retreated. Now he was satisfied to have the main islands of Japan covered by the agreement and no exchange of notes on that point would be necessary. But he wished to narrow the type of controversies falling within the agreement. Hughes, on the contrary, wished to make certain that questions affecting the security of island possessions could be brought into a conference under the treaty as well as questions directly arising out of the islands themselves. Balfour welcomed this attempt "to give the peace-making aspects of this instrument a wider scope." [13] Ultimately it was agreed to revamp the preamble. Article I was also somewhat altered to read as follows:

The High Contracting Parties agree as between themselves to respect their rights in relation to their insular possessions and insular dominions in the region of the Pacific Ocean.

If there should develop between any of the High Contracting Parties a controversy arising out of any Pacific question and involving their said rights which is not satisfactorily settled by diplomacy and is likely to affect the harmonious accord now happily subsisting between them, they shall invite the other High Contracting Parties to a joint conference to which the whole subject will be referred for consideration and adjustment. [14]

Eager to announce the treaty because of the prairie fire of rumor that was running through Washington, Hughes got permission to call a plenary session the next morning if Paris indicated its assent in time. Viviani called at the

[12] Harold and Margaret Sprout, *Toward a New Order of Sea Power* (Princeton, Princeton University Press, 1940), p. 174. Copyright, 1940, by the Princeton University Press.
[13] *Foreign Relations, 1922*, I, 23ff.   [14] Report of American Delegation, p. 44.

Hughes home that evening with a favorable message from Briand. The fourth plenary session of the conference was thus held on December 10, with Hughes reporting for the Committee on Pacific and Far Eastern Questions and Senator Lodge presenting the Four-Power Pact in his best literary style. While Hughes himself had written the treaty and fought it through, he gave Lodge the honor of presenting it, with a shrewd eye upon its approval by the Senate. Root and Underwood were also to have their moments in the spotlight. The chairman's fair division of honors contributed much to the complete harmony and good will that prevailed in the American delegation.

The nature of the treaty was a surprise to the public. While it was generally hailed as a welcome substitute for the Anglo-Japanese Alliance, politicians and editors scrutinized it suspiciously. When members of the American delegation reported, in reply to questions from the press, that the terms of the agreement covered the main islands of Japan there was an outcry against the supposed "guarantee" to Japan without any reciprocal guarantee to the United States. But the furor subsided because no one who read the treaty carefully could find any guarantee to Japan.

Then a reporter asked the President, at his regular press conference on December 20, whether he understood the main islands of Japan to be included in the treaty. Hughes had explained the whole controversy to Harding, telling him precisely what Balfour and Kato had said and what the final outcome had been. But Harding had forgotten these details. "As I see it," he replied to the press, "the quadrilateral treaty does not apply to Japan proper. The mainland is no more included in the provisions of the treaty than is the mainland of the United States." [15]

News of the President's contradiction of his own delegation flashed and re-flashed around the world. Foes of the treaty shouted with delight. Even the Administration itself, they said sarcastically, was torn between conflicting interpretations of Hughes' "simple and direct" agreement. Suspicion as to the whole document deepened. Some jumped to the conclusion that Hughes had kept the President in the dark as to the meaning of the treaty. Others assumed there had been an open break between the President and the delegation. The conference was thrown into commotion.

Hughes and the other American delegates met immediately. Fearing that Hughes might wish to resign, Root expressed his indignation and offered to go to the White House as mediator.[16] But Hughes was neither excited nor in a mood to resign. Knowing Harding, he surmised what had happened. After reassuring his fellow delegates, he hastened to the White House to see what could be done about Pandora's box that had been opened.

[15] Text of statement in Hughes Papers.
[16] Author's interview with CEH, Nov. 26, 1946.

Harding was apologetic. "I shouldn't have said anything about it to the press," he confessed in a tone of self-accusation. "But, Hughes," he added honestly, "when they asked me about it, I didn't want to appear to be a dub." [17]

They both laughed and agreed that Hughes should dictate a corrective statement to be issued by the White House. Honest words in a case of this sort are a poor cushion; but Hughes softened as much as possible the bump that his chief was bound to take. "He [the President] has learned from the United States delegates to the conference," the statement read, "that they have agreed to the construction which includes the homeland of Japan in the term 'insular possessions and insular dominions,' and has no objection to that construction." [18] It was a complete retraction.

Meanwhile Shidehara, encouraged by senatorial criticism of the treaty, revived his request for exclusion of the main islands of Japan from its provisions. Hughes objected because such action would expose the conference to criticism on the ground that it had approved a treaty meaning one thing today and another tomorrow, but it was found that Australia and New Zealand did not object to exclusion of the Japanese home islands. Ultimately Hughes accepted Shidehara's proposed supplement, insisting only that it be recognized as a change in the treaty and not a mere afterthought.

Thoroughly fatigued as the conference adjourned, Hughes sailed to Bermuda for a brief rest. The Senate took up the Four-Power Treaty in his absence, and part of his time there was spent writing messages and letters in its defense. Opponents of the treaty assumed that it was an alliance imposing on each of the parties at least a moral obligation to aid the others by military or naval force in case of aggression from an outside power. Lodge had made it absolutely clear in his presentation of the treaty to the conference that it had no such implications. The delegates had merely "substituted a four-power agreement to talk for a two-power agreement to fight." But some Senators refused to believe that Great Britain and Japan had given up their alliance for such a flimsy pledge on our part. They formally requested the President to submit all records, minutes, arguments, debate, and conversations relating to its negotiation. Harding cabled to Hughes his proposed refusal to comply. Hughes corrected the President's assumption that all available records had been handed to the Senate and suggested that, while refusing to disclose memoranda of informal and confidential conversations, the President assure the Senate "that there were no secret understandings or exchanges of notes and no commitments whatever except as appeared in the Four-Power Treaty itself. . . ." [19] "President's attitude seems to me exactly right," he commented. "The freedom of the Executive in negotiating treaties should not be impaired by yielding to demands of this sort which can serve no useful purpose but would be re-

[17] *Id.*   [18] Text in Hughes Papers.   [19] CEH to State Department, Feb. 19, 1922.

sented by foreign powers and create distrust of our ability to respect reasonable amenities of negotiations."

For several weeks the debate continued. It was asserted that the Japanese or British had drafted the treaty, with implications that the American delegation had been taken into camp. Hughes responded with a letter to Underwood disclosing his own authorship of the draft that was finally accepted and sharply denying that there was any basis for suspicion concerning it. "Its failure," he wrote, "would be nothing short of a national calamity." [20] In a letter to Lodge he branded the continued rumors of a secret understanding as "absolutely false" and expressed an indignant hope "that the American Delegates will be saved further aspersions upon their veracity and honor." [21]

The Senate's performance was very depressing. Hughes wrote to his friend Judge Hiscock:

I am at a loss to understand how those who have attained the high position of Senator can permit themselves to indulge in reckless characterization of other peoples and to manifest in a manner so injurious to the conduct of our foreign relations their opposition to the work of the conference. There is certainly cause for anxiety when the results of the most earnest endeavor under American auspices come so near to defeat at the hands of the Senate. . . . My solicitude in the matter transcends any personal feeling that I may have growing out of my relation to the matters under consideration, for we cannot protect our own interests and enjoy the prestige and influence which we should have in the world if we are thus betrayed in our own homes.[22]

The tirades of the Irreconcilables had the effect of rallying public support behind the treaty. One editor called Borah, Johnson, and their like "senatorial jackals" and accused them of introducing "the forensics of the gutter." Hughes was so angry that he thought this criticism was "entirely justified."

Eventually the Senate consented to ratification of the treaty, with a reservation asserting that it involved "no commitment to armed force, no alliance, no obligation to join in any defense"—all of which was obvious from the treaty itself. A majority came to realize that this Four-Power Pact was the cement of good faith that held together the settlements reached as to other issues. The consultation pledge afforded a means by which disputes in the Pacific could be settled if there was any will to settle them. But of much greater importance than the obligations it created were the obligations it removed. By destroying the Anglo-Japanese Alliance, Hughes detached the British from their tacit support of Japanese policy in the Far East and in effect aligned them with American policy. That is an achievement from which great historic consequences have flowed.

[20] CEH to Underwood, March 11, 1922.   [21] CEH to Lodge, March 21, 1922.
[22] CEH to Frank H. Hiscock, March 24, 1922.

Chapter 48

STABILIZING THE FAR EAST

THE DISTRUST and turmoil that were festering in China could best be dealt with, Secretary Hughes concluded, by giving American policy in that area the sanction of international law. Ever since Secretary Hay had proclaimed the open door in 1899, the United States had consistently sought to prevent the powers from seizing Chinese territory and carving China into spheres of influence. In 1921 the need was not to devise a new policy but to make this old policy effective against the postwar imperialism of Japan. Hughes' first move in that direction was to reiterate, in notes to London, Tokyo, and Peking, the intention of the United States "neither to participate nor to acquiesce in" any schemes to create monopolies or spheres of influence in China.[1]

At the Washington Conference, Balfour initiated the discussion in this sphere on November 11 when he handed Hughes a proposed five-power "arrangement" on China. In the meetings of the Far Eastern Committee that followed, Root was given the responsibility of drawing up a joint statement of principles. Hughes seemed always to be present at these sessions, however, and on January 17 he offered a resolution on the open door that, with slight changes, was to become Article III of the Nine-Power Treaty. Under the influence of Hughes and Root, this instrument was shaped into "the most categorical and aggressive affirmation of the Far Eastern policy of the United States yet on record." [2]

The principles underlying the Nine-Power Treaty were agreed upon early in the conference. The Japanese balked only when the Americans insisted on translating those principles into specific pledges and obligations. All Hughes' powers of persuasion, Root's experience and moderation, and Balfour's shrewdness as a mediator were required to bring the Japanese into line. That is not strange, for the treaty erected the strongest barriers ever raised against Japanese imperialism in China. It was possible to wring such concessions from Japan only because a spirit of mutual trust prevailed. Hughes had lifted all suspicion that the United States had aggressive intentions. Expecting condemnation, Japan had been welcomed to friendly discussions; her prestige had been upheld by the Four-Power Pact; she could not afford to withdraw from the

[1] *Foreign Relations, 1921,* I, 439–446.
[2] A. Whitney Griswold, *The Far Eastern Policy of the United States,* p. 322.

world community. In these favorable circumstances the negotiators were able to compel Tokyo to forswear policies which it had been pursuing since the outbreak of the war.

The treaty was signed on February 6, 1922, by representatives of the United States, Great Britain, Japan, France, Belgium, China, Italy, the Netherlands, and Portugal. For the first time China became a party to the agreement of the powers about herself. The signatories pledged themselves (1) to respect the sovereignty, independence, and integrity of China; (2) to give China the "fullest and most unembarrassed opportunity" to maintain an effective and stable government; (3) to use their influence to establish and maintain equal opportunity for the commerce and industry of all nations in China; (4) to refrain from taking advantage of conditions in China in order to seek special rights or privileges that would abridge the rights of citizens of friendly states, and from countenancing action inimical to the security of such states.

By Article II the powers were bound not to make any agreements among themselves or with other nations that would infringe these principles. Article III was Hughes' open-door provision committing the powers not to support their nationals in seeking any superiority of commercial or economic rights in China or any monopoly or preference that would close the open door to any legitimate trade or industry sponsored by the nationals of other powers. Spheres of influence were specifically condemned. China agreed to prevent unfair discrimination as to railway traffic. Finally, the powers pledged themselves to "full and frank" discussion if any one of them should raise the issue of violation of the treaty.

The language could not have been more emphatic in avowing respect for the open door and the integrity of China. But it was a mutual promise of self-discipline, not a guarantee to use force. Hughes and Root had given new buttressing to the traditional American policy.

The Secretary also took advantage of this treaty to end what appears to have been the only secret protocol in American diplomatic history up to that time. Former Secretary Lansing had signed an agreement with Viscount Ishii of Japan in 1917 giving countenance to Japan's "special interests in China." [3] Apparently Lansing had no intention of recognizing any special Japanese *rights* in China. He attempted to offset his concession by obtaining from Ishii a memorandum which pledged Japan "to refrain from taking advantage of conditions in China in order to seek special rights or privileges which would abridge the rights of subjects or citizens of friendly states, and from countenancing action inimical to the security of such states." But he permitted the memorandum to remain secret. Openly stated, it would have been an effective moral weapon behind American policy in the Far East. Remaining under

[3] *Ibid.,* p. 216.

cover, it was useless. The world assumed that the open-door doctrine had been distorted in Japan's favor, and Tokyo acted as if the secret pledge were non-existent.

Hating secrecy in public affairs and being loath to work under the handicap of this hidden protocol, Hughes laid a clever plot to bring it into the open. While Root was working out the principles to guide the Far Eastern Committee, the Secretary showed him the secret memorandum and asked him to embody it in the new treaty.[4] Root incorporated Ishii's secret pledge almost verbatim into the Nine-Power Treaty as Paragraph 4 of Article I. The Japanese could scarcely object, for after all they had agreed to it under cover. A much-criticized deviation from the open-door policy was thus eliminated, and the secret diplomacy into which Lansing had slipped was abandoned without revealing the existence of the suppressed document.

The public learned nothing about Hughes' shrewd coup in putting the secret protocol on record until 1938, when the State Department published the diplomatic correspondence related to the Washington Conference. But the impediment had been removed in 1922, and Japan had consented a year later to formal cancellation of the defunct Lansing-Ishii Agreement. The open-door policy had reached the zenith of its vigor.

To avoid any further resort to secrecy, Hughes induced the conference to provide for publicity concerning every treaty or agreement then in force or later entered into concerning China. Contracts giving concessions or franchises in China to the nationals of any of the powers were also to be brought into the light of day.

More delicate than any of the other Far Eastern issues that bedeviled the conference was the dispute between China and Japan over Shantung. At Versailles, Wilson had given way to the Island Empire's demands for control of Shantung, which it had wrested from Germany. China got only "the shell of the oyster." That settlement had aroused much bitterness in the United States and had been an important factor in the defeat of the Treaty of Versailles in the Senate. In the Far East it had kept hostility between China and Japan near the boiling point. Some readjustment was imperative if war clouds over the Pacific were to be dissipated.

China had refused to negotiate with Japan on the basis of the Versailles settlement or to take any step that would involve recognition of the wartime treaties Japan had wrung from her. Japan, being in the saddle, was eager for a settlement. Ambassador Shidehara approached Hughes on July 21, 1921, and said that if the Secretary could induce the Chinese to negotiate with Japan, his government would seek a settlement that would be satisfactory to China and all the other powers. Hughes asked what sort of terms Japan might be

[4] Author's interview with CEH, Nov. 26, 1946; *Foreign Relations, 1922*, I, 279n.

willing to make and was not satisfied with Shidehara's vague reply. A few weeks later he informed the ambassador that before approaching China he would have to know what the outcome was likely to be. If negotiations should be undertaken and fail, the outlook for the forthcoming conference would be worse and not better. Japan would have to have a satisfactory offer, therefore, if she expected him to have anything to do with it. But he would welcome a full statement by Japan, and if such a statement seemed to hold promise of a settlement he would suggest to China that negotiations be undertaken.

Shidehara came in with Japan's proposal on September 8. Hughes objected to various obscurities and said that he had reason to believe that China would not consent to the proposed joint ownership of the Shantung Railroad. He could not make a hopeful suggestion to China on this basis. Were the terms final? Shidehara said they were not. Hughes expressed his gratification and threw out the suggestion that it might be possible for Japan to offer a solution under which China could obtain complete ownership and control of the railroad by making compensation.[5]

While thus wangling the best possible terms out of Japan, Hughes also attempted to soften the Chinese. Peking was determined to inject the Shantung controversy into the conference itself. Hughes saw that a more practical approach would be necessary to achieve results. Japan was loath to permit reopening of the issue before any international body. And even if that hurdle could be cleared, China would be confronted by a group of powers—all of those present except the United States and the Netherlands—that had sanctioned the rape of Shantung at Versailles. Any attempt to force the issue into the conference in these circumstances might split it wide open and endanger everything it was attempting to do. Yet it was clear that the Sino-Japanese rupture would have to be healed if the conference were to achieve its aims. Hughes thought it doubtful that the Senate would approve a naval limitation treaty or any pact dealing with the Far East unless this threat to the peace could be removed. The best hope, he concluded, lay in direct negotiations between the Chinese and Japanese representatives to be carried on collaterally in Washington but not as part of the conference.

As the weeks passed, the Secretary increasingly turned his persuasive powers upon the Chinese in the hope of inducing them to negotiate. The Chinese resisted any compromise, insisting on full restoration of Shantung with no economic or political strings attached. When Balfour arrived in Washington, he and Hughes jointly offered their "good offices" to the disputants. Under heavy pressure in Peking as well as Washington, the Chinese finally caved in with the understanding that American and British observers would attend the direct

[5] *Foreign Relations, 1921*, I, 620.

negotiations. This idea of neutral observers sitting in to assure fair play between hostile negotiators is one of Hughes' significant contributions to diplomacy.

Hughes, Balfour, and the Japanese delegates met at the Pan American Building for the first of these sessions on December 1. They sat wondering what had happened to the Chinese delegates. Upon investigation, J. V. A. MacMurray, who was Hughes' right-hand man in all Far Eastern affairs, found the Chinese besieged in the bathroom of their Massachusetts Avenue Legation by an angry crowd of Chinese students who were opposed to direct negotiations with Japan. When Hughes heard of the siege, he telephoned the War Department and asked for a military escort to bring the Chinese delegates to the meeting if they wished to come. But MacMurray and a companion had no difficulty in bringing the beleaguered delegates out, and the conference went forward as scheduled.[6]

Thirty-six meetings were held before an agreement could be reached. After failure of the Japanese scheme for joint ownership of the Shantung Railroad, Shidehara got around to acceptance of Hughes' suggestion for restoration of the railroad to China in return for payments to be made over a series of years. But controversy continued over details of the arrangement. Several times an impasse was reached. On each occasion Hughes and MacMurray worked on the Chinese and Balfour on the Japanese until direct negotiations were resumed. The Chinese would not meet with the Japanese without American or British representatives present. At one point M. Viviani further bedeviled the negotiations by insisting that he or a French expert be admitted, although he had not been invited by either of the governments directly concerned.

When Hughes concluded that the Japanese had been pushed as far as they would go in making concessions, he turned all his persuasive powers upon the stubborn Chinese. The Secretary believed that if the conference should end without a settlement of the dispute, China would lose Shantung. She could not force the Japanese out. The idea of the United States going to war to put the Japanese out was unthinkable. Consequently, our own interests and those of China demanded support of the best compromise obtainable. After Shidehara had made numerous concessions, the question boiled down to this: Should China risk losing Shantung because the Japanese insisted on spreading China's payments for the railroad over at least five years and on employment of a Japanese traffic manager during that period?

Hughes invited the Chinese (along with Balfour) to his home on January 22 and talked to them with the utmost candor. The conference had produced a remarkable atmosphere of good will, he said. The Japanese had liberalized their original offer to an extent that had seemed beyond hope when the con-

[6] Author's interview with J. V. A. MacMurray, July 9, 1949.

ference opened. China's remaining objections were trivial beside the great advantage of regaining Shantung. It was "inconceivable," Hughes told them, that these objections should be allowed to stand in the way of a settlement. "Surely what China wants," he exclaimed, "is to see Japan out of Shantung." That fond hope of every Chinese could not possibly be attained by trying to "fire" the Japanese out. Only a conciliatory mood would bring the desired result. Continued standpattism might frustrate all that it was hoped to achieve in the conference for the good of China. Before making their decision, he declared, the Chinese should realize that if they chose to break off negotiations over trivialities and thus bring disaster upon themselves, they could not "count on any support either from public sentiment in the United States or from this Government." [7]

Balfour said afterward that he had never heard so "forceful an appeal." The Chinese must have been similarly impressed for they withdrew their last objections and signed the treaty with Japan in ample time to have it reported in a plenary session of the conference. Full sovereignty over Shantung was restored to China. Japanese troops were withdrawn. The railroad also went to China, with payments in Chinese treasury notes over a period from five to fifteen years. Japan retained a shadowy economic hold on the province, but the treaty was a substantial victory for China. It dried up the worst open sore in Far Eastern diplomatic relations and made it possible to consummate the other agreements that had been moving forward in the conference. In keeping with the prevailing spirit of accommodation, Balfour also announced that Great Britain would hand back to China the Weihaiwei leasehold on the Shantung coastline.

After the conference was over, Admiral Kato, back in Tokyo, candidly acknowledged that the Shantung settlement "was largely due to the good offices of Messrs. Hughes and Balfour" and paid a touching tribute to Hughes for "his unceasing care, intense earnestness and indefatigable industry as well as for the unalloyed sense of justice with which he discharged his duties." [8]

[7] Mills W. Lampson's memorandum of interview; Hughes Papers.
[8] Philadelphia *Public Ledger,* May 12, 1922.

Chapter 49

IN RETROSPECT

AFTER GERMANY, Italy, and Japan had scourged the world with new wars in the thirties and forties, the whole idea of limiting armaments by mutual pledge seemed to fall into disrepute. Men desperate for an explanation of these calamities looked back to the Washington Conference and saw that it had wiped out a formidable fleet of battleships. With ships, tanks, and airplanes once more the main source of security, they impetuously denounced the conference of 1921–1922 for having intoxicated the world with a false idealism. It has not yet emerged from the cloud cast upon it by this superficial judgment.

There is a basic fallacy, however, in trying to judge any international conference by events two decades after the completion of its work. History moves in cycles, and what is wise or possible in one period may be utterly unwise or impossible in another. To appraise the Washington Conference fairly, it must be kept in its own setting of events and trends. Its sponsors had to deal with the problems before them and could not be expected to forsake the prospect for peace in the decade ahead in deference to uncertain objectives related to a more distant future.

The first important point about the conference, then, is that it admirably met the demands of its own time. Its achievements evoked almost universal applause. The Senate approved the Naval Limitations Treaty by a vote of seventy-four to one, and twenty of the twenty-one Senators who were absent took pains to have it announced that, if present, they would have voted for the treaty.[1] The explanation is clear. When the conference met, as Balfour said, a "spirit of deep anxiety" overshadowed the Pacific. Twelve weeks later the war clouds had vanished. Confidence took the place of distrust. "The conference produced a complete change in the attitude of mind of the nations there assembled," said Lord Lee of Fareham, "and, if I may so describe it, made them think in terms of peace rather than in terms of war." [2] Balfour said the conference gave "an expectant world all that anybody possibly could hope for, and far more than experienced statesmen ever dared to expect." Sarraut

[1] *Congressional Record*, Vol. 62, Pt. V., 67th Congress, 2nd session, March 29, 1922, pp. 4718f.
[2] Speech to Royal Colonial Institute, London, May 9, 1922; Hughes Papers.

called it "the loftiest precedent of mankind." Speaking for Portugal, Viscount d'Alte dramtically exclaimed, "America has justified her leadership of the world." [3]

It is true that there was much disappointment in France, for the conference had not been able to deal with that country's vital problem of security in Europe. In Japan the navy clique and part of the press were hostile to the treaties on the ground that Japan had been exposed to Anglo-American domination. "The most miserable is Japan," wailed the *Yomiuri*, ". . . the days of her unrestricted freedom of action are at an end." [4] But it was the common verdict among the Japanese delegates, according to K. K. Kawakami, the leading Japanese journalist at the conference, "that the happy conclusion of the naval negotiations, so skillfully and so patiently engineered by Mr. Hughes, is a master-stroke of American diplomacy even greater than the announcement of his naval retrenchment program at the very first sitting of the Conference." [5] The liberal government then in power in Tokyo courageously supported the treaties, and a large majority of the people were said to rejoice in the brightened prospect of peace. Prime Minister Takahashi called the treaties "a blessing to all mankind." [6]

In both Great Britain and the United States some protests were made by the big-Navy advocates, but they seemed scarcely audible. Prime Minister Lloyd George told Parliament that the conference was "one of the greatest achievements for peace that has ever been registered in the history of the world." The *Times* of London thought the day on which the Naval Treaty was presented would be "a great day for all time." The *Daily Chronicle* hailed the treaty as "a unique contribution to world peace," and the London *Outlook* said that it was "magnificent."

Enthusiasm in the United States bubbled up in the press, the pulpit, and street-corner talk. "Much the greatest [conference] . . . of all time," said the *New York Herald*. "A monumental contribution to international understanding and human progress," declared the New York *Tribune*. "The way to measure the importance of the naval treaty," reasoned the *World*, "is to remember what would have happened had there been no agitation for disarmament, no Washington Conference, no Hughes proposals, and no agreement." [7] A "stupendous success—the results epochal," concluded Walter McLean in the Baltimore *Sun*.[8]

Walter Lippmann accurately saw in the conference the beginning of a new policy of Anglo-American cooperation. "For the first time," he wrote, "the

---

[3] *Conference on the Limitation of Armament*, pp. 366ff.   [4] Feb. 11, 1922.
[5] Kawakami, *Japan's Pacific Policy* (New York, Dutton, 1922), p. 28.
[6] *New York Times*, March 12, 1922.
[7] Quotations from Sprout, *Toward a New Order of Sea Power*, pp. 263–273.
[8] Feb. 20, 1922.

concert of powers in the East is not a concert of aggression, with America on the outside protesting, but a concert against aggression, with Japan on the outside resisting." It may well be, he added, that Hughes "has stopped the drift into a ruinous and indecisive war." [9]

Looking back to Hughes' opening speech, Senator Ransdell declared that "humanity breathed easier from that hour. I have never felt prouder of being an American citizen than on that occasion." [10] Indiana and New Jersey passed resolutions congratulating the Administration on the outcome of the conference. "If the world has hungered for a new assurance," said President Harding, "it may feast at the banquet which this Conference has spread." [11]

Nor was it a temporary intoxication. Three years after the conference the General Board of the Navy concluded that "the great accomplishment . . . was not in the fixing of a definite ratio of ships, with its attendant economies, but in effecting an agreement making aggressive warfare across the ocean more difficult." [12] The *New York Times* was still convinced that the conference was "a monument of peace-making, and no one who has the welfare of the human race at heart will attempt to undermine it." [13] Elihu Root's conclusion in 1925 was: "I think you will go far to find any public service to the world rendered with a higher order of ability or with more signal success than the service Mr. Hughes rendered in directing and controlling that Conference." [14]

Eight years after the event the New York *Herald Tribune* expressed a widely held view: "The Washington treaty stands as a monument to international accommodation and self-restraint, to cooperation in avoiding needless causes of national antagonism and in promoting peace." [15] The *World* then thought that the threat of conflict in the Pacific had vanished and that the conference still stood as "one of the great diplomatic achievements in modern times." [16] The least that can be said is that the conference put into effect a policy for which most of mankind was clamoring.

The second important point is that the conference did lay a proper groundwork for an indefinite period of peace in the Pacific. The Naval Treaty relegated rivalry among the powers to the economic sphere, and the Nine-Power Treaty provided a code of fair play to prevent commercial enterprises from evolving into political conquests. The Shantung settlement removed the poison from the well of Sino-Japanese relations. The Mandates Treaty settled the most irritating issue between Japan and the United States. The Four-Power Pact brought a sense of equality and, as Hughes said at the time, a "new state of mind" [17] in which friendly conferences were to take the place of naval competition. The limitation of navies fit into the picture as a sort of guarantee

[9] New York *World*, Jan. 29, 1922.   [10] *Congressional Record*, March 15, 1922, p. 3906. [11] *Conference*, p. 398.   [12] New York *World*, Dec. 11, 1924.   [13] April 8, 1924. [14] Speech of Nov. 10, 1925.   [15] Jan. 22, 1930.   [16] Dec. 18, 1929. [17] *Report* of the American Delegation, p. 88.

of good faith which made all the other agreements at once possible and meaningful.

Each country had to make substantial concessions to bring about these happy results. The United States' great concession was the scrapping of twenty-eight capital ships, thirteen of which were under construction. Great Britain's chief sacrifice lay in her abandonment of supremacy on the seas and in giving up her giant super-*Hoods*. Japan's concessions ran all the way across the board. In addition to her loss of battleships, she gave up her 10:10:7 demand, the Anglo-Japanese Alliance, her forged license for conquest in China, and her extreme claims in Shantung and the mandated islands. The treaties coming out of the conference unquestionably impinged more severely upon Japan's expansionist policy than upon the national policies of any other power.

It is sometimes said that the United States paid (in battleships) too high a price for the legal strait-jacket placed upon Japan. But this assumption, as we have already seen, rests on the false premise that the United States scrapped real ships while Great Britain and Japan merely burned their blueprints. Actually, Japan, with her smaller navy, scrapped sixteen ships, six of them under construction. The heart of the matter is that each of the three major navies was drastically reduced without disadvantage to any one of them. In this respect there were no victors and no vanquished at the conference.

Hughes had contributed only the principle of a proportionate reduction of naval strength and the idea of halting all building. It was the Navy that decided what ships each country would have to scrap to carry out this formula. If the American sacrifice could be shown to have been disproportionate, the blame would fall upon the admirals. But no such criticism is valid. The fact is that each country saved enormous sums of money without losing anything in terms of security. Completion of the 1916 program would have raised our Navy's annual operating costs alone by more than $200,000,000. Sixteen years after the conference a Congressman estimated that it had saved at least $4,000,000,000 for American taxpayers.[18]

Our relative naval strength could have been improved only by adding costly new shipbuilding ventures to the 1916 program, and Congress had emphatically rejected that policy before the conference was called. Eager as they were for relief from the burden of naval building, both Great Britain and Japan were determined to continue the competition in the absence of agreement. "Despite her financial burdens," wrote Hector C. Bywater, the distinguished British naval expert, "it is unthinkable that she [Great Britain] would have let the trident slip from her hands without making a strenuous effort to recover it."[19] Japan was still more energetic in pushing her ambitious pro-

[18] Congressman Robsion, *Congressional Record*, March 16, 1937, p. 2930.
[19] Baltimore *Sun*, Dec. 18, 1924.

gram of naval construction. Only our own Congress was hell-bent to disarm, unilaterally if necessary. What the conference did was to slow down the other powers to a pace that the United States could reasonably expect to maintain in the psychological climate of the twenties.

The absolute necessity of a naval limitation agreement from the American point of view is driven home with great force by subsequent events. The United States virtually abandoned naval building. All the other powers continued to add to their fleets vessels in the unrestricted categories. During the eight years from 1922 to 1930 Great Britain laid down or appropriated for 74 naval vessels; Japan, 125; France, 119; Italy, 82; and the United States, 11.[20]

Hughes had expected our Navy to be maintained at the 10:10:6 ratio. In October, 1922, he issued a direct warning against sacrificing by default the victory that had been won:

This Government has taken the lead in securing the reduction of naval armament, but the Navy that we retain under the agreement should be maintained with
sufficient personnel and pride in the service. It is essential that we should maintain the relative naval strength of the United States. That, in my judgment, is the
way to peace and security. It will be upon that basis that we would enter in future
conferences or make agreements for limitation, and it would be folly to undermine
our position.[21]

His sound advice was not followed. Because of the United States' failure to maintain the 10:10:6 ratio, Japan made a powerful bid for a 10:7 ratio in heavy cruisers and other auxiliary craft when the London Naval Conference met in 1930. She succeeded in getting a ratio a little better than 10:6 in light cruisers and destroyers and equality in submarines. Premier Hamaguchi in- duced the Diet to ratify this compromise but at the cost of violent reactions on the part of the military and his own assassination.

When the powers again met in conference in 1935, Japan demanded a "common upper limit" for all navies and walked out when she failed to get it. Assuming that the United States would never build up to treaty strength any- way,[22] Tokyo had previously renounced the naval treaties of 1922 and 1930. All restrictions on naval building thus came to an end in 1936, not because any mistake had been made at the Washington Conference, but partly because the United States' failure to maintain the sensible balance of strength there established had convinced Japan that if the naval race were resumed she could win it. Her conclusion was not without foundation, for naval building in Japan was pressing against the treaty ceilings, while depression-ridden America

---

[20] Senate Document 202, 78th Cong., 2nd session.
[21] Quoted by Representative Vinson, *Congressional Record*, Jan. 30, 1934, p. 1607.
[22] Ambassador Grew in *Peace and War—U.S. Foreign Policy, 1931–1941*, pp. 20f.

needed 102 ships that would cost $380,000,000 to restore the expiring treaty ratios.[23]

In one other vital respect Congress undercut the policy of good will and cooperation that Hughes had inaugurated. Our relations with Japan had reached a high state of cordiality. The American people had generously aided Japan after her "bewildering devastation" by the earthquake of 1923. The gratitude of the Japanese strengthened the good relations that had taken firm root at the Washington Conference. Then suddenly this hopeful amity was poisoned by rancor because Congress intemperately wrote a Japanese exclusion clause into the Immigration Act of 1924.

Immigration from Japan to the United States had been controlled since 1907 by the so-called Gentlemen's Agreement between the two governments. The agreement was not wholly satisfactory because it allowed too many exceptions and did not permit effective control at the ports of entry. The State Department recognized a need for tightening the agreement or for giving Japan a quota under the Immigration Act. Instead, California legislators demanded absolute exclusion of aliens ineligible to citizenship—a sly way of striking at the Japanese without naming them.

Ambassador Hanihara called on Secretary Hughes and said that it would be quite impossible to make the Japanese people understand the general friendliness of the Americans toward Japan if an exclusion provision should be enacted. He wished to impress upon the American Government how seriously the issue would be regarded in Japan. The Japanese counselor of embassy also informed the State Department that the influence of the conciliatory party, meaning that group of public men who were disposed to work in conjunction with the United States, would be at an end if the exclusion policy should become law.[24] The militarists would insist that, with the closing of the American door upon the Japanese, the open door in the Orient could no longer remain open.

Hughes expressed his deep concern over the exclusion movement in a letter to Albert Johnson, chairman of the House Committee on Immigration and Naturalization, on February 8:

The Japanese are a sensitive people and unquestionably would regard such a legislative enactment as fixing a stigma upon them. I regret to be compelled to say that I believe such legislative action would largely undo the work of the Washington Conference on Limitation of Armament, which so greatly improved our relations with Japan. The manifestation of American interest and generosity in providing relief to the sufferers from the recent earthquake disaster in Japan would not avail to diminish the resentment which would follow the enactment of such a measure, as this enactment would be regarded as an insult not to be palliated by

[23] Representative Vinson in *Congressional Record*, Jan. 30, 1934, p. 1607.
[24] Saburi to MacMurray, Jan. 9, 1923, memorandum in State Department.

any act of charity. It is useless to argue whether or not such a feeling would be justified; it is quite sufficient to say that it would exist. It has already been manifested in the discussions in Japan with respect to the pendency of this measure and no amount of argument can avail to remove it.

The question is thus presented whether it is worth while thus to affront a friendly nation with whom we have established most cordial relations and what gain there would be from such action.[25]

Hughes went on to show that if the exclusion section of the bill were eliminated, the effect would be to put immigration from Japan under quota. This would limit the number of Japanese immigrants to only 246 a year—fewer than were estimated to be coming under the Gentlemen's Agreement. "I am unable to perceive," he concluded, "that the exclusion provision is necessary and I must strongly urge upon you the advisability, in the interest of our international relations, of eliminating it."

The committee rejected the Secretary's plea and sent the bill to the House floor with the exclusion provision intact. One reason for this action, the committee report indicated, was the obscurity of the Gentlemen's Agreement, which consisted of diplomatic correspondence with Japan that had not been made public. Hughes felt this was a valid criticism. The meaning of the agreement had to be gleaned from a mass of diplomatic papers that he had not been able to submit to Congress without the consent of Japan.

When Hanihara called on March 27, the Secretary told him that he was troubled by two points in the committee report. The assertions that the Gentlemen's Agreement was secret and obscure and therefore ineffective, he said, ought to be met. Since the correspondence back of that agreement was long and detailed, there would be little point in merely producing it. Nor could the State Department properly undertake to outline Japan's activities under the agreement. Hughes cautiously suggested, therefore, without making a definite proposal, that the ambassador write him a letter setting forth the Japanese Government's understanding as to the intent and effect of the agreement and summarizing the agreement itself.[26]

Acting on Hughes' suggestion, Hanihara got the consent of his government and explored the problem with MacMurray. The State Department submitted a memorandum on the Gentlemen's Agreement to the Japanese Embassy. Hanihara finally completed his letter on April 10. It was an accurate résumé of the agreement, giving all the information of which the House had professed ignorance. In addition, Hanihara expressed his personal belief that Japan would willingly discuss proposed changes in the agreement. He recognized the right of the United States to control immigration into its own territories and denied any desire on the part of Japan to send her nationals where they were

[25] *Foreign Relations, 1924,* I, 217.   [26] *Ibid.,* II, 337f.

not wanted. His plea was merely for "that proper consideration ordinarily given by one nation to the self-respect of another, which after all forms the basis of amicable international intercourse throughout the civilized world."

The temperate and persuasive qualities of the letter were lost to sight, however, because of two ill-chosen words in the following paragraph:

> Relying upon the confidence you have been good enough to show me at all times, I have stated or rather repeated all this to you very candidly and in a most friendly spirit, for I realize, as I believe you do, the grave consequences which the enactment of the measure retaining that particular provision would inevitably bring upon the otherwise happy and mutually advantageous relations between our two countries.[27]

Seeking the State Department's approval, Hanihara took the letter to MacMurray, who relayed it to Hughes. In reading it the Secretary's eye rested momentarily on the words "grave consequences." "That is a very unfortunate phrase," he said.[28] But he decided to ignore it. The words were couched in a friendly text. Obviously they meant only that the happy relations between the two countries would be impaired by an exclusion act, which was the simple truth. Any suggestion that the phrase be changed, moreover, would have put him in the position of approving the remainder of the letter, and Hughes was determined not to assume that responsibility. Finally, if this restatement of the Gentlemen's Agreement were to reach Congress before the exclusion amendment came to a vote, there was no time in any event to seek revision of it. Hughes wrote to Hanihara that the statement was in accord with his own understanding of the arrangement between the two governments and sent copies of both letters to the interested committees of the House and Senate.

Two days later the House passed the immigration bill, including an exclusion provision, by a vote of 323 to 71. Meanwhile a section of the press had given an inflammatory meaning to Hanihara's words, "grave consequences." On April 14 Lodge took up the cry in the Senate. Asserting that the letter was a "veiled threat" to the United States, he induced the Senate to reject the Hughes-endorsed amendment recognizing the Gentlemen's Agreement. Even the Senators who had supported the department's point of view bolted, and the amendment went down by a vote of 76 to 2. Passage of the Johnson bill then followed by a majority scarcely less stupendous.

Hughes had had no idea that Hanihara's indiscreet words would be so blatantly misinterpreted.[29] The hapless ambassador went to the department in sackcloth and ashes carrying a copy of the *Congressional Record* in which he had underlined the unbridled ranting of the Senators. The idea of a threat, he said, was the furthest thing from his mind. He had not "in any part of his

---

[27] *Ibid.*, p. 373.   [28] Author's interview with J. V. A. MacMurray, July 9, 1949.
[29] Author's interview with CEH, Dec. 18, 1946.

body" the slightest feeling of unfriendliness or antagonism toward the United States. A few days later he wrote the Secretary a letter expressing his dismay over the hostile interpretation his words had been given.

Hughes accepted the explanation and expressed his deep regret over the incident and his feeling of complete assurance that no threat had been intended. It is unbelievable that any substantial number of Senators were really concerned about the alleged "threat." Rather, they were determined to adopt the exclusion policy in any event and seized upon the Hanihara letter to salve their consciences. A poll is said to have indicated a majority of fifty-four votes for exclusion in the Senate before the Hanihara letter was released.

President Coolidge attempted to avert the "grave consequences" of the incident by suggesting, while the immigration bill was in conference, that application of the exclusion clause be delayed for two years. In that period the State Department would negotiate with Japan a treaty so effectively restricting immigration that drastic legislation would not be necessary. Congress refused. Coolidge then bid for a one-year postponement, and was again rebuffed. Ultimately the President signed the exclusion measure because it was part of a comprehensive immigration bill and because a veto in the face of such overwhelming congressional support would have been a futile gesture. For the same reasons Hughes had not requested a veto.

Irreconcilable Senators whispered about the cloakrooms a tale that Hughes had written the Hanihara letter. His associates hotly denied it,[30] but the fact that he had suggested the letter in order to bring the agreement out into the open gave buoyancy to the rumor. Twenty years later Frederick Moore, who had been an adviser to the Foreign Office in Japan, asserted that the State Department had not only urged Hanihara to strengthen his "grave consequences" paragraph but had also approved the letter in its final form. "I have every reason to believe, and do believe," Hughes replied to an inquiry about this statement, "that the paragraph in question, and these words, were Hanihara's own and that their insertion was not advised, suggested, or approved, by any member of the State Department." [31] This was emphatically corroborated by MacMurray.[32]

Japan's reaction to the incident was prompt and violent. "No nation retaining the least trace of its self-respect," said the *Jiji*, "could tolerate the discrimination aimed at by the Johnson bill." As a people, the Japanese were deeply wounded in a way that is difficult for Americans to understand. Crowds picketed the American Embassy in Tokyo, some of them threatening to destroy American property and shoot Americans who would not leave Japan.[33] Suicides in protest against the Act were reported, and American goods were boy-

[30] William R. Castle's diary, 1924, pp. 178f.
[31] CEH to Miller Freeman, Aug. 31, 1944.
[32] MacMurray to Miller Freeman, Oct. 14, 1944.   [33] Castle's diary, 1924, pp. 203f.

cotted. The Japanese's sense of injustice brought gall and wormwood into relations that, since 1922, had been singularly happy.

The Secretary was badly jolted by the incident. Calling on President Coolidge while the latter was confined to his bed by illness, he declared that "it was enough to make a man resign." "Don't you ever think of leaving your position," Coolidge responded. "I agree with you in everything that you've done." [34]

In a letter to Judge Hiscock the Secretary got some of his disgust off his chest:

It is a sorry business and I am greatly depressed. It has undone the work of the Washington Conference and implanted the seeds of an antagonism which are sure to bear fruit in the future. Of course there is no danger of war. Japan cannot threaten anybody. She is overwhelmed with her economic difficulties as a result of the earthquake. She had no idea of making threats. That makes the situation all the worse because she feels that we have chosen to affront her at such a time. The question is not one of war but of the substitution of antagonism for cooperation in the Far East, with all that that involves. Our friends in the Senate have in a few minutes spoiled the work of years and done a lasting injury to our common country.[35]

Calling in Hanihara, Hughes sought to minimize the damage that had been done by saying that the Act did not indicate a lack of friendship on the part of the American people for the Japanese. When Japan lodged her formal protest against the Act, the Secretary again attempted to soothe her wounded feelings while upholding the right of Congress to terminate the Gentlemen's Agreement by unilateral action.

Hanihara resigned in humiliation, and his successor, Ambassador Matsudaira, arrived in San Francisco amid a storm of recriminations across the Pacific. Hugh Wilson, chief of the Division of Current Information, suggested that the occasion be used to rekindle amiability. Dejected and pessimistic, Hughes nevertheless said he was willing to try. Wilson prepared a statement and summoned a group of correspondents to the Secretary's office. When he spoke to them, every trace of Hughes' discouragement had gone. "Like a prophet," he preached the gospel of good relations. So impressed were the newsmen that they spread his message through their stories and communicated its substance to their home offices. Editorials appeared all over the country. Matsudaira got a friendly reception, and the idea that "there was nothing between Japan and ourselves except a state of mind" was widely broadcast. "This episode," Wilson wrote many years later, "caused one of the most extraordinary reversals of public opinion that I have ever seen." [36]

[34] Beerits' Memorandum, XXVII, 10.   [35] April 24, 1924.
[36] Hugh Wilson, *Diplomat Between Wars* (New York, Longmans, 1941), p. 188. Copyright, 1941, by Hugh R. Wilson.

In Japan, Shidehara, who had become Minister of Foreign Affairs, earnestly sought to calm the excitement of his countrymen, and some measure of cordiality was maintained. After Hughes left office, however, Secretary Kellogg let the United States drift into outright championship of China against Japan, even when China reneged on her treaty obligations. While Chiang Kai-shek was extending his conquests and consolidating his power by playing upon Chinese hatred of all foreigners and by inflicting violence and insults upon Americans and other Westerners, the United States and Great Britain seemed nevertheless to vie with each other for Chinese favor. Breaking away from the cooperative policy that had been established at Washington, the State Department suddenly negotiated a separate customs treaty with Chiang's Nationalists and began yielding to Chinese pressure for ending extraterritoriality. Alarmed by this division of the big powers in the face of China's repudiation of treaties, Japan sent Count Uchida to Washington in 1929 to find out whether the cooperative policy was dead. The only answer that he could get was that where concurrent action had not been agreed upon or had been tried and failed the United States considered itself free to act independently.

These deviations from the Hughesian policy of cooperation and even-handed justice necessarily weakened the liberal elements in Japan. In 1931 Shidehara's "friendship policy" was finally routed,[37] and the military launched its conquest in Manchuria. For a decade, however, the spirit generated at the Washington Conference had pervaded the Pacific, and it is clear that if the Hughes and Shidehara policies could have prevailed there would have been no attack on Pearl Harbor in 1941 and no war between the United States and Japan.[38] Incidentally, Shidehara returned to power in Japan after World War II and expressed the view that his country had been liberated—that the Japanese people were better off under American occupation than they would have been under a victorious Japanese military hierarchy.[39]

The invasion of Manchuria was the signal that a new policy in dealing with Japan was essential. Secretary of State Stimson saw that the gang then in control in Tokyo would respect only force and sought to find such force in collaboration with other governments and the League of Nations. Everywhere he was rebuffed. No nation was willing to use its economic or military strength to arrest aggression in the Far East. And the United States, racked by depression and weakened by neglect of the Navy, was neither inclined nor prepared to back its words with actions. The Nine-Power Treaty was at hand as an appropriate implement of pressure, but willingness to apply the pressure was lacking. Stimson could only fall back upon the lame device of refusing to recognize Japan's war spoils.

[37] Henry L. Stimson, *The Far Eastern Crisis*, p. 87.
[38] See *Documents on German Foreign Policy, 1918–1945*, Chap IV.
[39] Wayne Coy in *Washington Post*, March 9, 1947.

When the Franklin D. Roosevelt Administration took over the reins, the nonrecognition policy was reaffirmed. Secretary Hull, however, offered no leadership in collective resistance to Japan's imperialistic ventures.[40] Both Roosevelt and Hull clung to the twin policies of conciliation and arms reduction as tenaciously as Hughes had done under far more favorable circumstances. Three years after the conquest of Manchuria, the President instructed Norman H. Davis, chairman of the American delegation to the 1935 naval conference, to seek another 20 per cent reduction in navies in accord with the principles laid down in 1922. He wrote:

The Washington Naval Conference of 1922 brought to the world the first important voluntary agreement for limitation and reduction of armament. It stands out as a milestone in civilization. . . . The important matter to keep constantly before your eyes is the principle of reduction—the maintenance of one of the greatest achievements of friendly relations between nations.[41]

A few months later, when Japan scuttled the Naval Limitation Treaties, Secretary Hull expressed his "genuine regret" because those treaties had "safeguarded the rights and promoted the collective interests of all of the signatories." [42] Even with the protective treaty structure a shambles, the Administration made no immediate move to strengthen the navy.[43] To be sure, the President had drawn upon "pump-priming" funds in 1933 to finance the construction of thirty-two naval vessels and the following year Congress had passed the Vinson-Trammell Act authorizing a navy of treaty strength. But appropriations continued to lag. The Washington and London naval treaties had been dead three and a half years and Hitler and Japan had gone on the warpath before any move was made toward building ships in excess of the old treaty levels.[44]

Japan's undeclared war on China in July, 1937, pointedly demonstrated the weakness of the American position under these changed conditions. For a time it appeared that the United States might take the lead in resisting this aggression. On October 5 the League's Far Eastern Advisory Committee declared Japan guilty of violating the Nine-Power Treaty and the Kellogg Pact and called the signatories of the former into conference. The same day President Roosevelt made a sensational speech in Chicago urging the "peace-loving nations" to quarantine war "like an epidemic disease." When the delegates of the nine powers (excepting Japan) met in Brussels, however, the Americans declared that the purpose of the gathering was not to coerce the belligerents

---

[40] A. Whitney Griswold, *The Far Eastern Policy of the United States*, pp. 440, 445.
[41] *Foreign Relations, Japan, 1931–1941*, I, 282.
[42] *Peace and War*, pp. 12, 244.   [43] *Ibid.*, pp. 44, 316.
[44] Senator David I. Walsh, Senate Document 202, 78th Congress, 2nd session, p. 3.

but "to seek by agreement a solution of the present situation in China." [45] With Japan thumbing her nose at the conference, it was obvious that no conciliation was possible. After three futile weeks the conference adjourned with a mere reaffirmation of the principles of the Nine-Power Treaty. Here was final notice that only force could halt the Japanese militarists; yet it was not until 1941 and 1942 that large-scale naval building in the United States got under way.

Under the whip of war sentiment, the work of the Washington Conference was frequently derided, especially in the campaign of 1944. Speaking at the Democratic National Convention, Governor Kerr of Oklahoma accused the Harding Administration of having "scrapped and sunk more of our fleet than was destroyed by the Japanese at Pearl Harbor." [46] President Roosevelt, sick and weary, declared that "much of the strength of our Navy, and I ought to know it, was scuttled . . ." in the twenties.[47] Such distorted statements cut Hughes to the quick. Even before the campaign warmed up, he wrote to his son-in-law, Chauncey L. Waddell, from his winter retreat (he was then in retirement) in Tucson, Arizona:

Your letter is a better tonic than the Arizona air. I have been greatly distressed by the unjustified criticism of the Washington Conference and your letter is balm to a wounded spirit. I have realized that it was wise for me to keep quiet as anything I might say would bring bitter and demagogical rejoinders, and I should only extend and magnify a controversy in which I couldn't hope to have the last word. I have no doubt that truth will prevail after the present emergency is over and there is a better chance for a correct historical perspective.[48]

The outstanding fact that the critics ignored is that the conference changed a prospective 100 to 87 naval ratio as between the United States and Japan into a 100 to 60 ratio. Whatever disadvantage the United States suffered in the final showdown with Japan was not a result of the Washington Conference but is solely attributable to the failure of subsequent administrations to maintain the fair naval ratio which the conference fixed and to the delay in recouping our strength after the treaties had been thrown overboard. Roosevelt shares the blame for our naval weakness when war came because of his adherence to the Hughes policy of 1922 long after the amicable relations that had blossomed in the twenties had been upset by Japanese fascism.

World War II also brought criticism of the agreement restricting fortifications. Deploring the cost in American lives of recapturing our insular possessions in the western Pacific, politicians and armchair strategists stressed the

[45] Griswold, *op. cit.*, p. 460; see also *Documents on German Foreign Policy, 1918–1945*, Chap. IV.
[46] *New York Times*, July 20, 1944.
[47] David Lawrence in New York *Sun*, Oct. 23, 1944.
[48] Feb. 21, 1944.

great advantage that bases at Guam and the Philippines would have given us. The trouble is that this view wholly ignores the impossibility of acquiring such bases under conditions that existed in the twenties and thirties. Had the United States insisted on the right to fortify the islands, there would have been no naval agreement. We should then have been more thoroughly outclassed in the ensuing competition than we were under the treaty.

Japan naturally feared the building of American bases in Guam and the Philippines, as we would fear potentially hostile bases in Bermuda or the Galapagos Islands. Hugh Wilson, who served in Tokyo while the Washington Conference was in session and who made a study of the problem of fortifying Guam, expressed fear that "those fortifications would never be completed, at least they would not be completed before battle had been engaged between the Japanese and American fleets, unless we have available in Pacific waters a fleet of much greater preponderance than the present one." [49] Even if a clash could have been avoided, the Japanese would have ringed our base at Guam with bases at Saipan, Palau, and Truk (as they did during the war), so that it would have been useless.

The historic fact is, moreover, that the Naval Limitation Treaty did not delay the fortification of Guam. After Japan threw off the restraints of the treaty, the Roosevelt Administration had five years in which to fortify the island—years in which events were moving inexorably toward the Pearl Harbor disaster. But the Hepburn Board had estimated the cost of such a project at $326,216,000, and the danger of precipitating war with Japan had increased. Chairman Walsh of the Senate Naval Affairs Committee stated flatly after the war had broken out: "No direct request for the fortification of Guam was ever put before the committees of the Senate or the House." [50] A small appropriation for dredging the harbor and building a breakwater was requested in 1939, but Secretary of the Navy Edison and Admiral William D. Leahy told congressional committees that there was no intention of fortifying Guam.[51]

Obviously, then, nothing was lost by Hughes' concession to Kato on fortifications. That agreement did make it impractical for the United States to use force in support of its Far Eastern policy. But the decision not to use force for this purpose had been made by Theodore Roosevelt and Secretary Hay at the turn of the century and was merely continued by Hughes. With the country in an isolationist mood, he could not have reversed that policy. He recognized also, as previous and subsequent administrations have done, that the Philippines could not be defended against an all-out attack from Japan. The Philippines were made a little more secure, however, by a direct pledge from the

[49] *Diplomat Between Wars*, p. 145.
[50] *Congressional Record*, Aug. 24, 1942, p. A3369.
[51] *Ibid.*, May 7, 1942, p. A1811; also Walsh report, pp. 4ff.

Japanese, in the Four-Power Pact, to respect their status and submit any unsettled dispute to a four-power conference.

Hughes rightly concluded that this was the best he could do. There was not a remote possibility that Congress would appropriate the enormous sums required for bases that would make our position in the Far East entirely secure. Equally important was the fact that the whole network of treaties coming out of the conference scrapped distrust as well as the sinews of war. The United States could not at once bid for a new order of live and let live in the Pacific and then insist on building bases that would menace another power. Finally, it is not to be forgotten that Hughes exacted a price for his concession on fortifications. By giving up the right to fortify the Kuriles, the Bonins, the Loochoos, and Pescadores, Japan sacrificed potential submarine bases from which American trans-Pacific shipping could have been menaced. When the war came it was the Japanese bases in the mandated islands that made the recapture of the Philippines and the defeat of Japan so difficult. The United States could have been fully informed about these bases if Secretary Hull had enforced the inspection rights that Hughes had forehandedly passed along to him. "It was not the Washington treaties," as Sumner Welles has pointed out, "but the subsequent shortsighted policies of the major powers, that enabled Japan to flout her treaty obligations with impunity." [52]

Nor should we forget that the Washington Conference laid the groundwork for the Anglo-American partnership that saved the world from fascist rule in the forties. When the Four-Power Pact was under debate in the Senate, Borah interpreted a speech by Paul D. Cravath, Hughes' former law partner, as indicating, on the authority of delegates to the conference, that a secret understanding had been established between Great Britain and the United States. Cravath vehemently denied it. He had not talked with any member of the conference.[53] While Hughes was irritated by Cravath's indiscretion and Borah's suspicion, and while he diplomatically refrained from making a point of his coup at the time, what he had openly done was to break the tie between Great Britain and Japan and give new emphasis to the common interests between Great Britain and the United States. "I doubt," said Root, "if any formal treaty ever accomplished so much by doing so little." [54]

"Had it not been for the Hughes policies," Sumner Welles commented nearly three decades later, "the British-Japanese alliance would have continued and Britain and the United States would have started a naval race. Anglo-American relations would have been poisoned with disastrous consequences for the democracies when the Axis rose to power." [55] Thanks to the

[52] *Washington Post,* Sept. 7, 1948.   [53] Cravath to CEH, March 20, 1922.
[54] Address to American Society of International Law, April 27, 1922.
[55] *Washington Post,* Sept. 7, 1948.

Washington Conference, that potential misfortune was averted. When the great test came in 1941, Britain and the United States stood side by side in fighting Britain's former ally.

To summarize, the Washington Conference immediately dispelled the war clouds that had been rising in the Pacific by eliminating the worst sources of friction in that area; it "nailed open" the open door and gave the American policy of safeguarding the integrity of China the sanction of international law; it applied new pressure for Japanese evacuation of Siberia; it transferred the British from the Japanese side of the Pacific conference table to the American side; it held Japanese naval expansion in check for ten years; it saved billions of dollars for the taxpayers in each of the big naval powers; and, finally, it brought the United States back into world councils for the first time since the tragic debacle over the Treaty of Versailles. With all the Hughes treaties ratified by the Senate, America resumed a place of world leadership that had seemed impossible of attainment when the conference assembled.

By robbing these treaties of endurance, Japan minimized their impact on history. That was a tragedy for mankind. But it scarcely detracts from the stature of the man who planned this new order in the Pacific and brought it into being with such consummate skill. His performance proved to be the most effective blow that was struck for peace between the two great wars of this century. Since the conference effected the only general reduction of armaments in the history of the world, it will remain a challenge to statesmanship as long as big navies and national rivalries exist.

Chapter 50

PROTECTOR OF RUSSIA—FOE OF LENINISM

HUGHES' hatred of imperialism gave him a unique role—protector of Russia—that was almost forgotten in later years. Coming into office at a time when Russian industry and commerce were in a state of collapse and revolution was still rampant, Hughes feared that Russia was slipping into chaos of the sort that had made China easy prey for the imperialistic powers a few decades earlier. All the influence that he could muster was used to drive away the vultures while the Russian nation was going through its agony of rebirth.

The most dangerous threat came from Japan's continued occupation of large areas in Siberia and Sakhalin. The United States and Japan had jointly sent troops to Siberia in 1918—one of the strangest and least defensible missions ever assigned to American soldiers. The purpose loudly proclaimed at the time was to help a Czechoslovak force that had been isolated when Russia had dropped out of the war and was supposed to be fighting its way to Vladivostok. Actually, the Czechs had taken over the Trans-Siberian Railway, organized new governments in towns along the line, and did not intend to leave Siberia. Major General William S. Graves, who commanded the American expedition, later concluded that Washington officials knew this before he was given his orders and that the underlying purpose of sending troops to Siberia was to overthrow the Soviet régime,[1] although the War Department instructed him not to interfere in Russia's internal affairs. This cynical view of our Siberian adventure is consistent with President Wilson's flirtation with Admiral Kolchak, the counterrevolutionary who was trying to restore a monarchistic régime in Russia. On June 12, 1919, Wilson had agreed with the Allies, "To assist the government of Admiral Kolchak with munitions, supplies and food, to establish themselves as the government of all Russia." [2]

General Graves distributed American arms and supplies to Kolchak in accord with that agreement, but otherwise refrained from interfering with the course of the Russian Revolution. The expedition proved to be a "dismal tragi-comedy" which succeeded only in arousing the resentment of more than 90 per cent of the people of Siberia,[3] thus driving them into the arms of the

[1] Graves' *America's Siberian Adventure* (New York, Cape & Smith, 1931), pp. 346–355. Copyright, 1931, by William S. Graves.
[2] *Ibid.*, p. 355.   [3] *Ibid.*, p. 347.

Communists. The American troops were ingloriously withdrawn early in 1920, but the Japanese remained and continued to run riot.

The understanding had been that the United States and Japan would each send about 10,000 troops; Japan had sent 72,000. These invaders broke up local efforts to restore order, smuggled in goods disguised as military supplies, and maltreated the population. Anti-Soviet soldiers, under the protection of Japanese troops, "were roaming the country like wild animals, killing and robbing the people." The invaders were in complete control, and there were many indications that they intended to stay. The Island Empire appeared to be bent on Japonizing the entire Russian Pacific littoral.

In a stiff note to Tokyo on May 31, 1921, Hughes told the Japanese that their continued hold upon strategic centers of Siberia "tends rather to increase than to allay the unrest and disorder in that region." The issue presented, he said, was that of scrupulous fulfillment of the assurances given to the Russian people by the United States and Japan that the expedition of 1918 would not be used as "an occasion to occupy territory, even temporarily, or to assume any military or administrative control over the people of Siberia." Hughes' pointed indictment continued:

. . . in the present time of disorder in Russia, it is more than ever the duty of those who look forward to the tranquilization of the Russian people, and a restoration of normal conditions among them, to avoid all action which might keep alive their antagonism and distrust toward outside political agencies. Now, especially, it is incumbent upon the friends of Russia to hold aloof from the domestic contentions of the Russian people, to be scrupulous to avoid inflicting what might appear to them a vicarious penalty for sporadic acts of lawlessness, and, above all, to abstain from even the temporary and conditional impairment by any foreign Power of the territorial status which, for them as for other peoples, is a matter of deep and sensitive national feeling transcending perhaps even the issues at stake among themselves.[4]

Hughes frankly warned the Japanese that the United States would not recognize "any claim or title arising out of the present occupation." Nor would we acquiesce in any action which "might impair existing treaty rights or the political or territorial integrity of Russia." The Secretary went as far as any statesman could go (without making futile threats) in pressing the Japanese to pull in their horns.

When he called the Washington Conference, "the integrity of Russia" was given a prominent place on the agenda. The Soviet's Commissar for Foreign Affairs sent a slashing protest against Hughes' failure to invite Russia to the conference. Without acknowledging the note of the unrecognized Moscow régime, Hughes took upon himself the responsibility of protecting Russian interests.

[4] Report of the American Delegation (Arms Conference), p. 82.

"In the absence of a single, recognized Russian government," he announced, "the protection of legitimate Russian interests must devolve as a moral trustee-ship upon the whole conference." [5] It was regrettable that the conference, "for reasons quite beyond the control of the participating powers," was not to have Russian cooperation. But Hughes could not conceive of the conference taking any action that would be prejudicial to legitimate Russian interests or would encroach upon Russian rights.

After the conference opened, the Secretary had his aides draw up a resolution reaffirming the idea of moral trusteeship and taking a firm position against any "further violation of the rights of Russia and her citizens." [6] Ambassador Shidehara probably anticipated what was coming. The moment Hughes mentioned the Siberian issue in the Far Eastern Committee on January 23, 1922, the ambassador was on his feet reiterating Japan's "good intentions" and announcing that Japanese troops were soon to be withdrawn.[7]

Hughes accepted these assurances, reasserted the American policy laid down in the note of May 31, 1921, and again drove home the point that good faith required the "complete withdrawal of Japanese troops from all Russian territory." Spreading both Japan's pledge and his own statement on the conference record, he placed Tokyo under the necessity of withdrawing its troops or acknowledging its words to be fraudulent.

When the United States was invited to participate in the Genoa Conference of 1922, Hughes took advantage of the occasion to reiterate that "this Government, anxious to do all in its power to promote the welfare of the Russian people, views with the most eager and friendly interest every step taken towards the restoration of economic conditions which will permit Russia to regain her productive power." [8] Even though the United States did not send delegates to this conference, the Secretary made it plain that any move on the part of the powers to take advantage of Russia's prostration would meet with sharp disapproval in America.

A few months later Japan evacuated Siberia; three years later her troops left northern Sakhalin. Historians point out that by this time she had gained valuable concessions, and occupation costs had become heavy. But Hughes' skillful mobilization of world opinion against the Japanese venture was one of the factors that made it too costly to pursue. Challenging the Japanese militarists without any European assistance, he earned the lion's share of the credit for saving Russia from continued exploitation and possible dismemberment.

This statesmanlike intercession in behalf of a prostrate power reflected not only Hughes' desire to curb Japanese expansion but also a genuine interest in the welfare of the Russian people. His friendliness toward the Russians was

[5] *Foreign Relations, 1921*, I, 70.   [6] J. A. V. MacMurray to CEH, Jan. 12, 1922.
[7] *Conference on the Limitation of Armament*, pp. 139ff.
[8] *Foreign Relations, 1922*, I, 393.

further manifested by his aid to the movement which supplied $66,000,000 for the relief of suffering from the great Soviet famine of 1921–1922. But he could see nothing good for the Russians or for the world in Nicolai Lenin's Communist régime.

Wilson had not recognized the new Moscow government, and Hughes continued that policy in common with most of the foreign offices in Europe at that time. At St. Augustine in February, 1921, he was approached by Joseph Z. Dalinda, a Russian who was sponsoring a scheme to employ American engineers for the restoration of Russia's ruined industries. Hughes was cool and noncommittal. The following month the Soviet government suggested sending a special delegation to the United States to negotiate a trade agreement. The communication was crudely addressed to Congress as well as to the President and was released to the press before it was received.

"It is idle to expect a resumption of trade," Hughes replied, "until the economic bases of production are securely established. Production is conditioned upon the safety of life, the recognition of firm guarantees of private property, the sanctity of contract, and the rights of free labor." [9] Pointing to Russia's starvation and chaos, he insisted that her primary need was for relief and internal stability.

Through Secretary of Commerce Hoover, several American companies inquired of the State Department as to the possibilities of resuming business in Russia. "I do not think it advisable," Hughes replied, "to put any obstacle in the way of any American concern that desires to do business with Russia, or to endeavor to resume management of its property in Russia, always with the understanding that it is acting at its own risk. It is only through efforts of this sort that the difficulties in doing anything worth while under the present regime in Russia will be disclosed to the satisfaction of our business men." [10]

As to diplomatic relations, Hughes' stand was based on well defined principles and reflected no vindictiveness. He was not stiff-necked about recognizing a revolutionary government. "We are not concerned with the question of the legitimacy of a government as judged by former European standards," he wrote in reply to a letter from Samuel Gompers, president of the American Federation of Labor. "We recognize the right of revolution, and we do not attempt to determine the internal concerns of other States." [11] The Russians had a right to develop their own institutions. The Secretary also conceded that "long-continued acquiescence" on the part of the people in a régime actually functioning as a government should count heavily in its favor.

Beyond stability, however, was the all-important element of good faith. "Recognition," he said, "is invitation to intercourse. It is accompanied on the

[9] *New York Times,* March 26, 1921.   [10] CEH to Hoover, March 22, 1922.
[11] CEH to Samuel Gompers, July 19, 1923; Hughes Papers.

part of the new government by the clearly implied or express promise to fulfill the obligations of intercourse." Soviet Russia made no pretense of accepting such obligations. Hughes knew, as Root said, "that the fundamental doctrine of the men who govern Russia now is that it is their mission in the world to overturn and destroy the government of the United States, of England, of France, of all the civilized nations of the western world." [12] Moscow had a new code of ethics which elevated bad faith to the status of a policy. Hughes refused to match it by making self-deception or hypocrisy a guide to action.

The Soviet officials had openly and unconditionally repudiated all foreign debts owed by Russia, including $187,000,000 the United States had lent to the Kerensky government. They had also ruthlessly confiscated property belonging to American citizens. Hughes had not the slightest idea of slipping into the role of the harsh creditor. "The United States," he said, "is not seeking to press debtors who cannot pay beyond their means. But indulgence and proper arrangements are one thing, repudiation is quite another." [13] How could there be any faith in a régime that adopted repudiation and confiscation as policies? The honest-minded apostle of justice who was Secretary of State simply could not bring himself to the point of rewarding the authors of those policies with diplomatic recognition.

The chief reason for turning a cold shoulder toward the Moscow régime, however, was its sponsorship of subversive activities in the United States. The State Department gathered an abundance of evidence as to what the world revolutionists in control of the Russian government were trying to do on this side of the Atlantic.[14] Hughes' attention rested especially on Trotsky's declaration to the young Communists that "revolution is coming in Europe as well as in America, systematically, step by step, stubbornly and with gnashing of teeth in both camps. It will be long protracted, cruel and sanguinary." [15] In his statement of July 1, 1924, the Secretary made his position clear:

The essential fact is the existence of an organization in the United States created by, and completely subservient to, a foreign organization striving to overthrow the existing social and political order of this country. The subversive and pernicious activities of the American Communist Party and the Workers' Party and their subordinate or allied organs in the United States are activities resulting from and flowing out of the program elaborated for them by the Moscow group.[16]

To recognize Russia under these circumstances, Hughes concluded, would be to give the Communist régime an embassy in Washington as an official

[12] Root's Address of Nov. 10, 1925.   [13] *The Pathway of Peace*, p. 63.
[14] *Hearings, "Recognition of Russia,"* before Senate Foreign Relations Subcommittee, 1924, 68th Congress, 1st session.
[15] *The Pathway of Peace*, p. 64.
[16] Charles Cheney Hyde, "Charles Evans Hughes," in *The American Secretaries of State and Their Diplomacy*, ed. S. F. Bemis (New York, Knopf, 1928), X, 287. Copyright, 1928, by Alfred A. Knopf, Inc.

headquarters for its subversive activities. That he steadfastly refused to do. To summarize, he denied the Soviet recognition for three reasons: (1) insufficient proof that it had been accepted by the people; (2) its unwillingness to meet the obligations of international intercourse; (3) its persistent efforts to destroy the governments whose recognition it sought.

Senator Borah, for reasons that have never been fully explained, became the spearhead of the movement for recognition of the Soviet. His demands for a conference to iron out differences between Washington and Moscow boomed through the Senate. Hughes felt that, without indications that the Soviet régime was ready to modify its conduct, a conference would be futile. Preparing a terse statement to this effect, he took it to President Coolidge for approval.

"Why shouldn't I say that?" was the President's response.

"Of course you could," Hughes replied. "But would it be wise to expose yourself to the criticism that will rain upon the head of the person who makes this statement public?" [17] He felt that it was part of his job to shield the President, whenever possible, from brickbats aimed at the foreign policy they were pursuing.

"I guess you are right," the calm little Yankee said.

Hughes then issued his statement:

The American government . . . is not proposing to barter away its principles. If the Soviet authorities are ready to restore the confiscated property of American citizens or make effective compensation, they can do so. If the Soviet authorities are ready to repeal their decree repudiating Russia's obligations to this country and appropriately recognize them, they can do so. It requires no conference or negotiations to accomplish these results which can and should be achieved at Moscow as evidence of good faith.[18]

The Lion of Idaho roared his disapproval, and Soviet sympathizers protested so loudly that newsmen asked the Secretary if he would resign. Hughes snorted in the negative. His policy undoubtedly reflected the wishes of a majority in Congress and the country as well as those of the President. Secretaries Kellogg and Stimson later adhered to the same policy, and the latter reiterated Hughes' three chief reasons for withholding the hand of friendship. When recognition was finally accorded in 1933, it was upon the explicit pledge that the Soviet government would refrain from interfering in any manner in the internal affairs of the United States and would restrain all persons in its service and all organizations in receipt of any financial assistance from it from any act liable to injure the tranquility, prosperity, order, or security of the United States. Subsequent history heavily underscores Secretary Hughes' fears that, even if expressly given, such a pledge would rest upon bad faith.

[17] Author's interview with CEH, Dec. 10, 1946.   [18] Hyde, *op. cit.*, p. 286.

At no time, however, did his realistic understanding of the Communist dictatorship alter his interest in, or his friendship for, the Russian people. And he insisted on maintaining the amenities when dealing with Soviet representatives. When one of the latter came to the department seeking an interview in connection with a case before an American tribunal and the subordinate assigned to see him began letting off steam, Hughes cut him short. "Hold on," he said. "Mr. ——— has asked for an appointment with me. I cannot see him; but you must. He is entitled to a perfectly fair hearing and to be treated courteously." [19]

A decade later when the first Soviet ambassador, Alexander Troyanovsky, came to Washington, he called on Chief Justice Hughes in accord with time-honored custom. Their relations became "most agreeable," and on three separate occasions in the years that followed the Chief Justice and Mrs. Hughes were the guests of honor at large dinners at the Soviet Embassy. At the last of these fêtes in May, 1938, the two men sat together after dinner and surveyed at length the rising menace of Hitlerism in Europe, with the ambassador asserting rather emphatically that Hitler, as soon as he was ready, would attack France.[20]

To the end of his days Hughes remained alert to the menace of revolutionary and imperialistic Communism. He would neither countenance the despoilment of a prostrate nation nor compromise with bad faith. When the Russian people emerge from their era of terrorism, they may well count him one of their best friends during the dark days of Lenin.

[19] Hyde, *op. cit.*, p. 282.   [20] CEH, Notes, p. 317.

Chapter 51

THE FRIENDLY NEIGHBOR

SECRETARY HUGHES picked up the reins of foreign policy in Latin America with vivid memories of his 1916 presidential campaign. Some of his severest criticism had been directed at Wilson's handling of the Mexican imbroglio. As Secretary of State, his central aim in regard to Latin America was to replace Theodore Roosevelt's big stick and Wilson's erratic interventions by the stabilizing hand of friendship.

The United States' meddling in Mexico and its general overlordship in the Caribbean area had provoked widespread resentment among the Latin American peoples. During World War I most of them had supported the United States; but, with the war over and with Europe notably weakened in relation to the Western Hemisphere, suspicion as to the motives of the "colossus of the North" had been reactivated. This suspicion was fed by the presence of United States troops in Santo Domingo, Haiti, and Nicaragua. The American flag was flying in more countries than ever before. Hughes' firm policy was to bring the flag and the troops home while helping our Latin neighbors to maintain their own freedom and national stability.

Ten days after he became Secretary of State, Hughes first enunciated his aim at a luncheon given by Dr. L. S. Rowe, director general of the Pan American Union.

We have and will have no ulterior purposes with respect to the Republics of Latin America. We wish to help to a common prosperity, through the safeguarding of the opportunities of peace, the fostering of friendship and of mutually advantageous commercial intercourse. . . . We can have neither security nor peace, neither stability nor progress, unless reason rules and justice is assured. We are all collaborators in that greatest of endeavors and we are looking forward with the utmost confidence to an era of exceptional mutual benefits through our working together in a spirit of mutual trust.[1]

What had been done could not be undone overnight. No good would come from sudden withdrawal of our Marines, leaving to chaos the countries that had come to lean upon them for law enforcement. Lasting progress could be made only by eliminating the causes of unrest, preventing the growth of conditions prejudicial to the United States, and aiding our neighbors to settle their

[1] *New York Times,* March 15, 1921.

own disputes peacefully without imposing our will on them. Hughes summed it up by saying: "Our interest does not lie in controlling foreign peoples; that would be a policy of mischief and disaster. Our interest is in having prosperous, peaceful, and law-abiding neighbors with whom we can cooperate to mutual advantage." [2]

Two decades after this policy was put into effect, Professor Samuel Flagg Bemis of Yale University described it as the liquidation of imperialism. "Responding to the new situation," he wrote, "it was the policy of Secretary of State Charles E. Hughes . . . to liquidate the interventions of the United States in the Caribbean and Central America as promptly as political stability should seem to be established and the safety of foreign nationals reasonably assured." [3] Hughes heartily accepted this as an accurate statement of what he had tried to do. Others credited him with taking the first steps toward what became, under the second Roosevelt, the "good neighbor policy." [4] Certainly he emulated the good neighbor, though he had more difficult problems to meet in Latin America than Roosevelt and Hull encountered more than a decade later.

One reason for this similarity of the Hughes and Roosevelt policies in Latin America was Sumner Welles. As chief of the State Department's Latin American Division when Hughes took office, Welles immediately won his new chief's respect. His work proved him to be a diplomat of "exceptional ability, poise, and force of character." [5] Although Welles left the department early in 1922, he helped to shape Hughes' Latin American policy in its formative period. During a large part of the Roosevelt administration Welles was again in the department as Undersecretary of State.

Among the first fruits of the Hughes-Welles teamwork was the Central American Conference. The little countries south of Mexico were on the verge of war. Honduras and Nicaragua had accused each other of assisting revolutionists in the invasion of their respective countries. Salvador had also become involved, and Washington feared a general upheaval in the back yard of the Panama Canal. On a request from Nicaragua, Hughes first invited the Presidents of the three countries to a conference on the U.S.S. *Tacoma* in Fonseca Bay in August, 1922, in the presence of United States diplomats, and they succeeded in patching up a temporary agreement.

Seeking a more reliable means of settling such disputes, Hughes induced the President to call a conference of Central American countries. It met in Washington in December, 1922, with Hughes and Welles as the United States'

---

[2] *The Pathway of Peace*, p. 137.
[3] Bemis, *The Latin American Policy of the United States* (New York, Harcourt, Brace, 1943), p. 203. Copyright, 1943, by Samuel Flagg Bemis.
[4] James Grafton Rogers in *American Bar Association Journal*, July, 1941, p. 412.
[5] CEH, Notes, p. 327.

delegates exercising no right to vote. The Secretary was to make the opening address. When the day of the conference arrived, however, he had been so preoccupied with the reparations dilemma in Europe that he had nothing prepared. Calling in Welles, he hastily discussed the main points to be covered and dictated his speech—ten small pages—in precise, penetrating words comprehensively dealing with every essential point. While the speech was being typed he turned to other problems, but he was on time for the conference and delivered his address verbatim, with no manuscript before him, changing only about three words.[6]

"The Government of the United States has no ambition to gratify at your expense," he said, "no policy which runs counter to your national aspirations, and no purpose save to promote the interests of peace and to assist you, in such manner as you may welcome, to solve your problems to your own proper advantage. The interest of the United States is found in the peace of this Hemisphere and in the conservation of your interests." [7]

The conference produced a general treaty of peace and amity and eleven conventions dealing with the limitation of armament, extradition, agriculture, an exchange of students, and so forth. One convention set up a Central American Tribunal, the first court of arbitration in history. The United States became a party to the convention providing for international commissions of inquiry into a limited category of disputes not settled by diplomacy or arbitration. Another blow for stability was struck by reviving and tightening up the Tobar Doctrine of 1907. Each of the five republics pledged itself in specific detail not to aid or recognize any government coming into power in any of the other signatory countries by a *coup d'état*. They also agreed "not to intervene, under any circumstances, directly or indirectly, in the internal political affairs of any other Central American republic." Here was a model for the Treaty on the Rights and Duties of States that came into being at Montevideo in 1933.

The usefulness of the treaties was demonstrated when the failure of the presidential election in Honduras in October, 1923, threw that country into revolution. The Navy proposed that Marines be rushed in at once. Hughes would not tolerate it. Instead, he sent Welles to offer the good offices of the United States, and peace and order were restored. In the thirties the nonrecognition treaty broke down when a revolutionary government established itself in Salvador in spite of the disapproval of Washington and its neighbors. However, the Central American treaties kept the peace among these little nations "until they stepped into the larger Pan American peace structure set up at Montevideo and Buenos Aires in 1933 and 1936." [8]

Relations with Latin America were also much improved by the Senate's rati-

---

[6] Author's interview with Sumner Welles, Oct. 29, 1947.
[7] Address of Dec. 4, 1922; Hughes Papers.   [8] Bemis, *op. cit.*, pp. 208f.

fication of the treaty for payment of $25,000,000 to Colombia because of Roosevelt's seizure of the Panama Canal Zone. The treaty had been negotiated before Hughes took office, but he heartily approved it and sought to take full advantage of the clarified atmosphere on the Pan American horizon. The logical next step was the withdrawal of American troops from Latin American soil, and to this task the Secretary diligently applied himself.

Santo Domingo became the first test case. Wilson had sent naval forces to the Dominican Republic in 1916 to avert civil war. Hughes' study of the situation convinced him in 1921 that the time was opportune to seek withdrawal of these troops. His initial moves were to bring about the appointment of Rear Admiral Samuel S. Robison as military governor and direct the issuance of a proclamation to the Dominican people. The United States wished to withdraw its forces, the proclamation said, and turn over the administration of the republic's affairs to a responsible Dominican government established in accord with the Constitution of 1908. The plan was for the military governor to convene primary assemblies to prepare for an election and then to supervise the balloting to get a free expression of the popular will.

The Dominican people suspected a trick intended to prolong the occupation, and rejected Hughes' friendly gesture. He tried in vain to reassure them; then, instead of resenting their rebuff, he patiently sought a new approach. At the same time he curbed the rigors of the Navy's dictatorship. Six or seven young Dominicans had been imprisoned for publishing articles in the press attacking the application of the land law. Hughes denounced the sentences as "peculiarly unfortunate" and asked the Navy Department to suspend them at once and "to refrain, in the future, from taking official cognizance of purely political offenses of this character without the concurrence of the Department of State." [9]

In March, 1922, Francisco J. Peynado, former Dominican minister to the United States, came to Washington. He and the Secretary had no difficulty in modifying the evacuation plan so that it appeared acceptable in principle. Then Hughes sent word to the Dominican political leaders that they would be welcome in Washington if they wished to seek an agreement. When General Horacio Vásquez and Federico Velásquez arrived in Washington, they were in entire accord with the new evacuation plan. The President, at Hughes' request, appointed Welles commissioner to Santo Domingo for the purpose of ascertaining the wishes of the people and arranging for the final withdrawal. Welles had previously resigned as chief of the State Department's Latin American Division and had been succeeded by Francis White.

It was a proud moment for Hughes when President Vásquez was inaugurated on July 12, 1924, and a new era of independence began for the Dominican

[9] *Foreign Relations, 1922*, II, 37.

Republic. The American occupation forces were gradually withdrawn between June and September. Hughes had insisted that law, order, and constitutional government follow in the wake of the occupation; his liquidation of imperialism was not the abandonment of bankrupts to their fate but the rehabilitation of weak states so that they were capable of self-government.

The Secretary hoped to repeat this achievement in every country that was still occupied by American troops. In Haiti, however, the situation was less favorable. Frequent upheavals had left the people destitute and almost hopeless. In the last murderous orgy before American troops had restored order in 1915, former President Zamora and President Sam were both slaughtered, the latter being dragged from the French Legation, where he had taken refuge, and torn to pieces in the street. Reviewing this background of chaos and violence, Hughes sent John H. Russell, a civilian-minded brigadier-general, to Haiti early in 1922, with instructions to work in the closest cooperation with the local authorities. The new American High Commissioner was not satisfied merely to maintain peace and order. Agriculture and industry were revived; the currency was stabilized, the public debt reduced, and constructive public works undertaken. An American adviser attempted to establish a sound judicial system, and local government was strengthened. But, after a thorough investigation, Hughes was convinced that the withdrawal of American troops would plunge the country into bloodshed and revolution once more. He had to be content with a report of progress and a statement of his good intentions.

Nicaragua was a more hopeful case. American troops had been stationed in that country since 1912; order had been fully restored and a new electoral system set up by Harold W. Dodds, later president of Princeton University. Hughes told the Nicaraguans in November, 1923, that after the elections of the following year and the installation of the new President in January, 1925, the last of the Marine guard at the American Legation in Managua would be withdrawn. Meanwhile he offered to lend expert aid for the training of a Nicaraguan constabulary. A relatively fair and free election was held, and Carlos Solórzano was inaugurated president in February, 1925. Fearing an uprising from the defeated party, Solórzano asked that the withdrawal of the Marines be delayed, and the evacuation was not completed until a few months after Hughes had left office. A revolution followed, and President Coolidge sent the Marines back again.

In Cuba the Hughes policy took the form of forbearance. The significant thing about our relations with Cuba, he used to say, "was not that we went in but that we came out." [10] The Secretary was "vehemently implored" to rescue

---

[10] Charles Evans Hughes, *Our Relations to the Nations of the Western Hemisphere* (Princeton, Princeton University Press, 1928), p. 76.

Cuba from the corruption of the Zayas régime. While the reports he received from General E. H. Crowder, trusted American friend of Cuba, gave him many anxious hours and while intervention might have been justified under the Platt Amendment, Hughes preferred to use less drastic methods. By aiding the Cubans in straightening out their financial affairs and governmental machinery, he avoided any necessity for intervention.

Cuba was especially grateful to Hughes for his aid in getting the Isle of Pines Treaty ratified. Negotiated in 1904, the treaty had been pigeonholed by the Senate out of fear that the interests of American citizens in the island might be imperiled if our government definitely renounced all claim of title. The Secretary revived the treaty and interested a number of Senators in it over Borah's opposition. "The present undetermined status of the Isle of Pines," he wrote to Senator Robinson, "constitutes one of the few remaining questions capable of prejudicing the intimate relations between the United States and Cuba, and it is my earnest hope that the Senate in its present session will give its consent to the ratification of the Treaty." [11] The Senate responded in March, 1925, two months after this letter was written, with a vote of 63 to 14 for the treaty.

The Hughes policies in Latin America were given a secure philosophical base by his clear thinking about the Monroe Doctrine. Over the years people on both sides of the Rio Grande had made a practice of lumping together under the heading of the Monroe Doctrine all the ideas and practices by the United States that our neighbors found obnoxious. Secretary Olney's boast that "the United States is practically sovereign on this continent," Theodore Roosevelt's "Corollary" to the Monroe Doctrine, and Wilson's interventions were all linked in the public mind to President Monroe's famous declaration. Some went so far as to assume that a logical extension of the doctrine would sweep all the Caribbean area under the American flag. Such hateful connotations were a heavy liability for any national policy to carry.

Hughes took advantage of his address to the American Bar Association in Minneapolis on August 30, 1923, to strip our hemispheric policy of these excrescences. "The Monroe doctrine," he said, "is not a policy of aggression; it is a policy of self-defense. It was asserted at a time when the danger of foreign aggression in this hemisphere was very real, when the new American states had not yet established a firm basis of independent national life, and we were menaced by threats of Old World powers directed against republican institutions. But the achievements of the century have not altered the scope of the doctrine or changed its basis. It still remains an assertion of the principle of national security. As such, it is obviously not exclusive." [12]

He assumed that the United States would always reserve to itself the right

[11] *Foreign Relations, 1925*, II, 2.   [12] *The Pathway of Peace*, p. 120.

of defining, interpreting, and applying the doctrine. He made no effort to share its enforcement with the other American states, as Secretary Stettinius succeeded in doing in the "one for all and all for one" arrangement worked out at Chapultepec in 1945. Hughes was well aware of Wilson's failure to interest Argentina, Brazil, and Chile in a Pan American treaty incorporating the Monroe Doctrine.[13] While persistently seeking hemispheric cooperation, he went no further in this matter than to encourage the other American states to maintain "Monroe Doctrines" of their own, which would have the effect of common resistance to any outside aggression. His chief contribution to the doctrine was his hard pounding on the point that it does not "infringe upon the independence and sovereignty of other American States." There was nothing in it contemplating a "protectorate" over any other country. It gave "no justification" for intervention in the affairs of our neighbors. "I utterly disclaim, as unwarranted," he said, "the observations which occasionally have been made implying a claim on our part to superintend the affairs of our sister republics, to assert an overlordship, to consider the spread of our authority beyond our own domain as the aim of our policy, and to make our power the test of right in this hemisphere."

In an address to the American Academy of Political and Social Science at Philadelphia on November 30, 1923, in celebration of the centenary of Monroe's declaration, Hughes further outlined the constructive aspects of his hemispheric policy. First, he recognized "the equality of the American republics, their equal rights under the law of nations." Second, he pledged respect for their territorial integrity. Third, he emphasized that each state has "duties as well as rights," including the duty of protecting the rights which citizens of other states have acquired under its laws. Fourth, he offered "friendly assistance" to promote the stability and strengthen the independence of those sister republics which were especially afflicted with disturbed conditions. Fifth, the United States would aid the peaceful settlement of disputes between the governments of the Western Hemisphere. Sixth, he urged limitation of armaments. Seventh, he promised "mutually helpful cooperation" through the Pan American conferences. Eighth, the United States would not seek preferential trade rights but unconditional most-favored-nation treatment. Ninth, it would rigorously protect its special interests such as the Panama Canal.[14] In Hughes' hands the Monroe Doctrine thus became the foundation for a positive policy of helpfulness.

He saw no inconsistency between the confraternity of the Western Hemisphere and the United States' position as a world power. American interest in the integrity of China and Russia and in world peace were sprouts from the same root that produced the Monroe Doctrine. In these broader fields, the Sec-

[13] Henry P. Fletcher to CEH, Jan. 10, 1923.   [14] *The Pathway of Peace,* pp. 155–163.

retary said, the United States was "pursuing under different conditions the same aims of independence, security, and peace which determined the declaration of Monroe." The Monroe Doctrine expressed our firm intention to retain security in the Western Hemisphere, but it also left the door open to action on the world stage in any degree that our future security might require.

Welles thought that Hughes' "painstaking and authoritative elucidation" of the Monroe Doctrine was one of his greatest services to the country. "Secretary Hughes brought it home to the American public in a manner more convincing than ever before," he said, "that the Monroe Doctrine was solely a policy of self-defense. . . ." [15] Hughes also gave greater endurance to his own concepts of international justice and fair dealing by weaving them into the fringe of the venerated doctrine.

[15] Welles' *Naboth's Vineyard* (London, Payson & Clarke, Ltd., 1928), II, 922f.

Chapter 52

REMOVING CAUSES OF FRICTION

SECRETARY HUGHES carried his message of friendship to the heart of South America when he attended the centennial of Brazilian independence at Rio de Janeiro in 1922. The Emperor Dom Pedro II had been a prominent figure at the United States centenary in 1876. To return the emperor's courtesy, Harding named Hughes head of a delegation that included also Representative Stephen G. Porter, Admiral Hilary P. Jones, Major General Robert L. Bullard, and Justice Edward R. Finch of the Supreme Court of New York.

The sailing of the official party from New York on August 24 aboard the S.S. *Pan America* was somewhat delayed by a striking incident that had no direct connection with the trip. As Hughes joined in the embarkation ceremonies, a New York lawyer determined to see him arrived hurriedly at the dock and followed the official party. It was Grenville Clark. Clark kept a watchful eye on the Secretary as the procession boarded the ship and went to the main saloon where the greetings and speechmaking took place. Then he followed the Secretary to his stateroom. The door was open. Hughes was unfastening his valise when Clark, standing in the doorway, made known his presence with a knock.

"Clark, what are you doing here?" the Secretary demanded sharply. "You are not going, are you? You will be left."

"I must speak to you," Clark replied, "about your having signed the document for the landing of the cable at Miami."

"How did you know about that?" Hughes asked.

"Stabler telephoned Root about it at Clinton and Root phoned me half an hour ago and was extremely disturbed," Clark said. "It was understood, as you know, that the cable would not be landed until the last South American country had consented, and, as you know, Argentina has not yet consented."

The controversy had arisen out of a prolonged fight between the American and British cable companies serving South America. All America Cables, Inc., maintained cable connections between the United States and Buenos Aires by way of the west coast of South America, where it held some monopoly rights. The Western Telegraph Company, Ltd., operated a monopolistic cable system on the east coast of South America. Through an alliance between this British company and the Western Union Telegraph Company, the east coast cable had been extended from Buenos Aires to within three miles of Miami—a formidable threat to the All America Company. Elihu Root, Jr., counsel for All America, had found a line of precedents under which the United States had forbidden foreign companies to land their cables on our shores if they held monopoly rights in other foreign lands with the effect of excluding the cables of American companies. Reasserting this policy, President Wilson had sent a government vessel to prevent the cable off Miami from being landed.

Suit had been brought, and Judge Augustus N. Hand had ruled that Wilson had exceeded his constitutional authority. While the case was pending before the Supreme Court, the All America Company had appealed to Congress to grant the President the needed authority, and an exciting race had ensued to get the measure enacted before the court could hand down its decision. Congress had won; the bill had become law; and the contending parties, after a number of conferences with Secretaries Hughes and Hoover, had entered into an agreement under which monopoly rights were to be abandoned on both South American coasts. It was understood that the cable at Miami was to be landed but only after all the South American countries had granted to the respective companies the landing licenses contemplated by the agreement.

To avoid further delay, Hughes had signed papers lifting the ban on the Miami cable before he left Washington, although there was still a question as to whether the reply of Argentina fully met the conditions on which the agreement between the cable companies was based. On learning this, Root (who was in Clinton, New York) had made every effort to telephone the Secretary, and, being unsuccessful, had asked his partner (Clark) to locate Hughes in New York and try to have the action revoked.

Hughes replied to Clark that the points he raised were technical and that he (Hughes) would see to it that Argentina's consent was forthcoming. "You young men have had a great success in holding off the landing of that cable all these years," he said, "and you ought to be satisfied. Now you must leave the ship at once."

"That is not quite the point, Mr. Secretary," Clark replied. "The point is that you have signed the document for the landing of the cable before Argentina's clear-cut consent has been received; and neither you nor anyone can absolutely guarantee what Argentina will do. If it goes wrong, the agreement is not fulfilled, and we are put in an impossible position."

"You have heard what I have said," Hughes retorted impatiently. "Now you must leave."

"I am sorry, then," Clark blurted out, "but I am obliged to charge a breach of faith by the Department of State."

"How dare you?" the Secretary exclaimed, his face flushed from indignation.

"I am indeed sorry to have to make that statement," Clark came back, "but I must repeat it; that is precisely what it is, a breach of faith." [1]

Hughes struggled for self-control. After a brief pause he rang for the steward and instructed him to go immediately to the captain and say that Secretary Hughes wished the ship to remain at the dock for an hour or until he sent word.

"Now, Clark," he said as soon as the steward had gone, "we have both raised our voices and become emotional. Let's take a fresh start. Sit down here quietly and we will cool off and talk it over, and I want you to take your time about it."

Hughes listened with only brief questions while Clark reviewed the main points of the whole controversy and, while holding to his position, again expressed regret that he had felt it necessary to use such harsh language. The Secretary then replied that Clark had done right to see him under the circumstances and that he had made a mistake in signing the cable-landing license before the question of Argentina's compliance had been fully cleared up. But he felt that the Argentine message constituted a substantial compliance, and that if Messrs. Root and Clark saw the entire dispatch they might change their minds. The upshot was an understanding that, if the license had not already been sent to the British-Western Union combine, Leland Harrison at the department could use his discretion as to holding it up until Root could examine the full Argentine dispatch. Hughes gave Clark a message to Harrison, repeating it several times so that Clark could learn it by heart and deliver it by telephone as soon as he got off the ship. Root saw Harrison the next morning. The net result was to delay delivery of the license by only a single day. The incident served, however, to reassure the American company, to alert the department, and to give Clark a "lasting admiration" for Hughes' sense of justice and self-control. At the same time, Clark's firm and persistent course evidently did not interfere with Hughes' esteem, as was shown by their confidential relations in later years.

Except for hot weather, the trip to Rio was a fascinating interval for the overburdened Secretary. He and Mrs. Hughes were lodged in the beautiful Guanabara Palace, home of Brazil's former emperors, and extensively entertained. On the centennial day, September 7, they were guests of President Pessôa of Brazil in reviewing 40,000 troops at Campo Sãochristovão, with American bluejackets and Marines leading the parade. At noon the whole city joined in a great noise-making demonstration, and in the evening more than 100,000 persons marched down the flag-draped Avenida Rio Branco.

In the following week Secretary Hughes delivered four addresses to Brazilian audiences. At the dedication of the site for the American centennial monu-

[1] Mr. Clark's memorandum for author, Nov. 21, 1949.

ment at Rio he made one of his most positive statements on Latin American policy:

We shall also be glad to have this monument associated in the thought of our friends with a true appraisement of our North American ideals and aspirations. . . . We have our domestic problems incident to the expanding life of a free people, but there is no imperialistic sentiment among us to cast even a shadow across the pathway of our progress. We covet no territory; we seek no conquest; the liberty we cherish for ourselves we desire for others; and we assert no rights for ourselves that we do not accord to others. We sincerely desire to see throughout this hemisphere an abiding peace, the reign of justice and the diffusion of the blessings of a beneficent cooperation. It is this desire which forms the basis of the Pan American sentiment.

. . . We have institutions dedicated to freedom, and we desire not simply the independence of might but the independence which rests secure in a prevailing sense of justice. We have different stocks and traditions but we cherish the same aspirations; the same longings for liberty under law. The differences are superficial, the resemblances fundamental.

On the return trip aboard the battleship *Maryland* a heavy storm arose. The Hugheses stood on the bridge for several hours watching a seventy-five-mile-an-hour hurricane curl foam-capped hillocks of water over the deck. When they went to their cabin, the lunging sea tore away the port and poured a series of fourteen-inch jets of water in upon them. Butler Wright found Hughes, wearing shorts and a quizzical smile, standing in the middle of the room, with several inches of water swishing back and forth and various articles of clothing floating about. Mrs. Hughes was sitting in a corner convulsed with laughter. Wright never ceased to regret that the scene was not recorded for the benefit of those who talked about Hughes' austerity.

The most troublesome chasm that Secretary Hughes had to bridge in Latin America was that between the United States and Mexico. A long period of turmoil in the land of Montezuma and Cortes had come to an end in September, 1920, with a constitutional election. The time seemed ripe for resumption of diplomatic relations and settlement of the voluminous claims of American citizens against Mexico. Tedious and complicated negotiations were necessary, however, to secure a meeting of minds between the two governments.

The unprincipled confiscation of American properties under Carranza, in the face of his explicit assurances to the Wilson Administration, had brought demands for armed intervention after the Armistice of 1918. But the Mexicans themselves had overthrown and assassinated Carranza. With General Obregón's claims to power confirmed by the election of 1920, Hughes felt that a steadying hand was the first essential in dealing with Mexico. He sought a treaty guaranteeing the protection of American interests [2]—a treaty of amity and commerce to be signed coincidental with the resumption of diplomatic relations. In expounding his Mexican policy on June 7, 1921, he said:

The fundamental question which confronts the Government of the United States in considering its relations with Mexico is the safeguarding of property rights against confiscation. . . . Whenever Mexico is ready to give assurance that she will perform her fundamental obligation in the protection both of persons and of rights of property validly acquired, there will be no obstacles to the most advantageous relations between the two peoples.

But Obregón continued to angle for recognition with no strings attached. When he got around to making counterproposals on a wholly different basis, Hughes declined to consider them and asked for a statement of objections to his proposed treaty. The result was a complete impasse. Again the Secretary outlined his policy—a somewhat softened policy—in a speech before a mass meeting in Boston's Symphony Hall on October 30, 1922:

Our feeling towards the Mexican people is one of entire friendliness and we deeply regret the necessity for the absence of diplomatic relations. We have no desire to interfere in the internal concerns of Mexico. We do, however, maintain one clear principle which lies at the foundation of international intercourse. When a nation has invited intercourse with other nations, has established laws under which investments have been lawfully made, contracts entered into and property rights acquired by citizens of other jurisdictions, it is an essential condition of international intercourse that international obligations shall be met and that there shall be no resort to confiscation and repudiation. We are not insistent on the form of any particular assurance to American citizens against confiscation, but we desire in the light of the experience of recent years the substance of such protection, and this is manifestly in the interest of permanent friendly relations. . . . The problem is a very simple one and its solution is wholly within Mexico's keeping.

Under the constitution of 1917, Mexico had broken up her large landed estates and permitted villages to regain or to acquire communal lands. She had also nationalized subsoil deposits, including petroleum, thus claiming valuable property which, under previous Mexican laws, the owners of the surface rights believed to be theirs. Many Americans, including the oil interests, had suffered severely under these expropriation and nationalization programs. In 1921 the Mexican Supreme Court handed down five decisions reassuring pre-1917 owners against any retroactive application of the nationalization laws,[3] but the government was extremely reluctant to make the amends that these judgments demanded.

[2] CEH, Notes, p. 322.
[3] S. F. Bemis, *The Latin American Policy of the United States*, p. 215.

Secretary Hughes was in sympathy with the fundamental policy of the Mexican law, which was to break up the big estates and to curb exploitation. What he objected to was the confiscation of property owned by Americans as a means of carrying out this policy. There was no suggestion in his attitude that Mexico should change her constitution to please the United States. All he asked was that she respect her own laws in dealing with United States citizens.

An intermediary finally suggested the appointment of commissioners to talk over the problems between the two governments. Hughes induced the President to name Charles Beecher Warren, former ambassador to Japan, and Judge John Barton Payne, former Secretary of the Interior, and they went to Mexico City in the spring of 1923 with instructions to seek (1) restoration or payment for lands taken from American owners prior to May 1, 1917; (2) assurances against confiscation of subsoil interests in lands owned by Americans prior to the same date; and (3) an appropriate claims convention. Ultimately Mexico agreed to respect the rights of American surface owners or lessees to subsoil privileges where some positive act had been performed prior to promulgation of the 1917 constitution and to grant certain preferential rights to landowners and lessees who had failed to perform such positive acts. It was a compromise that Hughes believed to be fair to both countries.

There was no difficulty in reaching an agreement that all the agrarian lands expropriated by Mexico should be paid for at their fair value. The claims of American citizens arising out of Mexico's ten years of revolutions were to be adjudicated before a commission under a Special Claims Convention, and a broader category of claims by the citizens of both countries was to be heard by a second commission. Both governments were to be represented on each commission, with a neutral presiding commissioner to be selected, if possible, by mutual agreement. Hughes had given way on many details, but underneath his policy of friendly conciliation the hard core of principle had been preserved intact. Mexico had acknowledged her international obligations. The Colossus of the North had demanded, not a pound of flesh or even a reservoir of oil, but only a common variety of justice that was everywhere recognized in international law.

Hughes derived great satisfaction out of this liquidation of the chronic feud across the Rio Grande. When General de la Huerta sought to fan the embers of revolution on the eve of the election that brought President Calles to power, Hughes responded to the plea of the Mexican authorities for arms and munitions to put down the rebellion. His object was to help a neighbor maintain its own constitutional processes. Huerta's movement was not instinct with the aspirations of an oppressed people, he said, but with personal politics.[4]

[4] *Our Relations to the Nations of the Western Hemisphere*, pp. 52f.

The work of the claims commissions was disappointing to the United States. The State Department magnanimously accepted a Panamanian umpire for the general commission and a Brazilian for the special commission. The United States finally accepted a lump sum amounting to only 2.64 per cent of its original claims before the special commission. In 1941 the claims before the general commission (other than petroleum expropriations) were similarly settled for a lump sum of $40,000,000. Mexico's big neighbor had tempered justice with extreme leniency. Faith and charity had triumphed over dictation and punitive expeditions. Losses were unquestionably suffered, but they ultimately became an investment in good feeling throughout the Western Hemisphere.

Being a realist, Secretary Hughes did not rely wholly upon peace machinery and expressions of good will. The best way of preventing war in the American family of nations was to heal the festering sores that spread the infection. Accordingly, he devoted himself to all manner of prophylaxis intended to promote a healthy international environment.

These activities extended to Canada as well as to Latin America. In 1923 he suggested the creation of an American-Canadian commission to be composed of an equal number of distinguished citizens from each country who would examine and report the facts underlying any question that might arise between them. His thought was that each country would be kept so well informed about the problems and sensibilities of the other that the infliction of unnecessary injuries or indignities could be avoided.

In Latin America he repeatedly minimized friction by thwarting the schemes of Americans who were trying to exploit or bully their less sophisticated neighbors. His influence was used, for example, to curb the Army's high-handed dealings with the natives of Panama. Thirty-six protests against the conduct of United States officials in the Canal Zone were sent to the State Department by the Panamanian Legation. Hughes asked Francis White, chief of the Latin American Division, to summarize these cases and suggest what should be done. White did so with fine regard for the department's policy of equal justice to all men and all countries. The Secretary allowed himself only fifteen minutes to read White's seventy-two page report before the Panamanian minister called. Yet he discussed each case with amazing familiarity with the details and agreed to satisfactory adjustments.[5]

Governor Jay J. Morrow of the Canal Zone, who seemed to be the antithesis of his brother Dwight, rushed to Washington to protest against the new policy of treating Panamanians as if they were human beings. The State Department, he told its chief, did not understand the Latin Americans. The only way to

[5] Author's interview with Francis White, April 22, 1949.

deal with them, he said, with the air of an old experienced hand, was to hit them between the eyes. Hughes froze the Governor with a glance, and told him flatly that hitting between the eyes was not the policy of the United States and was not going to be.

A well known Congressman came to the department with a financial scheme that he hoped to impose on Honduras. White threw cold water on it when he discovered that it would yield a million dollars in profits to its promoters. In a huff, the Congressman said he would go straight to the Secretary. Hughes gave the legislator a chance to present his plan a few days later and told him candidly, "I do not think it will bear examination." The Congressman sputtered that of course the details could be changed, but Hughes only repeated his firm conclusion.

The Secretary was eager to see American capital and American experts honestly at work developing the resources of neighboring countries. "This sort of 'economic penetration,'" he said, "may be regarded as the highest expression, from the material standpoint, of international confidence and good will." [6] Yet his awareness of dangers in the flood of Latin American bond issues that international bankers were unloosing upon investors in the United States led to the adoption of a precautionary policy. Hughes could not attempt, of course, to ascertain the economic soundness of these loans. All he could do was to prevent them from being used to thwart American foreign policy. Especially ominous was the prospect of bond issues being floated in the United States to finance revolutions or other militaristic ventures in Latin America. Called into conference at the White House, the investment bankers agreed not to sell foreign bonds to the American public without giving the State Department full information about each issue and an opportunity to raise objections.

When misunderstandings arose as to what this policy involved, the department issued a press release emphatically disavowing any attempt to pass on the soundness of any bond issue, directly or indirectly. Bankers were instructed that no prospectus or contract should in any way refer to the attitude of the Government toward any proposed issue. Salesmen nevertheless managed to convey, in some instances, an impression that the Government had endorsed the foreign issues they were peddling to gullible investors, and the department's policy was severely criticized, especially when the depression of the thirties left many of the bonds in hopeless default.

The outcome was certainly lamentable, but the department took the only course open to it at the time. It could not have permitted international bankers to thwart its policies in dealing with other countries for want of information as to what those policies were. Subsequent Administrations did not abandon but further tightened controls over foreign financing in the United States and set

[6] *Our Relations to the Nations of the Western Hemisphere*, p. 58.

up the Securities and Exchange Commission to compel the registration of all securities offered for sale to the public.

After Hughes settled the conflicting territorial claims of Panama and Costa Rica, many countries vexed by unsolved boundary disputes knocked at his door. According to Sumner Welles, the United States' efforts in this sphere were "singularly successful so long as Mr. Hughes was Secretary of State." [7]

In the case of the dispute between Colombia and Panama, the Secretary's contribution was merely a suggestion that the two countries undertake direct negotiations, which proved to be successful. At the request of Brazil, Colombia, and Peru he made a detailed study of their three-way boundary dispute and offered his final recommendations at five o'clock on his last day in office as Secretary of State. Brazil had brought the controversy to a head by protesting to Peru against the latter's ratification of the Colombia-Peru boundary treaty of 1922. Hughes suggested that the protest be withdrawn and that ratification of the treaty be completed. The third step he recommended was a convention between Brazil and Colombia accepting the Apaporis-Tabatinga line, with Brazil granting Colombia perpetual freedom of navigation on the Amazon and other rivers common to both countries. Within two hours an agreement on this basis was closed. According to Dr. Rowe, the settlement brought "universal joy" throughout Latin America.

Far more troublesome was the dispute between Chile and Peru over the desert provinces of Tacna and Arica. This feud had hung like a dark cloud over Latin America for forty years. However, both countries appeared to be in a mood of welcoming the good offices of the United States, and after sounding them out Hughes invited them to send representatives to confer in Washington in the spring of 1922. Secretary and Mrs. Hughes gave the delegates a brilliant reception on May 12 with more than a thousand guests present. A few days later the conference opened in the Hall of the Americas before a distinguished gathering of notables. Hughes was doing his utmost to provide a favorable atmosphere. "The only relief for a troubled world," he told the opening session, "is in resort to the processes of reason in lieu of those of force."

The idea behind bringing the Peruvian and Chilean delegates to Washington was that they might be able to agree upon certain points to be submitted to arbitration. At the close of the war between Chile and Peru in 1883, the disputed territory had been held by Chile. Their peace treaty, the Treaty of Ancón, had provided that after ten years there should be a plebiscite to decide whether these provinces should "remain definitely under the dominion and sovereignty of Chile," or should continue "to constitute a part of Peru." No such plebiscite had been held, and this fact had become the center of the acrimonious controversy. Asserting that 80 per cent of the population of the district was Peru-

[7] *Naboth's Vineyard* (London, Payson & Clarke, Ltd., 1928), p. 934.

vian in 1894 when the vote should have been taken, Peru charged that Chile had willfully obstructed the plebiscite until she could transplant enough Chileans to constitute a majority.[8]

Hughes worked indefatigably to narrow the area of disagreement. Patiently he argued the Chileans into acceptance of arbitration on the question of whether a plebiscite should be held. At the same time he persuaded Peru to give up her demand that the arbitrator proceed to decide the future status of Tacna and Arica if settlement by plebiscite should be discarded. At last both countries accepted the Hughes formula and, on July 20, 1922, signed a protocol of arbitration.

They had proceeded on the assumption that the President of the United States would be the arbitrator. Hughes had attempted to discourage this, suggesting instead an independent jurist, such as Elihu Root, or a board of jurists. Both sides refused to budge, however, because it was clear that if the President were named, the actual task of arbitration would fall on Hughes. The Secretary yielded because his refusal would have upset what seemed to be the only possible basis for agreement. In a showdown he always sacrificed his own personal wishes to pressing public duty.

Hughes named William C. Dennis to aid him, and they examined enormous volumes of historical data and arguments submitted by Chile and Peru. The first question that had to be decided was whether a plebiscite should be held. Hughes' answer was Yes. The Treaty of Ancón provided that the people of Tacna and Arica should decide their own destiny in a plebiscite to be held *"after* the expiration" of ten years. No time limit had been fixed. Failure of the parties to agree upon the terms of the plebiscite could not, therefore, be regarded as a breach of the treaty.

His second task was to prescribe conditions under which the plebiscite should be held. He laid down detailed rules as to who would be entitled to vote and called for supervision of the balloting by a Plebiscitary Commission consisting of one representative from Chile, one from Peru, and a chairman to be named by the President of the United States. Hughes had explored the idea of using American troops to supervise the balloting but dropped it because of his belief that Congress would not agree and because Chile had insisted, as a condition to her acceptance of the arbitral agreement, that she should retain administrative control over the territory until the dispute could be settled.[9]

As the Secretary's award was submitted on his last day in office, the Plebiscitary Commission, at first headed by General Pershing, functioned without his supervision. But in any case its task was hopeless. Peruvian sympathizers in Tacna and Arica were intimidated; some were forcibly deported as the date

[8] *Arbitration Between Peru and Chile*, "The Case of Peru," I, 206–251.
[9] CEH, Notes, p. 334.

for the voting approached. After postponing the plebiscite several times, the commission decided that no impartial expression of the will of the people in the disputed territory could be obtained, and the effort was abandoned. The effect of Hughes' arbitration was nevertheless to break the legal impasse that had prevented agreement. By establishing the fact that the plebiscite section of the Treaty of Ancón was still valid, he had proved to the parties that further direct negotiations would have to be undertaken to obtain a settlement. His formula, which Chile and Peru had accepted in 1922, foresightedly called for continued negotiations under the good offices of the United States if the other steps undertaken should fail, and such negotiations went forward in Washington. Although he was again practicing law in New York, Hughes kept closely in touch with these negotiations, and repeatedly advised with the department through correspondence and personal visits.

The settlement that was finally achieved in 1929 gave Peru the northern province of Tacna, where most of her lost citizens lived, and Chile retained Arica, the southern province to which many Chileans had migrated. Neither contender was reduced to bitterness or frustration. Of course, no such solution had been open to Hughes in his role as arbitrator. His duty lay in fair interpretation of a treaty rather than formulation of a new policy, but the background of good will he created and his later advice contributed enormously to the final elimination of the Tacna-Arica tinder box.

Still another boundary dispute was pressed upon Hughes after he had returned to the bench. Guatemala and Honduras had negotiated for six months without agreeing upon an arbitration formula, although both said that if such a formula could be found only one arbitrator—Hughes—would be acceptable. Francis White suggested that they leave to Hughes the points they could not agree upon, and both assented. Their century-old controversy was thus submitted in 1930 to a Special Boundary Tribunal consisting of the Chief Justice of the United States as president and two distinguished Latin American jurists —Dr. Luis Castro Ureña of Costa Rica and Dr. Emilio Bello Codesido of Chile. Burdened though he was by the work of the Supreme Court, Hughes decided that he should accept the appointment in the interests of eliminating another source of international friction.

The tribunal's first decision was that it should sit, not as the International Central American Tribunal, but as a special boundary tribunal. Since it was impossible to find the line specified in the treaty between Guatemala and Honduras in some parts of the area in dispute, Hughes and his colleagues fixed a new line following natural boundaries in so far as they were consistent with settlement of the territory, actual possession, and other equities. Aerial photographs were used for the first time in a case of this sort, and the new line was drawn on detailed maps so as to leave no question whatever as to its location.

It was a line of convenience and common sense which proved satisfactory to both countries and brought an exchange of friendly notes between them.

Hughes' great interest in the settlement of international disputes of a juridical character led him to work for a hemispheric arbitration system. At the Havana Conference in 1928 he helped to commit the American republics to a policy of obligatory arbitration. The next step toward transforming this pledge into international law was taken at the special Pan American Conference on Conciliation and Arbitration at Washington in the winter of 1928–1929. Secretary Kellogg was nominally head of the American delegation, but Hughes wielded the "laboring oar." His problem was complicated by the fact that the Senate, over a long period of years, had consistently rejected every arbitration treaty that did not make allowance for Senate approval of each separate case to be submitted to arbitration. Reviewing this disheartening history with Coolidge and Kellogg, Hughes said that he was not willing to go through the farce of drafting a convention that would merely pledge us to arbitrate when and if two-thirds of the Senate might feel so disposed after a dispute had arisen. If the Senate's attitude in the past had to be accepted as final, he hinted, he would not serve as a delegate.[10] The upshot was complete agreement on the part of the President, the Secretary of State, and Hughes to fight for arbitration without senatorial apron strings attached.

In the arbitration section of the conference the chief question was whether the general principle of arbitration, to which all were devoted, would be riddled by exceptions. The parties finally agreed to arbitrate all international differences of a justiciable nature that could not be settled by diplomacy. Specifically included were disputes over (a) the interpretation of a treaty; (b) any question of international law; (c) the nature and extent of the reparation to be made for any breach of an international obligation. Only two classes of controversies were excepted from the obligation to arbitrate: (a) those within the domestic jurisdiction of any of the parties and not controlled by international law; and (b) "those which affect the interest or refer to the action of a State not a Party to this treaty." [11] This latter exception was Hughes' language designed to protect the Monroe Doctrine.

In case the disputants could not agree on the tribunal to handle a specific dispute, the treaty provided that each should designate two judges and they should select a fifth presiding judge or leave the choice to two judges of the Permanent Court of Arbitration at The Hague. It was a long plunge toward acceptance of obligatory arbitration of all justiciable disputes. Especially notable was the absence of any provision for senatorial domination of the procedure, but this was also an Achilles' heel. The Senate let the treaty gather dust for six years and then riddled it by a reservation requiring senatorial approval

[10] Beerits' Memorandum, XVIII, 42.   [11] *Foreign Relations, 1929*, II, 659–663.

of each separate agreement. All but five of the Latin American countries put the treaty into effect, although with many reservations.

As to conciliation, the conference decided to build upon the Gondra Convention that had been worked out at Santiago in 1923. The Gondra commissions of inquiry set up in Washington and Montevideo were now authorized to act also in a conciliatory capacity. They were to take up any controversy between the parties that could not be settled through diplomatic channels, and to propose a basis of equitable settlement within six months if no prior settlement had been reached. This treaty was ratified by the Senate.

Except for his work on the Guatemala-Honduras boundary tribunal, this was Hughes' final contribution to the cause of a peaceful Western Hemisphere. For nearly a decade the business of living amicably with our neighbors had claimed a large share of his time and interest. No one can examine the soil in which the good-neighbor policy is rooted without being struck by the quality and extent of Hughes' contribution to it. His evacuation of troops from two of the occupied countries and his patience in restoring good relations with Mexico provided the essential ingredient of mutual trust. His settlement of boundary disputes removed sources of friction in several different areas. His clarification of the Monroe Doctrine afforded a philosophical climate in which the new Pan Americanism could flourish. And the specific improvements he made in the means of peacefully settling disputes nourished the belief that justice could be substituted for wars within the American continents.

Chapter 53

THE HAVANA CONFERENCE

SECRETARY HUGHES looked upon the quinquennial Pan American conferences chiefly as friendship festivals. They were more significant for the interchange of ideas, for the promotion of understanding, and for extension of cultural and commercial relations than for any formal treaties that might evolve out of them. Men had to learn to work together and to discuss their differences dispassionately before they could devise means of settling all the major disputes among themselves. The warp of confidence and the woof of law had not yet been woven into the fabric of hemispheric solidarity.

Originally Hughes intended to go to the Fifth International Conference of American states at Santiago in 1923 as chief of the American delegation. An avalanche of work and a stubborn case of grippe changed his mind. Henry P. Fletcher was brought back from his ambassadorial post in Belgium to head the delegation. The Secretary had to be content with sounding the keynote in a message read by Fletcher. Two facts about the conference stand out. First, it set up a commission of jurists to codify international law. Second, it adopted the Gondra Convention, a "cooling-off" arrangement designed to assure both ample time and expert assistance for the settlement of international disputes. Hughes praised the treaty as an "entirely practical" attempt to assure the maintenance of peace in this hemisphere, and the Senate gave its consent.

It was five years later that Hughes, then a private citizen, singlehandedly bent a Pan American Conference to his will. At the request of President Coolidge he headed the United States' delegation to the Sixth International Conference of American States at Havana. Among the actors in this hemispheric drama who disembarked from the U.S.S. *Texas* one brilliant Sunday morning in Cuba's springtime of 1928 were President Coolidge, Secretary of State Kellogg, Hughes, Ambassadors Fletcher and Morrow, former Senator Underwood, Ray Lyman Wilbur, James Brown Scott, former Justice Morgan Joseph O'Brien, and Leo S. Rowe, director general of the Pan American Union. At the dock the visitors were greeted by President Machado, and two hundred thousand spectators cheered them as they passed through beautiful Malecon Drive to the Presidential Palace.

On the morning of January 16 the delegates assembled in the National Theater to hear the opening speeches of Presidents Coolidge and Machado.

Two days later the first plenary session was held in the Magna Aula, or Great Hall, of the University of Havana—a chamber of awesome dimensions as well as rich decorations. This was the organization meeting. Hughes was assigned to the Committees on the Pan American Union and Public International Law.

In spite of the warm welcome, a good deal of tension hung over Havana. For the first time the Latin American republics were ready to challenge the "Colossus of the North" on real live issues, and the issue that arose most persistently was nothing less than the United States' interventions in the Caribbean area. Smarting under the restrictions the United States had imposed on the importation of Argentine beef in order to keep out the foot-and-mouth disease, the Buenos Aires government was especially eager to exploit the mounting resentment against "Yankee imperialism." Forebodings of a clash could be seen in every gesture of the Argentines.

The outlook for trouble was doubtless one strong reason for the appointment of Hughes, who had an enviable reputation for successful dealing with the Latin Americans. The State Department made no bones about handing him a hot potato. In a "Special Political Memorandum" the department directed attention to the "vigorous anti-American propaganda" that had swept through Latin America during the previous year and warned that "certain delegates" might attack the policies the United States had been following. The most prominent instruction to Hughes and his fellow delegates was to strive to keep off the agenda all controversial subjects not already there and to resist the doctrine of absolute nonintervention.

Fully aware of the explosive possibilities, Hughes had accepted the assignment with misgivings.[1] Some feared that, under his negative instructions, he could do little more than "sit on the lid." Mistrusting suppression, however, he himself brought the intervention issue out into the open and faced it squarely. His opportunity came at the dinner given in honor of the delegation by the American Chamber of Commerce of Cuba on January 21. His theme was the same as it had been at Rio six years before:

It is the firm policy of the United States to respect the territorial integrity of the American Republics. We have no policy of aggression. . . . We do not wish their territory. . . . Nothing could be happier for the United States than that all the countries in the region of the Caribbean should be strong, self-sufficient, fulfilling their destiny, settling their problems, with peace at home and the fulfillment of their obligations abroad.

The delegates who had counted on pussyfooting from the United States were routed. A dispatch from Mexico City pronounced the speech the "finest expression of the American position that had been given in a quarter of a cen-

[1] CEH, Notes, p. 337.

tury," and the Nicaraguan delegate said that it "ought to convince our critics of the justice of the United States' efforts to establish peace in Nicaragua." [2] Argentina continued her baiting, but the Havana atmosphere had been cleared, and the conference went ahead with candid discussion of its numerous projects.

Social events lightened the delegates' labors. Will Rogers once told a New York theater audience how he and Mrs. Rogers, having invited Mr. and Mrs. Hughes and other guests to dinner in their Havana hotel suite, had debated whether "to serve or not to serve." Prohibition was still the law in the United States. Finally they put the cocktails off to one side where they would not be conspicuous. "When Mr. Hughes came in," Rogers said in his inimitable drawl, "he took one glance at the refreshments, parted his beard, drank a cocktail, and the party was a success."

Several radical reforms in the Pan American Union were urged as a means of goading the "Colossus of the North." Mexico contended that the chairmanship and the office of director general should be filled by rotation among the member countries in alphabetical order. And she wanted the governing board composed of special representatives who would not be subjected to the subtle influences that were supposed to sway Latin American ambassadors in Washington.

Instead of fighting these proposals, Hughes expressed entire sympathy with the idea of equalizing rights and privileges in the organization. The United States, he said, wished only to be a "co-worker and colleague, a true comrade." Without making any direct suggestions, he pointed out, however, the great advantage of leaving each country free to decide for itself how its representative in the union should be chosen. Either an ambassador or a special representative would act only under instructions from his government. Special agents would mean extra expense and the risk of divided counsel without in any way changing the nature of the Pan American Union. Responding to this logic, the delegates refused to rule ambassadors off the governing board, and the suggestion for rotation in the office of the director general was withdrawn.

The American delegation heartily supported the Mexicans' proposal that the Pan American Union should not "exercise functions of a political character." But Dr. Honorio Pueyrredón, head of the Argentine delegation, fought stubbornly to write into the preamble of the Pan American Union Convention a denunciation of international trade barriers. While Hughes sat silent, many Latin American delegates rose in committee to plead with Pueyrredón to abandon his intransigence. It was Argentina that was isolated. "The United States found itself in the Latin-American family," as William Hard wrote, "arguing against the stubbornness of what might be called the Colossus of the South." For Hughes did have his say before the controversy was over. "Let us

[2] *New York Times*, Jan. 23, 1928.

not destroy the Union," he declared, "by attempting to make it a tariff commission." [3] When the vote came, Dr. Pueyrredón stood utterly alone. The conference then went on to adopt, in the form of a convention, a sort of constitution for the Pan American Union. While the field in which it could operate was delimited in keeping with the nature of the organization, the union was placed on a firmer basis than ever before.

In spite of his reluctance to get out in front, Hughes emerged as the guiding spirit of the conference long before its dramatic close. Mark Sullivan's "confidential scout" at Havana wrote him:

Hughes is walking away with the conference. In courtesy he out-Latins the Latins. There are only two or three first rate intellects among the delegates and Hughes looms head and shoulders above the best of them. In committee meetings the Latins tie themselves into knots from which escape seems impossible, and then Hughes gets up and in ten words unravels the tangle. He has the knack of remembering names and when he makes a flowery allusion to Senor So-and-So, he completely disarms hostility. From the tributes I have heard I am beginning to sympathize with Mr. Hilles' wish to "draft him" [for the presidential nomination in 1928].[4]

While he made use of Latin techniques, he was not swept away by them. In one of the sessions a speaker waxed eloquent in Spanish on the subject of Mr. Hughes himself. Sensing the trend of the remarks, Hughes said to his interpreter, "Don't bother to translate anything until he gets to *pero*"—meaning "but."

The standing of the American delegation was further strengthened by its vigorous support of a Mexican resolution denouncing aggression and pledging the American states to "employ all pacific means to settle conflicts which may arise between them." Hughes popped up with an endorsement so warm that he almost swept the semihostile Mexican delegates off their feet. "It is my happy privilege to say for the United States of America," he began, "that we would join most heartily in a declaration that there shall be no war of aggression in America." With visible emotion, Dr. Gonzales Roa, sponsor of the resolution, rose and bowed his acknowledgment while the audience thundered its approval.

The great event of the conference evolved out of a clash of national interests in the Committee on International Public Law. The committee had before it twelve projects for the codification of international law that had been submitted by the Commission of Jurists as a result of its meeting at Rio de Janeiro in 1927. Seven of these concerning the status of aliens, treaties, diplomatic agents, consuls, maritime neutrality, asylum, and the obligations of states in

[3] Proceedings of Committee No. 1, Feb. 13; Hughes Papers.
[4] Sullivan to CEH, Feb. 6, 1928.

the event of civil strife were adopted with little fuss and few modifications. Two others entitled "The Fundamental Bases of International Law" and "States—Existence, Equality, Recognition" threw the delegates into a fracas over the question of nonintervention.

On this subject the jurists at Rio had forsaken the prosaic task of codifying law already in existence in an effort to condemn the United States' action in Nicaragua. "No state," they had declared with misleading simplicity, "may intervene in the internal affairs of another." There had been no attempt to define "intervene" or "internal affairs," and both expressions were variously interpreted. It was a fragmentary and ambiguous pronouncement that satisfied some of the Latin American delegates but brought vigorous dissent from others.

Dr. Victor Maurtua of Peru, to whom this project had been referred as reporter for the Committee on International Public Law, discarded the oversimplified nonintervention gesture. Before attempting to codify the law, he said, the conference should define the fundamental principles on which the law was based. Dr. Maurtua offered in lieu of the Rio jurists' formula the Declaration of the Rights and Duties of States sponsored by the American Institute of International Law. It was the work of leading jurists of Latin America and the United States and had been endorsed by Hughes in 1923 when he was Secretary of State. It proclaimed the right of every nation to independence and freedom to develop itself "without interference or control from other states, provided that in so doing it does not interfere with or violate the rights of other states." [5] Recognized also was the right of every nation "to exercise exclusive jurisdiction over its territory, and all persons whether native or foreign found therein."

Hughes firmly supported Maurtua because he feared that "the balanced precepts of international law were . . . in danger of being forgotten in the zeal for a trumpet call in defense of the ideal of liberty to which we are all devoted." But they were in the minority. Gustavo Guerrero, chairman of the committee, insisted that the Rio jurists' nonintervention statement should be the basis of the committee's discussion. Delegates from thirteen states adhered to this view, with the notable exception of the Nicaraguans and the Cubans. To the latter "intervention" was a word of hope for oppressed peoples.

The sizzling controversy was referred to a subcommittee that met behind closed doors with Hughes in the chair. He labored mightily for agreement and at one point was said to have obtained unanimous approval of certain rights and duties of states, but when it came to phrasing the resolution Pueyrredón and Guerrero held out for complete nonintervention. Hughes told them he was there to codify international law, not to write up political theories and doc-

[5] American delegates' report, p. 14.

trines as law. While he was willing to condemn the domination of one country by another, he was not willing to cover up basic disagreements with loose phrases or to let Pueyrredón turn the conference into a propaganda siren.

When no agreement could be reached in the subcommittee, Pueyrredón finally shifted his position. At a banquet given in honor of Colonel Lindbergh, who had flown his *Spirit of St. Louis* to Havana in a gesture of good will, Pueyrredón told Maurtua that since there was no chance of reconciling the conflicting viewpoints, the issue should be postponed for another conference.[6] An informal discussion followed. Hughes and Raul Fernandes, of Brazil, also members of the subcommittee, were seated in the same group, but Hughes withheld his reply to Pueyrredón's proposal until he could consult with various other delegates. Having done so, he gave his consent the following morning on condition that Guerrero, chairman of the full committee, would agree. Pueyrredón talked with Guerrero, and as the committee assembled the latter came down to Hughes' chair and said he was willing to drop the jurists' proposal.[7] The committee then unanimously agreed that the whole subject of intervention should go over to the next Pan American Conference in 1933.

Frustrated by the failure of his general strategy and under pressure from his own government, Pueyrredón resigned both as delegate to the conference and as ambassador to the United States. At Montevideo, en route to Buenos Aires, he denied that he had fathered the move to postpone consideration of the intervention issue and said that the initiative had come exclusively from Hughes.[8] Later he contended that his suggestion had been to end discussion in the committee and carry the dispute to a plenary session of the conference then in being. This adroit misstatement enabled him to dodge criticism in Argentina, but there could have been no misunderstanding; his whole point in suggesting the postponement had been that the matter should not be further discussed because there was no prospect of unanimity. Hughes informed the State Department that "the action taken was precisely in accord with Pueyrredón's suggestion." Dr. Maurtua declared himself to be "absolutely in accord with Mr. Hughes' version," [9] and their accounts were further sustained by Fernandes.[10]

The conference met for its last plenary session on February 18. The galleries of the Great Hall were packed with visitors and men of the press, although the conference seemed to have nothing more to offer than routine reports and addresses by dignitaries of the University of Havana. Late in the afternoon, however, the report of the Committee on Public International Law, with its

[6] Statement by Dr. Maurtua, June 19, 1928; Hughes Papers.
[7] Hughes to Francis White, May 14, 1928.
[8] Associated Press dispatch, April 12, 1928.
[9] Statement by Dr. Maurtua, June 19, 1928.
[10] Fernandes to Dr. Octavio Mangabeira, July 2, 1928.

proposal that the subject of nonintervention be left to the next Pan American Conference, brought the new chief delegate from Argentina, Dr. Laurentina Olascoaga, to his feet with an expression of regret that no agreement had been reached and a reaffirmation of his government's "irrevocable convictions" in this matter. The atmosphere of the Great Hall tensed as if a current of electricity had run through it. Delegates who had been drowsing sprang into action with the startled excitement of troops summoned from deep sleep to immediate battle.

The delegates from Haiti, Santo Domingo, Guatemala, and Colombia rose in rapid succession to record their hatred of intervention. Hughes and many others expressed regrets that a postponement had been necessary. A Guatemala delegate wanted to know why no agreement had been reached, which brought from Guerrero, the Foreign Minister of Salvador, the amazing reply that while the subcommittee had been divided apparently agreement now existed. If the conference were unanimous, as it appeared to be, he told the delegates, he could see no reason why the question of intervention should not be submitted to a vote. As a member both of the subcommittee and of the main committee that had explored the problem, he knew, of course, that no agreement could be attained. Apparently he was only airing his grievance; in any event, he offered no motion.

But Dr. Antonio Sanchez de Bustamente of Cuba, the chairman of the conference, apparently did not clearly understand the situation. To the surprise of the United States delegates, he asked Guerrero to draw up a formula of a general character. The Salvadorean then hastily jotted down a resolution ending with the previously discarded declaration: "No State has the right to intervene in the internal affairs of another." Its presentation to the conference brought thunderous applause from the galleries.

The debate was interrupted at this point by an invasion of the gorgeously gowned doctors of law, science, and philosophy from the University of Havana. While the professors spoke, however, the delegates whispered plans for renewal of the fight. Fernandes of Brazil and Olaya of Colombia came to Hughes and said that Guerrero was guilty of an intolerable breach of honor. Hughes replied that in spite of it he would not be placed in the position of trying to stop the discussion. He sent to Dr. Bustamente a request that he keep the conference in session under any and all circumstances "until this matter can be settled." [11]

When the debate broke out again, it raged more fiercely than before. Fernandes contended earnestly that there had been a misunderstanding—that while there was unanimous regret over the failure to reach an agreement there was no meeting of minds on the proposal now submitted for reconsideration. Spokesmen for Colombia, Costa Rica, Ecuador, and the Dominican Republic

[11] Author's interview with CEH, Dec. 3, 1946.

took the same view, but the effect was only to add fuel to the flames. Fiery speech followed fiery speech. One of the delegates, in denouncing the attackers, declared that they would take us back to life in the jungle—a red-flag phrase in Latin America. Hughes murmured, "Save us from our friends." Maurtua attacked Guerrero, and when Guerrero resorted to personal abuse in return an indignant Peruvian called him a "cheap watch salesman." Dr. Bustamente intervened to prevent the exchange from reaching a point where nothing but pistols for two would have been acceptable to wounded Latin American honor. For the galleries it was a Roman holiday. At last they seemed to have the Colossus of the North in a tight box where everyone could jab at him. Each hostile sally brought wild applause, while defenders of the United States were hissed. The anti-intervention faction appeared to be sweeping everything before it.

Hughes listened to the unrestrained abuse of his country in a state of rising agitation. He could see the achievements of the conference crumbling into rubble under the impact of this emotional temblor. The prestige of the United States appeared to be cracking dangerously. Could the impending disaster be averted? If the Guerrero faction had votes enough to pass the resolution, Hughes thought it would be better not to resist it. On the other hand, it would be a grave mistake to let this onslaught against the United States succeed if he had a fighting chance to prevent it. The strain on his discretion was terrific.

"I feel like Holmes when he was wounded at Antietam," Hughes whispered to Fletcher with a sigh that seemed to come from deep within him. "If I ever get out of this, I think I shall never love another country." [12]

Senator Underwood was pacing up and down the aisle saying, "Let me answer him." "No, Senator," Hughes replied; "I've got to deal with this myself." [13] As head of the delegation, he could not risk the appearance of having been put to rout.

At 8:00 P.M. the Great Hall was still ringing with the excited cries and applause of the noninterventionists. Every argument for the resolution had been made. Every epithet had been hurled. The Guerreristas were moving in for the kill. "The time has come," said the Costa Rican delegate to a companion, "for Mr. Hughes to speak." As a hush fell over the hall, he turned and saw that Hughes was already on his feet.

Over the years Hughes had learned patience and superb self-control. Now he demonstrated both. His rising was neither a moment too soon nor a moment tardy. Inside he was boiling with excitement and almost trembling with the awful realization of what hung upon his words. Never had he felt more keenly the responsibility of speaking for his country. Yet his appearance

---

[12] Author's interview with Henry P. Fletcher, Aug. 10, 1946.
[13] Author's interview with CEH, Dec. 3, 1946.

was that of easy self-command. It was the evening of a nerve-racking day, but he was as radiant as morning. "He was smiling. He glanced at the galleries with no anger, with no discontent, with no reproof. He stood erect, unembarrassed, wholly unapologetic, positively commanding, and yet utterly companionable. The effect was incredible. He dominated the hall by his mere rising." [14]

Necks were craned to see how the famous North American would react to the bludgeoning his country had taken. Ears were alerted to catch every word. Summoning the interpreter to his side, Hughes commanded, "Interpret sentence by sentence." It was too important to trust a translator's summary. Through all the resulting pauses he sustained the continuity and force of what he was saying. In the most direct and candid fashion he laid bare the details of the disagreement in the Committee on Public International Law and of the unanimous decision to postpone action until the next conference. Then he turned to an incisive analysis of United States policy:

There is nothing to conceal. There are no hidden motives. . . . I merely recognized that this was a question which needed time and further study to resolve in principles which all could accept, and that was the view which I supposed that all my colleagues on the subcommittee, and on the full committee as well, entertained. I gladly acquiesced in their decision. Now what is the situation when we come to the actual facts of the case? There is no one here who does not have enjoyment in the free air of independence. My country was nurtured in the desire for independence. One hundred years ago we declared the policy that all the American republics should be recognized in their independence. We have given our arms and our blood for the independence of the American republics and are always ready to do so. We yield to none in the establishment of the ideal of sovereignty and independence for every one of the American republics from the greatest to the smallest.

Recalling his support of the Mexican antiaggression resolution, he hammered home the facts underlying the policy he had followed as Secretary of State:

We do not wish the territory of any American republic. We do not wish to govern any American republic. We do not wish to intervene in the affairs of any American republic. We simply wish peace and order and stability and recognition of honest rights properly acquired so that this hemisphere may not only be the hemisphere of peace but the hemisphere of international justice.

After explaining the situation in Nicaragua, he continued:

Now what is the real difficulty? Let us face the facts. The difficulty, if there is any, in any one of the American republics is not of any external aggression. It is an internal difficulty. . . .

What are we to do when government breaks down and American citizens are in danger of their lives? Are we to stand by and see them butchered in the jungle [15]

[14] William Hard in New York *Herald Tribune*, Sept. 2, 1928.
[15] The phrase "butchered in the jungle" was modified in the official text, but Michael J. McDermott, who heard the speech, insists that this is the way Hughes spoke it.

because a government in circumstances which it cannot control and for which it may not be responsible can no longer afford reasonable protection? . . .

Now it is a principle of international law that in such a case a government is fully justified in taking action—I would call it interposition of a temporary character—for the purpose of protecting the lives and property of its nationals. I could say that that is not intervention. One can read in text books that that is not intervention. But if I should subscribe to a formula which others thought might prevent the action which a nation is entitled to take in these circumstances there might come later the charge of bad faith because of acceptance of a formula with one interpretation in my mind, while another interpretation of it is in the mind of those proposing the formula. So it was necessary to have a fair understanding.

Of course the United States cannot forgo its right to protect its citizens. . . . International law cannot be changed by the resolutions of this conference. The rights of nations remain, but nations have duties as well as rights . . . we cannot codify international law and ignore the duties of States by setting up the impossible reign of self-will without any recognition upon the part of a State of its obligations to its neighbors. . . .

I have made this statement merely to avoid any possible misunderstanding. I am too proud of my country to stand before you as in any way suggesting a defense of aggression or of assault upon the sovereignty or independence of any State. I stand before you to tell you that we unite with you in the aspiration for complete sovereignty and the realization of complete independence. I stand here with you ready to cooperate in every way in establishing the ideals of justice by institutions in every land which will promote fairness of dealing between man and man and nation and nation.

I cannot sacrifice the rights of my country, but I will join with you in declaring the law. I will try to help you in coming to a just conclusion as to the law; but it must be the law of justice infused with the spirit which has given us from the days of Grotius this wonderful development of the law of nations by which we find ourselves bound.

As Hughes sat down, the galleries that had previously hissed the name of the United States gave way to a frenzy of admiration. Everyone seemed to realize that Guerrero's shoddy gesture had been beaten. A moment later Guerrero arose, and a hush once more fell over the Great Hall. In a voice that could scarcely be heard, he withdrew his resolution, saying that it was unnecessary to insist on a vote "since every resolution of the Conference to be valid must attain unanimity." [16] The reversal of his position, like the change in the temper of the audience, was complete. Hughes had routed an emotional tornado by the sheer force of his personality, the cutting edge of his logic, and the deep sincerity of his convictions.

It was ten-thirty o'clock that night when the delegates arrived at the dinner party given by the mayor of Havana. The Cubans had been leisurely waiting, and the festivities went forward with no apparent loss of the convivial spirit. Meanwhile the press and official circles in many lands fairly gurgled with

[16] Foreign Policy Association, Information Service, April 27, 1928, p. 72.

delight over Hughes' feat of snatching at least a show of harmony out of the very jaws of discord.

The *Springfield Republican* declared that the events at Havana "revealed once more to the American people in the person of Mr. Hughes their greatest living statesmen." "If Mr. Hughes' previous history had been by some black magic obliterated," commented the New York *Sun*, "the Havana speech alone would stamp him as one of the greatest Americans." [17] After the event had seasoned a few months, William Hard penned this panegyric: "If I live to be a hundred years old I shall never expect ever again to see anybody so great, so grand, so god-like, as was Mr. Hughes at Havana . . . an American statesman for the first time in our history had told to Latin America the truth and had received in return an ovation. Few equal triumphs of individual personality can be found written anywhere on the roll of recorded human time." [18]

In expressing his and the President's "deep sense of obligation," Secretary Kellogg wrote: "It is really an accomplishment of surpassing importance to the United States. . . . I have never seen the press so united and so enthusiastic." "I have heard you many times," observed the Costa Rican minister, "but never like this." A sheaf of letters from distinguished men was sprinkled with such glowing terms as "great accomplishment," "wonderful piece of work," "enthusiastic expressions," "wonderful impression," and "saved the conference from failure." President Coolidge wrote with typical conservatism:

. . . you secured a decision on all questions on their merits, which left us nothing to fear. . . . It was a great service in creating understanding and friendly relations among the peoples of the western hemisphere.

Hughes himself went back to the practice of law with the feeling that he had never had a greater success in his life. As the years passed, he probably came to realize that his tour de force, much as it was admired, left a backwash of resentment among some Latin Americans. But he had saved the United States from humiliation and the conference from driving a wedge of ill will into the American community of nations. The conference at Montevideo in 1933 was to approve a Treaty on the Rights and Duties of States with a nonintervention provision, and at Buenos Aires three years later Secretary Hull would accept the doctrine of absolute nonintervention by any state acting alone. At that time, however, American troops were no longer in Haiti and Nicaragua and the Platt Amendment allowing intervention in Cuba had been abrogated. Hughes had prevented a premature plunge. His comments in his later years left no doubt, however, that he would have been happier about it if his Havana speech could have been devoted to hastening the end of interventions, as his persistent efforts as Secretary of State had been.

[17] April 11, 1928.   [18] New York *Herald Tribune*, Sept. 2, 1928.

Chapter 54

THE HARDING TRAGEDY

REVERBERATIONS of scandal began to come out of the Harding Administration before it was two years old. Finding the President an amiable man and a lenient chief, the Ohio Gang established itself in the Little Green House on K Street and set up a lively traffic in everything from the protection of bootleggers to illegal concessions and appointments to office. Harry Daugherty, the crony who had wormed his way into the attorney generalship in order "to protect Harding from the crooks," was himself the center of an ugly tangle of rumors.

As Harding discovered one betrayal after another, he sought desperately to save his Administration from open scandal. Charles R. Forbes, the dashing playboy who had been a favorite at the White House while he mulcted the Veterans' Bureau, was sent to Europe with the understanding that he would resign. Twelve days after the Senate launched an investigation of the bureau, Forbes' closest assistant, Charles F. Cramer, the legal adviser, shot himself.[1] Less than three months later Jess Smith, simple, bumbling influence man, committed suicide in the apartment he shared with Daugherty. Harding was terribly shaken.

Between this aspect of the Harding régime and the State Department was a gulf that seemed as wide as the Atlantic. Secretary Hughes was not one of the President's cronies. He never attended the drinking parties on the second floor of the White House. Only once did he join Harding's poker circle—when cruising down the Potomac on the presidential yacht. Thoroughly preoccupied by his own bailiwick, he knew nothing of the corruption that was seeping into high places in the President's official family.

What did worry Hughes in the spring of 1923 was the President's failing health. Returning to his office after a few weeks of illness, Harding looked suddenly old and exhausted. His blood pressure, he confided to Hughes, was 175. "We have been worrying about Mrs. Harding," the Secretary commented to his wife that night, "but I think it is the President we should be more concerned about. No man can carry the burdens of the Presidency with a blood pressure of 175." [2]

[1] Mark Sullivan, *Our Times,* VI, 241.
[2] Author's interview with CEH, Dec. 10, 1946.

As friend after friend stooped to treachery, the President's appreciation of Hughes' steadfastness and complete loyalty seemed to be heightened. "If you find the associations incident to your official life agreeable and adding to your happiness," Harding wrote in one of his personal notes to the Secretary, "I shall never cease to rejoice that it was my fortune to call you to the high position which you are filling with such notable success."

In June, 1923, the President attempted to relieve his nervous exhaustion and deep brooding by going out to the country to "bloviate," as he expressed it. Weariness grew upon him as he stumped across the continent and then took a boat trip to Alaska. Returning to Seattle, he was seriously ill, and when he reached San Francisco the doctors put him to bed with pneumonia. A few days later, on the evening of August 2, apoplexy struck him down and plunged the whole nation into mourning.

Hughes' telephone tinkled ominously and persistently about midnight. A voice from the State Department informed him that the President was dead. Allen W. Dulles and a companion drove to the remote Macsfolly farm near Kensington, Maryland, where the Hughes family was spending the summer, and took the Secretary to the department. He talked unceasingly about Harding: the burden of the Presidency had killed him; Harding had been an admirable chief and had many fine qualities, but he could never deny a request from a friend. Hughes repeated the story that Harding himself had told in a flash of candor during an off-the-record talk to the National Press Club.

"Warren," his father had said to him, "it's a good thing you wasn't born a gal."

"Why?" Warren had asked.

"Because you'd be in the family way all the time. You can't say No."

News of Harding's death was carried to Calvin Coolidge, the new President, at his father's farm at Plymouth, Vermont. Awakened by a telegraph messenger from Bridgewater, eleven miles away, Colonel John Coolidge toddled up the narrow stairs and aroused his son in a voice trembling with excitement. Coolidge read the message under a kerosene lamp. At 2:30 A.M.—thanks to the quick work of telephone linemen in tapping the trunk line at Plymouth Union—he was talking with Secretary Hughes, the highest official in Washington.

Hughes advised the new President (he insisted that Coolidge had become President the moment Harding died) to take the oath of office and come to Washington at once. Coolidge recalled that it was a special oath he must take. Hughes already had the Constitution at hand and dictated the oath to Coolidge's secretary.

"It should be taken before a notary," he reminded the President.

"Father is a notary," Coolidge quickly responded.

"That's fine," Hughes replied.[3]

While farmer John Coolidge administered the presidential oath to his son before eight persons in the combination living room and office of his quaint old home, Hughes notified members of the Cabinet and all the American ambassadors and ministers abroad. To Mrs. Harding he wired: "There are no words that can express the depth of our sympathy and grief. May God sustain and comfort you. . . ." To the press he said: "A quiet, brave, strong leader has fallen over-borne by the burden he was carrying." Between tasks Hughes paced the floor of his office, moody and depressed, talking volubly about Harding and Coolidge to anyone who might be on hand to listen. He was glad to have had the privilege of sitting in Cabinet meetings with Mr. Coolidge, he said, for he now realized that there was something back of the New Englander's impassive face.[4]

Harding's funeral train, crossing the country to Washington, brought in an emotional deluge. A few sordid rumors about scandal in high places had been whispered during the President's trip, but these were silenced by the tragedy. The people knew only that a kindly President of good intentions had broken under the strain of his exalted office. Many thousands, including the new President and members of the Cabinet, packed Union Station when the body arrived. The whole city was in mourning on August 8 when the President, the Chief Justice, the Cabinet, and even former President Wilson followed Harding's flag-draped casket from the White House to the Capitol for a brief ceremony under the great dome.

Officials then boarded the funeral train for Marion, where the fallen son of Ohio was to be buried. Hughes lay awake in his berth most of the night watching the crowds that lined the tracks and jammed the station of every town through which they passed. Again and again the pall of silence was broken by the strains of "Nearer, My God, to Thee" and other hymns. The nation's heart had been deeply touched.

On the return trip to Washington there was an unseemly scramble to get the new President's ear—a scramble in which Hughes did not participate. Under questioning by Chief Justice Taft, however, he did drop a bit of information that was of much interest to Coolidge. Under no circumstances would he (Hughes) run for the Presidency in 1924. Taft, who loved a little friendly gossip, hastened to pass the word along to the calm little Yankee who had inherited the Republican landslide.

What Hughes had said to Taft was merely a repetition of what he had been telling friends ever since 1916. With his prestige greatly enhanced by his work as Secretary of State, many were loath to give up the idea of seeing him some

[3] Author's interview with Allen W. Dulles, July 6, 1949.
[4] William R. Castle's diary, 1923, p. 121.

day in the White House, but his own convictions remained firm, as indicated by a letter to his former secretary at Albany, Robert H. Fuller:

. . . of course you understand that nothing in the world could induce me, even if the question should come up, and it is not likely to come up, to consider a candidacy. I have had enough of that sort of thing and under no circumstances would I be drawn into such a venture again. I greatly admire Mr. Coolidge and I believe that he will impress the country as a man of rare ability.

Coolidge was eager to give the appearance of carrying on the Harding policies, but he quickly turned his back upon the playboys, the hangers-on, the grafters, and the poker cronies. To those who had played upon Harding's inability to say No, Coolidge seemed almost incapable of saying Yes. Visitors found so little advantage in an interview with the President that they were often content to see his secretary instead. When Hughes went to the Executive Office in the afternoons with important State Department business, he would find the President alone, smoking a cigar and reading his papers.[5] Order, simplicity, and quiet dignity were to be the watchwords of the new régime.

Coolidge asked all members of the Cabinet to carry on. Shortly after his accession, he summoned Hughes to the White House and told him that he was the backbone of the Administration and "the greatest Secretary of State this country ever had."[6] During the next two years Hughes acted as a sort of premier, being consulted on all the important issues relating to the welfare of the country. The two men got along admirably together. While it was difficult to get a quick response from Coolidge, once his answer was given after careful deliberation he was not likely to change it, as Harding sometimes had done.

Several members of the Cabinet thought Coolidge should get rid of Attorney General Daugherty because of his failure to prosecute cases of suspected corruption. Coolidge resisted out of loyalty to Harding. "Mr. President," Hughes said to him one day at the conclusion of an interview, "if it would be of any help to you, I think I could arrange to have all members of the Cabinet place their resignations in your hands; you could then reappoint those you wish to retain."

"No, don't do that," Coolidge called across the room as he was making a hasty exit. "It might leave me alone with Daugherty!"[7]

The Senate's exposé of the oil scandals began in the autumn of 1923. At first Albert B. Fall's bold and aggressive defense of his oil leases seemed to undermine the extravagant charges that the newspapers were making. Fall had resigned as Secretary of the Interior some months before Harding's death. Many thought he was a victim of smearing. Both Coolidge and Taft suspected

[5] CEH, Notes, p. 253b.   [6] Castle's diary, 1924, p. 54.   [7] CEH, Notes, p. 253e.

a Democratic-Progressive plot to discredit the Administration. As for Hughes, he found it difficult to believe that Harding, lenient as he had been with his cronies, would have permitted them to sway his judgment in any matter affecting the nation's vital interests. His conviction on this point had been strengthened by the fact that the President had once stood by him (Hughes) in rebuking Fall for a false statement that had offended a foreign government.[8]

As the months passed, the Senate's relentless investigator, Thomas J. Walsh, wove a web of circumstantial evidence about the looters. Congress had set aside rich oil-bearing lands as reserves under control of the Navy. To prevent these natural reservoirs from being drained by adjacent private wells, Congress had given the Secretary of the Navy authority to make leases on the reserves when and if, in his judgment, the best interests of the nation required such action. The accommodating and gullible Secretary Denby had yielded that responsibility to the Interior Department under Fall's blandishments, and Harding had innocently signed the transfer order. Avoiding competitive bids, Fall had proceeded to lease to Harry F. Sinclair the Teapot Dome, from which the latter expected to garner a cool $100,000,000 in profits, and to Edward L. Doheny the fabulously rich Elk Hills reserve in California. Then he had obtained a $100,000 loan from Doheny.

As the magnitude of the scandal became unmistakably apparent, Harlan F. Stone, future Chief Justice of the United States, urged Coolidge to appoint a special prosecutor for the oil-scandal cases and suggested Owen J. Roberts of Philadelphia. When his advice was sought, Hughes heartily seconded this suggestion, although he then knew Roberts only by reputation. Coolidge responded by naming two special prosecutors, Roberts and Atlee Pomerene, an able lawyer and former Democratic Senator from Ohio.

With the smell of unprosecuted crime growing ever stronger, Hughes renewed his efforts to get Harry Daugherty out of the Cabinet. He and Hoover went to the White House together and tried to stiffen the President's backbone in this matter.[9] Similar pressure was coming from Senator Burton K. Wheeler and Senator Borah, who pressed his charges in a dramatic showdown with Daugherty at the White House. Coolidge was slow to act, but at last when Daugherty refused to give the Senate investigating committee certain papers in his office the President demanded his resignation. Stone then became Attorney General.

While these events were unfolding, Hughes was writing the Harding memorial address to be delivered before a distinguished audience in the House of Representatives on February 24, 1924. Timid friends suggested to him that stories about to break might make it advisable to tone down his estimate of his

[8] Author's interview with CEH, Dec. 10, 1946.
[9] *Id.;* Herbert Hoover to author, March 14, 1949.

dead chief. He refused to change a word,[10] for in writing the speech he had drawn only upon his personal knowledge of Harding. Recounting the achievements of the Harding Administration, he gave a warm personal appraisal of his subject: "President Harding had no ossification of the heart. He literally wore himself out in the endeavor to be friendly." At the same time Hughes was gently candid about Harding's shortcomings. A president, he said, "is under strong temptation to endeavor to be all things to all men. . . . The presidency is a super-office, but nature imposing her limitations upon the greatest has supplied no super-men to fill it." [11] Harding had given his life in the service of his country. No man could give more.

The speech was a masterpiece of careful statement. "There was not a sentence I would have wished to change in your wonderful eulogy," wrote the grateful Mrs. Harding. "I have heard all the memorial addresses in the House of Representatives for twenty years," Chief Justice Taft commented to a friend, "and I do not hesitate to say that none surpassed his." "It is a hard thing not to overpraise or undervalue," wrote George Wharton Pepper. "But even Pericles would admit that you did neither." [12]

In the years that followed the Teapot Dome exposé, some who did not question Hughes' personal integrity nevertheless accused him of having sat silent while rich oil lands were turned over to the robber barons. Could it be that he was negligent or a quiet accessory to the crime? The first pertinent fact is that the oil leases were never discussed or acted upon by the Cabinet. The charge occasionally heard that Hughes was in the Cabinet meeting when jurisdiction over the naval oil reserves was transferred to Fall is plain falsification. Coolidge was a faithful attendant at the meetings of the Harding Cabinet, and he heard nothing about oil leases.[13] Hughes issued a statement on January 31, 1924, when the issue was before Congress, to the effect that the oil leases had never been brought before the Cabinet for decision and that his opinion as to their propriety or legality had never been sought. Secretaries Hoover and Weeks made similar declarations. All these denials were reiterated when the New York *Evening World* raised the issue in the Hoover-Smith campaign in 1928, and Hughes added emphatically: "I had nothing whatever to do with any of them [the oil leases], directly or indirectly, and I knew nothing whatever about them." [14]

The only way in which Hughes could have discovered Fall's perfidy would have been to turn aside from his own pressing duties and attempt to investigate a fellow Cabinet member. Such an investigation in itself, not being requested by the President, would have been an act of disloyalty to him. Only an incorrigible busybody would have launched such a venture, and Hughes was

---

[10] Henry L. Stoddard, *It Costs to Be President*, p. 80.
[11] *The Pathway of Peace*, p. 303.　　　　[12] Letters in Hughes Papers.
[13] White House statement, Jan. 26, 1924.　　　　[14] Speech at Brooklyn, Nov. 1, 1928.

the antithesis of a busybody. When it became his specific duty to investigate corruption, he would strip to nakedness every wrongful act within the purview of the inquiry; but he was astonishingly tolerant of misconduct toward which he bore no responsibility. He had, as Everett Colby has pointed out, "none of the average reformer's passion for regulating the private life of the individual." [15]

This characteristic in Hughes has intrigued many of his closest associates. It was not indifference to how the world wags, for he lent a hand to innumerable reform movements. Nor was it any laxity in his moral code; no man in public life in our time has held himself more rigorously to a high standard of conduct. Rather, it was a deep reluctance to judge his fellow men unless it became his official duty to do so. In his old age he said frankly that if he had known what the Ohio Gang was up to he would not have joined the Harding Cabinet. But under no circumstance would he prejudge the men whom Harding had trusted or intrude into affairs that were not his business.

Now that passions have cooled, it is impossible to see that the oil scandal reflected upon Hughes in the slightest degree. He was an actor in that sordid drama only to the extent of urging clean-up operations. The Coolidge Administration as a whole was astonishingly successful in lifting its skirts above the scandal. At times there seemed to be more oil in the 1924 campaign than in the Teapot Dome and Elk Hills combined, and it was not the kind of oil one pours on troubled waters. But the men who would have been vulnerable to that sort of attack were no longer in office. Fall, Denby, and Daugherty were gone. Daugherty was later to be indicted (but acquitted) for misconduct of his office, and Fall, Forbes, and Alien Property Custodian Thomas W. Miller were on their way to prison. The Republicans were vigorously cleaning house.

Hughes met the oil-scandal issue as temporary chairman of the New York Republican State Convention on April 15, the first time he had ever participated in a political convention. His candor and sense of proportion had much to do with turning the public mind away from oil toward the rising tide of national prosperity:

Let it be understood that we do not condone wrong; we extenuate no crime. . . . We would bring to the bar of justice every dishonest official and every perverter of administration in or out of office. . . .

Neither political party has a monopoly of virtue or of rascality. There are crooks in every community and in every party. Now and then, one gets into office. Let wrongs be exposed and punished, but let not partisan Pecksniffs affect a "holier than thou" attitude. The corrupting currency may be found in Democratic satchels. One who is corrupt is as faithless to his party as to his government. Guilt is personal and corruption knows no party.

Today, counsel of eminent ability and unimpeachable integrity, selected from

[15] *Scribner's*, May, 1928, p. 564.

both the great parties by a Republican President, are taking appropriate legal proceedings by which all the questions which have been raised as to the leasing of the public domain will be threshed out, every public interest will be safeguarded and every guilty person punished. These cases are in the courts where they belong, and the courts will decide. It would be foolish, false and unpatriotic to breed distrust either of the integrity of the Government or of the soundness of American life. That would be to assail the honor of the hosts of officials devoting their lives with unselfish fidelity to the country's interests.

Although Hughes forbade his associates at the State Department to engage in politics, he himself became the right bower of Coolidge's campaign. According to Chief Justice Taft, Hughes' effort at Cincinnati was "far and away the best speech of the campaign." It was "as exceptional as the one you delivered for me in 1908," Taft insisted, "and . . . I verily believe it will be equally effective." [16] Hughes bore down upon both of Coolidge's opponents, John W. Davis and "Fighting Bob" La Follette, with more skill than he had employed in his own behalf in 1916. It was an easy Republican victory; the G.O.P. was riding the wave of postwar prosperity. Nevertheless, the voters who swelled the Coolidge landslide must have concluded that the Administration had successfully purged itself of the corruption it had inherited. In this they were right.

[16] Taft to CEH, Oct. 5, 1924.

Chapter 55

ECONOMIC POLICIES

PROSPERITY, in Secretary Hughes' credo, was an intimate companion to peace. Settlement of international differences without bloodshed undoubtedly came first. But men do not live on peace, and their best plans and intentions are likely to go sour unless their economic endeavors are reasonably successful. The economic well-being of the war-sick world thus commanded an enormous amount of Hughes' energy during the four years of his Secretaryship.

On his first survey of the United States' commercial policy he concluded that it ought to be revamped. Our treaty of commerce and navigation with Great Britain was more than a century old, and various other treaties were equally obsolete. New products, new trade practices, and new nations had come into being without any recognition in our commercial agreements. In pursuit of a comprehensive new policy Hughes induced the President to set up a committee of advisers from the State, Treasury, and Commerce departments. The model draft treaty worked out by these experts was first accepted by Germany.

There were four principal sections to the treaty. It threw numerous safeguards around the rights of the nationals of each party living in the territory of the other. It spelled out the rights, immunities, and status of consuls. It set up a nondiscriminatory shipping policy and committed the contracting parties to unconditional most-favored-nation treatment for the exports and imports passing between them.

The latter policy was revolutionary in its effect upon American foreign trade. The most-favored-nation clause in our treaties had theretofore been interpreted as being conditional; that is to say, a most-favored-nation treaty between the United States and France would not give France the advantage of a concession we might make to Belgium unless France should give us in return a concession equivalent to Belgium's. This traditional policy of exchanging favor for favor had led to much bickering and uncertainty and had hampered international trade with a network of special conditions. Equality of treatment had been retarded instead of being advanced.

Before writing the unconditional most-favored-nation principle into his model treaty, Hughes had taken the precaution of securing the approval of the President and of Senator Lodge, chairman of the Senate Foreign Relations Committee. When the treaty with Germany reached Lodge's committee, however, he ignored it. Thinking it unwise to begin negotiations with other countries until the Senate had made its position known, Hughes undertook to answer every argument raised against the treaty in a series of letters to Senator Lodge. The practice of granting special concessions for special concessions, he wrote, had upset the equilibrium of international trade. It did not in fact produce equality of treatment but merely afforded opportunity to bargain for such treatment. In defense of its own interests, moreover, the United States had become the champion of the principle of the open door in international commercial relations. Consistency with this principle demanded that we interpret the most-favored-nation clause unconditionally.[1]

When Lodge died in November, 1924, Hughes discovered that none of his communications on the treaty had been submitted to the Foreign Relations Committee. He renewed his campaign and got an invitation from Senator Borah, the new chairman, to argue his case before the committee on February 2, 1925. He did so in masterful fashion, covering every point in controversy so thoroughly and so convincingly that opposition crumbled.

The most vehement protest against the treaty had been directed at its provision for reciprocal national treatment, rather than most-favored-nation treatment, as to cargo, tonnage, harbor, pilotage, and quarantine charges imposed on shipping. The United States would be untrue to its own interests, one coterie of Senators said, if it should bind itself in fresh treaties not to discriminate in favor of its own shipping. Our idle vessels could be employed only by giving them a privileged status. To this Hughes replied that discrimination would beget discrimination. "We are constantly insisting upon equality of opportunity," he said, "and we cannot expect to be successful in removing discriminations against us when we think them injurious and at the same time insist on discriminations in our favor whenever we see fit." And since the maritime powers imported more from the United States than the United States imported from them, our own shipping would suffer most from any policy leaving the door open to favoritism by each country of its own ships.

The Senate as well as the committee saw the logic of Hughes' argument and a week later consented to ratification of the treaty, with a minor reservation. The Hughes policies as to both shipping and trade were consistently written into other commercial treaties after his resignation, and they are still in effect more than a quarter of a century later. When the Reciprocal Trade Agreements Act was passed in 1934, it specifically retained the unconditional most-favored-nation principle.

Under the stimulus of Hughes' driving energy, the American policy of the open door also underwent a significant evolution. We have seen that he used

[1] CEH to Lodge, March 13, 1924.

the Nine-Power Treaty to prop open the open door in China, and that he forced Japan to recognize our commercial rights in the Pacific mandates. Possibly more important was the part he played in giving American oil companies a stake in the petroleum reserves of the Near East.

Oil had become the object of intense international intrigue in the years following World War I. It was apparent that the next war would be fought with gasoline-driven machines and that the lands seized from the crumbling Ottoman Empire were among the world's richest petroleum storehouses. With Germany prostrate, the British had turned over to France the former German interests in the Turkish Petroleum Company, which claimed exclusive rights to exploit the vast oil deposits of Iraq. In short, an Anglo-French-Dutch monopoly had been created in a mandated area in which the United States had equal rights. Hughes was determined to break this monopoly.

While the British denied any intention of discriminating against American companies in the mandates of the Near East, they claimed that the oil fields of Iraq had been leased to the Turkish Petroleum Company before the war and that the lease was still valid. Secretary Colby had resisted this claim, and Hughes exploded it by showing that no valid lease had been made by Turkey. In 1914 the Grand Vizier of Turkey had given a vague concession to British, Dutch, and German interests, but they had not obtained the required approval of the parliament, and no effort had been made to exploit the concession. Hughes argued that monopolistic arrangements of this sort should not be tolerated in the mandated territories unless such prior rights could be established by convincing proof.[2]

In March, 1925, the British caved in and relinquished half their shares in the Turkish Petroleum Company to seven American companies. The Iraq Government, under British mandate, granted a concession to this expanded international concern—a tacit admission of the dubious character of the 1914 lease. The final settlement, which gave the American companies a 25 per cent share in the concession, was negotiated by the companies themselves, but it was Hughes' intervention in behalf of fair play that made the victory possible.[3] The importance of this outcome was amply demonstrated by the part that Near Eastern oil played in World War II and is playing in the mechanized economy of the present day.

The Secretary's adherence to the policy of equal opportunity was consistent even when it worked to the disadvantage of American companies. On one occasion the Latin American Division sent to his office a scheme to grant a concession to an American national in one of the Caribbean countries under our control. Hughes smelled monopoly and asked A. C. Millspaugh, the depart-

---

[2] *Foreign Relations, 1921*, II, 82–110.
[3] Author's interview with Allen W. Dulles, July 6, 1949.

ment's economic adviser, to review the proposal. Millspaugh confirmed the Secretary's suspicions that the scheme would have sanctioned in the Caribbean precisely what the department had protested against in the Near East. The concession was denied.[4]

When the Sinclair Oil Company complained that the department was not supporting its efforts to obtain an oil concession in Persia, Hughes outlined his policy in a letter to President Coolidge on November 8, 1923:

From time to time there has been some dissatisfaction expressed in business circles because this Department's attitude towards American business interests in the foreign field differs somewhat from the attitude in similar matters of the British, French and other European governments. The latter are not loath to interfere politically in support of the business interests of their nationals to a degree which is not followed by this Department. Our position is that we are always ready to give appropriate support to our nationals in seeking opportunities for business enterprise abroad, but we do not undertake to make the government a party to the business negotiations or use political pressure for the benefit of private interests in order to obtain particular concessions, or intervene in favor of one American interest as against another. We are persistent in our efforts to maintain the open door policy, or equality of commercial opportunity, but we do not attempt to assume obligations for the government, expressed or implied, which under our system we could not undertake to discharge.

American companies which might prefer a policy of more direct interference on their behalf by the government are inclined, in my opinion, to overlook the fact that American prestige and reputation for fairness has [sic] been enhanced, and consequently business opportunities of our nationals have been increased, by the correct policy which this government has followed. I find that in many parts of the world American business is welcomed largely because foreign countries realize that they can deal with American interests on a business basis without fearing political complications.[5]

Entangled with the Near Eastern oil problem was the larger question of the United States' relations with the new Turkish republic. The Allies had attempted to impose on Turkey an unconscionable peace treaty, the Treaty of Sèvres, depriving her of vast territories and reestablishing all the pre-1914 encroachments upon Turkey's right to control her own fiscal, economic, educational, and judicial affairs and even adding new concessions. Rallying under Mustapha Kemal Pasha in a furious nationalistic movement, the Turks had rejected the treaty, driven the Greeks out of Anatolia and Constantinople, the French from Cilicia, and the Italians from Konya. The war-weary Allies had brought about an armistice between the Turks and Greeks in October, 1922. Then followed the Lausanne conferences in which the United States was ably represented by Joseph C. Grew, the minister to Switzerland.

---

[4] A. C. Millspaugh to author, May 17, 1949.
[5] Foreign Relations, 1923, II, 717f.

Just before the first conference met in November, 1922, the British ambassador told Hughes that the Turks were preparing to expel the entire Christian population of Constantinople and asked that the United States join in an ultimatum to the Turks. Hughes replied that he was using his utmost influence to curb atrocities growing out of the Turks' extreme nationalism, but he would not attempt to pledge the United States to go to war. Only Congress could do that. The ambassador said he had suggested only a threat of war, and Hughes retorted gingerly that his government did not indulge in idle gestures and could not associate itself with imperial ambitions in the Near East.[6]

When the conference opened, Hughes' inability to protect the rights of the persecuted and decimated Armenians in Turkey left him in an embarrassing position. Before his appointment as Secretary of State, he had been the "principal supporting pillar" of the American Committee for the Independence of Armenia. Early in 1919 he and Lodge and others had appealed to President Wilson for a positive American policy of protecting the Armenians. The country had been aroused by the Turks' atrocities against this Christian minority during the war, and Hughes felt that if we were going to intervene in their behalf the time to do it was when we had a large army abroad and were able to carry out any policy adopted. When the problem fell into his own lap a few years later, the possibility of American military intervention no longer existed. Most of our troops had been brought home; the Armenians in the region that had once been thought of as an Armenian state had been practically exterminated; and the victorious Turks were ready to resume fighting at the drop of the hat for what they regarded as their sovereign rights. They would give no guarantee whatever as to Armenian minorities. Secretary Hughes thus found it necessary to abandon a cause that Citizen Hughes had earnestly fought for, and the Armenians in this country probably never forgave him for it.

The first Lausanne conference was a flat failure. Due in no small measure to the moderating influence of Hughes and Grew, the second conference succeeded in hammering out a peace treaty. The United States did not sign that pact but negotiated a separate treaty with the Turks reestablishing diplomatic relations on much the same basis that the European powers had accepted. The capitulations through which Turkey had been held in a sort of vassalage were abandoned in favor of very limited immunities for foreigners. American religious, educational, and philanthropic institutions existing in Turkey before 1914 were recognized, and equality of commercial opportunity and freedom of the Straits were guaranteed. For the most part, however, the victorious Turks succeeded in imposing their own terms upon the Western powers.

[6] *Foreign Relations. 1922*, II, 952ff.

The Secretary was not pleased with the treaty, but he knew that it was impossible to secure any better terms than the Allies had obtained, and he believed that our interests in the Near East would best be protected by resuming diplomatic relations with Turkey as quickly as the other powers did. Unlike Russia, Turkey was ready to meet her obligations as a member of the family of nations. There was ample reason for recognizing the new republic and for approval of the treaty, but the Senate finally rejected it in January, 1927.

Hughes strongly resented the charges in some newspapers that the State Department had been influenced in negotiation of the treaty by the oil concessions Turkey had given to a group of Americans headed by Admiral Colby Chester, retired. The department had nothing to do with securing the concession. It had been granted before the treaty negotiations began. Britain and France had raised a furor because the Chester concession was in conflict with their claims in the Mosul oil fields, but Hughes had resisted requests that he intervene. The Turks insisted that the Chester concession was valid and that it had been granted because the Americans did business on business principles without resorting to governmental pressures.

The impact of prohibition in the United States upon our foreign relations gave Hughes an especially baffling problem. One horn of the dilemma was the section of the National Prohibition Act forbidding foreign as well as American ships to carry intoxicating liquors into our ports or through our territorial waters. The other horn was the hovering of foreign-flag smuggling vessels just outside the three-mile limit within which our domestic law could be enforced.

American-owned vessels shifted to British registry were transporting vast quantities of forbidden intoxicants from the Bahama Islands to Florida ports. They often carried two sets of clearance papers—one indicating they were bound with liquor cargoes to Halifax, Tampico, or St. Pierre and the other indicating that they were proceeding "in ballast" to an American port. If caught with the liquor, the former papers were used; if they succeeded in disposing of their liquor before being searched, the latter papers were used. Small, fast boats from these rumrunners delivered liquor direct to the American shore. To break up this traffic, Hughes asked Great Britain to agree that the authorities of each country might search the vessels of the other at any point within twelve miles of the shoreline.

Meanwhile the prohibition zealots were insisting that the Government reach beyond the three-mile limit for rumrunners without waiting for the consent of other countries, and the Department of Justice seized a number of such vessels on the high seas. In the Tariff Act of 1922 Congress specifically authorized enforcement agents to board, search, and seize vessels beyond the three-mile limit. Hughes insisted, however, that rights on the high seas are controlled by international law rather than by domestic law. The United States had always contended that the sovereignty of other nations ended at the three-mile limit and had once paid damages under international arbitration for the seizure of a British sealing vessel in disregard of that limit. In a Cabinet meeting Hughes secured an understanding that in the future no foreign-flag ship would be molested beyond the three-mile limit unless it was sending intoxicants to shore by small boats or otherwise violating the law within our territorial waters. Enforcement agents nevertheless detained seven vessels captured beyond the three-mile limit. Hughes sharply reminded Attorney General Daugherty of the understanding in the Cabinet and expressed hope that the seven ships would be released.[7] A month later five of them had been returned to their owners.

The British turned a cold shoulder upon Hughes' suggestion of a treaty to aid the capture of rumrunners. Nor would they concede any right on the part of the United States to seize liquor boats found to be communicating with the shore for illegal purposes from beyond the three-mile limit. When the United States persisted in capturing such boats, Lord Curzon, the British Foreign Secretary, warned that it would create "a very serious situation." [8] Hughes cited a British precedent for seizures under similar conditions and held steadfastly to the policy he had announced.

The two governments exchanged hot words over the seizure of the *Henry I. Marshall*, until the British Foreign Office acknowledged that it was an American vessel improperly using the British flag. An American note, which Hughes referred to as a "sockdolager," then pressed London not to espouse the cause of any British ship similarly engaged in this unlawful liquor traffic. The Foreign Office did not reply.

The United States Supreme Court added heat to the controversy in April, 1923, by holding that, under the Volstead Act, foreign ships could not enter American harbors carrying liquor cargoes or ships' stores of intoxicants even if they were under seal.[9] Protests from all parts of the globe rained upon the State Department. The United States, the complaints said, was egregiously departing from international comity.

Of course Hughes accepted the court's decision as the law of the land, but he had previously complained that the Supreme Court's view of the Eighteenth Amendment was "unnecessarily rigid" and that it would result in "great harm to the interests of our commerce." [10] There was no sense in trying to impose prohibition on foreign ships. Racking his brain for some practical means of relieving international commerce of this unreasonable restriction, he concluded that the Eighteenth Amendment itself did not forbid ships to bring intoxicants

---

[7] *Foreign Relations, 1922*, I, 576f.   [8] *Foreign Relations, 1923*, I, 164.
[9] *Cunard Steamship Co.* v. *Mellon*, 262 U.S. 100.
[10] CEH to Harry M. Daugherty, Oct. 5, 1922.

within American waters if those liquors were sealed to prevent their consumption in the United States. Congress had gone further than it needed to go in providing for enforcement of the Amendment. It followed that Congress could remove the burden it had laid on foreign vessels. Indeed, Congress had already exempted from the penalties and forfeitures of the Volstead Act intoxicating liquors in transit through the Panama Canal, although the Amendment was applicable to the Canal Zone. The Supreme Court had noted this exercise of congressional discretion without objection. Hughes seized upon this fact to clinch his point. If determinations of this kind had not been removed beyond the legislative power, he reasoned, then they were still within the treaty-making power. In other words, he could straighten out the tangle over foreign ships bringing liquor into American ports by making treaties with the maritime powers.

Hughes also saw in this situation an opportunity to strike a blow at smuggling. The treaty that he offered to Great Britain and other powers in June, 1923, thus provided not only immunity for forbidden articles under seal on foreign ships in American waters; it also proposed to grant the authorities of each country permission to board and search vessels of the other suspected of importing forbidden articles, if such vessels should be caught within twelve miles of the shore. The Secretary was acting on the theory that one good turn deserves another.

But Curzon denounced the proposed liquor treaty in a House of Lords speech aimed directly at Hughes. Some American newspapers printed it in full. The Secretary took up the gage the next day at his press conference, speaking off the record to avoid clashing openly with Curzon over a supposedly domestic speech. "For three-quarters of an hour he shouted and pounded the table. . . ." [11] Then correspondents dashed to their typewriters, and wires to many parts of the world were soon sizzling with the Secretary's words. Through the press, he had replied to Curzon as effectively as if he had used Congress as a sounding board.

A change in the London atmosphere was immediately noticeable. In late summer Hughes discussed the treaty with Lord Birkenhead, former Lord Chancellor of England, at the American Bar Association's annual meeting in Minneapolis and later in Montreal. Returning to London, Birkenhead softened the attitude of his friend Curzon, and within a few months the Foreign Office submitted a counterproposal. It was so responsive to Hughes' original suggestion that a complete agreement was soon worked out. The Secretary did not like the British demand that search and seizures be permitted within one hour's run of the shore instead of a twelve-mile limit. That made the legality of each seizure depend upon the speed of the particular boat seized, but he agreed to

[11] Bertram D. Hulen, *Inside the Department of State*, p. 132.

it in deference to Britain's unwillingness to name any mileage figure that might conceivably compromise the three-mile limit. The treaty was signed on January 23, 1924, and the Senate consented to its ratification two months later. Before the close of the year six other countries had signed similar treaties.

Without any strain on our constitutional system, Hughes had eliminated an acute source of international friction and snatched from the smugglers the handiest device of their trade.

Chapter 56

THE STRUGGLE FOR POSTWAR RECOVERY

EUROPE'S ECONOMIC calamities resulting from World War I came to a head in 1922. Germany was prostrate under her burden of reparations. With her people in poverty and despair, production lagged, and the payments that the victorious Allies had anticipated to aid their own recovery were not forthcoming. "Look pretty much where you will today in Europe," Ambassador Houghton wrote to Secretary Hughes from Berlin, "you find men and women living under conditions of great hardship,—insufficiently nourished, insufficiently clothed, unprotected against the bitter cold of the approaching winter." [1] In a previous letter he had said, "It is a sort of quiet bleeding to death."

Across the Rhine from Germany, wounded France was sullen and defiant. Having been twice invaded in half a century, France's strongest determination was to make the Germans pay for the war to the last franc. Originally she had demanded 100 billion dollars, then 56 billion, then 33 billion—the figure fixed by the Reparation Commission. The fading hope of wringing any such sum out of Germany's inflation-ravaged economy made it increasingly evident that France would resort to coercive measures. All Europe seemed to teeter on the brink of ruin.

As early as April, 1921, Germany had appealed to the United States to mediate the reparations question and to fix the sum to be paid by Germany to the Allied powers. Then had come a plea for President Harding to nominate a commission of impartial experts to investigate Germany's capacity to pay. Hughes had declined to intervene, but he had informally acquainted the British and French ambassadors with Berlin's proposals. Neither London nor Paris was interested.

Hughes had been deeply worried about the outlook long before the crisis stage was reached. "The prosperity of the United States," he had said in one of his earliest speeches as Secretary of State, "largely depends upon the economic settlements which may be made in Europe, and the key to the future is with those who make those settlements." [2] A year later he told the United States Chamber of Commerce, "We have only begun to think internationally, and we find the attitude of the public mind to be still ill-adjusted to the magni-

[1] *Foreign Relations, 1922*, II, 172.　　[2] At Brown Commencement, June, 1921.

tude of our financial power and to the international interests which we have suddenly accumulated as the result of the World War." [3] After the arms conference was out of the way, the economic rehabilitation of Europe became his major interest.

In European capitals and among American economists there was a clamor for cancellation of all reparations and war debts. The $10,150,000,000 that twenty European countries owed the United States, largely for supplies obtained during and after the war, was a secondary millstone on the neck of Europe's economy. But Congress had set up the World War Foreign Debt Commission and instructed it that, in entering into debt-funding agreements, it should not cancel "any part" of the war debts and should not accept interest rates of less than 4½ per cent. With postwar disillusionment still running strong, there was no possibility of inducing Congress to wipe out these wartime obligations. Hughes insisted, with characteristic regard for political realities, that any gesture toward cancellation would destroy his only chance of being helpful.

In September, 1922, the Secretary reviewed the growing chaos in Europe with Myron T. Herrick, who was on leave from his ambassadorial post in Paris. Returning to France in October, Herrick took with him a definite suggestion from Secretary Hughes that the best way of dealing with the reparations dilemma was to let a group of eminent financiers determine what Germany could pay. The effect would be, Hughes thought, to break the deadlock among the politicians (all of whom were catering to sentiment in their own countries) and force the recognition of economic realities. But Premier Poincaré clung to the waning hope of obtaining fabulous reparations. At Hughes' request, Herrick again suggested an expert study, and on November 7 the Secretary took it up with Ambassador Jusserand in Washington.[4] The governments could not solve the reparations problem, he said, for they were committed; but they could ask a group of financial experts to work up a plan that would have a secure economic foundation. Governments could then accept the plan because of the favorable world opinion that would be marshaled behind it. Jusserand expressed himself as in agreement and said he would see if anything could be done along the line suggested.

Meanwhile conditions in Europe were going from bad to worse. Houghton reported from Berlin that the parliamentary system had broken down. Armed groups in Germany were "working toward dictatorship." The most active of these groups were headed by a young Austrian named Hitler, who was in control of 30,000 men. "By his vehemence and fanaticism," Houghton wrote, "he [Hitler] was rapidly becoming leader of a whole movement . . . following

[3] *The Pathway of Peace*, p. 252.   [4] *Foreign Relations, 1922*, II, 178f.

the pattern of the Fascisti in Italy. These people," he concluded, "seem to me to be slowly going mad." [5]

France was still determined to make her enemies pay whether or not it was economically feasible. There were rumors that France would seize the state coal mines in the Ruhr. Hughes saw Jusserand again and talked earnestly about the interest of the entire world in the economic rehabilitation of Europe. He expressed doubt that the French really intended to occupy the Ruhr because that course would not give them the reparations they sought. There was no pot of gold in the Ruhr that the French could pick up.

French occupation of German territories, Hughes continued, would create a situation "which would seem to make war at some time inevitable if it were not otherwise redressed." No one wished to see Germany escape her just obligations. But a point had been reached, he said, "where it was necessary to put sentiment aside." In the interests of peace France could not afford to drive her former enemy to desperation. Force would accomplish nothing, he concluded, but France could win the favorable opinion of the world by offering to be guided by hard economic facts.

Poincaré remained cool to the idea, and there was an angry outburst in the Chamber of Deputies because of the impression that America was trying to tell France what she should do. Meanwhile a clamor arose in the United States against the drastic measures that seemed to be taking shape in Europe. The newspapers sensed the crisis, and, knowing nothing of what Hughes had been doing under cover to avert it, belabored him for following a do-nothing policy. Some of them assumed that the United States should step in and prevent occupation of the Ruhr. Senator Borah called for an international economic conference. Germany proposed an agreement with Great Britain, France, and Italy not to engage in war for thirty years unless war should be approved by a vote of the people. Fantastic proposals were legion; none of them offered any real hope of arresting the course of events in Europe.

Hughes' brooding over the dismal outlook was mingled with fitful sleep through the night of December 26, 1922. Suddenly he was awakened by what he later described to Castle as "the voice of God" [6] directing him to talk in New Haven about the European situation. He was to address the American Historical Association on the evening of December 29 on "Some Aspects of Our Foreign Policy." It would be a golden opportunity to get before the world the plan he had urged upon the French. Advance copies of the address had already been distributed to the press, but an annex could be added. Hughes was out of bed in a twinkling and worked through the small hours of the morning.

---

[5] Houghton to CEH, Nov. 21, 1922.
[6] Diary of William R. Castle, Jr., 1922, pp. 178–181.

Before breakfast he telephoned the White House for an appointment, and by 9:00 A.M. he was reading the annex of his speech to the President. Harding warmly approved. Two days later, when the Secretary delivered his address at New Haven, its historical aspects were completely overshadowed by his novel plan for dealing with the critical present.

"The economic conditions in Europe give us the greatest concern," he said. "We cannot dispose of these problems by calling them European, for they are world problems and we cannot escape the injurious consequences of a failure to settle them." Reparations were the crux of the difficulty. Germany should not be relieved of paying for the consequences of her aggression, but, on the other hand, economic recuperation in Europe would be impossible without German recuperation. "There will be no permanent peace unless economic satisfactions are enjoyed," Hughes declared. "We should view with disfavor measures which instead of producing reparations would threaten disaster."

The weak part of the speech was its lack of any promise of substantial aid from the United States. As this country had not asked for general reparations, Hughes was unwilling to relieve Germany of paying the costs of the American army of occupation. He would not permit German reparations to be linked with the war debts of the Allies to the United States, and he did not think the United States should assume the role of arbiter. But the United States would use its influence to obtain a settlement of the reparations issue on its merits. When that was done it would be easier to determine the capacity of the Allies to pay their debts to the United States.

The Secretary threw his challenge directly to the statesmen of Europe: "Why should they not invite men of the highest authority in finance in their respective countries—men of such prestige, experience and honor that their agreement upon the amount to be paid [by Germany], and upon a financial plan for working out the payments, would be accepted throughout the world as the most authoritative expression obtainable? . . . I have no doubt that distinguished Americans would be willing to serve in such a commission."

The speech caused a sensation in spite of the mildness of Hughes' proposal. It prompted the London *Morning Post* to comment that "only the truth can make statesmen free." The *Sunday Times* (London) thought Hughes' suggestion went "down to the heart of most of the difficulties retarding the world's recovery." [7] But Poincaré was moved only to anger. By inference Hughes had condemned the occupation of the Ruhr before it had begun and brought pressure upon France for a more reasonable settlement. Feeling the heat of world opinion, Poincaré denied that he had received any suggestion from the American Government along the lines of Hughes' New Haven speech. [8] It was a sheer falsehood. Herrick had twice presented the idea to Poincaré, and, at the latter's

[7] Quoted in *Literary Digest*, Jan. 13, 1923.   [8] *Foreign Relations, 1923*, II, 46.

request, repeated it again in the form of a memorandum. Jusserand had likewise kept his government informed, and, through Jusserand, Poincaré had expressed to Hughes his "cordial appreciation" of the suggestion.[9] Jusserand was highly embarrassed by his chief's disingenuousness, and Hughes was especially irritated because he had kept his proposal secret for several months in the hope that the French would feel free to take advantage of it and claim the credit for initiating it themselves.

The French moved into the Ruhr early in January, 1923, and a new avalanche of "hectoring and abusive criticism" descended upon the Secretary of State. On one hand he was denounced for not pursuing a vigorous policy in Europe; on the other, for intermeddling in Europe's affairs. The Senate Foreign Relations Committee began to take a keen interest in the reparations issue. Hiram Johnson demanded the recall of the American "unofficial observer" with the Reparation Commission, and Lodge asked for and received full details on the activities of that official.

Lodge went to the department to discuss the repeated demands for an economic conference. Whatever we may think of the matter, Hughes told him, the Allied powers regard their war debts to the United States as part of the economic problem. "They do not want our advice," he added, "but merely relief from their debts. We of course could not arrange for a conference to discuss a subject and then decline to discuss what others considered relevant to that subject." [10] Since any mention of canceling the war debts chilled the marrow in congressional bones, the conference idea was dropped.

Under the lash of criticism, Harding asked Hughes to watch for a favorable opportunity to intervene in the European situation. Although the Secretary was hurt by the fury of many of his critics and although he longed to go back to the practice of law, he scrutinized each development with the faithfulness of a mother watching over a sick child. "Sometimes I wonder how the Secretary can stand the strain," Castle wrote into his diary, "as the Senate is behaving like the devil, trying to take on itself the conduct of foreign relations and attacking Mr. Hughes most unreasonably on all sorts of counts. He has been irritable lately, and had to be irritable unless he were Job himself.[11]

As the summer wore on, there was discussion in the department of the possibility of making the Rhineland a separate state in the Reich, of measures to end passive resistance in Germany, and of depressing the value of the franc to make France realize her failure. No one of the schemes held a glimmer of hope. Indeed, Hughes had previously concluded that any action suggestive of sympathy with Germany would enrage France and give her a chance to blame him for the failure of her venture. And to support France in any way might delay her withdrawal from an untenable position. He could only bide his time.

Meanwhile it was a comfort to know that some thoughtful observers understood and approved the policy he was following. George W. Ochs Oakes, editor of *Current History*, wrote to him:

I think that your course has been prudent, statesmanlike, wise and eminently just. . . . I am writing this letter solely to let you know that amid the chorus of expletives and criticism hurled at you, there are some Americans, whose knowledge of foreign affairs qualifies them to speak, who unqualifiedly endorse your course.

Hughes replied on February 20, 1923:

If I could talk to the country as one could in dealing with domestic affairs I should have little difficulty, for I feel so sure of the propriety of our course that I think I could carry the country if I could go into every detail and make "appeals to the people." But we cannot talk to our own people without enlisting the attention of the peoples abroad and then we create more troubles than we cure. In representing the country in its foreign relations, it is necessary to be *right*, not to be assured of approval of the Press of the moment in its hurried and often biased reviews, but of the calm verdict of the coming generation which will pass the final judgment upon our fidelity and intelligence at this critical time.

While the French tightened the thumbscrews on Germany, the British sent Stanley Baldwin, Chancellor of the Exchequer, to Washington at the head of a commission to settle their war debt. The conversations began on January 8, 1923, with Secretary Mellon as chairman of the American commission (of which Hughes and Hoover were also members) and with Ambassador Harvey as the chief intermeddler.

Harvey had been granted permission to return to Washington during the debt negotiations upon his own suggestion that his services might prove useful. The nature of the service Harvey would render came to light when Sir Auckland Geddes, the British ambassador, went to the Secretary's home and handed him a copy of a speech written by Harvey and sent to Baldwin for his use in addressing the two commissions the next morning. In a state of high indignation, Geddes averred that the Chancellor of the Exchequer was quite capable of making speeches without such assistance. Hughes read Harvey's suggested peroration, laughed at its audacity, and mollified Geddes by saying that it was solely a product of Harvey's overzealous interest in securing a debt agreement.

Baldwin delivered his own speech the next morning and made a very favorable impression on the American Commission. Britain planned to pay her entire debt, he said, and asked only a fair business settlement. The American Commission decided to go beyond the limits fixed by Congress and make the most liberal settlement that Congress might be expected to accept. The limit of what

Congress might be willing to do was left to the Senators and Representatives on the commission after sounding out the sentiment on Capitol Hill.

In spite of the conciliatory attitude on both sides, the negotiations reached an impasse on the question of interest rates. Prime Minister Bonar Law in London insisted that the American offer to reduce the interest rate from 4½ to 3 (later 3½) per cent did not go far enough. Baldwin sailed for home on January 20, and Hughes instructed Harvey to hasten back to London and explain to the Prime Minister that the United States had made its best offer.

Hughes then learned from Geddes that Harvey had told Bonar Law some months previously that Britain could expect settlement of her debt on the basis of 2 per cent interest.[12] That explained the Prime Minister's stand against the 3 per cent offer. In Washington, Harvey had also suggested to Sir Maurice Low that a great surprise was in store for Mr. Baldwin; namely, an interest rate of 1½ per cent on the debt. That tip had been passed along to the British negotiators, who began to think, along with Bonar Law, that the American Commission was merely fencing. The Secretary cabled to Harvey to see Bonar Law immediately and make him understand that no settlement could be reached unless the terms offered by the American Commission were accepted.

The impetuous Harvey threw into his interview with Bonar Law all his very considerable power of persuasion. But once more he slipped into reckless speculation. The American Government, he told the Prime Minister, intended to give Britain the right to raise a tax-free loan in the New York market. Geddes hastened to Hughes' home to learn the meaning of Harvey's latest brainstorm, and the Secretary could only lament once more that Harvey had spoken without authority. Together Hughes and Geddes went to Secretary Mellon's apartment to see if he could throw any light on the strange report from London. Mellon had never heard of such a proposal. With astonishing restraint, Hughes cabled Harvey that he should not discuss any departure from the terms offered by the American Commission.

Harvey was near the end of his rope. After his return to London, two hotels sent to the State Department substantial bills that he had incurred and left unpaid. Hughes sent them on to Harvey and later refused to visa vouchers covering "certain items"—meaning intoxicants—for which, under the law, the department could not pay. Harvey thought this was "very ungracious," considering his aid in the debt-funding negotiations, but in the end he apologized.

The Secretary was aware of Harvey's final influence in swinging Bonar Law and the British press behind the debt settlement. Yet it was a great relief when, six weeks after the death of President Harding, Harvey submitted his resignation without any suggestion from the State Department. Undoubtedly he knew that his maladroit ventures had been tolerated only because of the

[12] Memorandum of Interview, Jan. 21, 1923.

political debt that Harding owed him. Hughes accepted the resignation courteously, expressed appreciation for Harvey's services, and recommended
former Senator Frank B. Kellogg as his successor.

The debt agreement with Britain was approved by Congress, but it had little
effect upon the deepening chaos in Europe. By midsummer Hughes said that
"between the Supreme Court liquor decision . . . the delay of the French to
ratify the Naval Limitation Treaties, the pressure for action in the Ruhr situation, he really wished he was a woman and could cry." [13] A week later, however, the department celebrated France's ratification of the Naval Treaty and
the Four-Power Pact, and other patches in the international sky began to clear.
Lloyd George, the former British Prime Minister, started a fresh clamor for
an expert inquiry into reparations. Speaking at Montreal, he noted that the
ability of Germany to pay was still shrinking. "The greater the delay," Lloyd
George said, "the closer the situation approaches chaos. I hope that serious
consideration of Mr. Hughes' plan may be taken up even at this late date,
and I repeat that it is the best hope of a successful settlement." [14]

The next day President Coolidge endorsed the Hughes plan. The effect
was to give it new life. Lloyd George came to Washington, and at his own
suggestion arrived an hour early at the dinner Hughes gave for him so as to get
a firsthand explanation of the proposed inquiry. After their chat together he
was so perturbed over Great Britain's neglect of the Hughes plan that, even
though he was no longer in the government, he cabled London asking for
immediate consideration of it. Britain then took the lead in urging its acceptance. Belgium and Italy expressed approval. France yielded an inch but still
insisted that the amount of the German debt could not be changed and asked
that the inquiry be limited to Germany's "present" capacity to pay. The French
chargé went to the State Department to explain France's position and stayed
to hear a powerful argument against the course his country was pursuing.

In defense of their position the French handed Hughes a technical memorandum on France's rights under the Treaty of Versailles. "But we have
nothing to do with all this," he replied. "What we are interested in is whether
M. Poincaré wants to get any reparations." [15] If so, the investigation would
have to be broad enough to mean something. Finally, Poincaré said he would
let the inquiry of the experts extend as far as 1930. Hughes replied that a
study on that basis would be futile. Jusserand attempted to argue. "It is
absurd," Hughes retorted, "for two old friends, as we are, to discuss this matter.
You have reported what you were told to say and I know what I must do, so
there is an end to it." [16] Once more the deadlock appeared to be unbreak-
able.

[13] Castle diary, 1923, July 5.   [14] *New York Times*, Oct. 9, 1923.
[15] Castle diary, 1923, p. 181.   [16] *Ibid*, p. 212.

At last the Reparation Commission itself backed into an inquiry of the type Hughes had suggested. Meeting on November 30, 1923, the commission unanimously voted to create a committee of experts to consider means of balancing the German budget and stabilizing the currency. A second committee of experts was instructed to estimate the amount of exported capital and suggest means of returning it to Germany. Louis Barthou, president of the Reparation Commission, earnestly requested the aid of American experts on these commissions of inquiry, and Hughes consented, with the understanding that the experts could investigate all the economic conditions in Germany essential to balancing the budget and stabilizing the currency. French opposition had been routed by giving a different name to the investigation of Germany's capacity to pay.

As the American experts to serve on the first committee, Hughes recommended General Charles G. Dawes and Owen D. Young. Both were appointed, along with Henry M. Robinson as an expert on the second committee. The Dawes Committee brought in its first report in April, 1924, recommending that French troops be withdrawn from the Ruhr; that a bank be set up as a depository and fiscal agent of the German Government; that Germany pay the Allies $250,000,000 from railroads, industry, and loans the first year and increasing sums thereafter; and that the Allies and the United States should lend Germany $200,000,000. The powers unanimously accepted the Dawes Plan and called a conference to meet in London in July to put it into effect. Dawes hastened to write to Hughes: "If our work contributes in a measurable way to peace and good will on earth to no one, more than yourself, is it due."

But the end of the controversy was not yet in sight. Ramsay MacDonald had come into power in Great Britain, and Édouard Herriot in France. They were soon at loggerheads over whether the Allies should approach Germany about the proposed new protocol before agreeing among themselves as to how the Dawes Plan should be put into operation.

While this wrangling continued, Secretary Hughes sailed for London, not as a delegate to the forthcoming conference, but as president of the American Bar Association leading two thousand American and Canadian lawyers and many of their families on an Old World pilgrimage. Chief Justice Taft had induced the lawyers to select Hughes as their leader because of the prestige he would give the expedition. The coincidence of the pilgrimage with the reparations meeting caused the New York *World* to jeer at Hughes as a "super-pussyfooter" and to assert that "America has sneaked into Europe by the back door." [17] European editors seemed to take special delight in ridiculing the idea that such a ceremonial visit by the Secretary could have any influence on the ravenous struggle for reparations. But, as formal American participation

[17] Aug. 1, 1924.

in the conference was out of the question, Hughes welcomed the opportunity the pilgrimage afforded for face-to-face discussion of the Dawes Plan on an unofficial basis.

The trip brought many memorable hours. Aboard the *Berengaria*, which had become a sort of lawyers' paradise, there was an outpouring of good fellowship and numerous gay parties. At one of these, a dinner of Harvard Law School graduates, Dean Roscoe Pound summoned the leader of the pilgrimage and conferred upon him a "degree" in these words:

Charles E. Hughes—in diplomacy, like a planked shad, open and above board; in politics, like Caesar's wife, all things to all men; in international affairs, like the Venus de Milo, the greatest figure in disarmament; your spirit of aloofness we now know is as Mark Twain said about the rumor of his death—greatly exaggerated. In recognition of how we have come to regard you on this trip, we confer upon you the degree of Prince of Good Fellows, *ex Merito*.[18]

The extent of Hughes' unbending surprised even some of the lawyers who were closely associated with him. One afternoon as he was relaxing on the promenade deck a rather breezy young woman came up to him.

"Mr. Hughes," she said, "I don't know how we should address you. My father used to speak of you as 'Governor Hughes.' Afterwards I heard people saying 'Judge Hughes.' Now here on the boat I hear them say 'Mr. Secretary.' I don't know how you should be addressed."

A quizzical expression on Hughes' face gave way to a bland smile.

"Those who love me," he said, "call me Charlie!" [19]

Arriving in London, the Hugheses and many of their compatriots attended the Sunday services in Westminster Abbey while other visitors thronged Westminster Cathedral and old St. Paul's. Hughes lived over again the thrill of his first visit to the Abbey as a boy of eleven in 1873. How he had loved that trip! As his mind ranged back over half a century, he mused that few present that morning had visited this choice spot before he had.

The official program for the visitors opened Monday morning with a grand reception in Westminster Hall—the shrine of the common law. The visitors sat in semidarkness under the awesome spell of Westminster's high-timbered roof and the colorful glow of light from its great window. The very atmosphere seemed heavy with history. On one side stood members of England's junior bar in bob wigs and gowns. On the other side was a bank of county court judges wearing full curly wigs, violet stoles, and cuffs. Below were members of the English bar in full wigs, black silk robes, knee breeches, buckled shoes, and frilly cuffs; also the Canadian Privy Councilors in the gorgeous blue and gold of their rank. To the left were Secretary Hughes, Ambassador Kellogg,

[18] Hughes Papers. [19] Roscoe Pound to author, March 22, 1950.

Solicitor General James M. Beck, Justice Sutherland of the Supreme Court, and other distinguished Americans.

The hall was suddenly flooded with light upon the entrance of the Lord Chancellor's procession, giving added brilliance to the ceremony. The tipstaff led the march followed by bearers of the traditional mace and purse and by the Right Honorable Viscount Haldane, the Lord High Chancellor, stately in his black and gold robes. Next came the Lord President of the Council, a group of former Lord Chancellors, the Lord Chief Justice in scarlet and ermine, the Law Lords looking the part of knights about to take part in a splendid tournament, and the King's Bench judges garbed in scarlet. The trains of the great men of the bench were solemnly carried by bearers. The American visitors arose and stood in silence while the judges marched up the aisle and Lord Haldane took his place with the dignity of an old king.

The oratory began with brief addresses of welcome by Sir Patrick Hastings, the Attorney General, resplendent in his white frills; Sir Robert William Dibdin, president of the Law Society; and the Honorable Sir James Aikins, president of the Canadian Bar Association. Lord Haldane then delivered a major address, and Hughes and Sutherland responded in behalf of the American lawyers. Their plain morning dress was in sharp contrast to the elegant robes of the British judges. But Hughes stood on the raised platform with statuesque dignity, his eyes twinkling under heavy brow and his face an image of masculine strength and firmness. The words rolled from his lips with measured cadence. As was his custom, he spoke from memory, with every quotation exact and with a nice balance of tact, wit, and literary polish:

Of all international contacts, none could be happier than this. We have no political ends to serve, no differences to compose, no policies to advance, except the highest good of all—the policy of understanding and good will. The fact that we are here is more eloquent than anything we can say here. We come rejoicing in an amity which has become, I am glad to say, a fixed habit of two peoples intent on cooperation in the interest of peace. We come to tighten the bonds of friendship. . . .

We are not here to pay tribute to the corpus of the early law, still less to the formalism which has had so much to do with its development, but rather to the genius of the common law which brings us together with a definite realization of brotherhood. . . .

The fundamental conception which we especially cherish as our heritage is the right to law itself, not as the edict of arbitrary power, but as the law of a free people, springing from custom, responsive to their sense of justice, modified and enlarged by their free will to meet conscious needs, and sustained by authority which is itself subject to the law—the law of the land. If, as Mr. Justice Holmes has said, "the life of the law is not logic but experience," the life of the common law has been the experience of free men. . . . There is still the need to recognize the ancient right—and it is the most precious right of democracy—the right to be governed by law and not by officials—the right to reasonable, definite and proclaimed standards which the citizens can invoke against both malevolence and caprice. We of the common law respect authority, but it is the authority of the legal order. We respect those who in station high or humble execute the law—because it is our law. We esteem them but only as they esteem and keep within the law. . . .

This meeting of those who enjoy a common tradition and cherish a common purpose cannot fail to heighten our sense of responsibility, as we find our strength renewed, our ardor quickened and our hearts deeply stirred as we sit together at the fireside in the old homestead.

Hughes' happy phrase about "the old homestead" resounded through the press and through many comments from the bar. On Monday night he was the guest of the Pilgrim Society of Great Britain at a dinner in the Hotel Victoria. Responding to toasts by the Duke of Connaught and his grandnephew, the Prince of Wales, Hughes delivered another memorable address, concluding:

I believe that Gladstone remarked in a time of great difficulty that public men ought not to suffer disenchantment. They ought to know that ideals in politics are never realized. Their progress in public life is a continual process of disillusionment, but the greatest of all illusions is that we can serve and achieve without faith. It was faith which made firm the Pilgrims' resolve. It is faith that brings us hither on this delightful journey, an unquestioning faith that some day humanity will enjoy an enduring peace and the reign of justice, and to that end we gladly pledge our lives.

Balfour said that it was "the most important speech ever delivered before a British audience by an American statesman." [20] Years later Hughes himself thought that in these London speeches he had reached his "top speed."

On Wednesday he took Mrs. Hughes to lunch with King George and Queen Mary at Buckingham Palace. It was a delightfully informal luncheon. The King talked freely and had a good deal to say about President Wilson, Colonel House, and Ambassador Harvey. He had been amazed, he said, by the fact that President Wilson was always shadowed by a number of secret service men while he was in Europe. "I never think of taking such precautions," the King said. "Often I go riding in Hyde Park in the mornings with a single companion." One morning as the King was riding along Rotten Row, he related, he was recognized by two Americans. "Hey, there's the King!" one of them cried. "Oh, hell," the other exclaimed, "where's his crown?" The idea that he should have a crown on his head while riding horseback was a source of much amusement to His Majesty.

The following day the King and Queen entertained the visiting Americans at a garden party at Buckingham Palace. By prearrangement Secretary and Mrs. Hughes met the royal couple near the palace. The King asked Hughes to

[20] London dispatch by J. D. Whelpley.

accompany him, and the Queen asked Mrs. Hughes to accompany her. Taking different routes, the two parties began making their way toward the royal marquee, the almost solidly packed crowd opening paths before them as they approached. During this walk, the King told Hughes that if he saw anyone whom he wished to introduce he should not hesitate to do so. The Secretary was very pleased and picked out of the crowd several prominent Americans for presentation to His Majesty, taking care, however, not to abuse the privilege.

Tea was served at the royal marquee to a group which included Secretary and Mrs. Hughes, Premier MacDonald, Premiers Herriot of France and Hymans of Belgium, Ambassador Kellogg, the Duke of Connaught, Prince and Princess Arthur of Connaught, and Princess Beatrice. Then the King and Queen moved to another marquee and received the officers and committee members of the American Bar Association. The crowd was standing obediently behind a line about 150 feet away, without any guards or police in evidence. Some Americans were shaking their heads in admiration of this discipline when a little Brooklyn girl broke away from the crowd and ran to the Prince of Wales for his autograph. The King laughed heartily and said, "I'm afraid she will capture my son"—not dreaming that that honor would go to a Baltimore girl and that it would cost the Prince his throne.

One other youthful effort to take advantage of royal graciousness was less successful. The seventeen-year-old daughter of a visiting lawyer attempted to go through the reception line a second time, assuming that, among the thousands present, she could not be recognized as a repeater. Instead of greeting her, however, Queen Mary said tartly, "I have already seen you."

Interspersed among the ceremonies were a series of informal discussions with the leading statesmen of Europe. Ambassador Kellogg invited Premier Herriot, M. Theunis, the French Minister of Finance, Baron Moucheur of Belgium, and the Italian ambassador to lunch at Crewe House, and Hughes spent two hours with them, pleading that the Dawes Plan be given a chance to operate. Herriot seemed sympathetic, but he feared that any concession he might make would be used against him at home by Poincaré. Pressed by Hughes' relentless logic, Herriot clapped his hands to his head and cried, "I'll fall! I'll fall!" Hughes' rejoinder was that the Premier would fall anyway if he did not carry out the plan.

When Herriot returned to the Inter-Allied Conference, a new spirit—the will to succeed—permeated the deliberations. Herriot began to make concessions that inspired counterconcessions. Meanwhile Hughes went to Paris, and in addition to being elaborately entertained by the French bar, had a heart-to-heart talk with Poincaré on the necessity of pulling together. "Here is the American policy," he said, referring to the Dawes Plan. "If you turn this down, America is through." Poincaré responded favorably. The clouds of pessimism began to lift. Even the French press began to reflect new confidence, with the result of strengthening the hands of Herriot in London.

In Brussels, Hughes' visit with the Belgians produced similar results. At a dinner at the American Embassy in Berlin he talked with equal candor to President Ebert, Chancellor Marx, and Foreign Minister Stresemann just before the German delegates went to the London Conference. If Germany did not accept the Dawes Plan, he said, she could look for no further aid or sympathy from the United States. The Germans pledged themselves to carry out the new reparations scheme to the letter.

The bankers came close to upsetting the apple cart by insisting that a representative of J. P. Morgan & Company be appointed as general agent to carry out the Dawes Plan. Hughes objected on the ground that the plan would have to have the full confidence of Germany for success. Then the bankers tried to swing the appointment to Norman Davis. The Administration's choice was Owen D. Young, but the bankers opposed him unless he would agree to hold the post for three years. Young was not willing to do this, but he was appointed with the understanding that he would get the machinery running smoothly before turning it over to S. Parker Gilbert.

As Secretary Hughes sailed for home, he was widely credited with having brought success to the London Conference without having attended it. "The solution of this reparations question, if it is solved," said a London dispatch "will date, I believe, from Herriot's luncheon with Secretary Hughes." [21] The London *Times* said of the conference:

It has reestablished harmony among the Allies over the principal problem of Europe; it has taken France and Germany out of the cold atmosphere of frigid notes and curt conversations into that of amicable discussion; and it has sealed the participation, unofficial but extremely helpful, of the United States in the economic reconstruction of the Old World. The first tentative suggestion of Mr. Hughes in his famous speech at New Haven some 18 months ago . . . has now borne splendid fruit.[22]

The reparations adjustments thus effected saved Europe from economic collapse for six years. In the great depression of the thirties the whole flimsy structure of war debts and war penalties tottered and fell. Then it became evident that the Dawes Plan and the Young Plan had succeeded temporarily only because American and British investors had lent to Germany more money than she repaid in reparations. Actually it was these investors who paid the cost of rebuilding Europe. It would have been much better to have wiped out the war debts and to have confined reparations to such tangible German property as could have been removed without crippling the country. Vast sums

[21] New York *World*, Aug. 2, 1924.   [22] Aug. 18, 1924.

simply cannot be transferred from one country to another year after year, except in the form of goods, and the United States and other countries had raised their tariff rates to prevent a larger flow of imports.

There is no evidence that Secretary Hughes foresaw the inevitable breakdown of the postwar settlements or that he fully appreciated the significance of the United States' shift from the position of a debtor to that of a creditor nation. He continued to support the Republican tariff policy, which made payment of the war debts economically infeasible. While he was clear-headed and insistent in warning the French that they could not get milk and beef from the same cow at the same time, he never undertook to warn the American people that they could not collect on the war debts unless they were willing to receive a much larger volume of European goods.

In appraising Hughes' efforts to cope with the economic dislocations resulting from World War I, however, we must avoid any easy comparison with the Marshall Plan which followed World War II. In the latter case the United States poured billions into the European recovery effort because the folly of expecting war and rehabilitation loans to be repaid had then been pointedly demonstrated and because the shift of military power in Europe to Soviet Russia made it imperative for the free nations to stand together. There were no such compulsions to unity of effort in the twenties. Nor was the dominant economic position of the United States so marked as it has since become. If, as Winston Churchill has pointed out, a man of great authority had had "the wit, ascendancy, or detachment from public folly" to declare the hopelessness of trying to make a defeated nation pay the cost of a modern war, no one would have believed him.[23]

A bolder attitude on Hughes' part might have enhanced his stature in history, but he was mindful of what had happened when Wilson overplayed his hand. It was prompt recovery in Europe and not a futile showdown that he sought. Root looked upon Hughes' course as the "only possible curative policy." It proved to be only a palliative, but the fact remains that it was the most constructive step taken to rescue Europe from its economic chaos in the postwar years when there was still hope that a second world war could be averted.

[23] *The Gathering Storm* (Boston, Houghton Mifflin, 1948), pp. 8–9. Copyright, 1948, by Houghton Mifflin Co.

Chapter 57

THE WORLD COURT

HUGHES' passion for justice and his deep interest in peace predestined him to become a strong supporter of the World Court. To his way of thinking the settlement of international disputes over legal issues in the cool detachment of the courtroom was the first logical step in the substitution of world law for force. "The desire for peace," he said, "must be supported by the institutions of peace." [1] Of course, no international court could become a cure-all. But an independent tribunal of able judges could settle numerous disputes on the basis of facts and law, and it could give peoples a new consciousness of justice operating on an international scale.

The creation of an international court had long been a cardinal feature of American policy. Secretary Hay had tried to interest the First Hague Conference of 1899 in such a tribunal, and the conference had set up the Permanent Court of Arbitration. As this body was only a panel of arbiters, Secretary Root had attempted at the Second Hague Conference to convert it into a real international court composed of full-time judges. The project had failed only because no satisfactory method of electing the judges could be found.

In his 1916 campaign Hughes had picked up the world-court idea from Hay, Root, and Theodore Roosevelt and given it warm support. After the United States had entered World War I and again in the 1920 campaign, he had voiced his devotion to the cause of an international court. With much interest, he had followed the work of the Commission of Jurists which had assembled at The Hague on invitation from the Council of the League of Nations. The jurists, including Hughes' highly esteemed friend, Elihu Root, had brought forth a carefully devised statute to set up the Permanent Court of International Justice, and the Assembly of the League had approved it on December 13, 1920—the very day that Hughes agreed to join the Harding Cabinet. His earliest acquaintance with the World Court plan had convinced him that one of his major tasks as Secretary of State would be to win adherence of the United States to it.

Despite Mrs. Harding's efforts to dissuade him, the President acquiesced in this conclusion. The revolt in the Senate against the League of Nations suggested caution, however, and Hughes' preoccupation with the Washington

[1] *The Pathway of Peace*, p. 67.

Conference through most of his first year in office compelled delay. Meanwhile a disturbing incident put him in the light of being hostile to the court.

Root had sponsored a provision in the World Court statute authorizing the nomination of judges for that tribunal by the members of the old Hague Court of Arbitration. By this means it was hoped to confine the nominations to eminent lawyers and judges in the various countries instead of having governments select nominees for political reasons. Judges to serve on the World Court were then to be elected from the list of nominees by separate votes of the League Council and Assembly. In June, 1921, Sir Eric Drummond, secretary general of the League, sent out requests that members of the old Hague Court panel nominate American jurists for the new court, but the letters went astray.

By Harry James Westerman in the *Ohio State Journal*, June 11, 1923.

CHARLES VS. SIMEON

Hughes told his press conference at the time that if the requests for nominations should come to the State Department they would be forwarded and that the Hague Court judges would act in accord with their own judgment. That was the last he heard of the matter until about August 14, when Root wrote him a letter and Oscar S. Straus called at the department to ask if the communications had been received. Hughes had seen nothing of them, but he launched an immediate search. Two days later he replied to Root:

As soon as I received the latter [Root's letter of August 14] I had the files of the Department searched and found, to my great regret, that the communications from the Secretary General of the League of Nations, addressed to you, Judge Gray, Mr. Straus, and Mr. Moore had been received, placed on file, and not forwarded. How this happened I am unable to state. . . . Apparently the papers were received and filed without being referred to me and without appreciation of their significance.[2]

In belatedly sending out the League's invitations, Hughes also apologized to the other members of the panel. He was deeply chagrined. The primary fault lay, however, with the incompetent career service officer who had been letting all League communications pile up in a sort of dead-letter file.

As it was then apparent that the United States would not join the League, Root was uncertain whether the American group should attempt to nominate judges for the court the League had created. He cabled Drummond that he was trying to get his fellow panel members together "to determine whether under the circumstances we have authority to comply with your invitation."[3] When they met, Straus and Gray thought the nominations should be made in spite of the roadblocks the Senate had erected between Washington and Geneva. Root then went to Washington in September, 1921, and laid the panel's dilemma before Hughes.

The Secretary was then in the midst of his preparations for the Conference on the Limitation of Armaments. Realizing that treaties coming out of the conference would be worthless without the Senate's approval, he was wary of any step that might antagonize the Senate. The members of the Court of Arbitration, he reminded Root, had been appointed by the President, and any action by them would be regarded as in effect done by the United States Government. Consequently, he feared that compliance with the League's request "would involve serious risk of immediate controversy which might be very injurious to the success of the important policies the government is now pursuing. . . ."[4] At the same time, Hughes said, he had no request to make of the judges. He had spoken frankly because Root had raised the issue, but

[2] CEH to Root, Aug. 16, 1921.
[3] Reprinted by permission of Dodd, Mead & Company from *Elihu Root* by Philip C. Jessup. Copyright, 1938, by Dodd, Mead & Company, Inc.
[4] *Ibid.*, p. 426.

he felt that the judges should act on their own responsibility.[5] Root replied that he too was convinced that the nominations should not be made. With the consent of the other judges, he cabled to Drummond to convey the reluctant conclusion that the American arbitration judges were not entitled to suggest nominees for the new court.

Apparently Root's disclaimer of authority to make the nominations was his own idea. There would have been less embarrassment when nominations were later made by the same group, without waiting for the United States to ratify the World Court protocol, if Root had merely accepted Hughes' argument that it was inexpedient for the four Hague Court judges to act in the fall of 1921. Hughes never questioned their authority.

Unaware that Hughes was merely biding his time on the World Court issue, the pro-League forces unlimbered some of their heaviest artillery against him. Hamilton Holt directly accused the Secretary of preventing the American Hague judges from sending in their nominations. As the interests of the court were close to his heart, this sort of criticism was hard for Hughes to take. "What a wonderful thing it would be," he remarked, "to wear a mantle of complacency so thick and warm that you would never fear the cold comments of the world." But he was never to find such a mantle. In this instance, moreover, he could not divulge what his future strategy would be, and the disgruntled friends of the court had no means of reading his mind. His reply that Holt's statement was "in error" and that "the American Hague Judges acted in accordance with their own views of propriety" [6] was not enough to overcome an impression that Hughes and Root were out to scuttle the World Court.

While the critics were having their field day, Hughes worked quietly "through one of the most eminent and most influential friends of the League" to get a voice for the United States in the election of World Court judges.[7] His silence on the court issue was finally broken in a speech at Boston on October 30, 1922. By this time the Senate was less suspicious of his motives, and the Washington Conference treaties had successfully run the senatorial gantlet.

"We favor, and always have favored, an international court of justice for the determination according to judicial standards of justiciable international disputes," the Secretary said. "I believe that suitable arrangements can be made for the participation by this Government in the election of judges of the International Court which has been set up, so that this Government may give its formal support to that court as an independent tribunal of international justice."

A misinterpretation of this speech by Charles A. and Mary R. Beard demands correction because of the generally high standing of their historical

[5] CEH, Notes, p. 310.   [6] CEH to Holt, July 13, 1922.
[7] CEH to Edwin Gay, Aug. 1, 1922.

work. "Secretary Hughes," they wrote, "made a declaration in favor of a world tribunal standing on an independent basis. That was a concession but as nearly all the nations of the earth were operating under the League court, there was a distinct air of hauteur in the American call for another institution of international justice. Perceiving this paradox, perhaps, Harding himself then indicated a desire to participate in the existing World Court if it could be so constituted 'as to appear to be . . . a world court and not a League court.' . . ." [8]

At no time did Hughes have any idea of proposing "another" court.[9] He spoke of arrangements for the United States to participate in the election of judges "of the *International Court which has been set up,* so that this Government may give its formal support to *that* court." (Italics supplied.) His reference to "an independent tribunal of international justice" was clearly a description of the court then in being. The suggestion that Harding stepped in to swing his Administration away from an impracticable State Department scheme to set up a new world court is especially ironical, for it was Hughes who was pushing Harding faster than he wished to move toward the existing World Court.

It was no accident that Hughes' first blow for the World Court was struck in Boston. That locale gave him a natural opportunity to sugar-coat his advocacy of the World Court with complimentary references to Senator Lodge, who was still chairman of the strategic Committee on Foreign Relations. As Lodge was confined to his home by illness, Hughes sent him a copy of the speech. The Senator replied that it was "a very great speech indeed." Back in Washington, Hughes found a favorable opportunity to see Lodge and elaborate the Administration's hopes and plans for ratification of the World Court protocol, with reservations. The wily New Englander refrained from expressing opposition in the face of Hughes' persuasive arguments, but his subsequent action was to prove that silence had not given consent.

Putting the most favorable interpretation on Lodge's passivity, Hughes again pressed for action at the White House. Harding once more indicated his approval, but he was eager to dispose of the merchant-marine bill and several other items on the legislative calendar before sending up a message on the World Court. Hughes agreed to wait a little longer.

February, 1923, rolled around, and Harding had made no move toward sending a World Court treaty into the senatorial lion's den. Confined to his home by an attack of grippe, with time to think about the court problem, Hughes decided to thrust the issue before the President in a form that would stimulate action. If Congress should adjourn before considering adherence to

[8] *The Rise of American Civilization* (New York, Macmillan, 1930), II, 691f. Copyright, 1930, by The Macmillan Company.
[9] CEH Notes, p. 311*b*.

the court, he thought, another year would be lost. Despite his illness, he dictated a long letter to the President outlining the steps he believed to be necessary to make adherence to the court feasible for the United States.

Ever mindful of the bitter-enders in the Senate, the Secretary took special pains to show that the Permanent Court of International Justice was not a mere tool of the League. The court statute had not become effective, he asserted, upon its adoption by the Assembly but only upon ratification of a special protocol by the participating powers. The court was open to non-members of the League. Its judges were jurists of the highest caliber from many nations, including a distinguished American—John Bassett Moore. To be sure, the judges were elected through the machinery of the League. It was this provision, giving the small nations a veto on judges through the Assembly and the large nations a veto through the Council, which had made the organization of the World Court feasible. Arrangements could now be made, he thought, for the United States to share in the election of judges on a basis of equality with the other states. "I am profoundly convinced," he concluded, "that this Government, under appropriate conditions, should become a party to the convention establishing the Court and should contribute its fair share of the expense of maintenance." [10]

Hughes offered four "conditions and understandings to be made a part of the instrument of adhesion": (1) our acceptance of the court statute should not be taken to involve us in any relation to the League; (2) the United States should be permitted to participate, on a footing of equality, in any and all proceedings of the Council and Assembly of the League for the election of judges; (3) our share of the expenses of the court should be determined and appropriated by Congress; (4) the court statute could not be amended without the consent of the United States.

Harding sent a copy of the Hughes letter to the Senate on February 24, along with a brief endorsement. Lodge came back with a tricky question. Did the President favor an agreement obligating all powers signing the protocol to submit to the court all disputes (of a specified character) which could not be settled by diplomatic efforts? A Yes answer would be fuel to the faggots the committee was piling up around the protocol. An answer of No would leave the court open to attack as a weak tribunal lacking compulsory jurisdiction.

The statute of the court gave it jurisdiction over only such cases as the powers might voluntarily submit to it, unless they had signed the optional compulsory clause, as only fifteen of the forty-six signatories had done. In his letter to the President, Hughes had carefully avoided asking for acceptance of the compulsory clause, knowing that it would be futile. Replying to Lodge, he found satirical amusement in pointing to the Chinese wall that the Senate

[10] *Foreign Relations, 1923,* I, 10–17.

had built against obligatory arbitration or adjudication of international differences. "In the light of this record," he wrote, "it would seem to be entirely clear that unless the Senate changes its attitude it would be a waste of effort for the President to attempt to negotiate treaties with the other Powers providing for an obligatory jurisdiction of the scope stated in the Committee's first inquiry. . . ." Lodge's boomerang thus smacked the Senate itself.

Hughes carried his case to the country in a speech before the American Society of International Law on April 27, 1923. We have a direct interest, he said, in seeing that "the best practicable method of judicial settlement" is applied to other nations' controversies as well as to our own. The faith of the American people in fact-finding and the application of law had been demonstrated by the participation of their government in more than seventy arbitrations. But it was unnecessarily expensive to create a separate tribunal for every case, and that practice resulted in a series of "sporadic utterances by temporary bodies" instead of the orderly development of international law that could be expected from a permanent bench of judges. An established court, moreover, would eliminate the increasing difficulty of finding impartial arbiters after a controversy had arisen.

The plan of the court, he declared, "gives every assurance against a successful attempt by any *bloc* to manipulate or control the elections." To the complaint that the court set up by the League was not a world court, he replied, "It is not too much to say that there will be no world court if this court cannot be made one, and whether or not it is to be in the fullest sense a world court depends upon our own action." As to the argument that joining the court would be an "entanglement," he asked, "In what do we become entangled?" Judicial settlement of international controversies had been a feature of American policy since the foundation of the government. "We have never considered this to be an entanglement," he asserted. "If you are to treat participation in a permanent court of international justice as an entanglement foreign to our institutions, you must rewrite American history."

Nor was it necessary to await the codification of international law. "We shall make no progress toward the prevention of war," he said, "if we adopt a perfectionist policy. Whatever else we should have, we need at once a permanent court of international justice. No plan to promote peace can dispense with it. . . . I hope that the United States, in deference to its own interests and in justice to its ideals, will do its part." [11]

This speech is one of the finest expositions of an intricate political problem in the English language. Hughes' persistent critic, Hamilton Holt, called it "by all means the most lucid, logical and irrefutable argument for the court that has appeared anywhere." [12] Rereading the speech a generation later,

[11] *The Pathway of Peace*, pp. 65–88.   [12] Holt to CEH, April 28, 1923.

Judge Manley O. Hudson of the World Court was moved to write to Hughes, "It is a most accurate chart for us today, and I feel myself still inspired by your words of almost twenty years ago." [13]

The Secretary was constantly on guard against schemes to take the court out of its strictly judicial role. "The success of the Permanent Court of International Justice is too important," he wrote to Lewis Einstein, the American minister to Prague, "to permit it to be used for the purpose of dealing with questions which lie outside the appropriate determination of justiciable controversies. . . . We have steadily refused in this country to permit the Supreme Court to become a political agency and I feel that we must take a similar attitude with respect to the Permanent Court of International Justice." [14]

Hughes made another plea for the World Court in his address at the Kent Centennial Celebration at Columbia University on June 4, 1923. Two weeks later he told the alumni at Dartmouth College, "There is no path to the millennium other than the path of justice, and if we discard the best attainable instrumentalities of justice, to that extent we invite the decision of the sword."

When Coolidge succeeded to the Presidency, he too spoke out for the court, and both the political parties called for adherence to the protocol in their 1924 conventions. But the Senate committee continued to stall. Lodge had introduced a bill calling for a new world court in the image of the existing one, except that he omitted any mention of the League. "It does not change the character of the judges," Hughes commented, "to move them from one room to another." [15] On the day before Hughes left office, the House of Representatives expressed its confidence in the court by a vote of 301 to 28 without stirring the balky Senate to action.

Out of office, Hughes continued to pile up arguments for the World Court. He told the American Society of International Law, of which he had been elected president, that

We have come to realize that war is not to be ended by war, that the seeds of another conflict have been plentifully sown, and that the spirit of man emerged from the fire of the struggle still unpurified, more restless if not more passionate, and less amenable to restraint. . . .

It is precisely because we are dealing with civilization itself, which is nothing less than progressive self-restraint and an increasing capacity for cooperation to ensure the enrichment of the individual life, that we attach the greatest importance to the development of international law . . . the effort to promote the reign of law, as accepted, not imposed, may be after all the most important contribution to permanent peace.

. . . it is not correct . . . to speak of peace, or the mere absence of war, as our ultimate goal. We wish to have the peace, not of the lowest forms of life, but

---

[13] Hudson to CEH, Dec. 12, 1942.   [14] July 11, 1924.
[15] Castle diary, 1924, p. 151.

of the highest, with its inescapable longings and strivings. Peace is but an opportunity, and our chief concern is justice.

Int Washington, however, timorous Senators had found a powerful ally in Judge Moore, who had returned from The Hague fearful that the court might abuse its power of giving advisory opinions. The court had set a sensible precedent when the League Council had requested an advisory opinion on the dispute between Finland and Russia over Karelia.[16] Because Russia, not a member of the League, withheld its consent, the court had ruled that it could

By Edwin Marcus in the *New York Times*, January 25, 1925.

ANOTHER ECLIPSE?

not give an advisory opinion in that case. It had concluded, moreover, that in any event advisory opinions could be given only in open court in conformity with the rules laid down for the handling of other cases. Not satisfied to have these sound rules established by a seven-to-four decision of the court itself, Moore sought to make them forever binding by writing them into an American reservation to the court protocol to which the previous signatories would be asked to assent.

Senator George Wharton Pepper sponsored a resolution embodying Moore's ideas. President Coolidge hastened to ask Hughes' advice. "I have never been able exactly to determine," the President wrote, "whether Judge Moore thinks we ought to go into the Court or stay out of it, though I suppose he is in favor of adherence." [17] The next day Coolidge wrote to Hughes again to ask

[16] Denna Frank Fleming, *The United States and the World Court*, pp. 61f.
[17] Coolidge to CEH, Nov. 3, 1925.

"what possible authority there can be for the constant assertion that it [the court] has to declare the League law to be *the* law."

Hughes was cool to the Pepper-Moore draft. As to Judge Moore's elaborate reservation prescribing rules for the court in rendering advisory opinions, Hughes thought it was quite unnecessary, although he did not object to the principles laid down. "The United States," he wrote, with clear-headedness that seemed to be lacking in the Senate, "would not have responsibility for any opinion upon any question in the submission of which it did not take part." [18]

Nor did he see anything frightening in the "League law" bogey. There could be no "League law," he advised the President, except in the sense of agreements between members of the League or rules established by it, and in neither case could these deprive states outside the League of their just rights. The court was bound by its own statute to apply international conventions, international customs that had come to be accepted as law, and the principles of law recognized by civilized nations; it could also recognize judicial decisions and legal teachings as subsidiary means of determining the law. ". . . if we were to undertake to set up a Permanent Court of International Justice of our own making," he wrote, "we probably should not care to phrase its duty differently."

It was Judge Moore's voice, however, that prevailed with the Senate. After accepting Moore's ultracautious reservations, the Senate added one of its own. No American case should go to the World Court in any event without the consent of the Senate by a two-thirds vote. The Senate finally adopted its own emasculated version of the court protocol on January 26, 1926, nearly three years after Hughes' letter had gone to Capitol Hill.

Distasteful though the extreme reservations were, Hughes hoped that the other powers would accept the Senate's proposal. "The significant thing," he said, "is that the United States has reaffirmed its historic policy." [19] But the League powers countered with reservations of their own, and the United States remained outside the court. That is the price the country paid for rejecting Hughes' advice, for it is clear that his limited reservations would have been acceptable to the other powers.

In 1935 a modified proposal to take us into the court failed to get a two-thirds vote in the Senate. It was not until the United Nations came into being after World War II that the United States finally took its place in the International Court of Justice. Meanwhile Hughes had served as a judge on the international bench, and his unquenchable faith in the judicial settlement of disputes had given buoyancy to the continued struggle for a world amenable to law.

[18] CEH to Coolidge, Nov. 5, 1925.   [19] Speech of April 22, 1926.

Chapter 58

THE HUMAN ELEMENT

FROM the foregoing pages one might suppose that Secretary Hughes had little time to sleep and no time at all for the ordinary trivialities of living. Actually he crowded into his busy days a myriad of personal chores and pleasantries. He found time to "be with the boys" at college class reunions, to write old friends, to give advice to youths, to send greetings to dozens of gatherings, to speak for charitable causes, to have several portraits painted, and to joke about thousands of things that tickled his sensitive wit.

When Philip A. de László espied the Secretary in a white suit one summer day, he said that he would like to paint him in that attire and would make him a present of the canvas. Having sat for several portraits, Hughes at first replied that he could not spare the time that would be required, but later he consented on de László's assurance that it would not take more than two sittings. As he went to the Corcoran Art Gallery for the second sitting and discovered that the artist had obliterated almost everything he had previously done, Hughes was inclined to abandon the venture, feeling that the portrait could never be finished in the time allotted. At the end of the third sitting, however, de László handed over the finished canvas, and it is the best portrait of Hughes in existence.

The painting of the Hughes portrait that hangs in the Cornell Law School library gave its subject a different sort of experience. He and Simon Elwes, popular English artist, exchanged so many good stories and had such a good time together while Elwes was at work that the portrait acquired the air of a man about town. "All it needs is a boutonniere," Hughes remarked as he surveyed the finished painting, "to make me a boulevardier."

Old friends and new discovered that Hughes' office was a humming workshop but no ivory tower. When "Al" Smith called, the Secretary rushed out to the reception room to greet him and ushered the Governor into the inner office with a friendly arm around his shoulder. Such effusive greetings were rare, but several of Hughes' aides felt his arm on their shoulders as an expression of appreciation for some service superbly rendered.

The Secretary's prolific correspondence included numerous personal letters of advice, encouragement, and kind words to people in trouble. He found time to write thoughtful suggestions to mothers worried about their children, to

604

advise veterans as to their careers, and to comfort friends who had suffered misfortunes. Something deep within his nature seemed to drive him to a full utilization of his powers, and the satisfaction that came from these casual acts of kindness was not very different from that derived from great achievements.

Blessed with an outgoing disposition, he naturally distributed most freely the intellectual coin that he possessed in greatest abundance. It would not be accurate to assume, however, that advice and cheer were his only gifts. His letters to relatives, friends, and organizations sometimes contained checks despite his limited means at this time. When the bread of kindness cast upon the waters returned in tangible form, he was cautious about receiving it. Such tokens of esteem as flowers, fruit, and incidental items of food he accepted, but he returned a package of cravats and many similar gifts. His invariable rule of not accepting compensation for his speeches caused him to return checks sent for that purpose in ignorance or disregard of his wishes.

Yet he continued to make an astonishing number of speeches that had little or no relation to his work as Secretary of State. On October 3, 1921, he presided over and addressed a gathering commemorating the six hundredth anniversary of the death of Dante. In memory of Helen, he spoke for the national and local tuberculosis associations. He laid the cornerstone of the National Baptist Memorial to Roger Williams and Religious Liberty, and spoke repeatedly on university campuses. The insistent demand for his speeches never turned his head or gave him any easy sense of mastery. A week before he was to deliver his scholarly address at the James Kent Centennial he wrote to his son, "I am terrified by the preparations to hear the address, which is still in the works."

The advent of radio induced him to change his speaking technique. As governor and as presidential candidate, he had been accustomed to enthusiastic audiences who would applaud the crescendoes of an extemporaneous speech. The radio audiences demanded more restraint and precision along with a conversational tone. This (plus the necessity of supplying copies to the press) meant that radio speeches had to be prepared in advance. At the same time Hughes was keenly aware of the dislike of American audiences for the reading of speeches. Finding himself frequently addressing an audience physically present as well as a larger radio audience, he took to memorizing what he wished to say. His Notes give the best account of his method:

Fortunately I did not find it difficult to memorize a speech—even a long one. I have been blessed, to a fair degree, with visual or what is sometimes called a photographic memory. That is, having composed a speech, I find that reading it a few times—always from the same typewritten copy—fixes the type in my mind's eye so that in speaking I am almost reading the pages. When I wished to interpolate, introducing something that was suggested or required by the occasion, or paused to answer a question, I put a mental finger at the place on the page, and after the interpolation or interruption I could easily resume where I had left off. Reporters sitting before me with copies of my speech have flattered me sometimes by saying that I had reproduced the written speech with verbal exactness. But that is an exaggeration. To follow the written speech so that the reporters were satisfied that I was not delivering a speech different from the one given out, answered the purpose.

His speeches were always prepared under pressure. "Aside from the Historical Address at Brown University (1914) and my lectures on the Supreme Court at Columbia (which because of so many references and details had to be worked over for some time)," he tells us, "I do not recall an instance in which I prepared an address with the pleasing consciousness that I could work at leisure and completely satisfy my ambition. Time was always of the essence, and one demand had to be got out of the way to make room for another on its heels." At no time in his life, however, did Hughes make use of a ghost writer. On one occasion he did incorporate a brief memorandum on the Near East in a speech covering a wide range of subjects, but when a book of his speeches was published in 1925 this part of the address was dropped out.

Because of their heavy social schedule, an evening at home or a quiet meal together was a luxury for the Hughes family in this period. Even an illness that would mean confinement at home had some aspects of a happy interlude. In February, 1923, the family was stricken by grippe, and Elizabeth, in spite of her fever, was charmed by the opportunity of monopolizing her mother for more than a week. A good deal of bantering passed between the sick rooms, and Elizabeth captured some of it in a parody of Longfellow:

> Loud from his darkened bed chamber, the deep-voiced
>   neighboring Secretary
> Speaks, and in accents disconsolate answers the wail
>   of the Madame.

Elizabeth was the only fledgling left in the nest. When the family had moved to Washington in March, 1921, Catherine had found an excuse to remain in New York as a guest in her brother's home, because she was in love. Within a month she was engaged to Chauncey Lockhart Waddell of New York, son of Mr. and Mrs. Edwin J. Waddell of Greenfield, Ohio, and notified her parents by letter. While Mrs. Hughes had liked Chauncey from the beginning, this unexpected news prompted her to call the car and go straight to the State Department with the letter in her hand. It was the only time she ever broke in upon the Secretary's work at the office to discuss a personal matter. "Catherine is engaged," she told him, "to a fellow she has seen only half a dozen times." Hughes had met the fiancé only once and could not identify him among the several young men Catherine had introduced to him. But he seemed to have implicit faith in his daughter's judgment. He and Mrs. Hughes telephoned their congratulations and also sent a telegram. Then each wrote Catherine a letter, with Hughes looking back at his own romance as the source of his greatest satisfaction:

DEAREST CATHERINE,

I long to see you and tell you how glad I am that the great decision has been made and that for you life's real happiness has now begun. I have no fatherly words of wisdom—only thoughts of love. I have had only a glimpse of Chauncey—but Mother has told me how much she had admired him, and I am sure that he not only has your love but also that sincere esteem—by reason of qualities of mind and character—which underlies the love and faith that endure no matter what experiences life may bring. You cannot realize all that this means to you both, but Mother and I do. We are thinking of you and Chauncey and sending our choicest blessing, realizing the fullness of the happiness of our thirty-two years together. The day we plighted our troth is as bright in the memory as ever and we have been reviewing those days of long ago with the tenderest thought of you.

Tell Chauncey that he will have the welcome of a son—and of the winner of a great prize.

Love and kisses from
FATHER

The marriage took place on June 10, 1922, in the Bethlehem Chapel of the National Cathedral in Washington and was the first Cabinet wedding of the Harding Administration. A distinguished gathering, including the President and Vice President, kept eyes fastened on the vivacious bride in her crepe-basque satin gown elaborately embroidered with pearls while the "I do's" were said. Then followed a reception at the Pan American Building at which the Secretary and Mrs. Hughes beamed almost as happily as the bride and groom. Hughes was already fond of his son-in-law—an affection that was to grow with the years.

More placid than her sister, Elizabeth nevertheless lived in a state of entrancement when men and women of famous names came to the Hughes household. In 1916 she had not realized her dream of bathing in the White House fountain, but that disappointment had long since been swallowed up by the fascination of being daughter to the Secretary of State. During the formal dinner parties given by her parents, she could not resist the temptation of peering at the guests over the banister from a secluded position on the second floor.

"Elizabeth," her mother used to say, "you'll come down with a crash some night."

But her curiosity was stronger than any fear of embarrassment. Hughes was well aware of the spell that famous people cast on her, and when Lloyd George came to visit him, he called Elizabeth in for a five-minute chat with the dynamic little Welshman. She walked out on air, as only a girl of sixteen can.

Sparks of humor and whimsy helped to dispel any clouds that gathered in either domestic or official skies. When Charles Junior wrote to acquaint his parents with some difficulty he had encountered, his father admonished him: "If you run into a course of bad luck, remember your grandfather's story of the man who bought a lot of pigs for one dollar apiece and drove them a long way to market, selling them for seventy-five cents apiece. When asked where the profit came in he said he had the company of the pigs on the journey. You are getting a most valuable experience."

Selected as one of the "burnt offerings" at the Gridiron Club's semiannual dinner, Hughes replied to the invitation: "I suppose the victims must at least utter a groan, if desired, and I shall endeavor to say a word . . . as requested." If a dinner put him in a jocund mood, he would sometimes dash off nonsensical rhymes, at least one of which has survived in the mind of a friend:

> Wives of great men all remind us
> We can make our wives sublime
> And departing leave behind us
> All the rest at dinner time.

Sitting with Balfour at a banquet during the Washington Conference, Hughes facetiously recalled a story about Balfour being questioned in the House of Commons on the arrest of a sixteen-year-old watchmaker's apprentice for yelling "Bloody Balfour" in the streets of Dublin. Suave Mr. Balfour had answered, Hughes recounted, that there were certain inaccuracies in the report: the person arrested was not a watchmaker's apprentice, but a shoemaker; he was not a lad of sixteen, but a man of forty-six; he was not arrested for shouting insults, but for being drunk; and while it was true that the prisoner had shouted "Bloody Balfour" en route to the jail, His Majesty's Government did not regard that as sufficient cause for the man's liberation. Balfour was much amused, but instead of verifying the story, he said simply, "I wish I could think I had said that."

Requests that flowed into the Secretary's office were sometimes a source of amusement. One woman solemnly asked Mrs. Hughes to secure the autographs of delegates to the Washington Conference on a tablecloth. A general, who was afflicted with what Hughes called a bit of the "divine inflatus," sent in a plan to settle all Europe's troubles and then publicly announced that he could not comment on the plan because it was under consideration by the State Department. Hughes telegraphed to the general a bit sharply that he was going to tell the people what his (the general's) suggestion was, "as we could not have it thought that the Department was preventing the world's salvation." [1]

There was good nature as well as humor in his day-to-day contacts. "This is Papapou speaking," the Secretary boomed into his telephone one busy day. He was exchanging a long-distance greeting with his little grandson in New York, who preferred his own contracted version of "Grandpapa Hughes."

"Bring me a bale of hay," Hughes invariably commanded his waiter when taking breakfast away from home. If the waiter were observant, he could detect the flicker of a smile playing around the corners of the Secretary's mouth. And if he hastened to bring a bowl of shredded wheat, amicable relations were at once established.

Fond memories were occasionally stirred by a note or a greeting from old friends on the Supreme Court. When Hughes received a book from Justice Holmes, he replied:

MY DEAR MR. JUSTICE:

I have always been glad to receive anything at your hand—except a dissenting opinion. . . .

I suppose that you are still plugging away at the Fourteenth Amendment.[2]

Yes, Joseph H. Choate was right. One has to have his pleasure from day to day if he is going to get it at all. Hughes had an enormous capacity for sandwiching the little amenities of life in between his herculean tasks. These lighter moments may have had little to do with the deeper satisfaction that he found in work well done, but they added savor to life; and they were as much a part of the complex character of Charles E. Hughes as were his moral qualities and his mental powers.

[1] Castle diary, 1923, p. 135.   [2] CEH to Holmes, Nov. 24, 1924.

Chapter 59

RESIGNATION

THE YEAR 1925 made its debut upon the stage of time amid a normal American hubbub over Coolidge prosperity, prohibition, and flapper fashions. In Congress the most exciting issues were the McNary-Haugen bill and the soldiers' bonus. Except for the smoldering anger in Japan over the Exclusion Act, our foreign relations were placid. It was a favorable moment, Secretary Hughes concluded, to return to the practice of law.

The State Department as well as the policies it was following had become the lengthened shadow of Charles E. Hughes. In part that was because he kept his fingers on everything the department was doing and carried a very large share of the burden himself. But in part also it was due to the striking loyalty that he commanded. His example of diligence, his courtesy, and the little things he remembered about employees gave him a special hold on them. Michael J. McDermott, later press relations officer of the department for many years, was one of several hundred employees who had shaken the Secretary's hand on the day he took office.

"Mr. Secretary," McDermott had said, "I'm proud to serve in your administration."

Four years later, when the employees filed by to say farewell, McDermott was again in the line.

"Well, Mac," Hughes asked, "are you still proud?"

Such incidents were typical, and they became lasting bonds between Hughes and his aides.

"As long as I live," Castle wrote in his diary near the end of the Secretary's fourth year, "I shall consider association with Mr. Hughes one of the great privileges of life. It is inspiring to come into contact with his mind, the most perfect mental machine in the world; with his courage, which always dares to do the right thing. . . . If he was only mind he would be a leader, but not the great leader he is. I know no more splendidly human person, no one with a bigger heart or quicker sympathy."

Nor was Hughes' personal interest confined to the top-ranking employees in the department. A routine letter reporting to the Civil Service Commission that certain charwomen in the department were doing outside work in violation of the regulations brought an explosion when it reached his desk. Tossing the letter at the chief clerk with an angry gesture, Hughes said he would not tolerate such nonsense. If these women wished to work extra hours to earn additional money for their families, he would be the last person in the world, regulation or no regulation, to get them into trouble for it. Hughes had lifted morale in the department to a level that has seldom been equaled.

The relations between the State Department and Congress had also undergone something akin to a revolution. Hughes had in large measure subdued the unruly Senate by working with it instead of throwing treaties into its teeth. Never demanding the impossible, he made the treaties he did send up so reasonable that the Senate was virtually compelled to accept them. The result was to supplant hostility by trust and amicable discussion even though many differences remained unreconciled.

Out of Hughes' experience with Congress came a suggestion to bridge the gap between the Executive and the legislature. ". . . the separateness of the executive power under our system, while it has advantages which have been deemed to be of controlling importance," he said, "deprives the Executive of the opportunities, open to parliamentary leaders, of participation in parliamentary debates. . . . The Secretary of State, acting for the President, may negotiate an important treaty, but he has no opportunity to explain or defend it upon the floor of the Senate when its provisions are under debate." [1] To overcome this handicap, he suggested that Cabinet members be given the opportunity to speak personally in either house of Congress when important departmental measures and policies are under debate. The proposal was not original with him, nor did he succeed in getting it accepted. But it gave special point to his belief that our governmental system of divided powers can be made to operate more efficiently by the simple device of executive-legislative cooperation.

The fruitfulness of Hughes' cooperative attitude is a matter of record. During his four years as Secretary of State sixty-nine treaties were negotiated, not counting a few insignificant ones that were later withdrawn. Of these, sixty-three had been approved by the Senate when Hughes left office. Of the remaining six, four were later ratified. The only two that failed in the Senate were the general relations treaty with Turkey and the Geneva convention for suppression of obscene publications. In addition, the Senate turned a cold shoulder to two protocols—one providing adherence to the World Court and the other dealing with the relations of Costa Rica to the Panama Canal.

Hughes' only conspicuous failure in dealing with the Senate, therefore, was in respect of the World Court, and both the tests on this issue came long after his resignation. The Hughes record, said the *Christian Science Monitor,* "constitutes a chapter of cooperation between the Department of State and

[1] Address to University of Michigan, June 19, 1922.

the Senate without parallel in the relations between the executive and legislative branches . . . no administration ever had so great a proportion of its foreign treaties approved by the Senate." [2]

On the basis of his own experience, Hughes concluded that there was no need for changing the constitutional requirement of a two-thirds vote in the Senate for approval of a treaty. The rejection of the Treaty of Versailles had created a powerful argument for abolition of the two-thirds rule. While recognizing the disadvantages of an arrangement which sometimes results in minority decisions and which deprives the House of Representatives of a share in the treaty-making process, Hughes was more impressed by the vast scope of the treaty power. Whatever is pertinent to our international relations, he said, is within the sweep of the power to make treaties. If the President could ratify treaties with the advice and consent of only bare majorities in the House and Senate, he might unwisely commit the nation to policies that could not be changed, as domestic legislation may be. In Hughes' mind that danger outweighed the disadvantage of having a treaty occasionally rejected by the Senate.

Whether or not one agrees with this conclusion, the success of Hughes' way with the Senate is well established. He maintained congenial relations both with the Republican and with the Democratic members of the Committee on Foreign Relations. Individual Senators frequently called on him at the department, and he was always well informed as to what the committee was thinking and doing. Borah's accession to the chairmanship on Lodge's death was unquestionably disappointing to Hughes, and when the latter resigned shortly afterward it was widely suggested that Borah's enhanced power was the cause. Hughes steadfastly denied this, and there is no reason to doubt his candor; for he succeeded in establishing satisfactory working relations with Borah. It was a matter of principle with him not to let personal feelings disrupt the public business.

Hughes' decision to leave the Cabinet was taken shortly after the election of Coolidge to a new term in November, 1924. The relations between the two men were still close and cordial, although Coolidge showed no enthusiasm over the vigorous speechmaking campaign that Hughes had made in his behalf. When the Secretary reported on his journey, half expecting a warm expression of thanks, the taciturn Yankee, whose reputation for parsimony in all things was already well established, said with a slightly embarrassed smile, "Well, I hear you've been making some good speeches." That was all! Hughes knew that the President intended it as a genuine expression of gratitude, but was none the less amused by his restraint.

The Secretary's chief reason for resigning was that he had been working at

[2] March 9, 1925.

top speed with little relaxation and no extended vacation for eight years. Now he was worn out. As he approached the end of his fourth year in office, moreover, he had a strong yearning to earn some money. For twenty years he had been almost continuously in public service. His expenses as Secretary of State, as during his governorship, had greatly exceeded his $12,000 salary. With his sixty-third birthday approaching, he felt that his primary duty was to make a satisfactory financial provision for his family's future. Mrs. Hughes too was eager for relief from her heavy social burden. Having notified Coolidge of his intention in November, the Secretary formally tendered his resignation on January 5, 1925, to take effect on March 4.

When he told his family that he had handed his letter to the President, he was in high spirits. Nevertheless, he was a little surprised by Coolidge's ready acceptance of his resignation. Laughing a bit ruefully, he said, "I feel a little as if I had been fired." Then, in a serious voice, he added: "Much as I wish to return to private life, I have so enjoyed the wonderful cooperation of those fine men in the department that if he had said to me, 'Hughes, I earnestly ask you to stay,' I don't think anything could have driven me from the job!"

The President responded to Hughes' letter as follows:

I can well appreciate that you are personally entitled, after twenty years of public service, to seek some of the satisfactions of private life. But I cannot refrain from expressing my feeling of personal loss at the prospect of your retirement, and also the loss that must inevitably ensue when one of your ability and experience goes out of an office which he is so well qualified to fill.

I realize, however, that this is in the nature of things, and so wish to put my emphasis upon the appreciation that I feel for your loyalty at all times to me, your many expressions by word and deed of a friendship upon which I could not set too high a value, and the exalted character and disinterested nature of the important public service that has come so constantly under my observation. I trust that you may have a well-merited repose and that satisfaction which alone can come from a consciousness that the duties of this life have been well performed.

At Hughes' suggestion, Frank B. Kellogg was named to succeed him. Kellogg was a conscientious and hard-working lawyer with experience in the Senate and at the Court of St. James's, and Hughes thought he was the best man available. Whatever qualifications Kellogg may have had, they suffered by comparison with Hughes'. Amid the chorus of praise for the retiring Secretary were many minor notes of regret that Kellogg was not his equal.

"It is not too much to say," declared the New York *Sun*, "that in sheer weight of mental force, backed and buttressed by sound and rugged character, Mr. Hughes stands with the foremost figures of to-day, perhaps the greatest of all." [3] The *Evening World* said that Hughes had parroted the language of the

[3] Jan. 12, 1925.

Irreconcilables and that from this phase of his career even his well-wishers would prefer to "walk backward with averted gaze and hide the shame." [4] But the *World's* was a lonely voice. Sir Willmott Lewis, Washington correspondent of the *Times* of London, referred to Hughes as "the most compelling figure among the Foreign Ministers of the post-war period" [5] and said this fact was perhaps more clearly appreciated outside the United States. The London *Observer* concluded that "In the Conferences of Washington and London, American cooperation without the League did bigger things than the League without American cooperation." [6]

"Probably not since John Quincy Adams," asserted the *Forum*, "have we had a more capable director of our foreign affairs." [7] "It is something to be said on behalf of democracy, which often blunders," said the *Outlook,* "that during this most critical period after the war this self-governing people found a way of putting such a mind to work on the specially intricate problems of foreign affairs." [8] One of the most pertinent comments came from Arthur Brisbane of the *New York American*, which had fought Hughes so bitterly when he ran against Hearst for the New York governorship: "Mr. Hughes, working for the public for twenty years, has sacrificed not less than six million dollars, plus interest, by doing so." [9]

Eminent friends of the Secretary swamped him with congratulations. Chief Justice Taft declared: "He was a great Secretary, one of the ablest we have ever had, as he was a great Judge and a great Governor." [10] At a dinner on Lincoln's birthday Arthur Balfour scribbled a note on the back of an envelope and passed it over to Senator Fess: "Charles E. Hughes is the most dominating figure I have ever met in public life." [11]

Within the department and the Foreign Service the farewells were warm with sentiment. "I doubt if you can realize how deep and genuine is our feeling of regret at your going—how much loyal attachment will follow you into private life," wrote Hugh Gibson from Berne. "Since your resignation was announced I have heard nothing but regret such as I have never heard in regard to the going of any other public man." Hugh R. Wilson was so upset that he tried to persuade the Secretary to change his mind.[12] Still more touching was a letter in which "a humble, insignificant clerk" let herself go in a personal lament over the loss of her "beloved chief":

I wanted you to know that not only I but every other woman in the Department appreciated more than I can tell you the unfailing generous courtesy with which you went out of your way to greet us when you saw us around the Depart-

4 Jan. 12, 1925.   5 March 3, 1925.   6 Jan. 25, 1925.
7 January, 1923.   8 Jan. 21, 1925.   9 Jan. 12, 1925.
10 Claude M. Fuess, *Calvin Coolidge* (Boston, Little, Brown, 1940), p. 363, note 2. Copyright, 1940, by Claude M. Fuess.
11 Original in Hughes Papers.   12 *Diplomat Between Wars*, p. 173.

By Carey Orr in the *Chicago Tribune*, January, 1925.

COMPLETED WITHOUT A BLOT

ment. It meant a great deal more to us than you have any idea of and it was quite understood that to meet you in the morning meant a happy day.[13]

The friendly sentiments that affected Hughes most deeply were expressed at a luncheon on March 3 at Rauscher's given by the staff of the State Department. Undersecretary Grew spoke for the group:

> We are at the parting of the ways with our chief, who, through four strenuous years, has held in unstinted measure our admiration and respect, our devoted loyalty, and, what is more, our deep personal affection. . . . If any greater monument to his work can be erected than the specific achievements of the last four years, it may be found in the inspiring and enduring influence he has exerted upon those around him. Because of it we shall always be better servants of the Government, better men.
> During the last four years the Department of State has attained a cohesion, an enthusiasm and an esprit de corps which has never before been equalled; a department where every man and woman works for the joy of working, and knows that his work is being directed into the right channels to constructive ends.[14]

When Mr. and Mrs. Hughes and their daughter Elizabeth left Washington on March 6, almost the entire Cabinet and diplomatic corps were at the station. Mounting the steps of a coach, Hughes held an informal farewell reception. After the last hand had been shaken and the train began to roll, he settled into a seat with the comfortable thought that his public career was over and he was now a free man for the remainder of his days.

The passing years have given Hughes additional stature as Secretary of State. He is repeatedly bracketed with the most eminent men who have held this office—Jefferson, Madison, John Quincy Adams, and Elihu Root. Sixteen years after Hughes' resignation James Grafton Rogers ranked him among "the little handful of major statesmen this country has produced." [15] The final conclusion of Charles Cheney Hyde is that "We have to go back for more than a century to find his equal in that office." [16] Sumner Welles' estimate likewise verges on the superlative:

> In his sheer intellectual supremacy, in his enlightened recognition of this country's permanent interests, and in his constructive patriotism, Charles Evans Hughes towers above all but a few of the truly great Americans of the past century.[17]

Greatness consists of many facets, but it is possible in Secretary Hughes' case to single out a few of special significance. First, there was seldom any doubt about where he stood. Muddling through was contrary to his nature. If Hughes did not know what our policy should be in any given instance, he

---

[13] Louise E. Lacey to CEH, March 4, 1925.   [14] *New York Times,* March 4, 1925.
[15] *American Bar Association Journal,* July, 1941, p. 412.
[16] Prof. Hyde to author, July 15, 1947.   [17] *Washington Post,* Sept. 7, 1948.

By "J. N. Ding" in the New York *Herald Tribune*, 1925.

NO WONDER HUGHES RESIGNED

probed into the facts until he had the answer. His subordinates were never left to flounder in confusion. Second, he thought in global terms. Before launching a policy in Latin America, the Near East, or Europe he sagely anticipated its repercussions in other parts of the world. Never did he play off the prejudices or hostilities of one area against those of another. His aim was nothing short of the welfare of the world, and all his major policies, from the limitation of arms to European economic recovery and the liquidation of imperialism in Latin America, point in that direction.

Third, he built no dream castles but worked with the men, the facts, and the ethos of his time, without losing sight of his long-range objectives. No one understood better than he that statesmanship is the art of the possible. Working against a tide of disillusionment and isolationism that he could not stem, he nevertheless reasserted world leadership in those areas of policy-making in which passion had not subverted reason. His stern refusal to abandon international cooperation because perfection could not be attained kept hope alight and eased the approach to collective security when a new opportunity arose out of World War II.

Fourth, his policies had a moral quality about them that overreached national interests in the narrow meaning of that term. Diplomacy with him was not a game or a matching of wits for the advancement of one country at the expense of others. Rather, it was the direction of international relations in accord with sound principles. "Our greatest interest," he once said, "is international friendship. National prestige may be associated with power, but it is never heightened by a brutal assertion of it. Indeed, our national prestige is inseparably connected with the demonstration of our sense of justice." [18]

Hughes' passion for justice was no less in evidence in his foreign policy than in his work on the supreme bench. He held steadily before him, as Sir Willmott Lewis pointed out, "the concept of the State as the embodiment of justice rather than force, with its corollary of the reliance on justice rather than force for the vindication of national policy." [19] There was no place for imperialism, "dollar diplomacy," or power politics in this concept. "The principle, each nation for itself to the full extent of its power," he once said, "is the principle of war, not of peace." [20] If a nation is truly devoted to peace, it must first substitute justice for force in its own dealings with its neighbors.

Here is the core of Hughes' policy. He had the courage to dethrone "My country right or wrong" and to deny sponsorship to every American cause that he believed to be unjust. That high moral attitude fused into working principles, without any taint of self-righteousness, lifts Hughes into the select company of our best and wisest molders of foreign policy.

[18] Speech of Nov. 10, 1925.   [19] *Times* (London), March 3, 1925.
[20] *The Pathway of Peace*, p. 15.

Chapter 60

PRIVATE CITIZEN AGAIN

REST WAS the first item in Hughes' plan for his new era of freedom. With his wife and Elizabeth, he spent the spring of 1925 in Bermuda and then shifted to Lake George for the summer. Under this unusual pampering his reserve of strength was fully restored, and a thorough medical examination showed him to be in fine fettle.

The mood in which they returned to housekeeping in New York is suggested by a rhyme that he dashed off for Mrs. Hughes' birthday on September 14:

> We're two old birds at best,
> Building another nest,
> It's up a tall tree
> And between you and me
> Our Avenue beats all the rest.
>
> But why speak of age
> When we're only more sage!
> Is not wisdom the crown of life?
> My darling in truth
> Has perpetual youth,
> Richest blessings upon my dear wife!
>
> The years gliding by
> Only strength the tie
> That binds our hearts together.
> Our love, strong and true,
> Will pull us both through;
> We're ready for any weather.

His first resumption of activity was not money-making but speechmaking. No longer bound by official restraints, he poured out a Niagara of ideas. His audiences were the American Society of International Law, many bar associations, chambers of commerce, patriotic, literary, scientific and political gatherings, and colleges. The public servant who had retired to a life of peace and freedom soon found himself getting up at 5:00 A.M. to write speeches for which he consistently refused compensation.

The public loved it. Frederic William Wile suggested that America ought to elect Hughes toastmaster for life. "In language, power of expression and that ebullition that must mark the ideal toastmaster," Wile declared, "Hughes is

incomparable. He scintillates mainly because he likes to do that sort of thing.
. . . It comes naturally. He can lapse from the sublime to the ridiculous without a strain. He can tell stories as well as Choate ever told them and in the
next breath stir hearers to emotional enthusiasm with some appeal to their
moral or spiritual sense." [1] Apparently these traits had something to do with
the characterization of Hughes by a legal journal, *The Jealous Mistress*, as "a
cross between Jehovah and Bernard Shaw . . . a cousin to Mark Twain and
a brother of Santa Claus." [2]

It is in his speeches and civic activities that we find the best index to
Hughes' thinking during this period. He was soon to be assailed as a tool of
wealth blind to the interests of a democratic people. But the work he was doing
outside of his profession reflects a keen interest in the free society of which
he was a part and a sympathetic understanding of its problems. While he was
representing many big corporations at the bar, those associations cast no
shadow upon the strong current of liberalism that ran through the activities
he pursued for the love of it.

Addressing the American Bar Association as its president at Detroit on
September 2, he assailed the reactionary thinking that had caused Nebraska to
forbid the teaching of the German language and Tennessee to suppress the
doctrine of evolution:

> The most ominous sign of our time, as it seems to me, is the indication of the
> growth of an intolerant spirit. It is the more dangerous when armed, as it usually
> is, with sincere conviction. . . . We justly prize our safeguards against abuses
> but they will not last long if tolerance gets under way . . . the just demands of
> liberty are not to be satisfied even by a free and uncorrupted right of suffrage.
> Democracy has its own capacity for tyranny. Some of the most menacing en
> croachments upon liberty invoke the democratic principle and assert the right of
> the majority to rule . . . freedom is in danger of being slain at her own altars if
> the passion for uniformity and control of opinion gathers head. . . .
> I do not propose to discuss evolution, or a particular statute and litigation
> recently much advertised [the Scopes trial in Tennessee]. . . . I desire in a non
> controversial spirit to emphasize the vast importance of the freedom of learning in
> the hope that our people instinct with the spirit of liberty will not lay hands
> on our public schools and state universities to set obstacles in the path of knowl
> edge. . . . If we sum up the comforts, the conveniences, the privileges and the
> opportunities of our life in the twentieth century . . . we must realize that these
> benefits are due, not so much to governments, or politics, or the strivings and issues
> of campaigns, but to the ceaseless and unobtrusive endeavors, and the unquench
> able zeal, of the pioneers and their devoted followers in the quest of knowledge,
> who in the study of the earth and the universe have enlarged the inheritance of
> the race and vindicated the capacity and worth of the human spirit . . . freedom
> of learning is the vital breath of democracy and progress.

[1] *Evening Star* (Washington), April 27, 1925.   [2] October, 1925.

The speech as a whole was an inspiring appeal that the law be made "the servant of liberty wisely conceived" and "the expression of the righteousness which exalteth a nation." The assembled lawyers could scarcely contain their admiration. Columnist Walter Lippmann wrote: "It seems to me about the most useful speech that anybody has undertaken to make in America for a long time." [3]

Hughes' interest in education was closely related to his political philosophy. "The cure for the ills of democracy," he said, "is not more democracy, but more intelligence." [4] Nor were his efforts in behalf of freedom of learning confined to occasional exhortations. As a trustee of the University of Chicago, he joined with President Harry Pratt Judson and others in altering a provision in the charter requiring that two-thirds of the trustees and the president of the university be members of regular Baptist churches. During most of the thirty-eight years that he was a Fellow of Brown University he also worked for liberalization of its charter.

Hughes had been a member of the committee of nine selected in 1908 to reexamine Brown's charter of 1764 giving the Baptists substantial majorities among the trustees and fellows and requiring the president to be a Baptist. The committee had brought in powerful arguments for removal of all the denominational provisions from the charter. Conservative alumni had whipped up a storm of protest. One member of the board had argued with deep feeling that if Catholics were admitted to the councils of the university it would be a betrayal of the founders. Hughes had replied in friendly tone but with withering effect. One eyewitness reports that "his logic fell with the driving power of a sledge-hammer, relentless, crushing, pulverizing." [5]

So bitter was the opposition, however, that the committee had advised postponement of action. It was not until 1926 that the presidency of Brown was freed from the denominational requirement and broader representation was given to non-Baptists on the board of trustees. Hughes was a consultant to the committee which sponsored this compromise and helped to shape the bill which the General Assembly of Rhode Island finally passed. In 1940 President Henry M. Wriston of Brown revived the issue, and after a conference with Chief Justice Hughes, it was decided that the time had come for full achievement of the aims of the original committee. This time Brown's charter was completely stripped of all denominational requirements.

Hughes' hatred of bigotry led him to join with Newton D. Baker and S. Parkes Cadman in founding the National Conference of Christians and Jews. The conference was an outgrowth of a dinner sponsored by the Committee on Good Will between Jews and Christians on February 23, 1926. As

[3] Lippmann to CEH, Aug. 27, 1925, after examining advance copy.
[4] Speech in Faneuil Hall, Boston, June 17, 1925.
[5] Everett Colby in *Scribner's*, May, 1928, p. 560.

toastmaster and principal speaker, Hughes made a powerful plea for tolerance, freedom of learning, religious liberty, and interracial cooperation.[6]

The following year he sent out a letter which raised $25,000, and this served to launch the conference as a going concern. Adopting the broad aims that he had suggested—elimination of intergroup prejudices and promotion of justice, amity, understanding, and cooperation among Protestants, Catholics, and Jews —the conference soon became national in scope. In 1940 it presented a citation to Chief Justice Hughes for his work in bridging the gulfs between racial and religious groups. Responding, he pleaded for a "deep and abiding sense of human dignity and worth" and said that rancor and bigotry "are deadly enemies of true democracy, more dangerous than any external force because they undermine the very foundations of democratic effort."

In 1947 Hughes sponsored the application of the International Council of Christians and Jews for affiliation with the United Nations Educational, Scientific and Cultural Organization. Tolerance with him was not a policy but a deep-seated trait. His son's activity as chairman of the Mayor's Committee on Unity in New York from 1944 to 1948 and the extensive work of his daughter (Mrs. Waddell) in behalf of the United Negro College Fund enlisted his keenest interest and sympathy.

Meeting with other bar association presidents in New York, Hughes joined in urging the appointment of a joint committee to investigate ambulance chasing and other shady legal practices. When lawyers make the machinery of justice a device to snare the unfortunate, he declared, "the outraged sentiment of the entire Bar should find expression in investigation, condemnation and redress. It should clean house. . . . Our trouble is not simply in keeping the pestilence out of the temple, but in destroying it inside." [7] "We are ministers of justice," he said in another speech to the bar, "and no lawyer is worthy of any reputation in the profession, whatever his ability may be, if he does not regard himself first and last as a minister of justice in the community in which he practices." [8]

Several books by Charles E. Hughes came off the press in this period. *The Pathway of Peace* contains more than a score of his speeches while he was Secretary of State. In May, 1928, he delivered a series of lectures at Princeton University on "Our Relations to the Nations of the Western Hemisphere," and these were published in book form. His Sherrill Foundation lectures at Yale on "Pan American Peace Plans" in March, 1929, were also published.

The most important of these volumes is *The Supreme Court of the United States,* containing six lectures delivered at Columbia University in January and February, 1927. Hughes devoted many of his supposedly leisure hours to

[6] *New York Times,* Feb. 24, 1926.   [7] To Bronx bar, Jan. 25, 1929.
[8] *American Bar Association Journal,* May, 1926, pp. 323–326.

gathering and arranging his data. Addressing laymen as well as lawyers, he produced one of the few first-class books that have been written about the Supreme Court. While it is in no sense an "inside story" and H. L. Mencken complained that it ignored some of the court's "most gorgeous feats of nonsense," the book is infused with a fine understanding of the court and its constitutional function. Professor Felix Frankfurter of the Harvard Law School, later to be Hughes' colleague on the bench, called it "the most compact story of the foundations of the Court and an excellent description of the Court at work." [9] The stipend for the lectures went back to Columbia, along with all the profits from the book, which was in its fourth printing in 1947. A similar course was followed in regard to the Princeton lectures.

"Success in the democratic experiment," Hughes said in one of his speeches, "lies in the extent to which the strong are harnessed, with bit and reins and blinders, and are induced to pull the democratic cart on a straight road without running away or upsetting it." Taking him at his word, numerous professional and civic groups "hitched" him to their causes as soon as he was out of official harness. In addition to being president of the American Bar Association, the Legal Aid Society, and the American Society of International Law, he was named vice president of the Pilgrims' Society, later president of the Association of the Bar of the City of New York, and president of the American Judicature Society. He became a member of a committee to finance a memorial to Woodrow Wilson, his political opponent of 1916, and chairman of a New York group seeking to raise a million-dollar endowment fund to promote the study of American history. He accepted the chairmanship of the American Committee of the World Conference on Faith and Order, the vice presidency of the National Municipal League, a place on the National Advisory Committee for the Institute of Law at Johns Hopkins University, and the chairmanship of the committee sponsoring the Byrd expedition to the Antarctic. He was elected vice president of the Brown chapter of Phi Beta Kappa and was awarded the Rosenberger medal at Brown. The Roosevelt Memorial Association medal was also added to his collection in 1928.

"Now, once more with us," said the New York *Sun*, "we have Hughes the great lawyer and Hughes the citizen, whose untiring hands go out to every public task."

Yielding to pressure from both political parties, Hughes accepted the chairmanship of a commission to effect a reorganization of the government of New York State. As we have seen, his first efforts to give New York a modern administrative system had been made while he was governor. His campaign had been carried on by others after he left Albany, and in 1925 they had secured the adoption of a constitutional amendment. The Republican leaders

[9] *American Bar Association Journal*, April, 1930, p. 251.

of the legislature then set up an unofficial commission to work out an organizational pattern in keeping with this mandate from the people.

Former Speaker H. Edmund Machold had been informally selected to head the commission, but the choice aroused fear that the Republicans might give the reorganization a political twist. John W. Davis, who had been the Democratic presidential candidate in 1924, suggested that Hughes be drafted for the chairmanship. Hughes reluctantly consented, and, being nominated by Machold himself, was unanimously elected. His first act as chairman was to assure the people that the reorganization plan would be shaped to their interest "with no partisan taint about it whatever." [10]

Hughes had an able commission, with John Lord O'Brian as vice chairman and men like Henry L. Stimson, John W. Davis, Henry W. Taft, James W. Wadsworth, Nicholas Murray Butler, and Robert F. Wagner among the members. Subcommittees were named to bring in detailed plans and suggestions in various different spheres of governmental activity. On the basis of reports from these groups the executive committee of which Hughes was chairman shaped its conclusions. Forgetting his initial reservations, Hughes almost wore out his committee with long intensive sessions. Once the members rebelled when he tried to keep them in continuous session without any lunch. His seeming insensibility to the pangs of hunger when there was serious work to be done was one failing that his associates never quite forgave.

Thanks largely to Hughes' driving energy, the report was completed in late February, 1926, and won a remarkably favorable response. Nearly 180 departments, commissions, and bureaus were consolidated into eighteen administrative departments under control of the governor. The Water Power Commission and various other floating ribs were marked for abolition with transfer of their powers to the regular departments. The reformers also recommended creation of a full-fledged executive budget, a four-year term and more extensive removal power for the governor, and better salaries for the governor and department heads. The central idea behind the plan was to increase the powers of the governor for efficient management of the state's affairs. In this respect the Hughes Commission did for New York State what the Hoover Commission was to do for the Federal Government more than two decades later.

Governor "Al" Smith thought the report was a "wonderful piece of work" [11] and gave it his enthusiastic support. Not a word reflecting a partisan motive had entered into the candid discussions. So great was the prestige of the commission that the legislature hastened to accept not only the organizational pattern but also the recommended changes in the law. Many contributed to this happy outcome, but it was the deft hand of former Governor Hughes that turned a hopeful experiment into a glowing success.

[10] *New York Times*, Nov. 20, 1925.   [11] Smith's address of Dec. 17, 1926.

Hughes also maintained a lively interest in national affairs. On his trips to Washington to argue before the Supreme Court, he was frequently invited to the White House, and Coolidge talked volubly and frankly about problems confronting his Administration. Sometimes the calm little Yankee would talk for an hour or more, almost without stopping, trying out on Hughes ideas and policies that were taking shape in his mind. Hughes replied with equal candor.

The President importuned Hughes to lead the American delegation to the Conference on Naval Limitation at Geneva in 1927. Hughes replied that his duties as special master in the Great Lakes case made acceptance of such an assignment impossible. Although he was still intensely interested in abolishing provocative armament, it is quite probable too that he foresaw the failure of this 1927 venture. He was never inclined to beat his head against a stone wall when the possibility of accomplishment was nil. However, he did accept appointment as an American member of the Hague Court of Arbitration to succeed Judge Gray—the only position he ever held involving so much dignity along with so little work. It was in this period also that he headed the American delegation to the Havana Conference and was a delegate to the Pan American Conference on Conciliation and Arbitration.

Hughes' boundless activity led many to suppose that he was out to capture the Presidency in 1928. When he was a guest at the Gridiron dinner in December, 1926, the funmakers of the press tried to tease him into an admission by singing a ditty with this refrain:

> You're as welcome as the flowers in May.
> Do you think you will come back to stay?
> For the White House has not moved away—
> Do you think that you'll come back some day?

"It is very pleasant to be sung to!" Hughes responded in the best of humor. "But the political flowers that bloom in the Spring and wither in the Fall have nothing any longer, thank heaven, to do with the case. I am glad to be here as an equal in the full enjoyment of my constitutional rights as a private citizen,— in this place dedicated to the freedom of the press. It was not ever thus! I have been here as a burnt offering, but now I am clad in the comfortable asbestos of private life. . . .

"Chief Justice Taft once said that a constitutional lawyer was one who had abandoned the practice of the law and had gone into politics. Well, for anyone who has left his profession to go into politics, the happiest road is the way back. I am with you no longer as a servant but as one of the millions of masters in this fortunate land where the Government is so organized that everyone has a chance to talk but can do as little harm as possible."

One group of Hughes enthusiasts suggested that he run for the Senate by unseating Senator James W. Wadsworth in the New York primaries. Instead, Hughes threw his support to Wadsworth. On May 21 the Republican State Committee talked of drafting Hughes to run against "Al" Smith for the governorship, but he issued a statement saying that even if nominated he would refuse to run. Plans were then laid to make him temporary chairman and keynote speaker at the state convention, but Hughes sailed for Europe on June 16, announcing that he would not be back for the convention.

At last Hughes was back to his exhilarating routine of earlier years—renewing his strength and recharging his batteries by European travel. Taking Mrs. Hughes, Elizabeth, and her friend Polly Hoopes, he toured Italy, Switzerland, France, England, and Scotland as if he were once more an adventurous youth discovering new lands. All worries were cast to the winds. They climbed Mount Vesuvius and looked down into the crater. Traveling by motor, they reveled in the Italian countryside and little villages and then sought variety in the art galleries and cathedrals of the cities.

In Rome the veteran tourist and his party spent two weeks seeing the sights. Vice Consul David Bruce hired the best known local guide to show the party around, but it was Hughes who read the Latin inscriptions and did most of the talking about the monuments and shrines and the history connected with them. Although it was his first visit to Rome, he displayed such an astonishing knowledge of Roman history that the guide refused to take any pay for his services, saying that he had profited from the tour more than Hughes could have done.[12] Hughes called on Mussolini and had an informal chat with Pope Pius XI. Everywhere he was recognized. Relaxed and in a holiday mood, he was an easy mark for autograph hunters. When a laughing group of girls cornered him and then filed by in a line to get his autograph, he probably enjoyed it as much as they did.

Leaving Mrs. Hughes at Ábano-Terme for some treatments at the springs, Hughes took Elizabeth and Miss Hoopes to Venice. The fairy city of canals and palaces, throned on her hundred isles, was one of his first loves, and now its beauty stirred fond memories as well as new emotions. Whether they were feeding the pigeons at St. Mark's or gliding through the moonlight in a gondola, as opera stars in adjacent boats filled the night air with music, every moment was a joy. Hughes' happiness bubbled out in the form of reminiscences, jokes, and fascinating talk about the people and their customs.

Switzerland was always heavenly—the food, the wine, and the quiet serenity of the mountains. Reinvigorated by a motor tour through the Alpine haunts they loved so well, the Hugheses turned to Paris and London. Another motor tour took them through the English lake country into Scotland and then

---

12 David Bruce to author, Jan. 26, 1950.

down to the cathedral towns. They sailed for home on the *Leviathan* near the end of September more than ever delighted with the new-found freedom of private life.

On the return voyage Hughes blossomed out in an utterly new role so far as the public was concerned. He teamed up with Will Rogers, the Oklahoma cowboy-humorist, as an entertainer. In response to the President's appeal for funds to aid the victims of the Florida hurricane disaster, the captain of the *Leviathan* called a meeting of its distinguished passengers, and Hughes seconded Rogers' suggestion that the entertainers on board be organized into a troupe to raise money for the cause. Rogers was made chairman. Apparently the rope-twirling humorist was chary at first about adding Hughes to his troupe; the two had not previously met, and Rogers regarded Hughes as "a pretty cold blooded proposition" who might freeze a joke in its tracks. But, "calcalatin'" that somebody would be needed to make a serious appeal for funds, Rogers satirically billed Hughes for "Wisecracks" and himself for "Diplomatic Immunity."

"Well," Hughes responded, "I have been called everything else in my career but an entertainer, but I will do my best."

Rogers tells what happened:

We gave the concert and he was supposed to be the serious end of our program and then I was supposed to come along and blackjack them out of what they had. Well he got out there and he was making such humorous remarks and such entertaining observations that he almost forgot to mention what the appeal was to be for, but then he switched on them and all I had to do when I went on was to have a bushel basket to put the checks in.[13]

Rogers began his performance with the air of one whose thunder had been stolen. "Say," he exclaimed, "we asked this old guy up here to be serious!"

The show was repeated on the two following nights for the second-class and third-class passengers, with Hughes racking his brain for new jokes and Rogers complaining that Hughes had outclassed him. All told, the troupers collected $42,000. "It broke all records for any collection at sea," Rogers recounted, "and it was mainly due to the hearty cooperation of Mr. Hughes. Say, if he had been running for President then he would have carried that boat, Democrats and all . . . if ever a man was misunderstood in regard to being a real genuine good fellow it's this Mr. Hughes." It was the beginning of a fast but never intimate friendship between the judge and the comedian.

Back in New York, Hughes campaigned unsuccessfully for Wadsworth and for Ogden L. Mills, who had been nominated as the Republican candidate for governor. Talk of Hughes as a presidential nominee persisted through the early

[13] Rogers' column in *Atlanta Journal,* Oct. 17, 1926.

months of 1927 as the popularity of Coolidge waned. On May 20, Hughes issued a statement designed to set all speculation at rest:

There should be no doubt as to my own attitude. I am for President Coolidge, first, last, and all the time, and I believe that he will be renominated and reelected. I do not wish my name to be used in any contingency. I am too old to run for President and I would neither seek nor accept the nomination.

The speculation flared up again, however, as soon as Coolidge's cryptic "I do not choose to run for President in 1928" came sizzling over the wires from the Black Hills. Hughes was again spending the summer in Europe with his wife and Elizabeth, without a political thought in his head. After a restful trip through France, including the Pyrenees and the Riviera, he returned in September and found that Secretary Hoover was making an active bid for the nomination. Several Hoover supporters called on Hughes and let him know that if he intended to go out for the nomination he would have a fight on his hands. Hughes assured them that he was not in any sense a contender.

Charles D. Hilles, Republican National Committeeman for New York, sounded out the party leaders and announced on December 1, 1927, that the New York delegation would go to the convention prepared to back Hughes. A few days later that unwilling favorite son said once more that he would not accept the nomination. While he was strong and vigorous at sixty-five, he would be nearly seventy-one at the end of the term. That age would be a bar to renomination, he said, and a President needs more than four years to carry out his program.

"Besides," Hughes added, "I don't want the turmoil of being a presidential candidate. I had that turmoil once, and I don't want it again." [14]

Hughes declined, late in March, 1928, to make the keynote address at the Republican Convention. As in 1920, he refused to compromise his position by making a speech that might seem to encourage a nomination he did not want. When the delegates assembled at Kansas City, powerful elements in the party were still trying to stop Hoover. Mellon, Hilles, Senator Butler, and Chief Justice Taft had all gone to the White House hoping for some hint that the President was willing to be drafted.[15] Coolidge was willing, but he remained quiet because he knew that there was no popular demand for his renomination. In a last desperate effort to save the party from Hoover, Thomas W. Lamont of J. P. Morgan & Company went to Hughes' office. An important group at the convention was eager to see Hughes nominated and elected, he said. All that was necessary was for Hughes to give his consent, and this group would throw its full strength behind his candidacy.

[14] Richard V. Oulahan in *New York Times Magazine*, Sept. 9, 1928, p. 19.
[15] William Allen White, *A Puritan in Babylon*, p. 400.

"Do you think I could accept a nomination coming in that way?" Hughes asked, with resentment and courtesy vying for control of his voice. Before Lamont left, Hughes had squelched the last vestige of hope that he could be drafted by Wall Street.

After Hoover was nominated, Hughes gave him assurance of his support and then sailed, with his family and a companion for Elizabeth, for another summer of freedom in Europe. In Berlin he visited President von Hindenburg, took his family for an airplane ride over the city, and laughed at his daughter because she was frightened. Motoring to Dresden and Prague, they visited Tomáš G. Masaryk, the tall and courtly President of Czechoslovakia, in his old castle. After a conference with Chancellor Seipel in Vienna, they turned again to Switzerland. Always the Alps had to be included. At Saint-Moritz they celebrated Elizabeth's twenty-first birthday, and her father indulged his custom of writing a birthday rhyme, which reflects his gay mood:

> Elizabeth—! 'tis of thee
> Sweet age of liberty—
> Of thee I sing—
> Age of our daughter's pride
> Parents at last subside
> From each St. Moritz side
> Let freedom ring!

Before Hughes returned about the middle of September, he had been made honorary chairman of a lawyers' committee to aid Hoover. Eager to get Hughes back to Washington, the Hoover forces made another vain effort to induce him to run for the Senate. However, his high esteem for Hoover and his lifelong habit of resting his confidence in the Republican Party did impel him into the thick of the campaign in spite of his affection for "Al" Smith, the Democratic nominee.

In his first speech at St. Joseph, Missouri, on October 23, he drew a balance sheet of the two candidates' qualifications and found Hoover to be best fitted for the Presidency. At Chicago he assailed Smith's criticism of Coolidge's economy record. At Buffalo he gave new emphasis to Hoover's charge of "state socialism" against some of the Democratic proposals. At Worcester he lauded Hoover's record. In Brooklyn he took up the tariff, water power, and prohibition. So impressed were Hoover and his managers with the power of Hughes' speeches that they induced him to close the campaign—a privilege usually reserved for the candidate himself—with a radio broadcast from his New York apartment at 11:30 P.M. the night before the election.

Before listening to this speech, Hoover wired: "The effect your speeches has been the most profound of any campaign in our history. I hear them from [e]very town and village across the continent." His sense of obligation to his former colleague was further enhanced by the Republican landslide on November 6.

The greatest honor that was paid Hughes in these busy years was the unremitting demand for his services on the stump, in governmental tasks, at the bar, in the civic forum, in the universities, and around the festive board. When the Bronx County Bar Association met to honor Hughes on January 25, 1929, because he was soon to enter upon a new phase of his career, William D. Guthrie compressed a popular appraisal of the man into three words: "the perfect citizen."

Chapter 61

LEADER OF THE BAR

WHEN HE was not traveling in Europe, making speeches, or slaving over some public-service assignment, Hughes intensively practiced law. Rejoining his old firm, Hughes, Rounds, Schurman & Dwight, he had everything to his own liking, including his complete independence at the bar. The Hughes name itself was sufficient guarantee that his practice would be large, varied, and lucrative. There was also, as he wrote in his Notes, "the privilege of once more enjoying an intimate professional relation with my son."

A thousand friends swarmed into the huge ballroom of the Hotel Astor on November 10, 1925, to welcome Hughes back to the bar and signalize his service to the cause of international good will. It was a gay dinner, with all the sparkle, wit, and good fellowship that the great men of the law could give it. Irving T. Bush, the toastmaster, read congratulatory messages from President Coolidge, Chief Justice Taft, and Secretary Hoover. The chief address by Root was one of the finest tributes that one eminent American has ever paid to another.

"I think we are not so much here to do honor to Mr. Hughes," Root said, "as to thank him for having done honor to us. (*Applause.*)

"Mr. Hughes is a lawyer. I claim him for the Bar. If there be unworthy lawyers—and there are some—range them all together upon one side of the account and I will put Mr. Hughes on the other side of the account and thank you to pay me the balance in my favor. (*Applause.*)

". . . it is not merely what Mr. Hughes has done that has shed honor upon all, upon all of his countrymen. It is what he has stood for. He never sought an office; he never administered an office with a view to keeping it longer, or with a view to getting another. (*Applause.*) He never attempted to build up a personal political machine for his own aggrandizement. He never abandoned or suppressed an opinion which he thought ought to be expressed, in order to please anybody. He never hated or abused or imputed sinister motives to an adversary who differed from him. . . . He always thought about his job and never about himself. He subdued his idealism to the uses of mankind. He never sought popularity by glittering generalities or noble sentiments, rhetorical or otherwise. He sought always the best possible means for weak and prejudiced and quarreling mankind, in order that a step might be taken towards the probability

631

for betterment in the future. He never allowed the expediency of the moment to drive him off the bed-rock of sound principles of government and of international intercourse, in which he believed and which he openly and fearlessly and cogently declared and expounded.''

"If this is the happiest moment of my life," Hughes responded, "it is also the most embarrassing. Words are useless . . . to requite such kindness and generosity, and what would be more becoming than 'a great, sweet silence'? But that is denied me. You have sent me forth to the doubtful combats of public life. Sometimes I have returned with my shield, and at least once I returned upon it (*Laughter*), but I have always come back. While it is a privilege to hold public office, it is the life beyond the political grave that is the best. In one respect the servant of the people is like the Apostle—he 'dies daily.' And his paradise of the blest, to which his hope fondly clings, is the old home with the kindred spirits who have not been estranged or deluded by the temporary official accouterment. It is their welcome and confidence that he prizes most.''

The zest with which Hughes went back to the bar was thus matched by generous recognition on the part of his fellow practitioners. His first big case in this period was a suit involving about $18,000,000 brought in behalf of the receiver of the New York & Cuba Mail Steamship Company. A few weeks later the New York Attorney General retained him as a special deputy to protect the state's power rights in its boundary streams against encroachments by the Federal Government. In May he offered to help the United Mine Workers fight an injunction in West Virginia. Other big cases that were dropped into his lap involved land suits against New York City, alien property, railroad rates, taxes on "short sales" of stock, and the antitrust laws.

The comparative freedom of private practice was very satisfying after long years in public service. As Hughes sat in the Supreme Court waiting to argue his first case before that tribunal since his State Department days, John W. Davis asked if he was not a little envious of his former brethren on the bench.

"No," Hughes flashed back. "Can't you hear the clanking of their chains?" [1]

Taking only about half the cases that were brought to him, Hughes had an excellent opportunity of picking and choosing his clients. Any case that might involve a departure from his professional standards he rejected as a matter of course. "A capable lawyer," he once said, "has in his own office scales of truth which he uses before he resorts to the public weighing station." Furthermore, he declined to capitalize his special knowledge of American foreign affairs. While he was still in Bermuda in 1925, his son wrote to him that two oil magnates were eager to see him about proposals by the Russians to supply them with oil. "I think I should keep clear of matters . . . with which I dealt officially," Hughes replied. This became his invariable rule. Foreign interests

[1] Author's interview with Mr. Davis, Nov. 4, 1949.

THE DIFFERENCE BETWEEN WORKING FOR THE U.S.A.
AT $12,000 A YEAR

AND BEING YOUR OWN BOSS WHERE SOUND LEGAL JUDGMENT
IS APPRECIATED AND RESPECTED

By "J. N. Ding" in the New York *Herald Tribune*, 1925.

seeking his aid against the United States were turned down whether or not he had had anything to do with the matters in controversy as Secretary of State. His special knowledge of our foreign relations might unconsciously redound to the advantage of a foreign client in cases of this sort; such knowledge he would not sell for legal fees.

He was equally conscientious in not taking advantage of his former membership on the Supreme Court. Never would he permit lawyers to put his name on a brief (if he had no other connection with the case) on the assumption that it might carry weight with his former brethren on the bench. Nor would he pit Hughes the lawyer against Hughes the judge. If a case required arguments at variance with legal principles he had enunciated as Associate Justice, he declined to take it. This self-imposed rule did not, however, prevent him from arguing a case if he saw an honest distinction between the principle he had laid down for the court and the new point at issue.

The first question Hughes asked himself about a case submitted to his scrutiny was: Should it be argued? If he thought there was a valid argument to be made in behalf of a client, he never refused to take the case because that argument might be difficult or might arouse public criticism. It was evident that his assault upon the five-cent fare in New York on behalf of the Interborough Rapid Transit Company would bring the wrath of city officials and subway riders upon his head. But he was convinced that the company's demands for a seven-cent fare were just and reasonable and that the city's policy of pouring tax funds into the transit system was depriving the people of needed schools, hospitals, and other municipal improvements.

Arguing the case before the Supreme Court in Washington, in the presence of Mayor "Jimmy" Walker, political beneficiary of the nickel subway ride, Hughes contended that a more compensatory fare was required by the law and that it would benefit the city. "The policy which the city now asserts," he said, "will only impoverish its taxpayers, and yet the city and Transit Commission sit here opposing and blocking the company in its efforts to get fair compensation under a policy which would relieve the taxpayers of a burden." [2] Hughes lost the case on technicalities, and the city continued to pour vast subsidies into its subway systems to keep them operating on the five-cent fare, until Mayor O'Dwyer finally denounced that policy in 1948 as a means of "playing politics with the health of the people."

We can get some idea as to Hughes' fidelity to his clients and at the same time his high ethical standards by following him to Washington on one of his frequent trips to argue a case before the Supreme Court. In the "short-sales" tax case he was retained by William F. Unger, New York attorney, to make the argument. As they traveled to Washington together, Unger said, "I know

[2] *New York Times*, Jan. 16, 1929.

that you have many friends in Washington and I don't want you to feel obligated to take all your meals with me."

"I have only one purpose in making the trip," Hughes replied, "and that is to win this case. I do not intend to accept any social invitations but to spend my time discussing the case with you." [3]

During the next two days they took their meals together and walked together from the Mayflower Hotel to the Supreme Court, a distance of about three miles. For the greater part of this time Hughes insisted on talking about the case. He urged Unger to ask him questions in order to test his knowledge of the facts and the law. His former brethren on the bench would probably take great delight, he said, in trying to trip him up—a fear that proved to be unwarranted. Each morning he went early to the Supreme Court to read the authorities cited in Unger's brief. Hughes carried his absorption in the case so far that Unger was relieved when the ordeal was over.

The case was not reached for argument in the first session that Hughes and Unger attended. After the court adjourned they walked together down the corridor at the moment the Justices began to file across the hall from the old court chamber to the robing room. Chief Justice Taft, jolly and ponderous, espied Hughes, rushed over, and clapped him on the shoulder in his most jovial manner.

"Hughes, my boy, I am delighted to see you."

"Mr. Chief Justice," Hughes replied, politely but coolly extending his hand, "I am honored to see you."

Looking deflated, Taft proceeded with the other Justices to the robing room. Unger, unable to conceal his astonishment, asked Hughes why he had greeted the Chief Justice so coldly.

"I did it intentionally," Hughes replied, "as I intend to win my cases on their merits and not through friendship with the judges." [4]

On proper occasions Hughes could greet an old friend on the bench with both warmth and admiration, as indicated by the feeling that infused the notes passing between himself and Holmes. Taft too was an old and esteemed friend, but his effusiveness in greeting a lawyer about to argue before him embarrassed Hughes before other members of the court. Having been a judge himself, Hughes had only contempt for fawning, unctuous lawyers, and he would not permit even a suspicion to arise that he was practicing their art.

In the spring of 1927, owing to the pressure from his lectures on the Supreme Court, the hearings in the Great Lakes case, and his extensive practice, Hughes almost suffered a breakdown. "I argued my cases with difficulty," he later disclosed, "and one day, walking to my hotel from the Supreme Court I suddenly felt as though a curtain had fallen over my left eye. I went at once

[3] William F. Unger to author, May 20, 1949.   [4] Id.

to an oculist and found that this was caused by the breaking of a small blood vessel. Fortunately no serious harm was done, but I was strongly advised to slow up my pace. I followed this advice so far as possible and soon regained my usual vigor." [5]

Big corporations and wealthy clients beat a trail to Hughes' door because he was the best known and certainly one of the ablest lawyers in the country. In behalf of the meat-packing industry, he challenged the validity of a consent decree of 1920, which had enjoined the "Big Five" interests from handling foodstuffs other than meat. In 1928 he argued the WYG case against the Federal Radio Commission before the United States Court of Appeals for the District of Columbia, contending that the General Electric Company had acquired a vested interest in the transmission channel it had been using. We shall hear more of this case later.

In the Duke-Haskell case Hughes' task was to save his client, the estate of the late tobacco manufacturer, James R. Duke, from the payment of damages amounting to $24,000,000. Haskell had sued under the antitrust laws, alleging that he had had a contract with Duke for the exploitation of bauxite deposits in Quebec and that he had been "frozen out" by a conspiracy between Duke and the Aluminum Company of America. A jury in the Federal district court had awarded Haskell $8,000,000, and his attorneys appealed the case in an effort to have the damages trebled under the punitive clause in the Sherman Act. Hughes also appealed and won a decision to the effect that Haskell had failed to establish a contract of agreement. The Circuit Court of Appeals said that the trial judge should have directed the jury to return a verdict in favor of the Duke estate.

Fat fees came rolling into Hughes' office in very satisfactory volume. As he was a lawyers' lawyer, most of his fees were fixed by other members of the bar. In his best year his straight legal fees amounted to $400,000. At last material fortune was smiling upon him in most generous fashion. Hughes could have doubled this income by giving all his time to his practice, but he was never thrown off balance by the idea of piling up wealth. Instead of money-grubbing, he sometimes argued against the fees other lawyers fixed for him. His old friend Meier Steinbrink came to him with an important tax case to get an independent check on the conclusions that he (Steinbrink) had already reached as counsel. Hughes hastily reviewed the facts and the proposed action, said that it was legally and morally sound, and made one minor suggestion. Steinbrink thanked him and asked what his fee would be.

"Don't you talk to me about a fee," Hughes replied. "A man who fought and bled with me in those dog days in Washington [during the aircraft investigation] is welcome to my advice any day for the mere asking."

[5] CEH, Notes, pp. 365f.

Steinbrink remonstrated that his client was able and willing to pay. "If you refuse to name your fee," he said, "I shall have to fix it myself." But Hughes good-naturedly insisted that his fee was nothing and he would not change it.

The next day Steinbrink sent a check for $500. Hughes called him on the telephone and said he would not accept it. "How ridiculous," he expostulated, "to send me $500 for fifteen minutes of work! Even if I were making a charge, it would not be more than $150. I shall return at least $350."

Once more Steinbrink insisted that the expert knowledge Hughes had brought to bear on the case was worth $500 and that his client did not think the fee excessive.

"I'll tell you what I'll do, Steinbrink," came the voice of sweet surrender over the telephone, "I'm going to retain you to capitalize my time for the rest of my life." [6]

Hughes was delightfully surprised in May, 1929, by the appointment of his son to be Solicitor General of the United States. Having no idea that his son's name was under consideration, he had recommended Randall J. Le Boeuf, a former student at Cornell, for the place. It was all the more gratifying that "Son's" nomination at the early age of forty stood entirely on its own merits— that it had come with no wire-pulling in his behalf. The younger Hughes had had the advantage of eight years of professional association with his father, but he had never coasted on his father's reputation. He was making an independent career.

In Europe at the time, the elder Hughes was impatient to have the nomination quickly confirmed. On May 12 he wrote to Mrs. Hughes:

DEAREST WIFIE,
I am a little anxious about Charlie's confirmation. I do hope that my business connections will not stand in his way, and that the Senate radicals will not make a disturbance. If there should be the slightest occasion, tell Charlie to cable me fully. I should give up every retainer if it would help him, in case there is criticism on account of his relation to me and my relation to "big business." It is hard for some persons to understand that when a lawyer of the right sort takes a public place, he brings to the public the same loyalty and singleness of purpose that he displayed in his relations to his private clients. . . .
Love to all my flock—now in the hands of the tender shepherdess. . . .

C.

The effect of the appointment was notably to diminish the elder Hughes' income, for a large percentage of his big cases had been against the Government and he no longer took cases of this sort. He could not imagine himself arguing one side of a case while his son argued the other. On November 11, 1929, he wrote to Attorney General Mitchell:

[6] Author's interview with Judge Steinbrink, July 24, 1947.

In order to avoid any possible misapprehension, and confirming what I believe is well understood by you, I think it proper that I should say that the sole reason for my withdrawal from further relation to the matter of the proposed merger of the Standard Oil Company of New York and the Vacuum Oil Company (which was the subject of an interview with you last spring) was that, in view of the appointment of my son as Solicitor General, I did not feel at liberty to continue to deal with any matters which might be the subject of consideration by the Department of Justice.

I may add that I have adopted the same policy with respect to all other cases in which the Government has any interest.

The Great Lakes water diversion case was the biggest legal problem that Hughes handled in the 1925–1930 period, and he took it not as counsel but as special master. As it was a dispute between states, the suit was filed directly in the Supreme Court. Being in no position itself to conduct a trial in such an intricate and far-reaching controversy, the court appointed Hughes special master to take the evidence and make findings of fact, conclusions of law, and recommendations for a decree. It was the most important case that had ever been entrusted to a special master.

During the next year and a half Hughes spent many weeks taking testimony and writing his report. ". . . although I am no longer even under the illusion of making history," he wrote to Jusserand, "I have been busier and more anxious in my smaller world than when the fate of 'American imperialism' was in my hands. . . . We have already taken over ten thousand pages of testimony and I am about to go to Washington for another session." [7]

At the conclusion of the hearings Hughes asked the lawyers if there was anything else that should go into the voluminous record. Newton D. Baker, chief counsel for the complaining states, replied that he was not certain whether or not his group had covered a certain point. "Yes, you did," Hughes shot back, citing the name of the witness and the day on which the testimony was given. [8]

The case had grown out of Chicago's use of Great Lakes water to flush her sewage into the Mississippi River. Having reversed the course of the Chicago River by means of a canal connecting it with the Mississippi, the Chicago Sanitary District was drawing 8,500 cubic feet of water per second from Lake Michigan. This diversion had lowered the level of the Great Lakes and caused heavy losses to citzens of the adjoining states.

Hughes found unmistakable evidence of damage suffered by navigation and commercial interests, summer resorts, parks, and riparian property generally in the Great Lakes states. Chicago was impairing the navigability of the Great Lakes to save itself the expense of building sewage-disposal plants. The special master concluded that Chicago had no authority to make or continue the

[7] CEH to Jusserand, March 11, 1927.   [8] Baker to J. Reuben Clark, Jr., to author.

diversion in question, although he concluded that a permit granted by the Secretary of War allowing Chicago to take 4,167 cubic feet of water was valid. He thought the court should uphold this permit and dismiss the bill of the complaining states without prejudice to their right to sue to restrain any attempted unlawful diversion in the future.[9]

Relying heavily on the master's report, the Supreme Court decided to enter a decree that would compel Chicago to end its illegal drainage. The opinion written by Chief Justice Taft expressed the court's "obligation to the master for his useful, fair and comprehensive report"[10] and referred the case back to him with instructions virtually to work out the details of a final decree. Further hearings were held and Hughes filed his second report in December, 1929. In an opinion by Justice Holmes, the court sustained all that Hughes had done. In effect, he had functioned as a special Supreme Court in disposing of an original jurisdiction case of enormous importance.

The question of Hughes' compensation for this work did not arise until after he had become Chief Justice. Then Holmes sought the advice of the counsel who had served in the case. A conference of the lawyers was held, and their recommendations ranged from $60,000 to $125,000. Newton D. Baker reported this fact to Holmes and added: "The work done by him was of the highest possible quality, and any compensation the Court awards him will have been richly earned."[11]

Holmes took the letter into the conference and laid the matter before his brethren. Hughes said immediately that he would not accept any such sum as Baker had suggested. So far as he personally was concerned, he said, he would be glad to take nothing. But that would set a bad precedent. As the court would occasionally need to call upon highly skilled lawyers to serve as masters, there should be no precedent that might make them feel they ought to serve without remuneration. With that, Hughes left the room so that his brethren could make their decision unembarrassed by his presence. They fixed his fee at $30,000, plus expenses, and this he "gladly accepted."

The most significant fact about Hughes in these last years of his practice is that he never lost his sense of being a "minister of justice." While most of his clients were wealthy corporations, they came to him because they needed a powerful advocate in a legitimate cause or an independent opinion on intricate legal issues. No one exercised a shadow of control over his thinking. He was the independent lawyer nonpareil, who also possessed a sensitive conscience that money could neither taint nor petrify.

[9] Master's report, House Doc. 178, 70th Congress, 1st session, p. 105.
[10] 278 U.S. 367.   [11] Baker to Holmes, April 17, 1930.

Chapter 62

INTERNATIONAL JUDGE

WHEN JOHN BASSETT MOORE resigned as judge of the Permanent Court of International Justice in 1928, his mantle fell naturally upon Hughes. His proved capacity as a judge, his wide experience as Secretary of State, and his preeminence at the bar marked him immediately as the best choice. At The Hague he was also recognized as one of the warmest and oldest friends of the World Court. The two Americans who had done more than any others to take the United States into the court were Root and Hughes, and Root was now too old to be considered for a judgeship.

The real question was whether Hughes would accept such a nomination. Only three years had elapsed since he left public office to spend the rest of his days in "the comfortable asbestos of private life." There was no hankering on his part for new honors. Judge Moore suggested Edwin B. Parker as his successor, and Hughes (now one of the nominators by reason of his membership in the Hague Court of Arbitration) readily gave Parker his endorsement. It was Wickersham and Professor Manley O. Hudson of Harvard Law School who first urged Hughes to allow his name to be presented. Both argued that it was vital to have an American on the court, that Hughes' election would be assured, and that the election of any other American would be "very improbable." [1]

Hughes scouted these doubts and said that if there was fear that Parker might not be elected, his choice would be Wickersham. His own disinclination stemmed from the facts (1) that he was committed to act as delegate to the Pan American Arbitration Conference the following December; (2) that the election would be for only the unexpired two years of Judge Moore's term, and if it were known that he (Hughes) would not stand for reelection, as it should be known, the nations might prefer to choose a judge who would render longer service; and (3) that even two years abroad would give him a difficult personal problem because of Mrs. Hughes' desire to remain with her daughter until after her graduation from college. [2] The other nominators replied that service on the court would not prevent Hughes from taking part in the Arbitration Conference. Wickersham and Hudson also insisted that it would be all right to serve on the court for only two years, and as the annual session lasted

[1] Hudson to CEH, May 30, 1928.   [2] CEH to Taft, June 16, 1928.

only four months beginning in June, it would not seriously encroach upon his personal affairs.

The President added Newton D. Baker to the panel of the old Hague Court which was to make the nomination, and Baker immediately added his urgings to those of his colleagues. "I know nothing," he wrote Hughes, "that would do so much to make America's entry into the Court so likely as your presence on it as a judge." [3] Hughes replied on June 9:

I deeply appreciate the generous way in which you support the suggestion made by Mr. Wickersham and Professor Hudson. . . . I have thought the matter over carefully, and I should be willing to accept the decision of yourself, Mr. Root and Judge Moore on the question whether my name should be presented. If you and they deem it advisable that I should serve, I am too deeply interested in our relation to the Court to decline.

Taft was "perfectly delighted" to hear that Hughes had been induced to accept the nomination. "It will be a great triumph for this country if you enter the court," he wrote. "And I doubt not you will greatly enjoy the work." [4]

Root, Moore, and Baker sent in the nomination while Hughes was in Europe, and twenty-six nations joined in presenting his candidacy. On September 8, just before he left Europe, he was elected a judge of the World Court by unanimous action of the League Council and an overwhelming vote in the Assembly. Four names were submitted to the delegates of the forty-eight nations that were voting. M. Walther Simons got five votes; Hughes, forty-one. He immediately cabled his acceptance and issued a statement expressing his deep interest in the court.

The event brought from the press of many lands generous praise of Hughes' work for an orderly world. Latin America was especially pleased. The *Jornal do Brasil* said that it was Hughes' "masterful diplomatic triumph" at the Havana Conference that had induced so many powers to sponsor his candidacy as a World Court judge, and the *Jornal do Comércio* hailed him as "the great advocate of . . . the reign of law in the relations between nations." The *Handelsblad* (Dutch) said that in Hughes "the American type is represented at its best." [5]

Telegraphing the "deep satisfaction" felt by all members of the court, H. E. Anzilotti, its president, expressed the belief that Hughes' election would be "of the greatest advantage to the Court in the fulfillment of its task of promoting the cause of international justice." [6] "No one could do so much as you," wrote Justice Harlan F. Stone, "to establish in that Court the traditions which have characterized the English and . . . American Courts. . . ." [7] Judge Moore

[3] Baker to CEH, June 6, 1928. [4] Taft to CEH, June 22, 1928.
[5] Clippings in Hughes papers. [6] Dec. 9, 1928. [7] Sept. 11, 1928.

commented, ". . . you have shown again that you may be reckoned as some-what of a specialist in subordinating your private interests to public service." [8] Taking advantage of the occasion to "rediscover" Hughes, William Hard described him as "our most extreme and exalted specimen of age veering toward youth." [9]

As a World Court judge, Hughes was doubtful whether he should go ahead with his plans to campaign for Hoover. While his high regard for his former associate in the Harding and Coolidge Cabinets swung him to an affirmative conclusion, he discussed only domestic issues. He also continued his practice of law until May 1, 1929, when he sailed for Europe to take up his new duties.

Hughes' departure brought forth another chorus of praise from Pound, Wickersham, Scott, John W. Davis, and others. Arriving in London, he was given a hearty welcome, and once more he was the guest of honor at a dinner given by the Pilgrims of Great Britain. The Lord Chief Justice of England, Lord Henry Hewart of Bury, toasted Hughes as "one of the few prophets who are not without honor even in their own country" and mistakenly assumed that "the spiteful voice of calumny" had never been raised against him. Quoting Burke's famous words—"calumny and abuse are essential parts of triumph"—Lord Hewart went on to ask: "Is there nobody waiting to seize an opportunity of pouring out upon him the accumulated venom of a defeated and mortified egotism? Apparently not; but you can never tell what the future may bring forth; nor from what unexpected quarter an omission of that kind may be supplied." [10]

His remarks were almost prophetic, for Hughes was only nine months away from the worst orgy of mud-slinging that he ever experienced.

"It is indeed an odd distinction," Hughes told the Pilgrims, "to come to Europe on the invitation of almost all governments except my own. But I am happy to think that . . . I may be taken as representing not only the detachment and impartiality which should characterize a judge of the World Court, but the earnest desire of the great majority of my fellow countrymen to promote the cause of international justice. . . .

"I come to you, and to my new duty, accredited by a force that is stronger than governments, the force of public opinion demanding the just settlements of peace."

The next day Hughes wrote to his wife, "I was overwhelmed by congratulations." The Hague welcomed him on May 13. Two days later he took the oath of office in the high paneled courtroom, looking very distinguished in his robe and lace "bib" hanging from his collar. It was a great day for the court. With Moore's resignation and the death of Lord Finlay of Great Britain, some

[8] Oct. 1, 1928.   [9] New York *Herald Tribune*, Sept. 2, 1928.
[10] Copy of speech in Hughes Papers.

of the judges had previously been discouraged. Hughes brought in new buoyancy and confidence. Let Judge Max Huber, former president of the court, speak on this point:

When you came in with your immense legal and judicial experience, your broad conceptions of a real statesman and your personality which inspires unlimited confidence, the conditions of work in the Court were entirely changed. The whole atmosphere was changed to such a degree that my decision, otherwise beyond discussion for me, to withdraw from the Court at the end of the period, was considerably shaken.[11]

Hughes entered into the work of the court with enthusiasm that was tempered only by his dislike for writing opinions and by the fact that he had temporarily left Mrs. Hughes in New York. Fond of Holland and its people, he also found delight in his meals, in the exhilarating walks that he took, and in the almost unbelievable freedom from pressure. For once a leisurely institution slowed him down to its own pace. At last he was on easy street. "I am about as happy here as I could be anywhere without you, my dearest," he wrote to his wife. "Life here is pretty close to the ideal." A week later he wrote again:

How I dislike writing opinions! I prefer arguments—and let some one else have the responsibility of decision. But—once more—I must say how delightful I find the immunity of this life and these pleasant surroundings. . . . Certainly—for a "working man" I have found a good job and—knowing what other jobs are—I am content.

After Mrs. Hughes arrived, life at The Hague was still more stimulating. There was a good deal of entertaining, and the distinguished American judge and his wife were favorite guests as well as gracious hosts. The first reception given during the Economic Reparations Conference at The Hague that summer, with Briand and Snowden present, was an especially gala occasion. Before the summer was over, however, it was evident that Mrs. Hughes did not share her husband's enthusiasm for The Hague.

Some of the judges won Hughes' high esteem. B. C. J. Loder of The Netherlands, who had been the first president of the court, was a seasoned expert in international law. Huber of Switzerland was every inch a judge. Anzilotti, then president of the court, was an Italian jurist of wide experience in international law and an admirable presiding officer. But some of the others were men of little distinction and meager judicial attainments.

When the court was hearing a case to which states having no national on its bench were parties, it permitted the *ad hoc* selection of one additional judge to represent each such state. The practice was sometimes criticized as a means

[11] Huber to CEH, March 15, 1930.

of putting interested parties on the bench. But Hughes observed that it worked well and that some of the *ad hoc* judges were very able men. The important consideration, he thought, was to have every state taking a case before the court represented on the bench so that a judge from the losing state could assure his fellow countrymen that every point had been thoroughly weighed.

Hughes was favorably impressed by the court's thoroughness. It seldom took evidence aside from the documents submitted, but when the hearing began counsel could talk as long as they pleased without interruption. "How I envied them," Hughes said. It was the only court he had ever entered in which lawyers could ramble on without limit. He discovered that this was a great convenience for the judges; when the arguments were over, they knew all about the case. Every document had been read, all the evidence had been painstakingly reviewed, and weighty authority had been cited on every point.

With oral arguments closed, the court went into conference to dispose of preliminary questions, including that of jurisdiction. The day for submission of preliminary opinions was then fixed, and each judge proceeded to write his own conclusions without any consultation. This was "a rather thrilling experience," and Hughes reflected that it would be a fine thing for the judges of our domestic courts to write out opinions as the basis of their consultations. As a practical matter, however, he realized that such a judicial luxury could be enjoyed only by a court with plenty of time on its hands.

The tentative opinions were circulated among the judges; then came the consultation. Each question of fact and law was discussed without limit and voted on until the crucial point was decided. Two members were selected by secret ballot to join with the president of the court in drafting its judgment in accord with the majority vote. The judgment and award were circulated, and the full court met for further discussion until a majority could agree upon a judgment in final form. Any dissenting judges then had a chance to prepare opinions of their own before the judgment was finally reviewed, voted upon once more, and handed down. Hughes was a member of every drafting committee selected during his summer at The Hague.

A judicial atmosphere pervaded the court. "After sitting alone, with one's task, endeavoring to reach a conclusion as to the merits of a stubbornly contested dispute, wondering what one's colleagues think of the different points that have been laboriously argued," Hughes said, "one cannot but have a feeling of exaltation in reading the preliminary opinions as they come in, and in realizing to what extent the minds of men drawn from many countries move along the same lines of careful reasoning." [12] The court itself, he thought,

[12] Address to New York bar, Jan. 16, 1930.

was partly responsible for this. So thorough was its analysis of the facts and law that it was difficult for a judge not to deal with a case on its merits.

Returning to New York in September, 1929, Hughes felt that his work on the international bench had been "one of the most interesting experiences of my life." More than ever he was convinced that the United States ought to be a part of this agency that was making international justice a handmaiden of peace. To be sure, he saw two defects in the court. The election of its fifteen judges for nine-year terms, all expiring at the same time, opened the door to logrolling and made it possible to reconstitute the court with serious loss of prestige and continuity—a defect that was to be corrected in the new statute for the court adopted by the United Nations. The nominees for the court offered by the arbitration judges of some of the smaller countries were entirely unknown in international circles, thus exposing the Council and the Assembly of the League to the risk of choosing unfit judges. But these defects were minor compared to the high-grade judicial work the court was doing.

Having accepted the judgeship largely to bolster the confidence of the American people in the court, Hughes continued to urge his countrymen to ratify the protocol. "As a nation devoted to the interests of peace," he told the New York bar after a detailed analysis of the court's organization and procedure, "we have the utmost concern in this development. To hold aloof is to belie our aspirations and to fail to do our part in forming the habit of mind upon which all hopes of permanent peace depend." [13]

Hughes felt that there were two steps which could be taken to implement the pledge in the Briand-Kellogg Treaty for peaceful settlement or solution of all disputes that might arise among the signatories. The first, of course, was United States participation in the World Court; the second was consultation among the powers if any threat to the peace should arise. The latter suggestion was a direct outgrowth of the Four-Power Pact that he had negotiated in 1922. In that pact the Pacific powers had agreed to consult freely together on measures to be taken if the rights of any one of them should be threatened. What he now had in mind was a similar arrangement for the Atlantic powers. When he offered a general suggestion to this effect in a speech to the American Society of International Law on April 24, 1929, Secretary of State Stimson asked him to elaborate it. Stimson too felt strongly that the Briand-Kellogg Pact should be "supplemented by additional machinery to really make it effective." [14] But he feared that any conference of all the signatories would be unwieldy and the omission of some would be awkward.

Hughes did not think it would be necessary to invite all the signatories to such conferences. Most of the Latin American countries, for example, would

[13] Id.   [14] Stimson to CEH, Nov. 18, 1929.

not care to enter a conference dealing with European or Far Eastern disputes. "My suggestion," Hughes replied, "is that the supplementary pact should be, like the Kellogg pact itself, very simple and should provide only for conference and not for any coercive process." The text he offered was:

If there should develop between any of the High Contracting Parties any controversy which is not satisfactorily settled by diplomacy and there is a prospect of the disturbance of peaceful relations, the High Contracting Parties shall confer with one another fully and frankly in order to carry out the purposes of their said Treaty for the renunciation of war as an instrument of their national policy.

To that end, any one or more of the High Contracting Parties may invite the Parties to such controversy to a joint conference for the purpose of consultation and conciliation. The Party or Parties issuing the invitation may include therein any others of the High Contracting Parties; and any one of the High Contracting Parties, who may not be so invited, shall nevertheless be entitled on its request to participate in such a conference.[15]

Hughes thought his plan would avoid interference with the League of Nations. At the same time it would enable conferences to move swiftly in any area of disturbance without assembling delegates from the whole world. It was, he thought, the most positive device for keeping the peace that stood any chance of approval by the United States Senate. Unfortunately, the plan was never followed up. Had it been adopted, the nations bordering the Atlantic would at least have had on hand a skeleton that could have been clothed with power (if there had been the will to so clothe it) when Hitler launched his aggressions.

Having thoroughly enjoyed life at The Hague, Hughes was looking forward to returning in the summer of 1930 and was even thinking seriously of accepting another nomination at the end of the two years for which he had been elected. As he refused to take cases involving the Government after his son became Solicitor General, his practice had sharply diminished. Everything seemed to favor his continuance on the international woolsack, except Mrs. Hughes' dislike for living abroad. The wife whom he adored, who had been sweetly deferring to his wishes for forty-one years, finally put her foot down and said that if he were elected to the court again he would have to go alone. Of course his utter devotion to her would have prevented him from going alone. A showdown was happily averted by his nomination on February 3, 1930, to be Chief Justice of the United States.

Hughes resigned from the World Court on February 15 amid a chorus of regret from The Hague. Judge Loder lamented that the resignation was "a blow we shall not easily overcome." Judge Huber was certain that nobody "equivalent" to Hughes would take his place, "because even a great country can have but one best man." [16] Anzilotti, the president, insisted that Hughes

[15] CEH to Stimson, Nov. 23, 1929.   [16] Hughes Papers.

would remain a member of the World Court until the election of his successor in September and urged him to attend the summer session in spite of his new assignment. Concluding that the American people would not like their Chief Justice to sit in an international court to which this country had not yet given adherence, Hughes insisted that his resignation be effective at once. In spite of this, the Hague judges continued to claim him as a member and to pay his salary. He rejected it, and the sum was finally deposited to the credit of the court.

It was a matter of keen disappointment to Hughes that his service on the World Court was so brief. Until the end of his days he retained a lively interest in the court as an instrument of international justice. The spread of law-debasing fascism and communism and the kindling of passions that led to World War II were especially painful because they seemed to postpone the day when the World Court could operate in a hospitable climate. But Hughes took a long-range view of the court. It could render immeasurable service, he felt, if it did nothing more than apply the judicial process to disputes arising under the network of treaties governing international relations. What was needed basically was a willingness on the part of the peoples of the earth to accept justice rather than force in settling their disputes. Progress toward that end has been slow, but with the World Court retained by the United Nations as a going concern, and with American adherence to it, Hughes clung to the belief that a sound and promising start had been made.

Chapter 63

THE HIGHEST JUDICIAL OFFICE

Two decades had passed since the exalted office of Chief Justice of the United States had first been associated with the name of Charles E. Hughes. Five Presidents had weighed his singular qualifications to preside over the nation's highest court. Twice his simple adherence to what he believed to be his duty had stood between him and the office. When the call finally came in 1930, it was almost as if destiny had intervened, first to broaden his experience and temper his qualities and then to bring him to the Chief Justiceship fresh and vigorous in the hour of the court's greatest need for leadership.

Taft had noted, when he himself was elevated to the Chief Justiceship in 1921, the ironical circumstances that had kept Hughes out of the office. "I cannot but think," he had replied to Hughes' congratulations, "that I am to sit in a seat that would have been yours by right, had you not responded to what you deemed the highest call of duty, in two instances. I am conscious, too, how your preparation to fill the peculiar duties of the place would have been far better than mine. It is a source of great satisfaction to me, however, that you think I can fill the place acceptably." [1]

The first time that Hughes' response to "the highest call of duty" had denied him the Chief Justiceship was obviously in 1910. Taft's letter more than a decade later confirms the assumption that if Hughes had not accepted the Associate Justiceship in April, 1910, Taft would have named him Chief Justice after Fuller died in July of that year. Probably the second instance to which Taft refers was in 1916, when Hughes turned his back upon Chief Justice White's suggestion that Wilson would name him (Hughes) Chief Justice if he would remain on the bench and not run for the Presidency.

In 1921 Hughes had resented the speculation that he would head the Supreme Court, because he had put his hand to the plow as Secretary of State and did not intend to turn back.[2] In 1925, when Coolidge asked him if he wished to be Chief Justice as he was about to leave the State Department, he had tossed off a flat No because he did not take it seriously. At that time he was eager to get back into private life. In any event, Chief Justice Taft was then going strong. "I had no reason to doubt," Hughes commented later, "that he would outlive the time when by any chance I could be deemed available." [3]

[1] Taft to CEH, July 8, 1921.   [2] CEH, Notes, 1930–1941, p. 1.   [3] *Ibid.*

Taft was only five years his senior. The idea of ever being Chief Justice had thus been completely dismissed from Hughes' mind.

But when Hoover was elected in 1928, he seemed determined to bring Hughes back into public life. As President-elect, he asked Hughes to become Secretary of State. When Hughes declined, Hoover sent Henry M. Robinson, who had been one of the American representatives in formulation of the Dawes Plan, to urge reconsideration. Hughes agreed to think it over again for a few days, but his answer was the same. The President-elect was loath to accept a negative reply and telegraphed a further appeal saying, ". . . our Nation has no others who can give such competent guidance."

Hughes remained unmoved because he feared that if he resigned from the World Court, before he had even attended one of its sessions and following so closely upon Judge Moore's resignation, it might have unfortunate repercussions. "I do not feel that I could honorably resign to accept other appointment," he replied to Hoover. He was also reluctant to subject Mrs. Hughes once more to the heavy social demands that the Secretaryship entails, although this was a minor objection.

Some weeks before the inauguration Hughes visited the President-elect at the latter's home in Washington.

"I don't suppose you would care to go to England," Hoover said, obviously referring to the ambassadorship.

"No," Hughes replied. "There is certainly one man who does not wish any office, and that is myself." [4]

Hoover had other requests. Sending Hughes an advance copy of his inaugural address, the President-elect asked for criticism, especially of the section dealing with Latin America. Hughes strongly advised the deletion of two pages on the subject of intervention, which, he feared, "might largely destroy the good effects of your recent visit" to South America.[5] His counsel was followed.

Three weeks after his inauguration Hoover sought Hughes' help in organizing the new commission that was to delve into the appalling problem of enforcing the prohibition law. His suggestion was that Judge Moore be persuaded to return to the World Court long enough for the Law Enforcement Commission to be set up under Hughes' leadership. "I am led to write you in this vein," the President said, "because the opposition of Chief Justice Taft is such that it seems hopeless to secure Justice Stone, who would be willing to undertake the work if the Chief Justice approved—but at the moment this seems impossible. Outside of yourself and Justice Stone there is no man in the country who could adequately undertake this work. I have again canvassed the entire possible personnel and am most despondent about the whole enterprise,

[4] Ibid., p. 2.   [5] CEH to Hoover, Feb. 13, 1929.

although I am convinced that it is the outstanding necessity of the next four years." [6]

Hughes replied that Judge Moore could not resume his seat unless he (Hughes) should resign and Moore should be reelected. Even then the re-election could not take place before September, and the court was to meet in May. As there was no alternative to taking his seat at The Hague, Judge Hughes could only express his sorrow over the President's troubles. After Owen J. Roberts had also declined the thankless prohibition assignment, it went to Wickersham.

Chief Justice Taft failed rapidly in the last months of 1929. Visiting him on December 17 before filing a final report in the Great Lakes case, Hughes was shocked by the havoc that had befallen Taft's ponderous hulk. Shortly after they parted, Hughes went to Bermuda to spend the Christmas holidays, and Taft, desperately ill, sought rest in North Carolina. Near the end of January, Hughes learned that there was no hope for his old friend and that Taft was eager to see him (Hughes) in the seat under the eagle. "Hughes is young enough to wait," President Taft had said twenty years previously as he snatched away the prize that he had so recently held up before the young Governor of New York. Now at last he might redeem his implied promise by himself relinquishing the Chief Justiceship as death plucked him by the ear.

Taft had been fearful that, if he should die or resign, Hoover would advance Stone to the Chief Justiceship. That would be a great mistake, he wrote to his son, "for the reason that Stone is not a leader and would have a great deal of trouble *in massing the court.* . . ." [7] Late in January, however, Taft's powers were slipping away so rapidly that all hope for his recovery was abandoned, and it appeared that the best he could do was to resign while he was still capable of making a decision in the hope that his wishes would be respected. Robert A. Taft (later Senator) took word of his father's condition to the White House, and members of the Supreme Court informed Attorney General William D. Mitchell that Taft would resign as soon as the President indicated that he was ready to nominate a successor.

Mitchell reminded Hoover at their next meeting that he "would be con-fronted soon with the most important appointment that he would have to make as President, the appointment of a new Chief Justice." [8] From the first, Hughes was Mitchell's choice, but he did not wish to make a recommendation to the President without knowing that Hughes would accept the post. Having no authority from the President to make a direct inquiry, Mitchell sought the assistance of two members of the court. Justices Van Devanter and Butler dined with Hughes in his New York apartment on January 28 and subse-

[6] Hoover to CEH, March 25, 1929.
[7] Henry F. Pringle, *The Life and Times of William Howard Taft*, II, 1044.
[8] William D. Mitchell to author, Nov. 7, 1949.

quently held a long conference. Doubtless they conveyed to him Taft's wishes and urged him to accept the nomination if it should come. They came back to Washington convinced that he was willing and so informed the Attorney General.

Mitchell went to the White House and suggested Hughes for the place. Hoover asked him if he thought Hughes would acquiesce, and Mitchell said he felt sure of it.[9] The Attorney General concluded from what the President said at the time that he had independently decided that Hughes was the logical choice. Some years later Hoover confirmed this in a letter to Hughes:

I at once discussed the question of his [Taft's] possible successor with the Attorney General. To my great satisfaction, Mr. Mitchell urged your appointment. The question required no consultation with others. It was the obvious appointment.[10]

Mitchell left the conference with the understanding that the President would inform Hughes that the mantle of Marshall, Taney, Chase, and Taft was to fall upon him. Meanwhile the Attorney General got word to the court that Hughes would be nominated as soon as Taft's resignation came in. Presumably this was relayed to Taft.

Hughes was summoned to the White House as he was glancing over an opinion that he had prepared for an oil company. "Hold up that opinion," he said as he put down the telephone receiver. "It may not go out." [11] Even though the opinion was finished, it was never released. A mere request to come to the White House while the Chief Justiceship was under discussion was enough to put his legal advice beyond the reach of private clients.

This time there was no cancellation of the White House call, as there had been in 1910. Hughes went to Washington on January 30 and ate breakfast with the President early the next morning. Taft's resignation had not yet come in, but the President said that it would undoubtedly be forthcoming and that he wished to be ready to announce the nomination of a successor instantly "and thus prevent all the political pulling and hauling that takes place over an open vacancy." [12] He offered the place to Hughes.

At no time since he left the bench in 1916 had Hughes yearned to return. Confinement to the bench, he once said, made him feel like a bird in a cage. His present judgeship in the World Court did not rob him of the freedom he loved so much; the Supreme Court would. Certainly he would not have accepted an Associate Justiceship.[13] Nor would he reach out for the highest judicial honor. "There are various reasons why you should not nominate me," he told Hoover, "one of them being that I'm too old." With his sixty-eighth birthday less than three months away, he felt that the responsibilities

9 *Id.*   10 Hoover to CEH, Feb. 25, 1937.
11 Author's interview with Ernest L. Wilkinson, February, 1949.
12 Hoover to CEH, Feb. 25, 1937.   13 CEH, Notes, 1930–1941, p. 2.

of the Chief Justiceship were more than he should carry. A second reason was his reluctance to interfere with the career of his son, who would have to resign as Solicitor General after only eight months of service if his father should become Chief Justice. "Finally," Hughes said, "I think I've earned the right to finish life in peace." [14]

The discussion ran to great length, with Hoover advancing many reasons why Hughes should accept the post. The President was eager to keep Charles Junior in the government in some other equally important position. "It is your duty to take it," Hoover said flatly. "Your acceptance would bring confidence to the whole country and would meet great response on the part of the people." Finally he argued that Taft would more readily resign if he knew that Hughes would succeed him.

With Hughes' arguments against acceptance pretty well demolished, he laid down one final condition. "I don't want a fight over the nomination," he said. "I want you to ascertain whether my nomination will have support. I've been active in politics since 1916. As recently as 1928 I campaigned for you. I don't know whether this political activity has left sores. If you are convinced that the nomination will be confirmed by the Senate without a scrap, I will accept it. But I don't want any trouble about it." [15]

The President reassured him that there would be no difficulty about his confirmation. The two parted with the understanding that the matter was settled if no evidence of opposition were found.

Hoover had counted on Hughes' "sense of public service" to compel his acceptance. But the voice of conscience may have been less influential than that of his wife. Although she had opposed his continuance on the World Court, she strongly urged him to take the Chief Justiceship of the United States. To her, he was still "a man of destiny." To him, her wish, even when it took him by surprise, as in this case, was a powerful incentive to action.

Taft's resignation reached the White House on February 3, and Hoover announced it late that afternoon. Immediately the press began to speculate about Taft's successor. For some unknown reason George Akerson, presidential secretary, walked into the White House pressroom and whispered, "It's Stone." [16] That false report was flashed all over the country. Reporters were frantically writing stories about the promotion of Justice Stone when the President appeared and passed around slips of paper announcing the nomination of Hughes.

Akerson's blunder has never been fully explained, and it has given buoyancy to reports that the President originally wished to appoint Stone. Hoover and Stone were close personal friends. They went fishing and played medicine ball

[14] Id., p. 3; also, Hoover letter of Feb. 25, 1937, and CEH to Hoover, Mar. 8, 1937.
[15] Author's interview with CEH, Nov. 12, 1947.
[16] J. Fred Essary in the Baltimore Sun, June 3, 1941.

together, and Hoover had previously offered the Justice several assignments. One version of the story is that Hoover confided to Undersecretary of State Joseph P. Cotton a desire to make Stone Chief Justice. Cotton is supposed to have said that it would be a good idea to offer the position to Hughes first but that Hughes would decline and then the President could name Stone.[17] Hughes' acceptance was thus supposed to have embarrassed the President. Another version of the story has Hoover, with tongue in cheek, offering the Chief Justiceship to Hughes over the telephone. It is known that Cotton was eager to see Stone promoted in the hope that his place as Associate Justice might be given to Judge Learned Hand, but beyond this the story is sharply contradicted by known facts.

When the rumor first appeared in print some years later, it "greatly disturbed" Hughes. Because of its inconsistency with what had passed between himself and the President, he assumed that the report was inaccurate but remained silent. In 1937 the story first came to Hoover's attention, and he voluntarily wrote to Hughes an indignant and emphatic denial of it.[18] Hughes then cited another version of the story, and Hoover, digging into his presidential files, wrote a longer letter declaring that he had not discussed the matter with Cotton and that "no telephone conversation as to your appointment as Chief Justice ever took place." Later he declared, "There was not a shred of truth in that Cotton story."

Buttressing Mr. Hoover's denial is the fact that he said nothing about Stone to the Attorney General. Mitchell had heard from other sources rumors that Stone was interested in the Chief Justiceship and made incidental reference to those rumors when he went to the White House to urge Hughes' nomination. "The President expressed surprise," Mitchell relates, "and I realized that he had not been considering Justice Stone or anyone else but Mr. Hughes." [19] Certainly the President could not have offered the place to Hughes expecting him to decline, for Mitchell had assured Hoover, on the strength of the report he got from Van Devanter and Butler, that Hughes could be persuaded to serve.

Through Justice Van Devanter, Hughes dispatched a warm note of regret to Taft:

I cannot tell you how distressed I was at the news of your illness and that it seemed to be necessary for you to retire from the office that you have filled with such great distinction. . . .

It is with deep emotion, with the keenest sense of opportunity and responsibility, that I shall endeavor, if the Senate confirms my appointment, to follow in your footsteps, inspired and heartened by your example.

[17] Henry F. Pringle in the *New Yorker*, July 13, 1935.
[18] Hoover to CEH, Feb. 19, and 25, 1937.
[19] William D. Mitchell to author, Nov. 7, 1949.

I trust that in these difficult days you may find rest and happiness, with no cause for regrets, conscious of noble aims nobly accomplished.

Believe me, my dear Chief Justice, as ever

Faithfully yours,

Acclaim of the Hughes appointment was almost unanimous. His daughter, Mrs. Waddell, asked, "What in the world did you want to do that for?" But the press and the hundreds of letters that streamed into his office were full of enthusiasm. "Never," said the *New York Times,* "was there a clearer case of the office seeking the fit man." The Democratic *World* said the appointment "has been received with universal approval." ". . . in the future that beckons so invitingly," concluded the *St. Louis Post-Dispatch,* "the political skids of 1916 may be accounted a beneficent intervention." From Maine to California the editorials were studded with such phrases as "a noble figure," "the greatest lawyer in the world," "the man to whom the people turn instinctively," "our most distinguished private citizen." [20]

Justice Brandeis said, "Confirmation ought to be made at once and ought to be unanimous." Judge Cardozo declared, "There has been a great choice of a great man for a great office." On Capitol Hill both the Democrats and Republicans appeared to be well satisfied. Senator Pat Harrison thought the nomination would be "universally endorsed." "There is no objection to the confirmation of Mr. Hughes," said Senator George W. Norris, Insurgent chairman of the committee to which the nomination was referred. "I think it will be unanimously voted by the Judiciary Committee." [21]

For a few happy days the designation of Hughes to be the eleventh Chief Justice of the United States seemed to be everywhere recognized as a fitting climax to his eminent career of public service. After the first wave of favorable comment subsided, however, an ominous stir was felt in the Senate—the sort of uneasy wind that rises before a storm. The Insurgent Republicans and a coterie of Democrats were trying to summon courage to defy the inevitable. At first their protests were a barely audible murmur. On February 8, for example, Senator Norris handed to the press, without explanation, a list of fifty-four cases in which Hughes had appeared as counsel before the Supreme Court since 1925. It emphasized what everyone knew—that Hughes had argued cases for many big corporations and wealthy clients. Still, Norris disavowed knowledge of any organized effort to withhold confirmation.

In the late afternoon of February 10, Norris took a favorable report from the Judiciary Committee to the Senate floor and said that he wished to be heard briefly. Majority Leader James E. Watson asked for unanimous consent

[20] Hughes Papers and family book of clippings.
[21] New York *Herald Tribune,* Feb. 4, 1930.

for immediate consideration of the nomination. For a moment it appeared that Hughes would be confirmed with nothing more than a token protest from the Insurgent committee chairman. But Coleman Blease, the hate-belching spellbinder from South Carolina, arose to object, and the nomination went to the calendar.

Norris then went ahead with his protest. For two "fundamental reasons" he thought the nomination was unwise. After Hughes had resigned from the Supreme Court to run for the Presidency and after he had amassed a fortune in practice that had come to him by reason of his former high position, Norris said, the President had returned him to the judicial tribunal which he voluntarily left to engage in politics and the amassing of a fortune. The Senator feared that such a precedent would encourage political activity on the part of Supreme Court judges. In the second place, he said Hughes had represented "untold wealth"; he had associated with Wall Street and lived in luxury. ". . . it is reasonable to expect," Norris concluded, in a sweeping generalization untainted by any relationship to fact, "that these influences have become a part of the man. His viewpoint is clouded. He looks through glasses contaminated by the influence of monopoly as it seeks to get favors by means which are denied to the common, ordinary citizen." [22]

Norris' attack was comparatively mild, but it drew blood that set the whole pack of Insurgents howling at Hughes' heels. The next day Borah took up the cry. Just as Norris had imputed to the nominee the opinions and failings of his clients, Borah linked him to the sins of the Supreme Court, of which he had not been a member for fourteen years. In striking down an order of the Maryland Public Service Commission, the court had said that the rate of return allowed a Baltimore transit company should have been 8 per cent instead of the 6.26 per cent allowed by the commission.[23] Borah pontifically warned the Senate that Hughes was "associated in his views with the contention which is sustained by the majority," which, if carried to its logical conclusion, "must result in great economic oppression to the people of the United States."

Actually, Hughes had had nothing whatever to do with this case. The conclusion reached by the court was in conflict with views he had expressed as Associate Justice, and he had no sympathy with it.[24] As a matter of policy, moreover, his antipathy toward excessive utility charges had been demonstrated in his fight for 75-cent gas in New York and in his successful campaign as governor for an effective public-service-commission law. But the Lion of Idaho, tossing his shaggy mane, roared that the Supreme Court had become

[22] *Congressional Record*, Feb. 10, 1930, pp. 3372f.
[23] *United Railways* v. *West*, 280 U.S. 234.
[24] Author's interview with CEH, Nov. 12, 1947.

an "economic dictator" on utility rates and that the Senate should not permit the President to add to the court a man holding extreme views "which exalt property rights above all other rights."

Abetted by Senator Wheeler, Borah then turned a barrage upon Hughes' arguments as counsel in the WYG case. Here perhaps a scintilla of justification for his fears may be found. Hughes had argued before the Court of Appeals in Washington that the General Electric Company, by reason of prior appropriation and long-continued use, had acquired a property right in the electrical impulses along a certain broadcasting channel. Senator Clarence Dill later took up this case in more detail, read extensively from the brief (which Hughes had not written, although his name was on it) and denounced the nominee for trying to set up "the doctrine of squatter sovereignty of the air."

This is one of many instances in which Hughes had been retained to lay before the court a case worked up by other lawyers. In doing so he made an extreme argument in favor of protecting the company's investment in Station WYG. It was clearly special pleading—the kind of plea to which Hughes had given short shrift on the bench. But under our system of jurisprudence, it is a lawyer's duty to his client to advance every legitimate argument to support his case. The judge will decide which arguments ought to prevail.

Three years after the confirmation fight Chief Justice Hughes was to hand down an opinion in another radio case running directly contrary to his own argument in behalf of Station WYG.[25] Under his leadership, the court would uphold a Radio Commission order transferring a frequency from two stations in Illinois to a station in Indiana as a means of equalizing public service. "Those who operated broadcasting stations," he would say, "had no right superior to the exercise of this power of regulation. They necessarily made their investments and their contracts in the light of, and subject to, this paramount authority." The views of the judge would push aside the advocate's arguments. Such is the common experience of active practicing lawyers called to the bench. The Insurgents failed to distinguish between the advocate and the judge—failed even to look impartially at the record Hughes had already made as Associate Justice.

The contribution of Senator Blease to the debate was a dark hint that "political intrigue" was at work, because of certain cases pending, "to get Mr. Taft off that bench for the purpose of putting on this man whose opinions have already been written in many of the cases in the form of arguments." [26] Demagoguery has seldom sunk so low.

The chief target of Senator Carter Glass' attack was Hughes' opinion as Associate Justice in the *Shreveport Case*. That decision, Glass inaccurately

[25] *Fed. Radio Comm.* v. *Nelson*, 289 U.S. 266.
[26] *Congressional Record*, Feb. 11, 1930, p. 3451.

The United States Supreme Court in 1930

*As friends often saw him
off the Bench*

Still "dining for my country"

The fiftieth year of marriage, Venice, 1938

declared, stripped from the states every right they possessed to control "interstate traffic." Here was a most ironical assault. Hughes was denounced because he had taken a broad view of the commerce clause—a view that had been twice sustained by the court after his resignation. In passing the Transportation Act of 1920, moreover, Congress itself had asserted precisely the same power that Hughes had upheld in the *Shreveport Case*. The excitement of the confirmation fight had led eminent Senators to grasp any stick to beat a judge. Connally, Borah, and several others took up the *Shreveport Case*. Senator Ransdell of Louisiana was the only one who undertook to analyze the court's opinion impartially.

While the debate waxed hotter with each passing hour in the Senate, Hughes was in New York in a state of mental agony. Always thin-skinned to criticism in spite of his extraordinary poise in public, he felt that his toil and faithfulness of a lifetime were being smeared over by a sickly smudge that might leave his name tarnished as long as it would be remembered. If he could have foreseen this tirade of abuse, which apparently no one foresaw, he never would have permitted his name to be submitted.[27] Now that the fight was on, however, he would not turn back. Nothing that was said in the Senate gave him the slightest twinge of conscience. His anguish was that of the builder who sees the temple he has erected defiled and hacked by wild, unthinking men in pursuit of what they suppose to be a noble cause. For a time it appeared that the almost universal acclaim which had greeted his nomination had been thrown into a chaotic reversal by some giant hand of fate. Nights were sleepless, and days were a continuation of chafing and waiting for a vote that did not come.

Senators Robert F. Wagner and Royal S. Copeland of New York gave Hughes their support, although both were Democrats. Senator Frederick H. Gillett pointed out that if the criticism leveled against Hughes for arguing cases in behalf of wealthy clients were to be taken seriously, no great lawyer could ever be confirmed as Chief Justice. The most effective defense speech was made by Senator Otis F. Glenn of Illinois, who contended that the arguments raised against Hughes would have been equally applicable to Lincoln; for Lincoln's best client was the Illinois Central Railroad. At the conclusion of his admirable rebuttal, however, Glenn took the wind out of his own sails by defending great mergers and combinations as being necessary in the public interest.

As the debate went on, venom increasingly took the place of argument. Intoxicated by his own slander, Senator John J. Blaine said that whenever the evil and blighting influences of monopoly had sought counsel their paths had "all converged in the office of Mr. Hughes." With complete emancipation from facts, Senator Dill ranted about Hughes having sat in the Harding Cabi-

[27] Author's interview with CEH, Nov. 12, 1947.

By "J. N. Ding" in the New York *Herald Tribune*, February, 1930.

CONCEDED TO BE ONE OF THE OUTSTANDING JURISTS
OF THE WORLD

net with Daugherty, Fall, and Denby without ever indicating that he "smelled anything." Senator George complained about Hughes' defense of Senator Newberry. Wheeler put in a derogatory plug about the Interborough fare case. Norris again raked over the Baltimore fare case in monotonous detail, assuming without a shred of justification that it reflected Hughes' reasoning. Then came Senator Thomas J. Walsh with a statement that he was switching his vote for Hughes in committee to a vote against him on the floor. To justify this change of front, he told a distorted story of the aircraft investigation of 1918, reviving the false claim that Hughes had suppressed a telegram that would have exonerated Colonel Deeds.[28] It was obvious that he had not read the testimony. Hughes' conscientious work in the aircraft inquiry brought one dividend, however. Senator Claude A. Swanson told his colleagues that Wilson had turned to Hughes to get "an honest and impartial investigation" and that "one to whom President Wilson gave that confidence we can afford to trust."

In the late afternoon of February 13 Norris moved to thwart the nomination by sending it back to the Judiciary Committee. The motion went down by a vote of 31 to 49. The Senate then confirmed Hughes as Chief Justice of the United States by a vote of 52 to 26, with 15 Democrats and 11 Republicans taking the negative side.

Not since Jackson nominated Taney had the Senate raised such a furor over the confirmation of a Chief Justice. Never before had Hughes taken such a drubbing. In his political battles he had at least been able to exchange blow for blow. In this one-sided contest he had suffered in silence while a tornado of accusation ripped through the Senate without warning. If calumny and abuse are essential parts of triumph, as Burke said, certainly the new Chief Justice had those particular qualifications for a place in history.

"My appreciation of the honor of the appointment is outweighed by a deep sense of responsibility," he calmly remarked when the ordeal was over. "The ideals and principles relating to public service with which I entered public life twenty-five years ago, and which I have tried to exemplify in public office, I hold unaltered. In facing this new and most important task, I am heartened by the generous expressions I have received from all parts of our land. I wish to express my most grateful acknowledgments." [29]

Probably the Senate's orgy on this occasion will never be fully explained, but certain aspects of it are understandable. America was in the first throes of the great depression of the thirties. The Insurgents were striking more at the Taft court and the Hoover Administration than at Hughes as an individual. For the moment Hughes was made an unwitting symbol of the philosophy which they believed to be responsible for the country's economic convulsions.

[28] See pages 379–382.   [29] *New York Times*, Feb. 14, 1930.

The strange thing is that men who claimed to be "liberals" chose as their target one of the greatest champions of human rights in the current century.

Only the unprincipled demagogues cast any reflections upon Hughes' integrity. Most of his opponents paid respect to his impeccable character and his great achievements in the law. The fatal infirmity of their case was that they assumed Hughes was biased in favor of big corporations without making any effort to examine his record or his personal views. They ignored his work in the gas and insurance investigations, which at that time had given him the reputation of being such a dangerous radical that the leading trustees of his own university stayed away from the commencement that he was invited to address. They ignored his progressive record as governor, his devotion to human rights as a judge, his work in the Legal Aid Society, his magnificent defense of the five Socialists expelled from the New York Legislature, his great reputation for fairness and even-handed justice as Secretary of State, and even the spirit of liberty and equality that had infused his speeches. Closing their eyes to his life

By Clifford Berryman in the Washington *Evening Star*, February 24, 1930, when Hughes took his seat as Chief Justice.

of public service, they pretended to believe that he had sold his soul to the clients whom he had happened to represent momentarily at the bar.

No doubt many lawyers who are attached to great corporations most of their lives absorb the corporate point of view. But Hughes was never in that position. The very fact that he represented dozens of different clients in rapid succession—such varied clients as the State of New York, railway companies, and the United Mine Workers—makes it absurd to suppose that, chameleon-like, he acquired their intellectual predilections. "We liberals," Professor Chafee wrote, "cannot have it both ways. If we blame a prominent lawyer like Mr. Hughes for some of his clients, we are merely chiming in with those who constantly call the American Civil Liberties Union communistic because it has represented Communists along with the great many other defendants. . . . The doctrine of guilt by association is abhorrent enough in the criminal and deportation fields without being extended into the relation between lawyer and client." [30]

Beyond this is the fact that Hughes' convictions bearing upon the great constitutional issues of the day had not been acquired at the bar but in public service. And these convictions, which were amply spread on the record, showed him to be no mouthpiece of the moneybags but a seasoned champion of liberty and of a "marching Constitution." The favorite shibboleth of the old-school judges had been "freedom of contract." Hughes had demolished that bulwark of the propertied interests in the McGuire case. With Holmes, he had fought against the "yellow dog" contract in *Coppage* v. *Kansas* and pleaded for the right to a fair trial in *Frank* v. *Mangum*. Over Holmes' protest, he had written that grand declaration of freedom from peonage in *Bailey* v. *Alabama*. Any impartial investigator could have found overwhelming evidence that, on the bench (as he had indicated in the letter about his son's confirmation as Solicitor General), the people of the United States would be his only client.

The Insurgents got from the press a drubbing no less severe than that they had administered to Hughes. Under the heading, "The Senate at Its Worst," the New York *Herald Tribune* declared: "That 26 Senators should vote to reject so admirable a nomination as that of Mr. Hughes to be Chief Justice of the United States is a symptom of aggravated degeneracy in a body now habituated to disesteem and decadence." [31] As the years passed, several repentant Senators quietly expressed regrets for their conduct, and others sought to mitigate their error by commending Hughes' outstanding service on the bench.

"The decorations of our public servants," Hughes once said, "are mostly scars." [32] In the long run, however, he carried few if any scars from the

[30] Reprinted by permission of the publishers from *Free Speech in the United States* by Zechariah Chafee, Jr., pp. 358f., Harvard University Press, 1941.
[31] Feb. 14, 1930.   [32] Speech of May 14, 1924.

bitter debate over his confirmation. The prevailing view of his qualifications was never really shaken. That view seems to have closely approximated the opinion of Samuel Untermyer, the distinguished New York attorney. ". . . not since the appointment of Chief Justice Marshall," Untermyer said, "has a man of such outstanding ability, experience and judicial temperament been called to that exalted office." [33]

[33] *Springfield Republican,* Feb. 16, 1930.

Chapter 64

INSIDE THE SUPREME COURT

"POPULAR interest naturally centers in the Chief Justice as the titular head of the Court. He is its executive officer; he presides at its sessions and at its conferences, and announces its orders. By virtue of the distinctive function of the Court he is the most important judicial officer in the world; he is the Chief Justice of the United States."

So wrote Charles Evans Hughes, attorney at law, in 1928.[1] Now he occupied the office. On February 24, 1930, he met with his brethren in the robing room at the Capitol (how familiar it was), and Holmes administered the oath of allegiance. Everyone had a cordial greeting for the new chief. At twelve o'clock the Justices crossed the corridor and took their places on the bench. Hughes, bringing up the rear, waited at the clerk's desk while the traditional "Oyez, Oyez, Oyez! God save the United States and this Honorable Court" resounded through the courtroom. With a quaver in his voice, Holmes then expressed regret over Taft's resignation. "We are happy to know," he said, "that in his place is to sit our old associate, Charles Evans Hughes." [2] Charles Elmore Cropley, clerk of the court, administered the judicial oath, and the marshal conducted the new Chief Justice to his seat at the center of the bench. Smiling happily, Hughes grasped the hand of Holmes on his right and of Van Devanter on his left and bowed to the other Justices and the audience. Then the business of the court went forward.

Hughes took over the reins with the easy grace of one long familiar with his task, although he had never presided over a court before. His piercing eyes and finely chiseled nose, his broad forehead, his white beard and bushy brows, standing out in contrast to his black robe, gave him the appearance of Mr. Justice himself. Never has a man been more appropriately cast for the highest judicial role.

The first lawyer recognized by the new Chief Justice was his son. Charles Junior had resigned as Solicitor General immediately upon his father's confirmation, but the resignation did not become effective until April 1. And since it was the Solicitor General's prerogative to lead off in presenting lawyers

[1] *The Supreme Court of the United States* (New York, Columbia University Press, 1928), p. 56. Copyright, 1928, by the Columbia University Press.
[2] *Washington Post*, Feb. 25, 1930.

for admittance to practice before the court, father and son briefly faced each other across the short distance from bench to bar.

That evening the new Chief Justice went to his son's home to dinner. Feeling chipper, he greeted both his son and his son's wife, Marjorie Stuart Hughes, with a kiss.

"Well," he said, his whiskers parting into a broad smile, "I suppose this is the first time the Chief Justice ever kissed the Solicitor General, and certainly it is the first time the Chief Justice ever kissed the Solicitor General's wife." [3]

The Chief Justice decided to give up his legal residence in New York and become for the rest of his days a voteless resident of the District of Columbia. Accordingly, he purchased the large commodious house at 2223 R Street, Northwest, and moved into it in September, 1930. Once more he completely severed his political connections; there would be no underground politicking on his part; nor would he serve as a backstage presidential adviser. Hughes promptly shut out every conceivable influence that might interfere with efficient and detached judicial service.

The heavy work of the Chief Justiceship compelled him to organize his time and utilize his energy with maximum efficiency. The innate sense of order that had characterized his life was thus crystallized into an almost invariable routine. He arose at the same time every morning, refreshed and full of ideas. Often he would jot down notes about a case before the court while he was dressing. Always his mind was keenest in the morning. At 7:30 A.M. he ate a light breakfast and then walked one mile. People living on Massachusetts Avenue could set their clocks by remembering the time at which he passed their door each morning. On his return he would be panting with eagerness to get his accumulated ideas on paper. At precisely 8:30 A.M. he was at his desk writing an opinion, making notes on cases to be presented to the conference, handling his correspondence, or holding interviews regarding the business of the court. On session or conference days he left home at 11:30 A.M., arriving at the court in time to give a few additional minutes to administrative details.

About five minutes before noon the Chief took his place in the anteroom where the judges assembled. As the other Justices arrived, there would be a general round of handshaking and affable chatting. At precisely the right moment Hughes would say, "Brethren, the time has come." Two pages would part the drapes, and the Justices would mount the bench together on the stroke of twelve with scarcely a second of variation. Not once in eleven years did the Chief permit the court to be one instant late.

From two o'clock to two-thirty the brethren lunched together. For Hughes it was a period of complete relaxation. On the bench, however, he would not permit a moment to be frittered away. Taking out the gold watch given him

[3] Author's interview with CEH, Jr., Aug. 13, 1948.

by his students at Columbia a half-century before, he held each speaker to exactly his allotted time. It is said, with some exaggeration, that once he called time on a leader of the New York bar in the middle of the word "if." When John W. Davis asked how much time remained and Hughes snapped, "Exactly one minute and a half," counsel suavely replied, "I present the court with one minute and a half." Hughes appreciated the humor, but he didn't alter his practice. He would call a new case for argument if only three or four minutes remained before adjournment. Sometimes when further argument seemed unnecessary, he would pass a slip of paper down the bench for the concurrence of his brethren and then say, "The court does not wish to hear any further argument in this case."

After court adjourned he disposed of administrative details with great dispatch and by five o'clock was on his way home. He and Mrs. Hughes would then go for a stroll and return for an early dinner. The evening was given to study, general reading, and family relationships. Promptly at 10:00 P.M. the Chief Justice went to bed feeling thankful for his sense of *bien-être,* which he attributed largely to his regular habits and his emancipation from smoking.

The fortune that Hughes had made at the bar brought his family all the comforts and some of the luxuries of life. Mrs. Hughes beautifully furnished the living quarters of their R Street home. The faithful services of Mary Dudley, the cook, and Lois Jones, the chambermaid, helped to keep the household running smoothly, and a chauffeur drove the family's shining limousine. Hughes would have none of the austerity that the wealthy Brandeises imposed upon themselves. Yet there was no splurging in his household—just comfortable living befitting the station of the Chief Justice.

By 1930 the Hughes family had shrunk to two members. On December 19 of that year, Miss Elizabeth, the youngest daughter, was married to Mr. William Thomas Gossett in a quiet ceremony at the Hughes home, with the Reverend Dr. Harry Emerson Fosdick and Dr. William S. Abernathy officiating and with only members of the family present. As a lawyer in Hughes' New York firm, Gossett had won a high standing with the father as well as the daughter. Later he was to be a partner in the law firm of his brother-in-law, Charles E. Hughes, Jr., until he left in 1947 to become vice president and general counsel of the Ford Motor Company.

Busy, happy, and self-sufficient, the Chief and Mrs. Hughes gave only one night a week—Saturday night—to entertainment, except when they were invited to the White House. This came to be generally understood in Washington's social circles, with the result that the Hugheses were booked up for every Saturday, sometimes nearly a year in advance, with only three Saturday evenings reserved for their own annual dinner parties.

These were occasions for complete relaxation, for indulgence in a glass of champagne, and full enjoyment of friendly relations. The majesty of the Chief Justiceship had not dulled Hughes' sense of humor. In conference, to be sure, his stories usually had a bearing upon the point at issue. But at a party humor for its own sake was always in order. He could even relish jokes on himself. When an unusual outburst of laughter went pealing through the Hughes home at one of their parties, it was safe to assume that he or Mrs. Hughes had brought out the "shirttail letter." Addressed to Hughes by May Markson, "auction editor" of the *Des Moines News,* the letter gave details of a scheme to raise money for the Red Cross "by selling at a big public auction here, kitchen aprons made from the shirttails of famous men, and others." It concluded:

May we ask you to mail soon a shirt from your wardrobe to the Auction Editor, The Des Moines News, accompanying the same with an identification mark, and if possible, a short biography of the garment, as to what important events it has shared in your life?

Whatever your decision, please do not make this letter public.

Hughes framed the letter, and it became a prized possession of the family. Incidentally, his fan mail while he was Chief Justice was said to be exceeded in volume only by the President's and Huey Long's—when the latter was in the Senate. One fan merely drew a picture of the famous whiskers on a card, and it was delivered without name or address.

People were insatiably curious about him. While the Hugheses were vacationing in the White Mountains one summer, the Chief took his grandson Dick Waddell to see the Old Man of the Mountain. Soon after they alighted from their car, they found themselves in a group of sightseers who had just arrived by bus. Some of the bus passengers whispered about that the bewhiskered gentleman was Chief Justice Hughes. But he and his young companion were laughing so gaily that others were skeptical. One woman who was sure that the illustrious Chief Justice would never indulge in such undignified mirth said to Hughes with a contemptuous smirk, "They think *you* are Chief Justice Hughes."

In Washington one day a young man passed Hughes on the sidewalk, staring hard, and then waited for the Chief to catch up with him.

"You know," the young man said, "you look like Chief Justice Hughes."

"Yes," was Hughes' only reply.

"Are you Chief Justice Hughes?"

"Yes," he again replied, much amused.

"Oh, no you ain't," the young man chortled and hastened away.

Even Mrs. John Lord O'Brian failed to identify the Chief Justice one Sunday morning—over the telephone. To Hughes' request to speak to Mr.

O'Brian, she replied that he was in the bathtub. "Please tell him," Hughes responded, "that the Chief Justice wishes to talk with him." Suspecting a joke on the part of her friend Charles P. Sisson, who had promised to call that morning, Mrs. O'Brian exclaimed, "Now look here, Charlie, you can't fool me." After a pause Hughes ventured, "But this really is the Chief Justice." Mrs. O'Brian apologized, and she and the Chief enjoyed a good laugh over the incident the next time they met.

During the weeks when the court was in recess for the preparation of opinions, Hughes worked all day in his chambers at home, taking time out only for a brief lunch with Mrs. Hughes. His chambers consisted of two rooms on the first floor, one of which was occupied by his secretary, Wendell W. Mischler, once described by the Chief as a man of "tact and discretion" who gave "meticulous attention to every detail . . . and never-failing devotion to duty." Hughes' office, a pleasant, squarish room with books covering two walls, was simply furnished with two overstuffed chairs and a davenport. He sat at a plain, flat-topped mahogany desk in the high-backed chair which he had used as governor and which had been given to him by the State of New York. Close at hand were his dictionary and a shelf of reference books. Looking down on him at his left above the clock was a picture of Chief Justice White, and nearby an engraving of "The Right Honourable Thomas Lord Denham, Chief Justice of the Queen's Bench." Behind the door, as if relegated to a secondary place, was a likeness of John Stuart Mill. Facing the Chief Justice from a high mantelpiece across the room was a bronze bust of Lincoln—the most conspicuous object in the room. From these modest quarters the Supreme Court was to be directed for eleven years.

Only three of Hughes' former associates on the bench were still there—the ineffable and seemingly ageless Holmes, the genial and versatile Van Devanter, and the narrow and tenacious McReynolds. Even in his felicitation of the new Chief Justice, McReynolds reflected the crabbed pessimism that had settled upon him. "As you well know," he wrote, "you are returning to slavery. But somehow it seems the common fate to end one's days in chains of some kind." [4]

"Yes; I know that," Hughes replied in blithe spirit. "I have experienced freedom but even freedom has its illusions." [5]

Van Devanter was delighted by the return of his good friend to the bench. Their mutual esteem ripened as they resumed their work together. Hughes noted that in conference Van Devanter was as lucid as ever, but his "pen paralysis" had become almost an affliction. When several months slipped by without opinions assigned to him being circulated in the court, he got no more cases from the new Chief Justice. Sometimes Hughes found it necessary, as the end of a term approached, to take back cases that he had assigned to Van

[4] McReynolds to CEH, Feb. 1930.   [5] CEH's speech of May 8, 1930.

Devanter. But he did it with a flourish of good will that put no strain on their friendship. "You are overworked," he would say. "Let me relieve you of some of your burden."

Holmes was still a keen blade of the law. It was always a joy to work with him. Three days before Hughes' confirmation the Magnificent Yankee, who had been presiding over the court as senior Justice during Taft's illness, had written the new chief:

This pressing affair that I expect to turn over to you very soon has delayed a little my telling you what I hope you know without my telling you, that I shall welcome you with a double delight—that I am to have my friend near me again and that we are to have such an able and competent head for our work. It is most satisfactory and once again I can sleep in peace at home or by your side. I hope that you are as happy as I am.

Hughes had replied on February 13:

DEAR JUSTICE HOLMES,

I am still somewhat dazed by the flash of the unexpected, but nothing could give me greater pleasure than your welcome. I can say with deep affection and esteem, and, I am sure—in your view—without irreverence—"Thou shalt guide me with thy counsel." I am indeed happy to return to our delightful association which I trust will long continue.

                    Faithfully yours,
                    CHARLES E. HUGHES

Holmes did continue to take his cat-naps on the bench, and this was a source of no little amusement among his brethren. One day an old colored man wandered into the court while arguments were being made, settled into a front seat, and fell asleep. In the interest of maintaining the court's dignity, Hughes sent a page boy to wake the man up. Then he whispered to Holmes, with a twinkle in his eye, "We can't have that. Only Justices are allowed to sleep in this courtroom."

Nevertheless, Holmes was still full of zest and intense devotion to his task. Observing that the venerable philosopher and judge kept his notes of the arguments with the same care that he had demonstrated twenty years before, Hughes was amazed by his vigor. Nor was any abatement of his power evident in his opinions. Standing almost alone in his generation, he was ever of the present. "Within his breast," Hughes said, "he carries the secret of eternal youth, and he carries it with an incomparable grace." [6]

Holmes' ebullient personality continued to find expression in notes on the proof sheets of the brethren's opinions. On one of the Chief's first opinions

[6] Hughes' tribute to Holmes, *Harvard Law Review*, March, 1931.

he inscribed: "Wee-Mussoo OWH Ye crags & peaks, I'm with you once again." [7]

The new Chief Justice was on friendly terms with all the members of the court, having appeared before them frequently and having met them off the bench from time to time. Justice Stone, able, scholarly, and experienced, had been Attorney General in Coolidge's Cabinet during Hughes' last year as Secretary of State. Some of Stone's friends thought that he resented Hughes' accession to an honor that might otherwise have been his. But he offered his "heartiest congratulations" and worked along with the Chief without noticeable friction.

The friendship between Hughes and Justice Brandeis went back to the former's clerkship in the office of Walter Carter. Always eager to boost promising young lawyers, Mr. Carter had come to the door of the clerks' room one day with a keen-eyed, slender young man whom he introduced as "Louis Brandeis, the coming leader of the Boston bar." [8] Some years later the firm of Brandeis, Dunbar, and Nutter had been correspondent in Boston to Hughes' firms in New York. When the Boston crusader finally won his long fight for confirmation and took his seat on the supreme bench in June, 1916, Hughes had heartily welcomed him a few days before his own resignation.

Brandeis' poise and serenity in every discussion made him "a delightful companion." Nothing of importance escaped him because it might be minute; at the same time his mental vision ranged "far beyond the familiar worlds of conventional thinking." Basic differences between the two men not infrequently came to the surface, but these were always disposed of in a friendly fashion. More often they saw eye to eye. When Brandeis marshaled his legions of facts behind a thesis that Hughes had laid before the court in conference, the Chief would say to his intimates, "Brandeis weighs a ton." [9]

Another colleague who won Hughes' highest respect was Justice Owen J. Roberts of Philadelphia. Roberts succeeded Justice Sanford in May, 1930, after the rampaging Senate had rejected the nomination of another outstanding jurist, Judge John J. Parker of the United States Circuit Court of Appeals. A most engaging personality as well as a lawyer of ability, forcefulness, and forensic skill, Roberts had won national distinction in his prosecution of the oil-scandal cases. On the bench he was a strong judge, and Hughes found him a "most agreeable" companion throughout the eleven years they sat together. At no time was there any display of the Chief's affection for Roberts, but when the big Philadelphian broke his shoulder in a fall from a horse, the Chief visited him in the hospital every day, except Saturdays and Sundays, for three weeks.

Hughes had been well aware of the cleavage within the court. After he re-

[7] CEH, private papers.   [8] CEH, Notes, 1930–1941, p. 10.
[9] Author's interview with William T. Gossett, June 14, 1949.

turned to the bench he agreed with Holmes: "We are very quiet there, but it is the quiet of a storm center." Pierce Butler, McReynolds, Van Devanter, and George Sutherland formed a tight little bloc of conservatism. All were men of character and conviction, but their common emphasis on property rights drove them into a sort of judicial phalanx against various types of welfare laws that Congress and the states were enacting with increasing frequency. Of course, they did not invariably stand together. In his earlier days on the bench Van Devanter had written a number of liberal opinions, and Sutherland, a former senator from Utah, frequently took a broad view of civil rights and governmental powers. For example, Sutherland wrote the court's opinions sustaining the right of an accused Negro to counsel in a criminal case in a state court; [10] striking down a state license tax on newspapers; [11] and upholding the exercise of broad presidential powers in the sphere of foreign relations.[12] But the pattern of agreement among the "Four Horsemen," as the conservative Justices were flippantly called, was sufficiently consistent to make them a formidable power.

Butler was the most difficult man on the court. Tough-minded and unshakable in his convictions, he was always ready for intellectual battle. At the conference table he argued with typically Irish tenacity and force, sometimes with thrusts of wit and eloquence. Authoritarian by instinct, he brought all the power of an indefatigable and fearless personality to the support of his views. McReynolds shared Butler's inclination to make a fetish of the constitutional guarantee of property rights, and they (especially Butler) exerted a strong influence upon Van Devanter and Sutherland.

The four conservatives often conferred together as a little nucleus within the court. Their teamwork was stimulated by a common dislike for certain views held by Brandeis, and his elaborate and forceful exposition intensified opposition.[13] Butler was sometimes so ill-tempered in his outbursts aimed at Brandeis that the Chief would have to intervene to restore a judicial tone to the discussion. While Butler was the spearhead of the conservative bloc, McReynolds easily held first honors in acidity. The cantankerous bachelor from Tennessee felt in his bones that Brandeis was undermining the court. In addition he was bitterly anti-Semitic and declined many invitations to avoid meeting Brandeis socially. The Hugheses held two court dinners each year and carefully divided the Justices so as to avoid embarrassment and make it possible to invite other guests.

Other members of the court felt the sting of McReynolds' churlishness in a different manner. He liked to regard himself as a mentor of new Justices, and

[10] *Powell* v. *Alabama*, 287 U.S. 45.
[11] *Grosjean* v. *American Press Co.*, 297 U.S. 233.
[12] *U.S. v. Curtiss-Wright Corp.*, 299 U.S. 304.
[13] CEH, Notes, 1930–1941, p. 14.

if they did not care to be taken under his wing, they had to brace themselves for persistent ridicule of their opinions. "This statement makes me sick," McReynolds would say with reference to an opinion circulated in proof.[14] For Chief Justice Hughes, however, the splenetic Tennesseean had a good deal of deference.

At the opposite pole of judicial thinking stood Brandeis, Holmes, and Stone. Brandeis, at this period, was the most resourceful of the three. "As Justice Holmes became more and more conscious of the limitations of age he was inclined to depend upon the judgment of his close friend." [15] Taft had concluded that Holmes was "so completely under the control of Brother Brandeis that it gives Brandeis two votes instead of one." [16] While Stone often agreed with Brandeis, he was careful to maintain his independence, sometimes writing separate concurring opinions.

Left to themselves, these factions might have produced the worst judicial cacophony in our history. But the Chief Justice exerted a powerful moderating influence. In terms of judicial philosophy, as well as in the seating arrangement, he occupied the center of the bench. Roberts, too, charted an independent course somewhere near the middle of the stream. If Hughes and Roberts stood together on a controversial issue and could win the support of the four conservatives, the court would usually divide six to three. In other controversial cases, Hughes would win the support of the liberal wing, and the division would be five to four, with Roberts casting the deciding vote.

In voting on decisions and in writing opinions the Chief Justice has no more power than any other member of the Supreme Court. Because of his three special functions, however, he has a unique opportunity for leadership within the court: (1) he is the moderator of the conferences in which the judges make their decisions; (2) he presides over the open sessions of the court; (3) he assigns the cases to the judges for the writing of opinions. Through the exercise of these powers a strong Chief Justice may dominate the court. ". . . it is evident," as Hughes himself wrote when he had no idea of becoming Chief Justice, "that his actual influence will depend upon the strength of his character and the demonstration of his ability in the intimate relations of the judges." [17]

Hughes had thoroughly mastered the art of judicial administration. In his first period on the court he had learned from Chief Justice White what a presiding judge ought not to do. The unfortunate results of White's indecisive statements to the conference and the rambling debate that followed led Hughes to place great weight upon concise, forthright, and accurate statement of each

[14] Author's interview with Owen J. Roberts, May 21, 1946.   [15] CEH, Notes, p. 14.
[16] Henry F. Pringle, *The Life and Times of William Howard Taft* (New York, Farrar & Rinehart, 1938), II, 969. Copyright, 1938, by Henry F. Pringle.
[17] *The Supreme Court of the United States*, p. 57.

case and confinement of debate to the points at issue. Through these administrative devices that White had neglected, Hughes was able to reduce controversy to a minimum (and to accelerate the work of the court) without sacrificing freedom or fullness of discussion.

Preparation for the Saturday conference began a week in advance when each Justice received from the clerk of the court a copy of all the accumulated petitions for certiorari, jurisdictional statements, and motions. Often these papers would make a stack four feet high. Delving into them, the Chief's law clerk made extensive notes on every case. Hughes had the good fortune of being served in succession by four law clerks of exceptional capacity—Reynolds Robertson, Francis R. Kirkham, Richard W. Hogue, Jr., and Edwin McElwain. He relied upon these men for a comprehensive survey of the "certs." With the aid of his clerk's memoranda, he then focused his own photographic mind upon the records and briefs, inserting innumerable bookmarks and making occasional checks on the margins. Most of his attention was given to the records, as he preferred to go to the original source for his facts.[18]

The purpose of this first examination of the certiorari cases was to determine which the court would review in the interest of clarifying the law. Hughes could find no merit whatever in about 60 per cent of these petitions. Many of them were so obviously frivolous that he recommended denial without discussion in conference. His list of such cases (it was dubbed the "black list" by court personnel) was circulated among the Justices with the understanding that a simple request by any one of them would be sufficient to get discussion of a listed case in conference. In eleven years, however, the Chief's judgment as to these cases was not questioned more than half a dozen times.

The conference discussion was thus focused upon about 40 per cent of the applications for certiorari. In these cases Hughes made concise notes from his study of the record and his clerk's memoranda, usually confining himself to two five-by-eight-inch sheets for each case. Taking these notes, his clerk's memoranda, his marked copies of the records and briefs, and numerous lawbooks, Hughes would sit at the head of the conference table full of youthful exuberance and ready for any challenge. His thorough and obvious preparation was an effective warning to anyone who might disagree with him that he had "better know *all* the facts and know them well." [19]

With scarcely a glance at his penciled notes, Hughes would launch into case after case in rapid succession. Since a typical agenda for the Saturday conference would include twenty to thirty petitions for certiorari, half a dozen jurisdictional statements on appeal, a few miscellaneous motions, and ten to fifteen cases that had been argued during the week, only a few minutes could be given

[18] Edwin McElwain in the *Harvard Law Review*, Vol. 63, No. I, p. 13.
[19] *Ibid.*, p. 14.

to each "cert" if the conference were to reserve time for deliberation on the argued cases. The pressure for time put a special premium upon Hughes' knack for condensing facts. His brief analyses were nevertheless so complete, accurate, and objective that in many instances no other Justice felt any urge to supplement what he had said or to take exception to it. If a question were raised, Hughes would reach for one of his reference volumes full of white markers and either read or summarize the supporting data. "I do not remember an instance," Justice Roberts has reported, "when he was found to have erred in his original statement." [20]

The court always granted certiorari if four Justices so requested, and, not infrequently, if three, or even two, Justices strongly urged the grant. Nevertheless, about 80 per cent of these petitions were denied. The phrasing of the denials and all other *per curiam* decisions was left almost entirely to the Chief Justice. Hughes gave a good deal of attention to this phase of his work, believing that clear expression of the reasons for the court's summary decisions would discourage lawyers from bringing frivolous cases to the supreme bench.

Except at the beginning of a new term, when several conferences were necessary to dispose of the petitions for certiorari accumulated during the summer, Hughes always insisted on finishing all the business before the conference at a single session. This kept the court abreast of its work. Stone sometimes complained that the Chief was a taskmaster, and Brandeis left the conference if it ran beyond the scheduled closing hour of 4:30 P.M. On such occasions Brandeis would pick up the old-fashioned green bag in which he carried his papers and say to the Chief, "Your jurisdiction is at an end. You know how I am going to vote in this case." [21] His vote would be cast accordingly. Beneath these superficial protests against the intensity of Hughes' methods, however, there was deep appreciation of his adherence to system and his prodigious industry. Brandeis used to say that Hughes was the greatest executive genius he had ever encountered in law, in business, or in government.[22]

The cases which the court agreed to take soon came on for argument, with Hughes in the presiding chair. In this role he was nothing short of superb. His long experience at the bar, his close study of judicial conduct, and his native courtesy had given him an impeccable set of courtroom manners. With his urbanity, dignity, and resourcefulness in meeting every situation, he "radiated authority." [23] Apparently no one has mastered the art of presiding over the court to the extent that Hughes did.

To argue before the Hughes court was a trying experience for any attorney. The Chief always seemed to know as much about the case as counsel did, or

[20] Justice Roberts' memorial address before the New York bar, Dec. 12, 1948.
[21] Author's interview with CEH, April 30, 1946.
[22] Author's interview with Henry P. Chandler, Dec. 8, 1949.
[23] Justice Frankfurter in the *Harvard Law Review,* Vol. 63, No. 1, p. 4.

even more. That was not due solely to his unusual memory but also to his systematic use of his notes. If counsel moved expeditiously from one main point to another, with neither oratory nor evasiveness, Hughes was likely to sit and drink it in. But few lawyers made that kind of argument. Since there is no real Supreme Court bar, most of the lawyers who came before the court (except the Solicitor General and his staff and the senior partners of a few large firms) were relative strangers to it. Hughes had the faculty of sizing up these men "a split second after the first word was uttered," [24] and he saw to it that neither nervousness nor shallowness of thinking on their part should deprive the court of expert analysis of the crucial issues.

Breaking into a windy harangue by counsel, the Chief would concisely state the point the lawyer should have been making and ask if that was the gist of his argument. If the lawyer assented, Hughes would say, "Now the court would like to hear you on these other points." It irked him to have counsel evade a question by saying that it would be answered at the appropriate point in his argument. When such a reply was made to other members of the court, the Chief often rephrased the query and usually got a responsive answer. But he never harassed counsel. His questions were asked solely for the purpose of eliciting information and keeping peripatetic lawyers on the beam. "I know of no instance," said Justice Roberts, "where a lawyer had reason to feel rebuked or hurt by anything that the Chief Justice said or did." [25]

Sometimes the intensity of an argument before the court was too much for a lawyer to endure. Solicitor General Stanley Reed once fainted while arguing a case before his brethren-to-be. One day a private practitioner completely lost the thread of his argument and began to babble incoherently. Hughes tried to aid him by asking simple questions about the case. Seeing that this further bewildered the lawyer, Hughes took the brief and completed the argument that counsel was unable to make. "Isn't your argument so and so," he would ask in his most kindly manner as he went along. The baffled lawyer could only assent and express his unbounded appreciation.[26]

Not infrequently the tension in the courtroom was broken by flashes of humor. A utilities lawyer argued that a rate-making question had been left in "a state of confusion." Unable to suppress a pun, Hughes cut in with, "It was left in the State of California, wasn't it?"

When an attorney argued a tax case which turned on whether a jig-saw picture was a game or a puzzle, Hughes asked with a twinkle in his eye, "Would the court in that case be a game?"

"No, your honor," the attorney drawled. "The court is a puzzle."

There were other occasions when the utmost restraint was necessary to

[24] Edwin McElwain in the *Harvard Law Review*, Vol. 63, No. 1, p. 16.
[25] Justice Roberts' memorial address before the New York bar, Dec. 12, 1948.
[26] Author's interview with Randolph Paul, Feb. 9, 1950.

maintain the dignity of the court. One day a young man arguing before the nine patriarchs of the law got himself tangled in a complicated sentence and exclaimed, as if dictating to his secretary, "Strike that out!" A New York attorney argued so vehemently that his false teeth popped out of his mouth. With amazing dexterity he scooped up the errant dentures almost before they hit the counsel's table in front of him and flipped them back into his mouth, with scarcely a word interrupted. Not a smile ruffled the dignity of the bench, but the Justices' pent-up mirth broke into gales of laughter when they reached safe havens of privacy.

Cases on which arguments were completed were presented to the conference the following Saturday. In preparing for this task Hughes would extend, and, if necessary, revise, the notes he had previously made on each case. Former Justice Roberts gives us a vivid picture of how the Chief laid an argued case before the conference:

> His presentation of the facts of a case was full and impartial. His summary of the legal questions arising out of the facts was equally complete, dealing with the opposing contentions so as to make them stand out clearly. When this had been done, he would usually look up with a quizzical smile and say, "Now I will state where I come out," and would then outline what he thought the decision of the Court should be. Again in many cases his treatment was so complete that little, if anything, further could be added by any of the Justices. In close and difficult cases, where there were opposing views, the discussion would go round the table from the senior to the junior, each stating his views and the reasons for his concurrence or his difference with those outlined by the Chief. After the Chief Justice had finished his statement of the case and others took up the discussion, I have never known him to interrupt or to get into an argument with the Justice who was speaking. He would wait until the discussion had closed and then briefly and succinctly call attention to the matters developed in the discussion as to which he agreed or disagreed, giving his reasons. These conference sessions lasted from twelve o'clock sometimes until six, sometimes until six-thirty in the evening. . . . It is not hard to understand that, at the close of such a conference, most of the Justices were weary. The sustained intellectual effort demanded was great. The way the Chief Justice came through these difficult conferences was always a matter of wonder and admiration to me.[27]

It has sometimes been assumed that Hughes was domineering and even schoolmasterish in dealing with his brethren. The idea is absurd to anyone who knew the court from the inside. No man of any intelligence would have attempted to dominate Brandeis, Butler, or Roberts. Hughes recognized that the court was composed of judges of wide experience, deep learning, independent views, and profound convictions. Everyone's brains, as he used to say, were on the table. It was ridiculous to suppose that the brethren could be swayed

---

[27] Justice Roberts' memorial address before the New York bar, Dec. 12, 1948.

from any settled habits of thinking by high-powered arguments or emotional appeals. Consequently, Hughes made no such appeals. We have Stone's word that the Chief's influence upon "the efficiency and morale of the Court . . . cannot be exaggerated." But Stone attributes that influence solely to Hughes' "passion for the prompt and faithful performance of the work of the court" and to his "painstaking care and unflagging energy." [28]

Nor did the Chief Justice solicit support for his views outside the conference. He had only contempt for the kind of chief who would take a judge aside and say, "Can't you see the tight spot we're in; you've got to help us out." He knew, of course, that the four conservatives conferred together on specific cases. But he would neither join their circle nor sponsor a rival one. While his door was always open to any member of the court who wished to discuss any kind of problem, he reserved his views of cases before the court (with one or two exceptions) for expression at the conference where all the Justices would be present.

"What his conclusion was," Justice Roberts said, "none of us knew until he announced it at conference. He neither leaned on anyone else for advice nor did he proffer advice or assistance to any of us, but left us each to form his own conclusions to be laid on the table at conference in free and open discussion. A nice sense of propriety undoubtedly brought about this practice. . . . I am sure that this calculated course greatly strengthened his position and authority with his brethren." [29]

Hughes' mere presence tended to keep the discussions on a high-minded plane. "This high personal quality," says Roberts, "pervaded all the deliberations of the Court. Strong views were often expressed around the conference table, but never in eleven years did I see the Chief Justice lose his temper. Never did I hear him pass a personal remark. Never did I know him to raise his voice. Never did I witness his interrupting a Justice or getting into a controversy with him, and practically never did any one of his associates overstep the bounds of courtesy and propriety in opposing the views advanced by the Chief."

If discussion among other members of the court deteriorated into wrangling, Hughes would promptly cut it off. Every Justice had complete freedom to speak his mind, and rebuttals and general discussion were permissible. But as soon as heat began to supplant analysis and reason, the Chief would say, "Brethren, the only way to settle this is to vote." [30]

Regardless of how deep the controversy might run, Hughes closed the door upon it as soon as the conference was over. As Justice Frankfurter has pointed out, "he had no lingering afterthoughts born of a feeling of defeat, and thereby

[28] *American Bar Association Journal*, July, 1941, p. 407.
[29] Justice Roberts' memorial address before the New York bar, Dec. 12, 1948.
[30] Author's interview with CEH, Dec. 3, 1946.

avoided the fostering of cleavages." [31] One day the court rejected a decision proposed by Hughes just before the judges went to lunch. Without once alluding to the case, the Chief sat by the junior member who had taken the lead in opposing his view and chatted in his most fascinating manner throughout the lunch period. Grousing over a defeat was as foreign to his nature as gloating over a victory.

Aside from his genius for pulling the court together, the rules of the conference gave Hughes the dominant role. It is often erroneously assumed that in these conferences the Chief Justice gives his verbal opinion last. "On the contrary," the most eminent authority has written, "it is the tradition and regular practice for the Chief Justice to lead the discussion of each case by stating his opinion first and then to call for the views of the other Justices in the order of seniority. The mistaken notion is due to a confusion of the order of discussion with the order of voting. When the discussion has reached the point where the Justices are ready to vote, the Chief Justice calls the roll in the inverse order of seniority and thus casts the last vote." [32] The important point is that in each case the judges were faced with the question of agreeing or disagreeing with the Chief, and no one was inclined to disagree with him unless driven to it by some basic conviction.

Division in the court was also held in check by the ingenious reasoning that Hughes frequently advanced to give the contending factions common ground on which to stand. In some cases in which agreement had seemed impossible, dissents were thus avoided.[33] Hughes often modified his own opinions in order to win additional support for them if that could be done without compromising the integrity of the position the majority had taken. And when other Justices seemed fairly close together in the views they had expressed, he would suggest insertions or a little blue-penciling to avert a split decision. In these efforts he was highly successful because of the great respect within the court for his judgment.

While it is true, therefore, that Hughes was the dominant influence in the court, it was not because of any domineering attitude on his part. He "ran the court as it was never run before." [34] But he did it through the thoroughness of his work, the clarity of his statements, the power of his intellect, and the considerate treatment of his colleagues. It is his fellow workers who have most frequently described him as "the greatest of a great line of Chief Justices." [35]

In the assignment of opinions Hughes again followed principles that buttressed the court as an institution. This important function is left entirely to

---

[31] Justice Frankfurter in the *Harvard Law Review,* Vol. 63, No. 1, p. 3.
[32] CEH, Notes, 1930–1941, p. 15.
[33] Author's interview with former Justice Roberts, May 21, 1946.
[34] Edwin McElwain in the *Harvard Law Review,* Vol. 63, No. I, p. 26.
[35] Justice Roberts' memorial address before the New York bar, Dec. 12, 1948.

the Chief Justice, except when he is in the minority, in which case the assignment is made by the senior Justice in the majority group. The Chief Justice may
write all the major opinions himself or he may distribute them among the
Justices whose views are closest to his. Hughes did neither. "My most delicate
task," he wrote in his Notes, "was in the assignment of opinions. I endeavored
to do this with due regard to the feelings of the senior Justices and to give to
each Justice the same proportion of important cases while at the same time
equalizing so far as possible the burden of work. Of course, in making assignments I often had in mind the special fitness of a Justice for writing in the
particular case." [36]

Laying great store upon this "deployment of his army," Hughes would sit
down at the end of each Saturday conference with his law clerk and a chart
showing the position each judge had taken in each case. After pondering and
trying various combinations, he would indicate his decisions by writing the
number of each case opposite the name of the Justice who was to write the
opinion. Most of the assignment slips were delivered that evening in deference
to the eagerness of the brethren to know promptly what opinions they would
write. But there were two exceptions. Justice Cardozo had suffered a heart
attack before his appointment to the Supreme Court. Knowing that Cardozo
went to work on his opinions immediately after getting his assignment on
Saturday night, the Chief made a practice of withholding Cardozo's assignment
slip until Sunday.[37] To keep Cardozo from suspecting that his health was being
shielded, Hughes also held back the assignments of Justice Van Devanter, who
was a neighbor of Cardozo in a Connecticut Avenue apartment house.

Hughes assigned to himself those cases which he believed to be of such importance that the country would expect the pronouncement of the court to come
from the Chief Justice. But he also took a large number of run-of-the-mine
cases. His constant practice was to write as many opinions as other members
of the court in addition to his administrative load.

Sometimes he would assign a line of cases in a single field to one Justice,
but he was careful not to carry specialization to extremes. To do their work
properly, all members of the court had to be at home with tax law, admiralty,
civil rights, and various other branches of the law. "Every judge," he said,
"should have a chance to demonstrate through the writing of opinions the wide
range of his reasoning powers and not be kept before the public as an extremist
or specialist working in one particular groove." [38] If the court were sharply
divided, he tried to avoid extremes by assigning the opinion to the Justice
nearest the center, as when he gave Roberts the Agricultural Adjustment
Administration case.

[36] Chapter XXIII, p. 16.   [37] Author's interview with CEH, April 30, 1946.
[38] Id., Oct. 17, 1946.

When a Justice with a reputation as a liberal voted with the majority on the conservative side of a question, he usually got the opinion to write. The same was true in the case of a conservative voting on the liberal side. Hughes' constant effort was to enhance public confidence in the entire court as an independent and impartial tribunal.

In writing his own opinions the Chief set an example in both promptness and systematic workmanship. First, he reexamined his combined set of notes plus any memoranda he might have made on points emphasized in the conference. Then he outlined the points he would cover in his opinion and the order in which he would deal with them. His writing began only after this pattern had taken definite shape in his mind and he had thought out precisely what he wished to say.[39] A first draft was then scratched out in longhand with little regard for paragraphing or any refinements. As soon as one section was completed, he would call Mischler and dictate from this rough draft. While Mischler was typing the first section, the Chief would scribble out another segment, continuing that process until the opinion was completed. This first draft went to the printer with few changes. Corrections were made on the proof sheets, but Hughes never rewrote his opinions in proof.

The qualities that he sought to infuse into his opinions were accuracy, clarity, conciseness, and power. These were the four corners of good judicial craftsmanship. It was not the function of a judge to write literature. The struggle for catch phrases, rhetorical flourishes, and stylistic effects too often led to obscurities and equivocal statements. Hughes was fond of turning a subtle phrase in his speeches, but not in his opinions. The test of a good opinion was not whether it beguiled the public but whether it made the court's judgment unmistakably plain to the lower courts and the bar.

As he wrote, Hughes felt that he had a lawyer representing each party to the case looking over his shoulder and saying, "Now, you son of a gun, don't dodge this point." That is why he always made it evident in his opinions that every important point had been considered. The losing party should know precisely why he had lost. A Hughes opinion thus exudes an inexorable quality. As Chief Justice Arthur T. Vanderbilt of the Supreme Court of New Jersey has pointed out, Hughes put into his opinions "the feeling of the pulsating, rhythmical, irresistible argument rolling on toward its predetermined end . . ."[40] His directness, simplicity, and vigor made each major opinion that he wrote an orderly march of facts to the music of reason.

The Chief followed a strict rule of not sitting in cases involving former clients or in cases in which a former partner was counsel. Under our system each judge decides for himself when he is disqualified, and the standards used to guide such decisions differ widely. Justice Brandeis, for example, did not

[39] *Id.*, May 28, 1947.   [40] *New York University Law Review*, October, 1950.

think it necessary to withdraw when the court heard cases involving corporations in which he had investments. He thought Hughes was too meticulous about disqualification. "Oh, Chief Justice," he would say, "there is no need to disqualify yourself because of some association in the remote past. No one will have the slightest question as to your impartiality." [41] But Hughes held to his rule.

Having argued the Duke-Haskell case, he stepped aside when another suit involving the Duke estate reached the high bench. For this he was severely abused by an ill-tempered Pennsylvania lawyer, who had the temerity to write the Chief Justice that he should either sit in the case or resign and make place for "a more courageous individual." Instead of ignoring the insult or "blowing his top," Hughes wrote to his impertinent critic a thoughtful letter on disqualification, in which Brandeis concurred. No matter who may be appointed to the bench, the Chief explained, he will be confronted by some cases in which he is not qualified to sit. If a judge should take part in a decision when he is disqualified, the letter continued, "he would, indeed, be subject to just criticism and might even in a grave case be subject to impeachment. If the judge is disqualified, the question is not one of courage but of propriety and honor." The fact that the withdrawal of one Justice may, in rare cases, leave the court evenly divided, he wrote, makes it the clearer that the deciding vote should not be cast by a disqualified judge.

In the second year of the Hughes period the spotlight seemed to focus on the court's most venerable member. Holmes celebrated his ninetieth birthday that year—March 8, 1931—and everywhere he was lionized. In the evening, as he sat in his library listening to tributes on the radio, he heard the Chief Justice say:

He has abundantly the zest of life and his age crowns that eagerness and unflagging interest with the authority of experience and wisdom. . . . We place upon his brow the laurel crown of the highest distinction. But this will not suffice us or him. We honor him, but, what is more, we love him. We give him tonight the homage of our hearts.

Deeply moved, Holmes philosophized for a moment about the "little finishing canter" in the race of life and concluded with a priceless quotation from a Latin poet: "Death plucks my ears and says, Live—I am coming." [42]

When the court began its new term the following October, Holmes was slipping fast. "While he was still able to write clearly, it became evident in the conference of the Justices that he could no longer do his full share in the mastery of the work of the Court." [43] His drowsiness during arguments was so

[41] Author's interview with CEH, Nov. 26, 1946.
[42] Francis Biddle, *Mr. Justice Holmes* (New York, Scribner's, 1942), p. 193. Copyright, 1942, by Charles Scribner's Sons.
[43] CEH, Notes, 1930–1941, p. 11.

uncontrollable that his head would droop almost to the papers on his desk; then he would start up suddenly, writing with concentrated effort to keep awake. The Chief shielded him whenever possible, giving him only the easier cases. But Holmes' brethren began to fear that he would bring criticism upon the court. In January, 1932, a majority of them asked the Chief Justice to request Holmes' resignation.

Hughes was in a quandary. His brethren had asked him to perform the most distasteful duty he ever had to face—a task he would never have undertaken on his own initiative. Instinctively his mind played upon the numerous attempts of the court in the past to ease senile judges from its bench. After the first argument of the legal-tender case following the Civil War, the court had been afraid that Justice Grier would cast the deciding vote at a time when he was no longer able to address himself to the issues involved. A committee of judges, including Justice Field, had waited on Grier and urged his resignation. Years later Field himself had tarried on the bench after he was too old to meet the responsibilities of a judge, and his brethren had deputed Justice Harlan to remind the old man of what his committee had said to Grier. Harlan had aroused the venerable Justice as he was vegetating on a settee in the robing room. Did not Justice Field remember that he was one of the committee which had waited on Justice Grier? Did he not recall what the committee had said on that occasion? Suddenly alert, his eyes once more blazing with the fire of youth, the old man had retorted, "Yes! And a dirtier day's work I never did in my life." [44]

Harlan had related this experience to Hughes. Certainly it did not lighten the "highly unpleasant duty" now laid upon him. He consulted Justice Brandeis, Holmes' closest associate on the court, and Brandeis agreed that the time had come for the Magnificent Yankee to step down.[45] On Sunday, January 11, the Chief summoned all his tact and went to see the grand old man at his home. Gradually coming to the point of his visit, he told Holmes that he was under too heavy a burden; a man who had been forty-nine years on the benches of his state and nation should not strain himself by continuing to carry the load when his strength was no longer equal to it.[46]

Holmes was the soul of equanimity. Without the slightest indication of resentment, he requested Hughes to get out from the bookshelves the applicable statute and wrote his resignation with his usual felicity of expression. On Monday the aged jurist was full of sentiment as he sat with his brethren for the last time. Hughes wrote him a letter which all the Justices signed—a letter warm with affection and regret over the necessity of his leaving. "My Dear Brethren: You must let me call you so once more," Holmes replied. "Your more than

[44] *The Supreme Court of the United States*, p. 76.
[45] CEH, Notes, 1930–1941, p. 11. [46] Author's interview with CEH, Jan. 7, 1946.

kind, your generous, letter touches me to the bottom of my heart." Seldom have government circles witnessed a more tender parting.

To Hughes' great satisfaction, President Hoover named, as Holmes' successor, Chief Judge Cardozo of the New York Court of Appeals. "I am delighted," the Chief Justice wrote to his son, who had once been Cardozo's law clerk, "with the appointment of Cardozo. I had hoped that this would be possible." Ever since Hughes had met Cardozo as a lad in knickerbockers at Long Branch, they had been friends. Frequently they had met at the bar in New York, and when Cardozo went on the bench he followed a self-imposed rule of waiting twenty-four hours before making a decision in any case argued by this particular friend so as to avoid being overwhelmed by the power of Hughes' intellect and personality. In return, Hughes regarded him as "one of the outstanding jurists of his time, a rare spirit with whom it was a privilege and constant delight to be associated." [47]

With Cardozo's accession to the supreme bench early in 1932, there was to be no break in the membership of the court for more than five years.

[47] CEH, Notes, 1930–1941, p. 12.

Chapter 65

ORGANIZING THE COURTS FOR EFFICIENCY

HUGHES' passion for efficiency was felt throughout the federal judicial system. "We do not blink the fact," he said in one of his first speeches as Chief Justice, "that the greatest need in this country today is improvement in the administration of justice, especially of the criminal law." [1] Not content to re-energize the Supreme Court, he stimulated the lower courts to minimize delays, simplify procedure, and make "equal justice under law" a living reality.

Chief Justice Taft had inaugurated two great judicial reforms for the sake of efficiency. The Jurisdictional Act of 1925 had made it possible for the Supreme Court to concentrate its efforts upon cases involving questions of public importance and to keep its calendar up to date. To survey the work of the lower courts, Taft had also brought into being the Conference of Senior Circuit Judges, with the Chief Justice as its chairman. But the great tasks of devising a control mechanism for the judicial system and of improving procedure in the lower courts were still in their initial stages when Hughes took the helm.

One of the most pressing needs was the expediting of appeals in criminal cases. Congress passed two Acts giving the Supreme Court authority to prescribe rules for the federal courts with respect to proceedings in criminal cases after verdicts or pleas of guilty. A careful study of federal practice and procedure was laid before the Supreme Court, and Hughes took the matter up with the Senior Circuit Judges. The court promulgated its rules as to criminal appeals on May 7, 1934.

With the ice thus broken, there was a tremendous drive for procedural reforms in civil cases. For many years the American Bar Association had urged Congress to give the Supreme Court the same authority to provide for uniformity in federal procedure in actions at law as had been given with respect to equity practice. But a great deal of opposition had come from lawyers who wished to retain the practice with which they had become familiar in the state courts. Hughes threw his influence strongly on the side of modernization, and Attorney General Cummings brought the weight of the Roosevelt Administration behind the reform.

Congress responded in its Act of June 19, 1934, authorizing the Supreme

[1] Address to American Bar Association, Aug. 21, 1930.

683

Court to prescribe general rules to govern civil actions at law and, at its discretion, to set up a uniform system of procedure both for actions at law and suits in equity. Despite much opposition, the court decided that it would proceed at once to obtain a unified system, so far as that could be done without violation of any substantive right.

"It is manifest," the Chief Justice said, "that the goal we seek is a simplified practice which will strip procedure of unnecessary forms, technicalities and distinctions, and permit the advance of causes to the decision of their merits with a minimum of procedural encumbrances. It is also apparent that in seeking that end we should not be fettered by being compelled to maintain the historic separation of the procedural systems of law and equity." [2]

In devising the new rules the Supreme Court named an advisory committee of experienced practitioners and specialists from the law schools. The committee's preliminary draft of rules was widely distributed for the criticism of judges and lawyers before being adopted, with some changes, by the court. It became effective in 1938.[3]

The new Federal Rules of Civil Procedure have brought an enormous improvement in the administration of justice. The pretrial proceedings alone have helped to clear many federal court calendars by encouraging amicable settlements and stripping the cases that go to trial down to the real issues. The rule permitting examination of defendants as to their assets has eliminated a great deal of legal finagling. Not least in importance is the fact that these rules came from within the judicial system instead of being imposed upon it by legislative action. It was Hughes' hope that a tradition could be developed for leaving changes in procedural rules entirely to the courts.

Early in the Hughes period the Supreme Court also simplified various practices of its own. Hughes insisted that the court keep abreast of its work even though it had to dispose of about a thousand cases a year. To him, "justice delayed was justice denied." [4]

More important than rules was the human factor. "The spectacle of a weak and incompetent judge in action, or in inaction," Hughes said, "does more to undermine public confidence than abuse of the institution by hostile critics." [5] In cases where conscientious judges were swamped with work, he persistently sought additional judgeships through the Conference of Senior Circuit Judges. Under Hughes' stimulation, the conference also instructed the senior judge in each circuit to assign judges who had relatively little work to help out in other districts that were overburdened. The result was speedier trials in many jurisdictions.

Behind these improvements a larger idea was taking shape. It was the idea

[2] Address to American Law Institute, May 9, 1935.   [3] 308 U.S. pp. 645–788.
[4] Justice Stone in *American Bar Association Journal*, July, 1941, p. 407.
[5] Asheville address, June 9, 1932.

of binding an array of separate courts, each operating independently with no effective check on its work, into a well managed judicial system. The people were complaining over the law's delays and occasional maladministration. If the courts could not put their own house in order, there was danger that Congress might sweep the judiciary under some sort of executive or legislative supervision, thus impairing judicial independence. Some judges were also complaining because they had to go hat in hand to the Attorney General for stationery, supplies, and office help. The Department of Justice itself was eager to be relieved of its duties of making budgets for the courts and buying their supplies. Under the impact of these pressures, Hughes began to vitalize the Conference of Senior Circuit Judges as "the nucleus of a supervisory organization" [6] and to project the conference idea into the circuits.

One of his first moves was to secure complete statistics on the work of the courts. The conference concluded that the gathering of statistics would have to be carefully supervised and suggested that a unit for tabulation of court statistics be set up in the Department of Justice. Meanwhile Hughes was advancing a proposal that a conference of federal judges be held in each circuit to deal with local problems of administration. Such voluntary conferences were already being held in some of the circuits. They afforded an admirable opportunity for bringing district and circuit court judges together, along with members of the bar, to consider their common problems.

At the invitation of Chief Judge John J. Parker, Hughes attended a conference of the judges of the Fourth Circuit at Asheville in June, 1932, which gave attention to various problems of efficiency in the judicial system. "I think that we should . . . put aside for a while the order of the day," he said, "in order to observe how the department to which we belong is working and what we can do to make it work to better advantage. We must do our duty as judges of particular cases, but we are more than that—we are guardians of an institution." [7] His plan was to have ideas of general interest that might be developed in the circuit conferences relayed to the annual gatherings of senior circuit judges in Washington. By this means national attention could be focused on the needs of the courts, while decentralized supervision would help to work out local problems and keep the judges on their toes.

While this evolution was going on, Attorney General Homer Cummings got out a bill to create an administrative office of the United States courts. Cummings' laudable object was to give the courts the management of their own housekeeping and better supervision of their work. His plan called for a director of the new agency with broad powers not only over administrative details but also to examine the dockets of the various courts and to recommend to the Chief Justice of the United States temporary assignments of

[6] CEH, Notes, 1930–1941, p. 38.   [7] *Asheville Times,* June 9, 1932.

judges to help clear up overloaded dockets outside their own districts or circuits. In this respect the bill was reminiscent of a provision in the court-packing bill of 1937 which called for a proctor to survey judicial calendars and authority for the Chief Justice to send judges wherever they might be needed most. Both measures would have made the Chief Justice a sort of czar over the federal judiciary.

Hughes laid the measure before his brethren of the Supreme Court without committing himself. It aroused general hostility. Brandeis was emphatically opposed to it. Apparently the chief objection of the brethren was that the measure would lay too heavy a burden on the Chief Justice, who was already overworked.[8] The Chief Justice would not have time to comb over the budget figures or to settle all the disputes that would arise over the temporary assignment of judges away from their home districts. Consequently, he might become an easy target for attacks that would reflect upon himself and upon the Supreme Court.

Hughes remained temporarily silent as this opposition to the bill developed; he did not wish to appear unwilling to assume the new burdens if Congress or others thought he should do so, and he was heartily in favor of pulling the federal courts administratively closer together by any appropriate means. In September, 1938, when Cummings came before the Judicial Conference with a plea for endorsement of his bill, Hughes was ready with a reply. He strongly approved the idea of freeing the courts from any reliance upon the Department of Justice for housekeeping services. Independent courts should not be beholden to the chief litigant before them for services essential to their operation. The opportunity of effecting this reform ought to be seized, he said, while an Attorney General willing to relinquish this power was in office.

There was definite need, moreover, for improvement in the work of federal judges. With district judges entirely free from supervision in 85 to 90 per cent of their work, their conduct sometimes became "czar-like and arbitrary." The bar was pressing for more supervision, and since the courts were peculiarly responsible for the maintenance of our form of government, it was of vital importance to keep their work in good standing before public opinion.

The trouble with the bill, as Hughes saw it, was not its aim but its method. He thought that better supervision of the courts could be achieved without the objectionable concentration of power in himself. "Instead of centering immediately and directly the whole responsibility for efficiency upon the Chief Justice and the Supreme Court," he said, "I think there ought to be a mechanism through which there would be a concentration of responsibility in the various circuits." [9] What he suggested was the creation of a judicial council in each circuit composed of judges who could supervise the making of budgets

[8] CEH, remarks to Conference of Senior Circuit Judges, Sept. 30, 1938.   [9] *Id.*

and thresh out local problems without ever coming to Washington. As for the nation as a whole, the Conference of Senior Circuit Judges could act as a judicial council. It would need a permanent organization to do the administrative chores and keep statistics, but that agency would be a servant of the conference and the circuit councils instead of looming up as a potential master over district judges. The Supreme Court could be left entirely out of the picture.

With this magic touch of decentralization, Hughes eliminated most of the opposition to the Cummings proposal. But he did not wish the modified plan to go to Congress as "the Chief Justice's bill." To avoid that possibility, the conference agreed to the appointment of a committee to work out the problem and draft a bill in accord with Hughes' suggestions. Chief Justice D. Lawrence Groner of the United States Court of Appeals for the District of Columbia became chairman of the committee, with Senior Circuit Judges Parker, Stone, Evans, and Manton as members. Working with the Attorney General and the Judiciary Committees of the House and Senate, the committee drafted a bill that was enacted on August 7, 1939.

This Act brought into being the Administrative Office of the United States Courts, which has been a powerful agent in improving the quality of federal justice. It functions as a secretariat for the judicial system and is directly responsible to the Conference of Senior Circuit Judges (now the Judicial Conference of the United States), thus greatly expanding the influence and usefulness of that body. Hughes' idea of decentralized control was spelled out in the Act. A council of circuit judges was set up in each circuit and directed to meet at least twice a year. District judges were put under obligation "promptly to carry out the directions of the council as to the administration of the business of their respective courts." While there was no interference with the independence of judgment in the lower courts, the circuit judges were thus empowered to maintain a constant supervision over the work of the courts in their circuits.

Hughes became chairman of the committee named by the conference to supervise the Administrative Office. The plan he had outlined seemed to be coming to fruition without a hitch. When he suggested the name of an outstanding lawyer to head the Administrative Office, however, he ran into stout opposition. Justice Reed proposed as rival candidates several lawyers who were associated with the Executive branch, one of them sponsored by Thomas G. Corcoran, the ubiquitous fixer then in high favor at the White House. This maneuver won the support of the three other Roosevelt appointees to the court. With Justice Butler ill, the court was thus deadlocked, and for some weeks it was unable to make an appointment. At last the Chief, at the suggestion of Grenville Clark, brought Henry P. Chandler of Chicago to Washington to meet the members of the court, and he proved to be an acceptable compromise. Some of the judges were indignant over this little revolt against Hughes' leadership, but Chandler proved to be a happy choice; he set up the Administration Office with a combination of tact and skill that have made it a bulwark of the judicial system.

"This plan has rich promise," Hughes said. "The courts are now equipped to manage their own affairs and will have the correlative responsibility." [10]

Judges immediately felt the monitory hand of the conference. It instructed the Administrative Office to obtain reports from all district judges as to delayed cases and motions, also the titles of cases that had been at issue more than six months. Easy-going judges could no longer let procrastination drain the substance out of justice. Now they were answerable to a better informed public as well as to their fellow judges. Courts that were two or three years behind in their work began to hustle. Those that were actually overworked were given more judge power. Without any great expense or any loss of judicial independence, the courts were brought into a manageable system with remarkable improvement in the quality of their work.

Although many men share the credit for this achievement, it was Chief Justice Hughes who gave the new concept of judicial integration its distinctive touches and supervised the establishment of the essential machinery. This work gives him a high place among the architects of our judicial system.

While the Supreme Court was left untouched by this evolution in the judiciary system, it too experienced a momentous break with the past. After sitting for seventy-five years in the old Senate chamber in the Capitol—that "unique and hallowed spot"—the court moved in 1935 to its new marble temple across the plaza from the Capitol. For the first time the court had a home of its own—a magnificent structure symbolizing in stone and steel the idea of a permanent institution for the settlement of legal disputes in accord with constitutional principles.

The new building was a fulfillment of Taft's dream, but Taft did not live to see construction undertaken. Hughes succeeded him as chairman of the Supreme Court Building Commission and spoke for the court at the laying of the cornerstone in October, 1932. In spite of the depression that had paralyzed the nation, in spite of widespread misgivings and world unrest, he saw in the project an expression of confidence that "our people have political instincts and convictions which are not likely to be uprooted." We have pride and hope on this occasion, he said, "because we believe, without underestimating adverse influences, that the spiritual resources of the Nation, from which each generation draws anew its conceptions of fair dealing, are unwasted, and because we

[10] Address to American Law Institute, May 16, 1940.

Photo P. Stephens, Yonkers, N. Y.

The Hughes children and their families

This picture was taken in 1938 for the golden wedding anniversary of the Chief Justice and Mrs. Hughes

In retirement at eighty

From a letter to his daughter: "You will receive a photograph, under separate cover, of the old man 'as is.' Mother is very desirous that you have it."

find in this building a testimonial to an imperishable ideal of liberty under law." [11]

One important decision concerning the building was literally handed down from the bench. A letter passed to the Chief Justice during an argument contained the architects' suggestion that the words "EQUAL JUSTICE UNDER LAW" be inscribed in the main frieze of the west portico and "EQUAL JUSTICE IS THE FOUNDATION OF LIBERTY" in the east portico. Hughes approved the first motto and passed the letter along the bench to Van Devanter with a note about the second: "I rather prefer 'JUSTICE THE GUARDIAN OF LIBERTY'." "Good," replied Van Devanter, and the east portico inscription was changed accordingly.

When "EQUAL JUSTICE UNDER LAW" began to gleam out from the white marble above the eight classical pillars at the front of the building, Herbert Bayard Swope accused the Chief Justice "of having permitted tautology, verbosity and redundancy, each of which is an abomination in good usage." [12] Hughes replied:

Immediate judgment. Indictment quashed.
The distress which led to your complaint may be somewhat alleviated if for a moment you will free yourself from the tyranny of the blue pencil and consider the history of the law. "Equal Justice" is a time-honored phrase placing a strong emphasis upon impartiality,—an emphasis which it is well to retain. [He quoted the phrase from two dictionaries, from Jefferson's first inaugural and from great opinions of the court.]
There is a long history in that phrase. Try to bear with it. [13]

One day in 1934 the Chief learned to his astonishment that his own likeness had been chiseled into the stone of the pediment above the front entrance, without either the knowledge or consent of the building commission. Nine figures stand out from the pediment. In the center is Liberty Enthroned, holding the scales of justice, with Order and Authority on guard on either side. To the left of this symbolic trio is a likeness of·Taft when he was a student, Elihu Root, and Cass Gilbert, architect of the building. Just to the right of Order is Chief Justice Hughes in a thoughtful mood; Robert Aitken, the sculptor of the pediment; and Chief Justice Marshall represented in his boyhood.

At first the court felt uncomfortable in its magnificent new chamber, with its walls of Ivory Vein marble from Spain, its rich red velour hangings, and its twenty-four columns of tinted Old Convent Siena marble from Italy. The elegance of its new home seemed strangely out of keeping with the compactness and simplicity traditionally associated with the court. Some of the Justices resented the change, and several declined to use the beautiful suites the

[11] *New York Times,* Oct. 14, 1932.   [12] Swope to CEH, Jan. 25, 1935.
[13] CEH to Swope, Feb. 4, 1935.

new building provided for each. The Chief continued to write his opinions at home and used his new office only for appointments and administrative work.

Visitors who flocked to the Supreme Court in increasing numbers seemed to be more interested in its luxurious surroundings than in the work it was doing. But its distinctive new home gave emphasis to its status as a separate, coordinate branch of the government. Established in a sort of shrine to the majesty of the law, the court would be better fortified for the great struggle that was soon to ensue over its right to function as an independent agent of justice.

Chapter 66

MARCHING CONSTITUTION

ONE of the most striking characteristics of Hughes' work on the bench was his high degree of objectivity. He was neither a crusader, standpatter, nor reactionary; he was an open-minded judge. Butler and McReynolds held doggedly to a *laissez faire* conservatism. Brandeis, too, according to his biographer, "was inclined by the pressures and drives of his own nature to translate his own economic and social views into the Constitution itself." [1] In a large measure Hughes succeeded in freeing his judicial reasoning from any social or economic pattern.

A student asked the Chief Justice whether he regarded himself as a "liberal" or a "conservative." He replied: "These labels do not interest me. I know of no accepted criterion. Some think opinions are conservative which others would regard as essentially liberal, and some opinions classed as liberal might be regarded from another point of view as decidedly illiberal. Such characterizations are not infrequently used to foster prejudices and they serve as a very poor substitute for intelligent criticism. A judge who does his work in an objective spirit, as a judge should, will address himself conscientiously to each case, and will not trouble himself about labels." [2]

No man can attain complete objectivity. His judgments will necessarily be guided by his convictions and his concept of the society of which he is a part. Loyalties to groups, methods, and ideas are likely to color his conclusions. The human mind does not operate independently of its experience. But Hughes' basic intellectual loyalty was to the idea of justice itself. No sympathy for any group, no interest in economic theory or social reform could stand against this powerful incentive. "His decisions," as Judge Joseph M. Proskauer has said, "were legal decisions and not determinations of non-legal controversies. They reflected the ideals of the judge and not of the philosopher or economist." [3] Emotionally as well as intellectually Hughes was driven toward judicial conclusions. For him, justice was not the means to an end; it was the end.

Closely related to his passion for justice was his ingrained respect for facts. Holmes used to say that he hated facts, although he used them skillfully when

[1] Alpheus T. Mason, *Brandeis* (New York, Viking, 1946), p. 580. Copyright, 1946, by Alpheus T. Mason.
[2] Asheville speech, June 9, 1932.
[3] Address at Hughes Memorial Services in Supreme Court, Nov. 4, 1949.

occasion demanded. Brandeis liked facts and marshaled armies of them to support his theses. Hughes trusted facts and sought them out as a guide to the course he would take. In his early days at the bar it was said that he "believed in God but believed equally that God was on the side of the facts." His chief predilection was for exhaustive investigation before he would attempt to draw any conclusions. Yet Hughes never lost himself in any uncharted wilderness of facts. He knew how to balance the details of a case and "the felt necessities of the time" with the facts of history and constitutional law. His pursuit of facts was nothing less than a search for the bedrock of truth.

The Chief's judicial thinking was also influenced by an unshakable belief in the American constitutional system. That system made it possible for the people to use government as an agency for their own advancement. At the same time it was a bulwark against tyranny. Its basic guarantees were justice and freedom of the human spirit. Believing that the best hope of mankind lay in the protection of these principles and rights, the Chief Justice set his course by the star of constitutional democracy. The system underlying our way of life was infinitely more important than any conflicting expedient that might be advanced to cope with temporary problems.

Hughes felt a special responsibility upon the courts to safeguard this American heritage. The nature of this duty he outlined in his address to the conference of federal judges of the Fourth Circuit at Asheville on June 9, 1932, in words that should long be remembered:

The supreme exercise of the judicial power of the United States is in maintaining the constitutional balance between State and Nation and in enforcing the principles of liberty which the Constitution safeguards against arbitrary power. This is an extraordinary demand upon judicial intelligence, but it is an integral part of our system, and the duty imposed upon our judges cannot be escaped. We cannot perform this duty in a narrow, technical spirit. Our dual system requires recognition of appropriate State power as well as Federal power. It demands freedom for state authority to meet local needs. It demands opportunities for experimentation and progress. We must ever keep before our minds the illuminating phrase of Marshall, "that it is a *constitution* we are expounding." That Constitution was made, as Justice Matthews observed, "for an undefined and expanding future, and for a people gathered and to be gathered from many nations and of many tongues." We should be faithless to our supreme obligation if we interpreted the great generalities of the Constitution so as to forbid flexibility in making adaptations to meet new conditions, and to prevent the correction of new abuses incident to the complexity of our life, or as crystallizing our own notions of policy, our personal views of economics and our theories of moral or social improvement. We should be equally faithless to our duty if we failed to remember that it is an *American* constitution we are expounding. It is permeated with American ideals, infused with an American conception of liberty.

We cannot take the great phrases of the Constitution and disregard their historical background and fundamental purposes. These purposes were so expressed as to permit a broad range for new methods and achievements, but they were expressed in limitations. These limitations were imposed so as to safeguard rights believed to be fundamental. As Madison said, the tribunals of justice would be "in a peculiar manner the guardians of those rights"; they were to be "an impenetrable bulwark" against encroachment upon them either by legislative or executive power. The extent of these fundamental rights is a subject of perennial debate. But that they exist is a postulate of our system that cannot be ignored. They are limitations, as I have said, in the interest of liberty, requiring a measure of freedom of opportunity which even legislatures must respect. We would be as faithless to our judicial obligation in failing to recognize these boundaries of power because of individual conceptions of the value of new social schemes resting upon coercion by a class, or upon unrestrained legislative will, as we would be in tightening conceptions to reenforce particular economic views. . . . It is a highly difficult, but I think not an impossible task, to escape the errors of the extreme constructions which either would nullify, or would extend beyond their fundamental purpose, the great guarantees of individual liberty.

It is from this philosophical background that his work on the bench must be judged.

Tax laws ran afoul of Hughes' constitutional doctrines more frequently than any others; yet the period of his Chief Justiceship was marked by the tapping of many new sources of revenue and by the virtual abolition of intergovernmental tax immunities. His contributions to tax law are indicative of his belief in a marching Constitution.

Depression-emptied treasuries had given new popularity to sales taxes accompanied by "use taxes" on goods consumed within the state after being purchased outside—the purpose being to prevent evasion of the sales tax. To the surprise of many who knew how jealously it had guarded interstate commerce from all state-imposed burdens, the court upheld these levies. Hughes had previously written an opinion that sustained a Minnesota tax on cattle shipped from another state and held in stockyards for resale, on the ground that interstate commerce had come to rest.[4] When the use tax made its bow before the high bench, he reiterated that doctrine, got agreement, and assigned the opinion to Cardozo.[5]

But the Chief adhered literally to the doctrine that a state could not, in any form or under any guise, directly burden interstate business. When the court in 1940 appeared to relax this principle in *McGoldrick* v. *Berwind-White*,[6] he vigorously dissented with the concurrence of Roberts and McReynolds.

[4] *Minnesota* v. *Blasius*, 290 U.S. 1.
[5] *Henneford* v. *Silas Mason Co.*, 300 U.S. 577.   [6] 309 U.S. 33.

For nearly a decade the Hughes court frowned upon double taxation. Its general thesis was that under the due-process clause of the Fourteenth Amendment a state could tax only property within its territorial jurisdiction or intangible property in the state where its owner was domiciled. To be sure, the court recognized some exceptions. Hughes wrote an opinion upholding a West Virginia tax on bank deposits and accounts receivable even though the steel company challenging the tax had plants, sales offices, and bank accounts in other states. The tax was saved by the fact that the company's business was completely directed from its Wheeling headquarters.[7] The Chief Justice also upheld New York in taxing the profits of a Massachusetts resident from the sale of a "right" appurtenant to his membership in the New York Stock Exchange, on the ground that the right by nature was localized in New York.[8] In 1939, however, when the court began to permit two states to tax the same intangible property and to let other states reach beyond their boundaries for revenue, Hughes consistently dissented.

It was an evolutionary process that swept away most of the labyrinth of intergovernmental tax immunities which had grown out of Marshall's thesis that the power to tax is the power to destroy. At first Hughes followed Holmes' reasoning in *Gillespie* v. *Oklahoma*,[9] giving the states and their agencies liberal immunity from federal taxation. He and Holmes led the majority in denying Congress the right to tax the sale of a motorcycle to a city,[10] with Brandeis and Stone dissenting. With a bare majority of the court, the Chief also clung to the precedents forbidding federal taxes on production of oil and gas from state school lands leased to a private company.[11] But a ferment was at work within the court, and Hughes himself became a part of it.

As early as 1931 Hughes spoke for the court in reversing a judgment that Congress could not tax profits from the sale of municipal bonds.[12] He accepted the doctrine that federal taxation of the interest from state and municipal bonds is forbidden, but that did not justify multiplication of immunities. "The power to tax should not be crippled," he said, ". . . by extending the constitutional exemption from taxation to those subjects which fall within the general application of non-discriminatory laws, and where . . . there is only remote, if any, influence upon the exercise of the functions of government." Three years later he again led the court in holding that railway trustees appointed by, and acting for, a state must pay the federal income tax.[13] Constitutional immunity from federal taxation, he said, was not a necessary result of being a state officer.

---

[7] *Wheeling Steel Corp.* v. *Fox*, 298 U.S. 193.
[8] *N.Y. ex rel. Whitney* v. *Graves*, 299 U.S. 366.   [9] 257 U.S. 501.
[10] *Indian Motorcycle Co.* v. *U.S.*, 283 U.S. 570.
[11] *Burnet* v. *Coronado Oil and Gas*, 285 U.S. 393.
[12] *Willcuts* v. *Bunn*, 282 U.S. 216.   [13] *Helvering* v. *Powers*, 293 U.S. 214.

In 1938 Stone spoke for the court in extending this principle so as to sweep away the entire maze of fine-spun immunities shielding government employees from taxation.[14] Millions of new taxpayers began to swell governmental revenues without the slightest loss of prestige or power to any federal or state agency.

Meanwhile Hughes and four of his brethren had upheld a nondiscriminatory West Virginia tax on a corporation doing work for the Federal Government.[15] Other Hughes opinions cleared the way for state taxation of contractors and their employees working on federal projects. After six years of such judicial erosion, Hughes also agreed to reexamine the precedents shielding private interests operating on public lands. In 1938 he wrote an opinion which upset both the Gillespie decision and *Burnet* v. *Coronado Oil and Gas* for which he had been in part responsible. "Mere theoretical conceptions of interference with the functions of government" could not give a cloak of immunity, he said. "Regard must be had to substance and direct effects." [16]

Finally, the court also swept away the immunity from income taxes that federal judges had long enjoyed. In the interval while Hughes was not a member of the court it had decided, in *Evans* v. *Gore*,[17] that judges' salaries could not be taxed because the Constitution forbids reduction of their compensation during their term of office. Holmes and Brandeis had vigorously dissented. In 1936 Congress had circumvented this decision by applying the income tax to the salaries of judges to be appointed after the law became effective. A test case came up to the supreme bench in 1939, and everyone except Butler agreed that the Act was constitutionally sound.[18] Hoping to avoid a direct repudiation of the court's previous judgment, Hughes assigned the opinion to Frankfurter, whose dislike for breaking away from precedents was well known. Frankfurter skillfully laid *Evans* v. *Gore* on the judicial relic shelf instead of consigning it to a dishonorable grave.

When the opinion was circulated, the Chief suggested that *Evans* v. *Gore* be made to appear a "less casual" decision. "I am ready to sign your opinion without changing a comma," he told Frankfurter. "If I had been on the bench when *Evans* v. *Gore* was decided, I think I should have voted with Holmes and Brandeis. Personally I am not concerned about having to pay the tax." But in deference to the judges who had been on the bench when the previous decision had been made he thought it would be well to put into the opinion the historical justification for *Evans* v. *Gore*. Accordingly Justice Frankfurter inserted a few lines about Chief Justice Taney's letter to Secretary of the Treasury Chase

---

[14] *Graves* v. *O'Keefe*, 306 U.S. 466.
[15] *James* v. *Dravo Contracting Co.*, 302 U.S. 134.
[16] *Helvering* v. *Mountain Producers Corp.*, 303 U.S. 376.
[17] 253 U.S. 245.   [18] *O'Malley* v. *Woodrough*, 307 U.S. 277.

saying that, while no federal judge would be qualified to sit in such a case, the application of the Civil War income taxes to judges' salaries was unconstitutional.

Out of approximately 350 opinions that Hughes wrote for the court as Chief Justice, thirty-nine are especially significant in their bearing upon the powers of the states. In thirty-two of these he sustained the state law or action that was challenged; in seven (including four tax cases) he administered a lethal dose of constitutionalism. Three times he dissented because a majority liquidated state laws he believed to be valid.

His self-restraint in passing upon state legislation was reflected in the first opinion he wrote after returning to the bench. The court held that Ohio was within its rights in denying its own supreme court the power to invalidate legislation if more than one judge dissented. ". . . it is not for this Court to intervene to protect the citizens of the State from the consequences of its policy," Hughes wrote in reply to a taxpayer's appeal, "if the State has not disregarded the requirements of the Federal Constitution." [19]

The cool logic of another Hughes opinion protected the powers of three governors against legislative irregularities. In defiance of gubernatorial vetoes, the lawmakers of New York, Minnesota, and Missouri had attempted to redistrict those states in accord with an Act of Congress reapportioning among the states the seats in the House of Representatives. The court ruled, in a test case from Minnesota, that the Constitution gives state legislatures no redistricting power outside the regular procedure of enacting a law, which the governor could veto. In case of a stalemate over redistricting, where the number of seats allotted to the state had been reduced, it would have to elect all its representatives at large. [20]

Hughes spoke for the court in upholding the New York workmen's compensation law, [21] a Louisiana Act for the purchase of books to be lent to children in private as well as in public schools, [22] an Oklahoma statute licensing cooperatives in competition with private business, [23] and a Nebraska law guaranteeing bank deposits. [24] Other Hughes opinions gave the green light to Texas in limiting the size and weight of trucks engaged in interstate traffic over its highways; [25] to Oregon in revoking the licenses of dentists for unprofessional conduct; [26] and to Minnesota in subjecting sexual perverts to examination akin to lunacy proceedings. [27]

His liberal view of the state police power is pointedly illustrated by his

[19] *Ohio ex rel. Wadsworth* v. *Zangerle*, 281 U.S. 74.   [20] *Smiley* v. *Holm*, 285 U.S. 355.
[21] *Staten Island Rapid Transit Co.* v. *Phoenix Indemnity Co.*, 281 U.S. 98.
[22] *Cochran* v. *Louisiana*, 281 U.S. 370.   [23] *Oklahoma* v. *Lowe*, 281 U.S. 431.
[24] *Abie State Bank* v. *Bryan*, 282 U.S. 765.   [25] *Sproles* v. *Binford*, 286 U.S. 374.
[26] *Semler* v. *Dental Examiners*, 294 U.S. 608.
[27] *Minnesota* v. *Probate Court*, 309 U.S. 270.

opinion sustaining Florida's regulation of sponge fishing by her citizens beyond the three-mile limit in the Gulf of Mexico. "If the United States may control the conduct of its citizens upon the high seas," he wrote, "we see no reason why the State of Florida may not likewise govern the conduct of its citizens upon the high seas with respect to matters in which the State has a legitimate interest and where there is no conflict with acts of Congress." [28] Even unseaworthy vessels could be brought under state regulation, the court held, so long as there was no collision with federal laws enacted under the commerce clause.[29] Hughes abhorred a vacuum of power.

Two interesting state cases give emphasis to the Chief's high standing with his brethren. Shortly after returning to the bench, he wrote a scholarly opinion holding that a Nebraska homestead law, as applied to a citizen of Norway, was not invalid because of conflict with an ancient treaty of amity and commerce between that country and the United States.[30] By way of expressing his approval, Holmes dipped into *Hamlet* and saluted the Chief with the admiring words of Ophelia about the Prince of Denmark:

> The courtier's, soldier's, scholar's
>   eye, tongue, sword,
> The expectancy and rose of the
>   fair state.
>   Yes Sir,
>   O. W. H.

Holmes had left the bench when the Chief wrote his learned opinion to the effect that the Principality of Monaco could not sue the State of Mississippi, without its consent, for the redemption of bonds that the state had repudiated.[31] But four of the other judges penciled generous comments on the proof sheets: "A skillfully drawn, masterly and judicious opinion. I agree." G. S. "Complete and convincing. I agree." W. V. "Yes. Handsomely done." L. D. B. "I agree. A notable opinion." B. N. C.

Only two state regulatory measures were wiped off the books by Hughes' opinions. Florida had passed a law subjecting private carriers engaged in contract hauling to a special tax and requiring them to obtain certificates of public convenience and necessity. Haulers of agricultural products and fish were exempted. The court concluded that "the constitutional guarantee of equal protection of the laws is interposed against discriminations that are entirely arbitrary." [32] The other case involved an Arkansas statute providing that no money paid or payable to any resident of the state as the beneficiary of a life-insurance policy could be seized through judicial process for the payment of

[28] *Skiriotes* v. *Florida*, 313 U.S. 69.
[29] *Kelly* v. *Washington*, 302 U.S. 1.
[30] *Todok* v. *Union State Bank*, 281 U.S. 449.
[31] *Monaco* v. *Mississippi*, 292 U.S. 313.
[32] *Smith* v. *Cahoon*, 283 U.S. 553.

any debt.[33] The profit of a business, Hughes pointed out, could thus be withdrawn from the pursuit of creditors by investing it in life insurance. The statute was condemned as an arbitrary interference with the "obligation of contracts."

The right-wing foursome dissented.

The Chief was also one of the majority which struck down the Oklahoma law regulating the ice business.[34] Declaring the manufacture and sale of ice to be a public concern, the legislature had forbidden anyone to engage in it without obtaining a license from a state commission. A licensed ice company sought an injunction for the purpose of driving an unlicensed dealer out of the business. Justice Sutherland's opinion for the majority recognized that "all businesses are subject to some measure of public regulation" but concluded that a statute denying to individuals the right to engage in "an ordinary business" of this kind offended against the due-process clause.

Brandeis, with the concurrence of Stone, strongly dissented on the ground that the decision as to when a private business should be converted into a public one ought to be left to the legislature. In the exercise of the court's power under due process to strike down measures that are "arbitrary, capricious or unreasonable," he said, "we must be ever on guard, lest we erect our prejudices into legal principles." This criticism has often been repeated, and subsequent judicial thinking leans strongly toward the broader rights of legislative experimentation for which the minority contended. Hughes himself thought the case was near the border line.[35]

The Chief's willingness to examine challenged statutes in a largeness of spirit was especially evident when the states' emergency measures enacted to mitigate the hardships of the depression were denounced before the high bench. The first major case of this kind involved the fate of the Minnesota Mortgage Moratorium Law of 1933. It was solely an emergency measure designed to postpone execution sales after mortgages had been foreclosed, thus extending the redemption period so that property owners would have a chance to save their homes. The law was attacked as an unconstitutional impairment of the "obligation of contracts."

"Emergency does not create power," the Chief Justice said in a sweeping opinion upholding the Act.[36] But "emergency may furnish the occasion for the exercise of power." A state could not adopt as its policy the repudiation of debts or the destruction of contracts or the denial of means to enforce them. "But it does not follow," he declared, "that conditions may not arise in which a temporary restraint of enforcement may be consistent with the spirit and purpose of the constitutional provision and thus be found to be within the

[33] *Worthen* v. *Thomas*, 292 U.S. 426.
[34] *New State Ice Co.* v. *Liebmann*, 285 U.S. 262.
[35] Author's interview with CEH, Jan. 2, 1947.
[36] *Home Building and Loan Association* v. *Blaisdell*, 290 U.S. 398.

range of the reserved power of the state to protect the vital interests of the community . . . if state power exists to give temporary relief from the enforcement of contracts in the presence of disasters due to physical causes such as fire, flood or earthquake, that power cannot be said to be non-existent when the urgent public need demanding such relief is produced by other and economic causes."

Reviewing all the cases directly bearing on his problem, the Chief Justice swept onward to his conclusion:

It is manifest from this review of our decisions that there has been a growing appreciation of public needs and of the necessity of finding ground for a rational compromise between individual rights and public welfare. The settlement and consequent contraction of the public domain, the pressure of a constantly increasing density of population, the interrelation of the activities of our people and the complexity of our economic interests, have inevitably led to an increased use of the organization of society in order to protect the very bases of individual opportunity. Where, in earlier days, it was thought that only the concerns of individuals or of classes were involved, and that those of the state itself were touched only remotely, it has later been found that the fundamental interests of the state are directly affected; and that the question is no longer merely that of one party to a contract as against another, but of the use of reasonable means to safeguard the economic structure upon which the good of all depends.

It is no answer to say that this public need was not apprehended a century ago, or to insist that what the provision of the Constitution meant to the vision of that day it must mean to the vision of our time. . . . the statement that . . . the great clauses of the Constitution must be confined to the interpretation which the framers, with the conditions and outlook of their time, would have placed upon them . . . carries its own refutation. It was to guard against such a narrow conception that Chief Justice Marshall uttered the memorable warning—"We must never forget that it is a *constitution* we are expounding" . . . "a constitution intended to endure for ages to come, and, consequently, to be adapted to the various *crises* of human affairs." . . .

With a growing recognition of public needs and the relation of individual right to public security, the court has sought to prevent the perversion of the [contracts] clause through its use as an instrument to throttle the capacity of the states to protect their fundamental interests. This development is a growth from the seeds which the fathers planted. . . . The principle of this development is, as we have seen, that the reservation of the reasonable exercise of the protective power of the state is read into all contracts and there is no greater reason for refusing to apply this principle to Minnesota mortgages than to New York leases.

"Yes. Strongly put and interesting," Brandeis wrote on the proof sheets. "I approve of changes proposed. I gladly concur in this memorable opinion."

Sutherland wrote the dissenting opinion, with the concurrence of Van Devanter, McReynolds, and Butler, reading the Constitution "with exact literalness like a mathematical formula." It was a narrow victory for forward-marching constitutionalism. But there was wide rejoicing throughout the country over the broad scope and realistic tone of the Chief Justice's opinion. He spoke in deliberate, judicial terms the language that was on the lips of legislators, editors, and leaders of the Roosevelt Administration.

Hughes also took the lead in sustaining the law under which New York was fixing the price of milk in order to curb destructive price-cutting. Once more the court divided five to four. Justice Roberts is said to have paced the floor of his home until the early morning hours in the process of deciding which way he would turn. When he voted to sustain the act, Hughes promptly concluded that he (Roberts) was the best man to write the opinion. "It is clear," the court asserted, "that there is no closed class or category of businesses affected with a public interest. . . . The Constitution does not secure to anyone liberty to conduct his business in such fashion as to inflict injury upon the public at large, or upon any substantial group of people." [37] Due process was no absolute bar to price-fixing.

Nebbia v. *New York* is sometimes said to reflect a sharp breaking away from the doctrine of the Oklahoma ice case. Hughes did not so regard it. To be sure, the court abandoned Sutherland's obiter dicta about a business being "charged with a public use." But in the Oklahoma case Liebmann's right to sell ice had been upheld against what a majority of the court believed to be an arbitrary and capricious restriction. In the Nebbia case no one had been denied the right to sell milk. Perhaps the difference is only one of degree, but a reasonable mind trying to strike a balance between individual liberty and governmental power to act in the public interest can support both decisions without inconsistency.

The great test of the court, so far as state police powers were concerned, came in *Morehead* v. *New York ex rel. Tipaldo* [38] in which the right to fix minimum wages for women was at stake. In 1923 the court had stricken down the District of Columbia minimum-wage law in *Adkins* v. *Children's Hospital* [39] by the slender margin of one vote. Its action had been widely criticized, and some states had enacted similar statutes in spite of the Supreme Court. Under the New York law, Morehead had been sent to jail to await trial for failing to pay the prescribed minimum wage and sought release on a writ of habeas corpus. New York resisted it on the ground that its law was distinguishable from the statute the court had invalidated. A majority of the court wished to deny certiorari, but Hughes, Brandeis, Stone, and Cardozo voted to take the case, and that was sufficient to put it on the docket.

From the beginning it was obvious that Roberts would cast the deciding vote. His opinion in the Nebbia case strongly suggested that he would not again impale a state police regulation upon due process unless the invasion of liberty

[37] *Nebbia* v. *New York,* 291 U.S. 502.   [38] 298 U.S. 587.   [39] 261 U.S. 525.

under it were beyond the pale of reason. The time was ripe for a bold assault upon *Adkins* v. *Children's Hospital*. But counsel for New York missed his opportunity. Meekly accepting the Adkins ruling, he asked the court only to differentiate the two statutes. Roberts thought that reasoning was disingenuous and voted with the conservatives.

Writing for the majority, Butler simply clung to the Adkins decision. This meant that the court benightedly looked upon minimum-wage laws as transgressing "the right to contract about one's affairs." The opinion provoked a powerful dissent from Hughes and another from Stone, Brandeis, and Cardozo. Butler then wrote additional arguments into his opinion. Its reactionary tone was very distasteful to Roberts, but he held to the position he had taken. The result was to subject the court to the severest drubbing it had experienced in many years. For in thus limiting the power of the states to cope with economic problems, while preventing congressional intervention in local affairs, it had created a dangerous power vacuum.

Hughes had not broken new ground when he urged his brethren to sustain the New York statute. As Associate Justice, he had riddled the freedom-of-contract doctrine, and in the case of the paper-box factory girl, he had thrown his support to the Oregon minimum-wage law.[40] *Adkins* v. *Children's Hospital* had been decided when he was not a member of the court, and Hughes looked upon it, as he did upon the Dred Scott decision, the income tax cases, and *Lochner* v. *New York*, as a self-inflicted wound for the court. Since four of the brethren were committed to the Adkins decision, however, he concluded that he would have a better chance of clearing the path for minimum-wage legislation if he made no direct assault upon that precedent.

There was a calculated difference between the District of Columbia and New York statutes. In the District, Congress had required a "living wage." Trying to avoid the shoals of due process, New York had added the idea of a "fair wage" corresponding to the reasonable value of the services performed. It was a slender distinction, but Hughes thought it was substantial enough to justify the court in taking a fresh look at the problem. The weakness of his case was that the New York Court of Appeals had found no material difference between the two statutes, and the Supreme Court usually considers itself bound to accept a state court's interpretation of a state law.

"The validity of the New York Act," he asserted, "must be considered in the light of the conditions to which the exercise of the protective power of the State was addressed." Women did not have equality in bargaining power. "Freedom of contract" as applied to them was illusory. Necessity forced them to accept whatever wages were offered. The legislature had found that harsh and over-reaching employers had been cutting wages, reducing purchasing power, threat-

[40] CEH, Notes, 1930–1941, p. 32; also p. 313 this volume.

ening the stability of industry, and forcing women to go on relief at the expense of the taxpayer in order to live decently. "We are not at liberty," the Chief Justice continued, "to disregard these facts."

Citing numerous decisions upholding different regulations affecting employment, he drove home his point:

> While it is highly important to preserve that liberty [of contract] from arbitrary and capricious interference, it is also necessary to prevent its abuse, as otherwise it could be used to override all public interests and thus in the end destroy the very freedom of opportunity which it is designed to safeguard. . . . In the statute before us, no unreasonableness appears. The end is legitimate and the means appropriate. I think that the act should be upheld.

Brandeis, Stone, and Cardozo joined in the Hughes opinion, but in Stone's separate dissenting opinion they also hinted that the Adkins case should be overruled even though its reconsideration had not been asked.

The issue was finally settled in March, 1937, when the court reversed its previous decision and found the minimum-wage law of the State of Washington to be constitutional.[41] Roberts joined the four Justices who had dissented in the New York case to make a new majority of five. Since the highest court of Washington had sustained that state's minimum-wage law in spite of the Adkins decision, that precedent had been directly challenged. And the majority in the Tipaldo case had felt the lash of public opinion from the bar, the press, and indirectly from the electorate when it returned the Roosevelt Administration to power by a landslide vote in 1936. It is impossible to determine all the influences that weigh upon a judge, but in any event Roberts had in his Nebbia opinion a well-marked trail by which he could, and did, return to the Hughes camp.

In writing the majority opinion Hughes took note of the ironical fact that the Washington law had been in effect for twenty-three years. It was almost identical with the Oregon statute which he and Holmes had championed in 1915 and which had been sustained by an evenly divided court two years later.[42] Meanwhile the court had invalidated the District of Columbia, Arizona, Arkansas, and New York minimum-wage laws and probably discouraged the enactment of similar statutes in many other states. Certainly it was time to sweep away the inverted pyramid of confusion that the court had built up on the insecure basis of due process.

"In each case," the Chief Justice said, "the violation alleged by those attacking minimum wage regulation for women is deprivation of freedom of contract. What is this freedom? The Constitution does not speak of freedom of contract. It speaks of liberty and prohibits the deprivation of liberty without due process

---

[41] *West Coast Hotel* v. *Parrish*, 300 U.S. 379.   [42] *Stettler* v. *O'Hara*, 243 U.S. 629.

of law. In prohibiting that deprivation the Constitution does not recognize an absolute and uncontrollable liberty . . . the liberty safeguarded is liberty in a social organization which requires the protection of law against the evils which menace the health, safety, morals and welfare of the people."

The new majority concluded that *Adkins* v. *Children's Hospital* "was a departure from the true application of the principles governing the regulation by the State of the relation of employer and employed." The correct view was to be found in Holmes' dissent in that case. "What can be closer to the public interest," Hughes asked, "than the health of women and their protection from unscrupulous and overreaching employers? And if the protection of women is a legitimate end of the exercise of state power, how can it be said that the requirement of the payment of a minimum wage fairly fixed in order to meet the very necessities of existence is not an admissible means to that end?" The legislative response to the evils of the "sweating system" could not be regarded as arbitrary, he said, "and that is all we have to decide." The Adkins decision was flatly overruled.

Sutherland solemnly admonished his brethren that the judicial function "does not include the power of amendment under the guise of interpretation." But he spoke for only a minority.

The court's about-face on this vital issue is generally attributed to President Roosevelt's court-packing plan, which was announced in the interval between the two decisions. Actually that assault upon the court had no bearing whatever on the outcome, as will be shown in a later chapter. The West Coast Hotel case did, however, clinch the victory of the liberal-minded men within the court. With a few exceptions, state police powers have since been broadly interpreted.

The Hughes record as a whole shows a tolerant recognition of state powers. While holding fast to the basic freedoms, he used his influence to loosen the restraints upon social experimentation. In very large measure he succeeded in diverting the court from intermeddling in local economic and social policymaking to the role of guardian of an ordered liberty and the federal system.

Chapter 67

BALANCE WHEEL OF POWER

No MEMBER of the Supreme Court since the days of John Marshall has written as many opinions of far-reaching import as did Chief Justice Hughes in the fateful decade of the thirties. The nation was in a ferment. Economic dislocations, new social pressures, and changing political concepts sent a parade of constitutional issues into the highest court. As Marshall was called upon to give the Constitution the vitality of a workable organic law, Hughes was destined to adapt the great charter to the bewildering requirements of an economic and social transition.

One of the most delicate aspects of this task arose out of the repeated appeals to the courts to save public-service corporations from the consequences of rate regulation. On this subject the Hughes court had inherited from its predecessors mostly confusion and controversy. While there was general agreement that confiscatory rates could not stand under the due-process clause and the direct prohibition in the Fifth Amendment against taking private property for public use without just compensation, the Justices were far apart in their ideas as to what was confiscatory and what was not. Back in 1898, in *Smyth* v. *Ames*,[1] the court had laid down the rule that a utility is entitled to a fair return and that such a return should be calculated on the "fair value" of the property used for the convenience of the public. But the yardstick suggested by the court for measuring fair value was so all-inclusive that it multiplied confusion.

Conservative judges were inclined to interpret "fair value" as meaning the cost of reproducing a utility. After World War I greatly increased reproduction costs, this formula often led to exorbitant charges. Hughes had been the first judge to speak for the Supreme Court in rejecting the cost-of-reproduction formula when it gave utility property a speculative value. In working out the *Minnesota Rate Cases*[2] in 1913, he had pointedly exposed the injustice of valuing land in accord with the estimated cost of "reproducing" it.

When he returned to the court as Chief Justice, it was leaning toward general acceptance of the cost-of-reproduction formula. At every step it was being challenged, however, by Justice Brandeis, who had developed the "prudent investment" theory and was pressing for its acceptance by the court. Hughes threw his influence against commitment of the court to either theory. While he

[1] 169 U.S. 466.   [2] 230 U.S. 352, 445, 450, 454.

agreed with Brandeis that the original cost of property devoted to public use was in most instances the best guide to its "fair value," it was not for the court to fix a rigid formula. Legislatures and rate-making bodies should be left free to adjust or change their formulas to meet changing conditions. Under some circumstances, moreover, a regulated utility might have real value that would not be reflected by the "prudent investment" formula. It was property of which a person could not be deprived without due process of law—not merely an original investment.

The Chief Justice tried to extricate the court from its tangle in two important cases. When a Los Angeles gas company attacked rates fixed by the Railroad Commission of California, the court refused to upset those rates because the company's value had been fixed on the basis of historical costs after examination of all the relevant data. "We do not sit as a board of revision," Hughes said, "but to enforce constitutional rights. . . . The legislative discretion implied in the rate making power necessarily extends to the entire legislative process, embracing the method used in reaching the legislative determination as well as the determination itself. . . . The Court may not interfere with the exercise of the State's authority unless confiscation is clearly established." [3]

Here was plain notice that the court would not thrust down the throats of rate-making bodies either the "prudent-investment" or the "cost-of-reproduction" yardstick. Brandeis put aside championship of his own particularistic formula and concurred. Butler dissented and gave vent to his fury both on and off the bench. Only Sutherland joined him.

The Chief realized that his course left a great responsibility upon rate-making bodies and that it might throw a heavy burden upon the courts. But he felt that the mistake of imposing a rigid formula from the bench must be avoided. And what labor was too great if it might "serve to buttress in any degree the institutions of an ordered liberty?" [4]

In a later opinion the court sustained the Chicago telephone rates fixed by the Illinois Commerce Commission. Trying to show that those rates were confiscatory, the company had swelled the record with expert testimony as to the cost of reproducing its system. Hughes swept it all aside. "Elaborate calculations which are at war with realities revealed by the financial history of the business," he said, "are of no avail in determining the adequacy of the rates prescribed for a public utility corporation." [5]

This time Sutherland agreed, and wrote on the proof sheets, "A hard job well done." Butler concurred in the result. Cardozo suggested that one paragraph be taken out; yet he concurred "in this extraordinarily fine opinion." Brandeis too was pleased and gave a copy of the opinion to Lord Keynes when

[3] *L.A. Gas & Electric Co.* v. *R.R. Comm. of California*, 289 U.S. 287.
[4] Address to American Law Institute, May 6, 1937.
[5] *Lindheimer* v. *Illinois Bell Telephone Co.*, 292 U.S. 151.

he came to Washington as an illustration of how the United States was meeting its economic problems.

To the embarrassment of his critics, who had assumed that he would favor exorbitant profits for utilities, Hughes consistently upheld rate-making bodies in allowing a 7 per cent return on the "fair value" of the property.[6] Since a unanimous court, with Cardozo as spokesman, invalidated gas rates yielding a return of only 4.53 per cent,[7] presumably the "line of confiscation" fluctuated, according to differing circumstances, between that figure and 7 per cent.

Another mounting problem for the court was the mushroom growth of administrative agencies that were impinging upon the rights and lives of the people. As one of the original fathers of this movement, Hughes was not hostile toward its progeny. He recognized

that this development has been to a great extent a necessary one. Activities of vital importance to the public could not be left unregulated where legislatures were powerless to supply the details of regulation. Experience, expertness, and continuity of supervision, which could only be had by administrative agencies in a particular field, have come to be imperatively needed. But these new methods put us to new tests, and the serious question of the future is whether we have enough of the old spirit which gave us our institutions to save them from being overwhelmed.[8]

The controversy over the constitutionality of fact-finding by such bodies was settled by Hughes' opinion in *Crowell* v. *Benson* [9] handed down in 1932. An injured worker had been awarded benefits under the Longshoremen's and Harbor Workers Compensation Act of 1927. The claim that only the courts could make a final determination of the facts relating to the alleged injuries was rejected. If the deputy commissioner's findings were supported by evidence and within the scope of his authority, the Chief Justice said, without dissent, the courts should not interfere.

Harmony among the judges was shattered, however, when Hughes asserted that the courts had a right to determine the facts for themselves in deciding whether they had jurisdiction in the case. Brandeis made a vehement attack upon this view and was joined by Stone and Roberts. Sutherland, too, was at odds with the Chief in conference, but when he saw the finished opinion, he scribbled on the proof sheets: "I congratulate you upon a beautiful piece of work. You have effectively disposed of the proposed dissent. I fully concur."

The battle of wits between Hughes and Brandeis on this issue was renewed in the St. Joseph Stock Yards case.[10] The question before the court this time was whether the rates fixed for the company by the Secretary of Agriculture

---

[6] *Wabash Valley* v. *Young*, 287 U.S. 488; *Clark's Ferry* v. *P.S.C. of Penn.*, 291 U.S. 277.
[7] *West Ohio Gas Co.* v. *P.U.C. of Ohio*, 294 U.S. 63.
[8] Address to Federal Bar Association, Feb. 12, 1931.
[9] 285 U.S. 22; see also *Shields* v. *Utah Idaho Central R.R.*, 305 U.S. 177.
[10] 298 U.S. 38.

were confiscatory. The court had no difficulty in deciding that they were not. But the question of how far judicial review should go brought these two giants of the law into one of their sharpest controversies. The Chief Justice contended that the court could redetermine the facts when a constitutional right depended upon factual findings. Brandeis was willing to grant this as to personal liberty but not as to the protection of property rights.

If a legislature acts directly in fixing rates, Hughes declared, those rates are subject to scrutiny in the courts to make certain that the limits of legislative power have not been transgressed. The legislature could not preclude such scrutiny by making any finding of its own. Nor could Congress frustrate judicial review of the acts of its agents by authorizing those agents to find that they had kept within their powers. Some of these quasi-legislative agencies were expert and impartial; others were not. An unscrupulous administrator might be inclined to say, "Let me find the facts for the people of my country, and I care little who lays down the general principles." If the Constitution were to be maintained as the supreme law of the land, Hughes insisted, the court would have to intervene where the evidence clearly showed that the agency's findings were wrong and that constitutional rights had been infringed.

Brandeis agreed that, when constitutional rights were at stake, every question of law could be carried to the courts. Moreover, "a citizen who claims that his liberty is being infringed is entitled, upon habeas corpus, to the opportunity of a judicial determination of the facts." But in dealing with property, he declared, "a much more liberal rule applies." In these instances Congress was free to leave the final ascertainment of facts to an administrative tribunal.

To this Hughes replied: "You've no right to split the due process clause for the purpose of judicial convenience." [11]

Under the Fifth Amendment no distinction whatever is made between the human right to liberty and the human right to retain property. Hughes marshaled all his persuasive powers to prevent the court from writing such a distinction into its constitutional doctrines. In his opinion he declared:

It is said that we can retain judicial authority to examine the weight of evidence when the question concerns the right of personal liberty. But if this be so, it is not because we are privileged to perform our judicial duty in that case and for reasons of convenience to disregard it in others. The principle applies when rights either of persons or of property are protected by constitutional restrictions. Under our system there is no warrant for the view that the judicial power of a competent court can be circumscribed by any legislative arrangement designed to give effect to administrative action going beyond the limits of constitutional authority.

Hughes emphasized that the court should give due weight to administrative findings. His only point was that the court must not wear any blindfold in-

[11] Author's interview with CEH, Nov. 12, 1947.

vented by Congress to prevent it from seeing an invasion of constitutional rights by way of clearly erroneous findings. While he carried a majority with him, Stone and Cardozo joined in Brandeis' concurring opinion.

The most spectacular fight over the conduct of administrative agents came in the Morgan cases.[12] Secretary of Agriculture Henry Wallace had found the rates of commission men for selling livestock on the Kansas City market to be exorbitant and had fixed maximum rates under the Packers and Stockyards Act. Morgan and others went to court with a complaint that they had not been accorded a fair hearing. The first time the case reached the supreme bench in 1936 it ordered the lower court to give the commission men an opportunity to show the nature of the hearing accorded them. ". . . there must be a hearing in a substantial sense," the Chief Justice said. "And to give the substance of a hearing, which is for the purpose of making determinations upon evidence, the officer who makes the determinations must consider and appraise the evidence which justifies them."

Secretary Wallace was then put on the stand in the lower court, and his testimony clearly showed that no fair hearing had been given. The evidence had been taken under his predecessor. "Sketchy and general" arguments had been heard by Assistant Secretary Tugwell. Wallace himself had then dipped into the bulky record, read the briefs and transcripts of the oral arguments, and conferred with the department's prosecutors in the case. Accepting the prosecutors' findings (save for the alteration of some rates), he had given the commission men no opportunity to be heard on those findings before issuing his order. Requests for a rehearing had been denied.

When this situation was laid before the Supreme Court, it held the Wallace order invalid and pointedly rebuked his department for laxity of procedure.[13] "The right to a hearing," Hughes said, "embraces not only the right to present evidence but also a reasonable opportunity to know the claims of the opposing party and to meet them. The right to submit argument implies that opportunity; otherwise the right may be but a barren one." The Chief Justice repeated what he had said in his previous opinion: that it was good practice to have an examiner receive the evidence and prepare a report as a basis for exceptions and argument, but this was not required procedure. The Secretary himself might conceivably hear evidence in some cases and make his own findings. But he could not accept as his own the findings "prepared by the active prosecutors for the Government" and impose those findings upon the commission men without giving them an opportunity to argue their objections. "That is more than irregularity in practice," the court said; "it is a vital defect." Only Justice Black dissented.

Wallace pretended that the court's criticism was aimed solely at the absence

[12] *Morgan* v. *U.S.*, 298 U.S. 468.   [13] 304 U.S. 1.

of a trial examiner's report. He wrote a complaint to the Chief Justice and told the Senate that the error the court had criticized had been "committed not by this administration but by the preceding one." [14] In a public statement he accused the Chief Justice of indulging in "cloudy phraseology," [15] and the Solicitor General asked for a rehearing on the ground that the court had contradicted itself. Of course, the court had done nothing of the sort. Hughes might have written more clearly than he did in the second opinion, but a careful reading shows unmistakably that he was striking at the irresponsible practice of having one man hear the evidence, a bureau make the findings, an official hear the arguments, and another official make the decision. In a sharp *per curiam* opinion the court denied a rehearing, again spelled out the "vital defect" in Secretary Wallace's procedure, and declared that the Government's allegation of conflict between the two previous opinions was "wholly unfounded." [16]

It has been generally assumed that the $700,000 paid into the District Court by the commission men while awaiting the outcome of the case would go back to them under the Supreme Court's ruling. The lower court did so decide after the Supreme Court had tossed the case back to it a second time, but the Government again appealed. The Supreme Court said through Justice Stone that the fund should be held until the outcome of new rate-fixing proceedings could determine who was entitled to it.[17]

Not infrequently the court administered judicial correction to itself. These were always occasions for soul-searching on the part of the Chief Justice. Laying great store upon clarity and stability in the law, he was loath to see the court throw down a previous decision. The court, as Justice Frankfurter once said, "did not sit like a kadi under a tree dispensing justice according to considerations of individual expediency." General adherence to its own rules and precedents was indispensable to the idea of a government of law. Yet if experience and deliberation convinced Hughes that a previous decision was out of line with sound legal or constitutional doctrines, he would frankly face the necessity of correcting it.

Such a necessity arose in *Erie Railroad Company* v. *Tompkins*,[18] and the Supreme Court met it by discarding a doctrine to which it had given faithful adherence for nearly a century. The facts of the case were simple. Tompkins had been injured by a swinging freight car door on a passing train, and a federal court jury had awarded him damages of $30,000. The Court of Appeals had affirmed. Ordinarily that would have settled the issue. The Supreme Court granted certiorari only because the case came up to it after years of brooding

[14] Department of Agriculture release, May 12, 1938.
[15] *New York Times*, May 8, 1938. [16] *Morgan* v. *U.S.*, May 31, 1938.
[17] *U.S.* v. *Morgan*, 307 U.S. 183. [18] 304 U.S. 64.

by several of its members over the inconsistent practice of applying different versions of the common law in the federal and state courts.

Tompkins had got his case into a federal court because he was a citizen of Pennsylvania and the railroad that injured him happened to be incorporated in New York. The first Congress had provided in Section 34 of the Judiciary Act of 1789 that in such cases of diverse citizenship, where no question of federal statutory or constitutional law was involved, the federal courts should rest their decisions on "the laws of the several States." A question had arisen as to whether this meant only state statutes or included also the decisions of state courts, which some lawyers insisted were not laws. The Supreme Court had directed the lower federal courts to follow the decisions as well as the statutes of the state in which they sat. The result was that the federal courts applied different versions of the law in every state.

In 1842 the Supreme Court had decided in *Swift* v. *Tyson* [19] that the federal courts were bound to apply only the statutes of the state in which they sat and could interpret the common law in accord with their own judgment. This might create two different versions of the common law in each state, Justice Story acknowledged, but it would have the virtue of promoting uniformity of federal decision. The court hoped that the new "federal general common law" would gradually supersede state common law and thus evolve into an accepted un-written law for the whole country. But in this it was disappointed. The only result was to build up conflicting versions of the unwritten law in each state. If two persons riding side by side were injured in the same accident, one claiming diversity of citizenship might go into the federal court and obtain damages while the other, confined to a state court, might be entitled to nothing. Equal protection of the laws became impossible.

Holmes and Brandeis had tried to overthrow *Swift* v. *Tyson* before Hughes returned to the bench.[20] Charles Warren, historian of the Supreme Court, had showed from examination of the original documents that Story had given an erroneous interpretation to Section 34 of the Judiciary Act in 1842.[21] As new cases arose, the conference of judges threshed out the advantages and disadvantages of reverting to the earlier rule. Each time the conviction that the 1842 precedent was wrong seemed to take firmer root. When *Erie* v. *Tompkins* brought the issue into sharp focus in 1938, Hughes laid the case before the conference with the comment, "If we wish to overrule *Swift* v. *Tyson*, here is our opportunity." [22] Every judge except Butler and McReynolds agreed that the time for a change had come.

The Chief Justice recognized Brandeis' leadership in bringing about the change by assigning the case to him. The dean of the court responded with a

[19] 16 Pet. 1.   [20] *Southern Pacific Co.* v. *Jensen,* 244 U.S. 205, 222.
[21] *Harvard Law Review,* Vol. 37, pp. 49, 51–52, 81–88.
[22] Author's interview with CEH, June 4, 1947.

closely reasoned opinion showing that, "There is no federal general common law." To the surprise of his brethren, however, he did not stop with a reversal of the court's error in 1842. "If only a question of statutory construction were involved," he wrote, "we should not be prepared to abandon a doctrine so widely applied throughout nearly a century. But the unconstitutionality of the course pursued has now been made clear and compels us to do so."

Hughes was disturbed by this. He could see no point in dragging in a constitutional argument when the court was merely correcting its own misinterpretation of the Judiciary Act.[23] To be sure, *Swift* v. *Tyson* had departed from sound constitutional theory, but it had set up only a judge-made rule. The court was always free to rectify its mistakes whether or not a constitutional doctrine were involved. The Chief consulted Brandeis and learned that he had originally written his opinion without reference to any constitutional issue. Stone had induced him to change it by arguing that *Swift* v. *Tyson* had stood so long that Congress must be regarded as having accepted its doctrine. Consequently, it was necessary to invoke the Constitution to undo what the Supreme Court and Congress had jointly done. Hughes replied that there was no evidence that the issue had ever come squarely before Congress—that in fact only the court was at fault. For the sake of harmony in so important a decision, however, he and a majority of the brethren agreed to go along with the Brandeis opinion as circulated. Only Justice Reed insisted on writing a separate opinion, saying that the constitutional argument was surplusage, although the Chief Justice and apparently several other members of the court shared that view.

One writer has assumed that the judicial revolution effected by *Erie* v. *Tompkins* was a result of Justice Black's lone dissent in the Gamer case two months before.[24] But in this dissent [25] Black did not even mention *Swift* v. *Tyson*. More conclusive is the fact that he got no support from Brandeis, who voted with the majority. The court was brooding over a reversal of *Swift* v. *Tyson* long before Black came to the bench, and it is absurd to suppose that his lone dissent in the Gamer case had any influence on the momentous decision in *Erie* v. *Tompkins*. Most of the credit for this overturn goes to Justice Brandeis.

Hughes' disposition to keep the law attuned to the needs of the time may be seen in a notable opinion dealing with the Sherman Antitrust Act. To him, the virtue of the Sherman Act, like that of the Constitution, lay in its broad generalities. It was not to be interpreted in a spirit of narrow literalness but used with shrewd discrimination to protect the public interest against monopoly and the destruction of competition.

In the early thirties the coal-mining industry was in a state of acute de-

---

[23] *Id.*   [24] Wesley McCune, *The Nine Young Men*, pp. 31–32.
[25] *N.Y. Life Insurance Co.* v. *Gamer*, 303 U.S. 161.

moralization. Several investigations had revealed a surplus capacity within the industry, cutthroat competition that was depressing both prices and wages, a breakdown in collective bargaining, heavy financial losses for the operators, and violence and disorder among the miners. A group of producers who controlled 73 per cent of the commercial production in their area formed a collective selling agency, with authority to set prices for coal from all the cooperating mines. The agency continued to meet sharp competition from mines in other areas and from other fuels, but it was prosecuted under the Sherman Act.

The Supreme Court refused to upset the venture, with Hughes writing in his most vigorous manner. A cooperative enterprise is not to be condemned as an undue restraint of trade, he asserted, because it may effect a change in market conditions, where the change would mitigate recognized evils and would not impair, but rather foster, fair competitive opportunities. The restrictions imposed by the Act were not mechanical or artificial. Its general phrases did not seek to establish a mere delusive liberty. "Reality must dominate the judgment," Hughes insisted. For "when industry is grievously hurt, when production concerns fail, when unemployment mounts, and communities dependent upon profitable production are prostrate, the wells of commerce go dry." [26] The Sherman Act did not require companies to merge in order to correct marketing abuses.

It was a statesmanlike application of the antitrust law in full accord with the needs of the times. "I agree entirely," Brandeis wrote on the proof sheets. "You have made our position clear and persuasive." Sutherland praised the opinion as "excellent, timely and helpful," and Cardozo as "a fine piece of work." Only McReynolds dissented.

A few months after Hughes had returned to the bench, with much opposition from the unions, he handed down a decision that made labor leaders sit up and rub their eyes. The court sustained an injunction under the Railway Labor Act of 1926 forcing the Texas and New Orleans Railroad Company to disestablish its company union and reinstate the Brotherhood of Railway and Steamship Clerks as collective bargaining agent.[27] Anyone familiar with Hughes' defense of the right of collective bargaining in *Coppage* v. *Kansas* back in 1915 would have expected this decision in 1930. Labor was taken by surprise because it had listened to the misleading tirades of the self-styled liberals in the debate over Hughes' confirmation.

"Freedom of choice in the selection of representatives on each side of the dispute is the essential foundation of the statutory scheme," the Chief Justice said. ". . . it is of the essence of a voluntary scheme, if it is to accomplish

[26] *Appalachian Coals* v. *U.S.*, 288 U.S. 344.   [27] 281 U.S. 548.

its purpose, that this liberty should be safeguarded." Collective bargaining would be a mockery if the workers had to organize under employer coercion.

Nor was there any doubt as to the constitutional authority of Congress to prohibit such coercion. "The power to regulate commerce," Hughes asserted, "is the power to enact 'all appropriate legislation' for its 'protection and advancement.' . . . Exercising this authority, Congress may facilitate the amicable settlement of disputes which threaten the service of the necessary agencies of interstate transportation." Here is the precursor of Hughes' famous opinion in the Jones and Laughlin case, but that can be best discussed in a later chapter.

"You have made this matter entirely clear," Brandeis wrote on the Texas and New Orleans proof sheets. Van Devanter thought the opinion was "as near perfect as is humanly possible." Said John P. Frey of the American Federation of Labor: "It may well be that those who believe that the Chief Justice is over-conservative in his attitude toward human relations in industry are mistaken." [28] A news commentator said that Hughes had "shown himself to be just the sort of Chief Justice that his opponents insisted he never could be." [29]

The Texas and New Orleans opinion did not mean that the Chief Justice was pro-labor. Rather, it indicated a disposition on his part faithfully to enforce a policy laid down by Congress within its constitutional powers. His conclusions were no less forthright when he felt that the law compelled a decision against labor. Such a case reached the high bench in 1939 after the country had experienced an epidemic of sit-down strikes. Because the Fansteel Metallurgical Corporation had indulged in unfair labor practices and resisted organization of its employees, a group of them had seized its plants and fought furiously against dislodgment. After two pitched battles, many had been arrested and fined or sent to jail for violation of a court injunction. The strikers had been discharged for their misconduct, but the National Labor Relations Board had ordered them reinstated with back pay. Hughes wrote for the court an almost blistering denunciation of this attempt to condone the strikers' "highhanded proceeding without shadow of legal right." [30]

The employer's conduct was reprehensible, the opinion said, but it did not make him an outlaw or deprive him of the right to possession of his property. The remedy for the employees was a complaint to the NLRB. They also had the right to strike, "but they had no license to commit acts of violence or to seize their employer's plant." "To justify such conduct because of the existence of a labor dispute or of an unfair labor practice," Hughes declared, "would be to put a premium on resort to force instead of legal remedies and to subvert the principles of law and order which lie at the foundations of

[28] *International Labor News Service*, July 19, 1930.
[29] Oliver McKee, Jr., in *Outlook and Independent*, Oct. 7, 1931, p. 171.
[30] *NLRB* v. *Fansteel Metallurgical Corp.*, 306 U.S. 240.

society. . . . There is not a line in the statute to warrant the conclusion that it is any part of the policies of the Act to encourage employees to resort to force and violence in defiance of the law of the land."

Justices Reed and Black, dissenting, fell back upon the flimsy argument that both sides had erred grievously and that the courts should "not interfere with the normal action of administrative bodies."

The Fansteel decision was a powerful stroke for "ordered liberty" and helped to counteract the perilous doctrine that labor unions can do no wrong. It was followed by another notable decision to the effect that Illinois could restrain picketing conducted "in a context of violence." [31] In this instance Hughes assigned the opinion to Frankfurter. Black and Reed wrote separate dissents, with the support of Douglas, thus opening a breach between the Roosevelt appointees to the court that was to be greatly widened with the passing years.

In two labor cases involving the Sherman Act, Hughes found himself in the minority. The first of these, *Apex Hosiery Co.* v. *Leader,*[32] brought him into a memorable clash with Stone. The case arose out of a sit-down strike. Only eight of the company's 2,500 employees had been members of the union when the strike began, but union men from other factories descended upon the company's plants and held them for nearly two months, wrecking the machinery and completely stalling operations for a longer period. Stone condemned the strike as a "lawless invasion" resulting in "destruction of . . . property by force and violence of the most brutal and wanton character." Still he concluded that, in willfully preventing any movement of 134,000 dozen pairs of hosiery awaiting shipment, largely to other states, the strikers had not restrained commerce within the meaning of the Sherman Act.

To Hughes (who was joined by Roberts and McReynolds), this was an unwarranted contraction of the antitrust laws. In the Clayton Act Congress had given labor immunity to antitrust restraints in carrying out its "legitimate objects." The Chief Justice bore down on the fact that violence and willful obstruction of interstate shipments were not "legitimate objects." Where, then, could the immunity be found? Stone had taken refuge in the historic meaning of "restraint of trade," but Hughes pointed to the fact that the Sherman Act also condemns conspiracies in restraint of "commerce among the several States." "Commerce" had a definite meaning in American law. It embraced "commercial intercourse in all its branches, including transportation. . . ." Plainly there was a conspiracy here. Certainly there was restraint, and it was admitted that the restraint acted directly upon interstate commerce. Hughes unmercifully exposed the tangled logic on which the majority relied:

[31] *Milk Wagon Drivers Union* v. *Meadowmoor Dairies,* 312 U.S. 287.
[32] 310 U.S. 469.

It would indeed be anomalous if, while employers are bound by the Labor Act because their unfair labor practices may lead to conduct which would prevent the shipment of their goods in interstate commerce, at the same time the direct and intentional obstruction or prevention of such shipments by the employees were not deemed to be a restraint of interstate commerce under the broad terms of the Sherman Act.

This Court has never heretofore decided that a direct and intentional obstruction or prevention of the shipment of goods in interstate commerce was not a violation of the Sherman Act. In my opinion it should not so decide now. . . .

Once it is decided, as this Court does decide, that the Sherman Act does not except labor unions from its purview,—once it is decided, as this Court does decide, that the conduct here shown is not within the immunity conferred by the Clayton Act,—the Court, as it seems to me, has no option but to apply the Sherman Act in accordance with its express provisions.

In the Hutcheson case [33] the court took another long leap toward freeing labor from the restraints of the Sherman Act. This was a secondary boycott case, the carpenters' union having launched a boycott against Anheuser-Busch beer because the company had given the machinists' union work the carpenters thought they should have. If the court followed its previous decision in *Duplex Co.* v. *Deering*,[34] it would have to rule that the Sherman Act prohibited such union conduct. Speaking for a majority, Justice Frankfurter avoided that result, without overruling the Duplex decision, by "reading the Sherman Law and Section 20 of the Clayton Act and the Norris-LaGuardia Act as a harmonizing text of outlawry of labor conduct."

This strained telescoping of different Acts passed at different times for somewhat different purposes shocked the legal profession.[35] The court had joined together what Congress had put apart. Many authorities believe that the old court, in its Duplex decision, had emasculated Section 20 of the Clayton Act, providing that none of the routine labor union activities specified should be held to violate any federal law. But if Congress had thought so, as Justice Frankfurter assumed, it could have reversed the Duplex decision. It could have written Section 20 of the Clayton Act into the Norris-LaGuardia Act. Instead, it deliberately restricted the latter Act to the control of injunctions in labor disputes. It said not a word about relieving unions from liability to prosecution under the Sherman Act for secondary boycotts.

Because of his "forked" opinion in the Apex Hosiery case, the Chief Justice refrained from writing a dissent in the Hutcheson case. But he conferred with Roberts and joined in his dissenting view, "that no court has ever undertaken so radically to legislate where Congress has refused to do so."

This clash high-lights two diverging concepts of the judicial function. In

---

[33] *U.S.* v. *Hutcheson,* 312 U.S. 219.   [34] 254 U.S. 443.
[35] Charles O. Gregory, *Labor and the Law*, p. 273.

justification of the technique he had employed in the Hutcheson opinion, Justice Frankfurter cited Holmes' belief that if the legislature had "intimated its will, however indirectly, that will should be recognized and obeyed." ". . . the change of policy that enduces the enactment may not be set out in terms," Holmes had said, "but it is not an adequate discharge of duty for the courts to say: We see what you are driving at, but you have not said it, and therefore we shall go on as before."

Hughes was much less trustful of judicial acumen in reading the legislative mind. If the change of policy was not set forth in the law itself or indicated in its legislative history, how could judges be sure of what Congress was "driving at"? In a note to Frankfurter three weeks before the Hutcheson opinion came down, the Chief offered a substitute for Holmes' explanation to Congress:

DEAR JUSTICE FRANKFURTER:
Just a word "off the record"—prompted by your quotation from Justice Holmes but with humble deference to judicial technique:
"We have a notion that you may have had this in mind, but you stopped short of covering it, and we can't extend your statute so as to add what you left out. We await your pleasure." [36]

A strong bond of friendship had grown up between Hughes and Frankfurter, the chief legatee of the Holmes tradition. That friendship remained unruffled by any intellectual differences; still Frankfurter's acceptance of what he believed Congress was "driving at" and Hughes' more cautious policy of "awaiting the pleasure" of Congress suggests a wide difference in approach to the judicial task.

[36] CEH's private papers.

Chapter 68

GUARDIAN OF FREEDOM

A SINGULAR devotion to civil liberties had marked Hughes' advance to the headship of the judicial system. His soul-searching over the pardon cases at Albany, the tolerant spirit that infused *Bailey* v. *Alabama* and *Frank* v. *Mangum*, and his courageous defiance of popular prejudices to defend the five Socialists expelled from the New York Legislature had revealed the consistent liberality of his thinking in this sphere. The Chief Justiceship was to bring this dominant quality to full flower.

It was a crucial moment in the development of constitutional safeguards for civil liberty when Hughes returned to the bench. Even such basic rights as freedom of speech and freedom of the press seemed to hang by a slender thread when challenged by state governments. In 1920 the Supreme Court had sustained a wartime statute in Minnesota forbidding the advocacy of pacifism.[1] Holmes had acquiesced, and Brandeis, dissenting, had said he saw "no occasion to consider" whether this encroachment upon freedom of speech violated the Fourteenth Amendment. Two years later, in upholding the Missouri Service Letter Law, the court had said flatly: ". . . neither the Fourteenth Amendment nor any other provision of the Constitution of the United States imposes upon the States any restrictions about 'freedom of speech' or the 'liberty of silence' . . ."[2] Both Holmes and Brandeis had concurred.

Curiously, it was McReynolds who had been spokesman for the court when, in 1923, it had found enough freedom in the Fourteenth Amendment to knock out the Nebraska law forbidding the teaching of the German language.[3] Holmes and Sutherland had dissented. Then had come the Gitlow case in which the court assumed "for the present purposes" that "freedom of speech and of the press—which are protected by the First Amendment from abridgment by Congress—are among the fundamental personal rights and 'liberties' protected by the due process clause of the Fourteenth Amendment from impairment by the States."[4] It was the first time the court had transfused these basic guarantees from the First into the Fourteenth Amendment, and the transfusion seemed rather inconclusive, for the effect of the decision was to uphold the New York Criminal Anarchy Act and to suppress a Socialist pamphlet.

[1] *Gilbert* v. *Minnesota*, 254 U.S. 325.   [2] *Prudential Insurance Co*. v. *Cheek*, 259 U.S. 530.
[3] *Meyer* v. *Nebraska*, 262 U.S. 390.   [4] *Gitlow* v. *N.Y.*, 268 U.S. 652.

Holmes' dissent showed that by this time he and Brandeis had firmly embraced the Fourteenth Amendment as a shield to free speech, although he thought that principle might "be accepted with a somewhat larger latitude of interpretation than is allowed to Congress" under the First Amendment.

In 1927 the Criminal Syndicalism Act of California had been upheld,[5] but a little later the court had used the due-process clause to reverse a conviction under the Criminal Syndicalism Act of Kansas.[6] Such was the state of the law when Hughes came to the bench a second time. Under his powerful influence the pendulum might easily have swung backward or forward. His decision to push it vigorously forward is one of the most significant facts in our recent constitutional history.

On three successive Mondays in the late spring of 1931, Hughes spoke fluently and inspiringly for free speech, free thought, and freedom of the press. Twice he spoke for a majority of the court in overthrowing state policies of suppression. The man who had been denounced as "the greatest champion of property rights" was leading the way into a new era of civil liberties.

First came *Stromberg* v. *California*.[7] In a Communist camp a nineteen-year-old girl of Russian parentage, but American-born, had daily raised a red flag bearing the hammer and sickle and taught children to salute it as an emblem of opposition to organized government. California had convicted her under a vague "red-flag" law—a characteristic tool of suppression. Hughes insisted that she had a right to display a red flag so long as she did not "incite to violence and crime and threaten the overthrow of organized government by unlawful means." Stripping the case to the naked issue of freedom, he declared:

The maintenance of the opportunity for free political discussion to the end that government may be responsive to the will of the people and that changes may be obtained by lawful means, an opportunity essential to the security of the Republic, is a fundamental principle of our constitutional system. A statute which, upon its face, and as authoritatively construed, is so vague and indefinite as to permit the punishment of the fair use of this opportunity is repugnant to the guarantee of liberty contained in the Fourteenth Amendment.

It was the sweep of the decision that gave the country a lift. Hughes made it clear that free speech was not to be cramped into any kind of narrow brackets. Instead of forcing citizens to curb their speech in accord with state rules, legislatures would have to accommodate their rules to a free market place of ideas. Only McReynolds and Butler failed to go along.

In the celebrated case of Douglas Clyde Macintosh four of the strongest men ever to sit on the supreme bench—Hughes, Holmes, Brandeis, and Stone

[5] *Whitney* v. *California*, 274 U.S. 357, 373.
[6] *Fiske* v. *Kansas*, 274 U.S. 380.   [7] 283 U.S. 359.

—stood together and lost.[8] The majority, with Sutherland as mouth, denied citizenship to this Canadian-born professor of divinity at Yale University, because his pledge to fight in defense of the United States was qualified—he would fight only if he believed the war to be morally justified. To the majority, this meant that he was not attached to the principles of the Constitution.

Three years previously the court had denied citizenship to Rosika Schwimmer, and Holmes, dissenting, had made his classic plea for "freedom for the thought that we hate." [9] This time he joined Hughes in a quite different line of reasoning. The question was not, the Chief said, whether it was right to deny citizenship to applicants who refused to bear arms, but whether Congress had prescribed such a test. Where did the arms-bearing requirement originate? The statute itself provided only that applicants for citizenship should take an oath that they "will support and defend the Constitution and laws of the United States against all enemies, foreign and domestic, and bear true faith and allegiance to the same."

This naturalization oath, Hughes showed, is substantially the same as that required of civil officers. Certainly men with religious scruples against war could not be deemed disqualified for public office because they would have to take an oath to defend the Constitution. The bearing of arms was not the only important method of defense, even in time of war. "I think that the requirement of the oath of office should be read in the light of our regard from the beginning for freedom of conscience," the Chief Justice said. And since Congress had "reproduced the historic words of the oath of office in the naturalization oath," it should be read in the same way.

The practice of excusing conscientious objectors from military service further suggested that Congress had not expected every naturalized citizen to tote a gun. ". . . in the forum of conscience," Hughes pointed out, "duty to a moral power higher than the state has always been maintained. . . . The essence of religion is belief in a relation to God involving duties superior to those arising from any human relation. . . . There is abundant room for . . . maintaining the conception of the supremacy of law as essential to orderly government, without demanding that either citizens or applicants for citizenship shall assume by oath an obligation to regard allegiance to God as subordinate to allegiance to civil power. . . . The Congress has sought to avoid such conflicts in this country by respecting our happy tradition."

This powerful dissent won the support of the country and became the law of the land in 1946, when the Supreme Court overruled both the Schwimmer and Macintosh decisions.[10] Although Hughes was no longer on the bench, the court specifically went back to his dissent of 1931 and rested in his conclusion

---

[8] *U.S.* v. *Macintosh*, 283 U.S. 605.
[9] *U.S.* v. *Schwimmer*, 279 U.S. 644   [10] *Girouard* v. *U.S.*, 328 U.S. 61.

that Congress had not "set a stricter standard for aliens seeking admission to citizenship than it did for officials who make and enforce the laws of the nation."

On June 1, 1931, the Chief Justice completed his trilogy on freedom with an opinion which had the effect of wiping the Minnesota press-gag law off the books. It was the first time that the guarantee of liberty in the Fourteenth Amendment had been used completely to obliterate a state law. The Chief met with fierce opposition within the court, and Butler, Van Devanter, McReynolds, and Sutherland dissented. The decision stands out, however, as one of the great landmarks in the history of civil rights.[11]

The newspaper that Minnesota had suppressed was a vicious little scandal-sheet called *The Saturday Press*. Its vilification campaigns had been aimed chiefly at city officials of Jewish origin in Minneapolis. After much provocation, officials had moved against the publisher under a state law of 1925 providing that "malicious, scandalous and defamatory" newspapers and magazines could be enjoined as a "public nuisance." The Supreme Court of Minnesota had upheld the conviction, but from the center of the supreme bench in Washington, D.C., the state's action had the appearance of violating a great principle to punish a little scandalmonger.

Hughes found it "impossible to conclude" that freedom of the press "was left unprotected by the general guaranty of fundamental rights of persons and property." To be sure, it was not an "absolute right," and the state could punish its abuse. But this Minnesota statute condemned publications that officials might deem to be "malicious" without even requiring proof of malice. It permitted defense, not on grounds of truth alone, but only on the ground that the truth was published with good motives. Instead of prescribing punishment for libel, its aim was the suppression of newspapers that might be exposing political scandals. And after a newspaper had been suppressed, its publisher could be placed under court order for continued good conduct. "This is the essence of censorship," the Chief Justice exclaimed.

The government could forbid publication of the sailing dates of troop ships, he reasoned; it could protect community life against incitements to violence and uphold requirements of decency. But it could not suppress a publication to stop criticism of public officials. Laying great stress on the almost complete absence of "previous restraints upon publications" for a century and a half, he concluded:

The importance of this immunity has not lessened, . . . the administration of government has become more complex, the opportunities for malfeasance and corruption have multiplied, crime has grown to most serious proportions, and the danger of its protection by unfaithful officials and of the impairment of the funda-

[11] *Near* v. *Minnesota*, 283 U.S. 697.

mental security of life and property by criminal alliances and official neglect, emphasizes the primary need of a vigilant and courageous press, especially in great cities. The fact that the liberty of the press may be abused by miscreant purveyors of scandal does not make any the less necessary the immunity of the press from previous restraint in dealing with official misconduct.

Stromberg v. *California* and *Near* v. *Minnesota* set the pattern for the Hughes court in shoring up civil liberties. In 1936 Sutherland wrote for the court in knocking out Huey Long's tax on the gross receipts of the larger Louisiana newspapers that were opposing him.[12] It was an obvious device for curbing freedom of the press. Two years later Hughes extended the doctrine of *Near* v. *Minnesota* to handbills, circulars, and tracts. Alma Lovell of the Jehovah's Witnesses had been sentenced to prison for fifty days for violating a city ordinance in Griffin, Georgia, forbidding the distribution of circulars or "literature of any kind" without permission of the city manager. The court was unanimous in recognizing this sweeping prohibition as an invasion of freedom of the press. The Chief Justice said:

We think the ordinance is invalid on its face. Whatever the motive which induced its adoption, its character is such that it strikes at the very foundation of the freedom of the press by subjecting it to license and censorship. The struggle for the freedom of the press was primarily directed against the power of the licensor. . . . Legislation of the type of the ordinance in question would restore the system of license and censorship in its baldest form.

The liberty of the press is not confined to newspapers and periodicals. It necessarily embraces pamphlets and leaflets. These indeed have been historic weapons in the defense of liberty, as the pamphlets of Thomas Paine and others in our own history abundantly attest. The press in its historic connotation comprehends every sort of publication which affords a vehicle of information and opinion.[13]

Freedom of assembly had a no less exalted standing in the court's scale of values. When Dirk De Jonge was sentenced to prison for seven years for helping to conduct a Communist Party meeting in Portland, Oregon, Hughes drew an unerring line between criminal conduct and peaceful assembly. The meeting had been an orderly protest against the shooting of strikers—until the police broke it up on the ground that it was sponsored by an organization advocating criminal syndicalism. Whatever the objectives of the Communist Party might be, the Chief Justice said, De Jonge still retained his right to make a speech and take part in a peaceful meeting:

The right of peaceful assembly is a right cognate to those of free speech and free press and is equally fundamental.

These rights may be abused by using speech or press or assembly in order to

---

[12] *Grosjean* v. *American Press Co.,* 297 U.S. 233.
[13] *Lovell* v. *City of Griffin,* 303 U.S. 444.

incite to violence and crime. The people through their legislatures may protect themselves against that abuse. But the legislative intervention can find constitutional justification only by dealing with the abuse. The rights themselves must not be curtailed.

. . . The holding of meetings for peaceful political action cannot be proscribed. Those who assist in the conduct of such meetings cannot be branded as criminals on that score.[14]

Sutherland made it clear in a proof-sheet note that he concurred because the opinion was carefully drawn "so as to safeguard the right of free speech & peaceful assembly without giving sanction to abuse of these rights." Brandeis wrote simply, "Yes Sir. This is grand."

The court again in 1939 went on record for freedom of assembly after Mayor Hague had attempted to prevent the Congress of Industrial Organizations from holding a public meeting in Jersey City.[15] An ordinance giving full discretion to the director of safety to grant or withhold permits for public meetings was held to be invalid on its face. There was no opinion of the court, but Roberts and Stone wrote separate opinions and Hughes partly concurred in both; McReynolds and Butler dissented. The following year the court overturned an Alabama statute forbidding "loitering and picketing," with Justice Murphy writing the opinion and only McReynolds dissenting.[16]

An opinion by Justice Roberts took the sting out of a Connecticut law requiring the approval of a welfare official for the solicitation of money for religious or charitable purposes.[17] No such strait-jacket could be placed on religious freedom, the court said. By this decision it completed the process of incorporating the entire First Amendment—freedom of religion, freedom of speech, freedom of the press, and the right of peaceful assembly—into the word "liberty" in the Fourteenth Amendment.

Attorneys for Tom Mooney dropped an enormous record, including twelve volumes of testimony, into the lap of the Supreme Court in 1934. Near the end of the summer Hughes called his secretary to New York and dictated an analysis of the celebrated case for presentation to the conference. The court concluded that Mooney should seek a writ of habeas corpus from California's highest court before sending his case to Washington.[18] The Chief laid a good deal of store upon the judicial proprieties. At the same time he jarred the California authorities by declaring that due process could not be satisfied "by mere notice and hearing" if in truth the court and jury had been deceived "by the presentation of testimony known to be perjured." His *per curiam* opinion was an invitation to Mooney to send his case back if he could not get justice from California.

[14] *De Jonge* v. *Oregon*, 299 U.S. 353.
[15] *Hague* v. *C.I.O.*, 307 U.S. 496.
[16] *Thornhill* v. *Alabama*, 310 U.S. 88.
[17] *Cantwell* v. *Connecticut*, 310 U.S. 296.
[18] *Mooney* v. *Holohan*, 294 U.S. 103.

Tyranny from any source found its nemesis in the Hughes court. The Chief was fond of quoting William Pitt's penetrating observation. "Where law ends, tyranny begins." Then he would assert, "And it is our business to see to it that when law begins, tyranny shall end." [19] In *Sterling* v. *Constantin* [20] he applied this rule to the Governor of Texas who was trying to enforce his edicts by martial law.

In the dark days of the depression Texas had sought to reduce the flow of oil from wells capable of producing five thousand barrels a day to a mere two hundred barrels. The legality of the order had been challenged, and a federal court had issued a temporary injunction against its enforcement. By way of retaliation Governor Sterling had shut down all the wells in several counties and tried to justify this resort to martial law by declaring that "insurrection and riot" in the oil counties were beyond civil control.

A three-judge federal court had found "no insurrection or riot in fact . . . no closure of the courts, no failure of the civil authorities," nor any condition resembling a state of war. In these circumstances, the Supreme Court concluded, the Governor could not interrupt the ordinary judicial procedure by military force. Hughes' opinion said:

It does not follow from the fact that the Executive has this range of discretion, deemed to be a necessary incident of his power to suppress disorder, that every sort of action the Governor may take, no matter how unjustified by the exigency or subversive of private right and the jurisdiction of the courts, is conclusively supported by mere executive fiat. . . . What are the allowable limits of military discretion, and whether or not they have been overstepped in a particular case, are judicial questions.

The Governor's duty, Hughes concluded, was to aid the process of having rights determined, not to thwart it. The logic of this sound limitation on martial law—imposed upon governors for the first time in this Hughes opinion—would have saved the court from sanctioning the expulsion of the Nisei from the West Coast in World War II [21]—if the court had then been willing to apply it.

Hughes was always on guard against racial discrimination in the courts. The broad tolerance of his earlier opinions had ripened into unalterable convictions. After putting on the mantle of Chief Justice, he seized the first opportunity to speak his mind on this subject. A federal judge in the District of Columbia had refused to permit the questioning of jurors as to their racial prejudices, and the all-white jury thus selected had convicted a Negro of first-degree murder. Hughes reversed the judgment, with the comment that "no surer way could be devised to bring the processes of justice into disrepute" than to "permit it to

---

[19] Address to Federal Bar Association, Feb. 12, 1931.
[20] 287 U.S. 378.   [21] *Korematsu* v. *U.S.*, 323 U.S 214.

be thought that persons entertaining a disqualifying prejudice were allowed to serve as jurors." [22]

The well-known Scottsboro case involving rape convictions against seven Negroes came twice to the supreme bench. The first time Hughes took the lead in reversing the convictions because the trial judge's appointment of counsel for the men had been a mere gesture.[23] Only Butler and McReynolds resisted this conclusion. In line with his policy of asking conservative judges to write liberal opinions, the Chief assigned the case to Sutherland.

Alabama tried the Scottsboro boys in another county, and they came back to the Supreme Court under death sentences with a plea that Negroes had been systematically excluded from jury duty. The statute itself did not discriminate against Negroes. But in Jackson County, where the indictment had been drawn, residents for more than half a century could not remember that any Negro had been called for jury service. In Morgan County, where the trial had been held, no Negro had ever been on a jury, although a large number were qualified to serve. This testimony in itself, Hughes said, "made out a *prima facie* case of the denial of the equal protection which the Constitution guarantees." [24]

The chief significance of this opinion lies in its realistic handling of the facts. The Supreme Court of Alabama had relied upon fiction—the fiction that if no Negroes were called it was because none was qualified. Hughes cut through that flimsy pretense by giving weight to facts that the state court had ignored. Nor did he require elaborate proof of intent on the part of the administrative officials to discriminate; that inference was drawn from the overshadowing fact that Negroes were never summoned as jurors.

Here is a striking illustration of the need for the Supreme Court to discard clearly prejudiced or incompetent fact-finding by lower courts or administrative agencies when necessary to protect a constitutional right. "That the question is one of fact," Hughes said, "does not relieve us of the duty to determine whether in truth a federal right has been denied. . . . If this requires an examination of evidence, that examination must be made. Otherwise, review by this court would fail of its purpose in safeguarding constitutional rights." All the brethren concurred, including Justice Brandeis, who a year later was vehemently to challenge this doctrine when the Chief Justice reiterated it in a case involving property rights.

The Chief's indignation boiled over when a shameful third-degree case came up to the high bench from Mississippi.[25] Three ignorant Negroes accused of murder had been tortured until they confessed and then convicted solely on the basis of the confession. One of the men had been hanged to a tree and then systematically beaten until he signed a statement dictated to him. The

[22] *Aldridge* v. *U.S.*, 283 U.S. 308.   [23] *Powell* v. *Alabama*, 287 U.S. 45.
[24] *Norris* v. *Alabama*, 294 U.S. 587.   [25] *Brown* v. *Mississippi*, 297 U.S. 278.

By Daniel R. Fitzpatrick in the *St. Louis Post-Dispatch*, February, 1937.

STILL A PLACE OF REFUGE

others had their backs cut to pieces with buckles on the ends of leather straps. ". . . the transcript reads more like pages torn from some medieval account," Hughes wrote in his opinion, "than a record made within the confines of a modern civilization which aspires to an enlightened constitutional government."

Fairly scorching the authorities responsible for this outrage, he continued:

The rack and torture chamber may not be substituted for the witness stand. The State may not permit an accused to be hurried to conviction under mob domination —where the whole proceeding is but a mask—without supplying corrective process. . . . It would be difficult to conceive of methods more revolting to the sense of justice than those taken to procure the confessions of these petitioners, and the use of the confessions thus obtained as the basis for conviction and sentence was a clear denial of due process.

Hughes, Brandeis, Stone, and Cardozo joined Roberts in an opinion freeing Angelo Herndon, who had been sent to prison for eighteen years after conviction under an ancient Georgia statute of attempting to incite an insurrection.[26] Herndon had been advocating "self-determination for the Black Belt," but there was no real evidence of insurrection.

In 1938 the Chief Justice wrote a strong opinion holding that a Negro student was entitled to admittance to the law school of the University of Missouri. The state admitted that the student, Lloyd Gaines, was scholastically qualified to take up the study of law. Missouri also acknowledged her obligation to provide Negro students with educational opportunities substantially equal to those provided for white students. But this obligation had been met, it was contended, by the declared intention of the state to set up a law school for Negroes "whenever necessary or practical" and meanwhile by paying the tuition of its colored law students at the universities of adjacent states to which they could be admitted. Hughes brushed aside this subterfuge. "Manifestly," he said, "the obligation of the State to give the protection of equal laws can be performed only where its laws operate, that is, within its own jurisdiction."[27] Nor could the discrimination be excused by its alleged temporary character. With only McReynolds and Butler dissenting, the court decreed that the University of Missouri law school should open its doors to Gaines.

Abuse of the "separate but equal" formula again brought a rebuke from the Chief Justice in *Mitchell* v. *United States*.[28] Congressman Arthur Mitchell had been compelled to give up his Pullman seat as the train on which he was traveling crossed the line into Arkansas. Confined to an "old combination" coach assigned to Negroes, he had been denied various accommodations available to white passengers. Hughes said the discrimination was unmistakable and

[26] *Herndon* v. *Lowry*, 301 U.S. 242.
[27] *Missouri ex rel. Gaines* v. *Canada*, 305 U.S. 337.   [28] 313 U.S. 80.

repeated his conclusion in the McCabe case twenty-seven years before. If separate facilities were provided, they had to be substantially equal in spite of differences in demand on the part of white and colored passengers.

The Chief was also alert to racial discrimination and denial of civil rights in examining the *in forma pauperis* cases.[29] The law gives every citizen a right to proceed in any federal court without payment of fees, upon his execution of a pauper's oath. Consequently, murderers, madmen, bank robbers, and illiterates of all sorts who believe they are victims of injustice may address themselves directly to the Supreme Court. In Hughes' day all such unprinted documents addressed to the court, some of them scrawled illegibly in pencil, went to the Chief Justice and were reported upon by him at conference before any printing costs were incurred. Most of them were completely frivolous, but Hughes scanned them patiently because the smell of injustice could occasionally be detected despite the inadequacies of the petition.

Perhaps the most notable of these cases was *Bob White* v. *Texas*.[30] White, an illiterate Negro, filed a petition for certiorari *in forma pauperis* after his second conviction in Texas on a charge of raping a white woman. The meager papers he submitted gave the court no understanding of the underlying facts. Certiorari was denied. On a petition for a rehearing, however, the Chief somehow sensed that an injustice had been done and sent for the record.[31] It revealed that Texas Rangers had wrung a confession from Bob White by third-degree methods. A rehearing was granted; the court took the case and summarily set aside the conviction. Two irate Texans connected with the prosecution called on the Chief and accused the court of arbitrary conduct. He suggested that they file a petition for rehearing. Their petition failed to wash out the horror of the coerced confession; so the court reiterated its stand in an excoriating opinion by Justice Black. As a jury was being empaneled to try White a third time, he was shot by the husband of the complaining witness, and the killer was exonerated on the prosecutor's assertion that he had been forced to take the law into his own hands because the Supreme Court had thrown out the confession and the state did not have enough evidence to convict White without it. Such lawlessness in the name of law was sufficient to keep Hughes vigilant in examining the *in forma* cases.

As it became known that victims of injustice might win a case before the Supreme Court without a high-priced lawyer—sometimes by merely writing a letter to the court—crude petitions to the high bench were greatly multiplied. After the court ordered a new trial for an inmate of Alcatraz who had been denied the right of counsel,[32] a veritable bombardment of petitions came

[29] Edwin McElwain in *Harvard Law Review*, Vol. 63, No. I, p. 24.
[30] 309 U.S. 631; 310 U.S. 530.
[31] Edwin McElwain in *Harvard Law Review*, Vol. 63, No. I, p. 25.
[32] *Johnson* v. *Zerbst*, 304 U.S. 458.

out of that institution. Most of these went to the District Court at San Francisco and the Ninth Circuit Court of Appeals and got scant consideration because of their lack of merit. The Solicitor General did not bother to file opposing briefs in the "Alcatraz cases" that reached the Supreme Court. Disturbed by this casual attitude, Hughes induced his brethren to grant certiorari on a highly informal petition from two convicted bank robbers who had been given the brush-off in the District Court. Counsel was appointed, the cases were argued and sent back to the lower court with instructions to hold proper hearings in *all* cases,[33] including *in forma* pleas from Alcatraz. About the same time the Solicitor General made it a rule to file a brief in every case before the Supreme Court in which the United States was a party. The effect of the Supreme Court's vigilance seemed to permeate throughout the judicial system.

With all his zeal for the protection of civil rights, Hughes consistently resolemnized the marriage of liberty and order in his constitutional doctrines. When five Jehovah's Witnesses were convicted of parading on a public street in Manchester, New Hampshire, without a license, the court held that the state had a right to control the use of its highways for the public convenience and safety.[34] "Civil liberties, as guaranteed by the Constitution," Hughes said, "imply the existence of an organized society maintaining public order without which liberty itself would be lost in the excesses of unrestrained abuses."

In the flag-salute case of 1940 the court was compelled to choose between two important rights.[35] The children of Walter Gobitis, a Jehovah's Witness, had been expelled from the public schools at Minersville, Pennsylvania, because of their refusal, on religious grounds, to salute the flag. The question was whether the right of the state to use the flag-salute ceremony for training its youth in citizenship should supersede the right of the individual to follow the dictates of his conscience in such matters.

To most of the Justices, it was not a new issue. The underlying question had been settled when a unanimous court had concluded in 1934 that the University of California was within its rights in expelling conscientious objectors who refused to take a prescribed course in military training.[36] Cardozo had written a concurring opinion with the support of Stone and Brandeis. Four times the court had also unanimously found that it was not beyond the power of the states to make attendance in the public schools conditional upon saluting the flag.[37] Stone, Brandeis, Cardozo, Roberts, and the Chief Justice had all joined in these decisions.

When the Gobitis case arose, Hughes reiterated the established doctrine

[33] 312 U.S. 275, 342.   [34] *Cox* v. *New Hampshire*, 312 U.S. 569.
[35] *Minersville School District* v. *Gobitis*, 310 U.S. 586.
[36] *Hamilton* v. *Regents*, 293 U.S. 245.
[37] See Justice Frankfurter's dissent in *West Virginia* v. *Barnette*, 319 U.S. 624.

that a state had a right to prescribe its own curriculum in its free public schools. If it wished to require a salute to the flag, as a symbol of liberty, that was its own affair. It was not an encroachment upon religious scruples. The liberty protected by the due-process clause did not extend so far as to require settlement of this question of educational policy in the courtroom.

Not a word of opposition to this view was uttered in the conference discussion. As several of the brethren left the room together, someone said that the Chief ought to write the opinion, presumably to clinch a settled issue. At Roberts' suggestion, Frankfurter turned back and repeated that idea to Hughes.

"No," the Chief replied emphatically, "I'm going to assign it to you."

Frankfurter wrote a persuasive opinion, and only when Stone failed to initial it did the brethren learn that he was writing a lone dissent on the ground that the required salute was an encroachment upon religious faith.[38] Within three years, however, this view became law. Justices Black, Douglas, and Murphy dramatically reversed their previous conclusion and joined a new majority in uprooting a West Virginia flag-salute requirement. Hughes, then in retirement, felt so strongly that the court had gone astray in this case that he broke his self-imposed rule not to discuss current decisions of the court in order to write his congratulations to Frankfurter on his powerful dissenting opinion.

While he thought Jackson had written a strong opinion for the majority, Hughes concluded that Frankfurter had "knocked out one of the main props of the decision in pointing out that the State, under the unanimous decision in *Pierce* v. *Society of Sisters* and other cases, could not constitutionally make attendance in its public schools compulsory." [39] The Chief was confident that Cardozo, Brandeis, and Holmes would have held to Frankfurter's position.

The Gobitis case is the only instance in which Hughes has been accused of voting against civil liberties. Actually his vote should not be so regarded here, for he upheld what he believed to be the prior right of the state to impose a condition upon the privilege of attending public schools. The decision gives emphasis to his restraint in not undercutting legislative policy with due process, unless basic rights were actually impaired.

Hughes' entire record in this field makes him one of the greatest modern exponents of civil liberties. Joseph Percival Pollard concluded as early as 1934 that Hughes had shown a "greater fondness for the Bill of Rights than any Chief Justice this country ever had." [40] While avoiding the distorted view that the entire Bill of Rights was absorbed into the Fourteenth Amendment, he made the fundamental freedoms living law in the states as well as the nation. The arch of due process had been chiefly used to shelter property rights. Hughes

[38] Author's interview with CEH, Nov. 12, 1947.   [39] CEH to Frankfurter, June 17, 1943.
[40] *North American Review*, April, 1934, p. 357.

found under its protective expanse ample room for those human rights that are traditionally associated in the American mind with "liberty." Under his leadership, the court made freedom of the press and of religion, free speech, and free assembly so much a part of the law binding upon the states that they are never likely to be endangered so long as independent courts sit. To his everlasting credit also, he refused to eclipse the constitutional guarantee regarding property while he was amplifying the guarantees as to life and liberty.

Chapter 69

THE NEW DEAL IN COURT

THE MOST dramatic and far-reaching struggle involving the court came over the use of federal power to control the national economy. The depression of the thirties had thrust upon the government numerous obligations that it had never before assumed. Swept into office on a pledge of drastic action, President Franklin D. Roosevelt had launched a series of bold experiments with little regard for the limits of federal power. From the first days of the New Deal it was obvious that our constitutional system was undergoing a wrenching such as it had not experienced since the Civil War.

In the dark days of 1933, however, officials were thinking only of pulling the country out of the hole it was in. The banks had been closed to avert general panic. Industrial production was at a low ebb. Unemployment had reached an appalling total. Agriculture was being crushed by its own unmanageable surpluses. People were losing their homes, their savings, and their faith in the future. In the face of these conditions the country welcomed heroic measures.

The new Congress fell at once into the role of the little lamb to Roosevelt's Mary. Meeting in extraordinary sessions in March, 1933, it rushed through the President's emergency banking bill in a single day. In the turbulent weeks that followed the statute books burgeoned with legislation creating the Civilian Conservation Corps, the Tennessee Valley Authority, the Home Owners Loan Corporation, and the Agricultural Adjustment Administration for the control of farm production. To the AAA bill Congress also attached the slapdash Frazier-Lemke scheme to save farm mortgages from foreclosure and an amendment to inflate the currency and give the President broad powers to change the gold content of the dollar. Finally, came the National Recovery Act with its vast grant of power to the President and trade associations to harness business and industry under codes that could be enforced as law. In a little more than three months our sick and halting free economy had been brought under centralized national control.

Congress had not legislated in the ordinary meaning of the term. Rather, it had responded to the demands of the executive branch for power to meet an emergency. Most of the bills enacted had come straight from the White House. All of them had been drafted under great pressure—some by men with little

731

experience in government. Veteran legislators had warned their colleagues that no such heedless unleashing of federal power could be sustained under the Constitution, but the prevalent feeling was that if constitutional obstacles were in the way, the reckoning would have to be left to less critical times.[1] Some of the young men who surrounded the President believed that the country was in a revolutionary era. In this expansive mood they felt no necessity for shaping their "new instruments of power" to the constitutional doctrines that had found acceptance on the bench. The Supreme Court was *passé*, and the idea that it might interfere with the forward march of the New Deal was heresy.

As between the principals in the approaching struggle, relations were cordial and friendly. Roosevelt had made his debut in public life as a member of the New York Senate the year that Hughes had left Albany to take his seat on the supreme bench. As a young anti-Tammany Democrat, F. D. R. had supported Hughes' reforms and had even crossed the party line to vote for the Republican Governor.[2] In later years Louis Howe had served as liaison between them. Howe had been an indefatigable Hughes supporter at Albany long before he became Roosevelt's closest political adviser. He appears to have kept Hughes' stock at a high figure in the presidential book in the early years of the New Deal.

On the eve of his inauguration in 1933 the President-elect had written to the Chief Justice:

May I tell you how very happy I am at the thought that you will administer the oath to me. In addition to our long time friendship and to my admiration and respect for you, I think it is interesting that a Governor of New York is to administer the oath to another Governor of New York.

I am looking forward with great satisfaction to our coming association and to seeing more of you than I have had the opportunity of seeing for many years.[3]

Hughes had replied:

It gives me the greatest pleasure to receive your letter. It will be a high privilege to administer the oath of office and you will enter upon your great task with my heartiest felicitations and my earnest wish that you will have a most successful administration.

I am glad to have the suggestion that you repeat the oath in full instead of saying simply "I do." . . .

I cordially reciprocate the sentiments of friendship which you so kindly express, and I especially prize the opportunity of being associated with you in our great American enterprise.[4]

[1] Carl Brent Swisher, *American Constitutional Development*, p. 877.
[2] F. D. R. to CEH to author, interview of May 28, 1947.
[3] F. D. R. to CEH, Feb. 25, 1933.   [4] CEH to F. D. R., Feb. 28, 1933.

Hughes did administer the oath with great dignity on that historic March 4; then the two men went their separate ways. Roosevelt sent Howe to consult the Chief Justice about a very important appointment in the State Department, and the executive and judicial heads occasionally chatted amiably at official receptions. That was the extent of their relationship. As constitutional issues began to loom large on the horizon, the President let it be known that he would welcome a chance to talk over these problems with members of the Supreme Court. One of his intimates gave that message to Justice Stone. Before his inauguration F. D. R. had written to Justice Cardozo: ". . . I hope that I can have at least in part the same type of delightful relations with the Supreme Court which I had with the Court of Appeals in Albany." [5] Intimations of the same desire reached the ears of the Chief Justice, although he was not directly approached.[6] Stone had been shocked by the suggestion, and any alert observer could determine that Hughes' concept of judicial duty would never sanction a back-stage discussion of issues or cases that were to come before the court for adjudication.

Through the newspapers Hughes was aware of the New Deal's unprecedented recovery program. The closer integration of society thus contemplated seemed to have his sympathy. On June 7, 1933, he told the graduating class at Deerfield Academy, including his grandsons, Charles E. Hughes, 3d, and Henry Stuart Hughes: "Now one increasingly finds himself controlled by a social urge. Economic independence is now difficult, if not impossible, to realize. We cannot save ourselves unless we save society. No one can go it alone." But the Chief was too much absorbed in his own task to give any detailed attention to the type of legislation Congress was passing, and another year was to elapse before any major New Deal law would come under his scrutiny.

A slight jar to the Administration's confidence was felt in February, 1934, when a unanimous court ruled that an economy measure was invalid in so far as it reduced the pay of retired judges of the lower federal courts.[7] Roberts' opinion pointed out that retired judges could be recalled to active duty; consequently, they still held the office, and, under the Constitution, their salaries could not be diminished. *Lynch* v. *United States* [8] was a further warning that the Supreme Court was not overawed by the so-called Roosevelt revolution. The court decided unanimously that Congress had overreached its power in taking away certain contractual rights under the War Risk Insurance Act, and Hughes diplomatically assigned the opinion to Brandeis.

When the "hot-oil" cases were argued in December, 1934, the court got

---

[5] *F. D. R.: His Personal Letters 1928–1945* (New York, 1950, Duell, Sloan & Pearce), III, 307. Copyright, 1950, by Elliott Roosevelt.

[6] Author's interview with CEH, May 28, 1947.

[7] *Booth* v. *U.S.*, 291 U.S. 339.   [8] 292 U.S. 571.

an extremely unfavorable impression of New Deal methods. To his great credit, Assistant Attorney General Harold M. Stephens (later Chief Judge of the United States Court of Appeals for the District of Columbia) volunteered the information that the Petroleum Code had been enforced for about a year without a penal section. In a revision approved by the President, the section imposing penalties had been inadvertently left out, and the mistake had not been discovered until shortly before the "hot-oil" cases were argued. Men had been arrested, indicted, and held in jail for violating a law that did not exist.

The elusive character of the codes stimulated searching questions from the bench. Brandeis wanted to know who promulgated these codes that had the force of law. Stephens said it was the President.

"Is there any official or general publication of these executive orders?" Brandeis persisted.

"Not that I know of," Stephens replied.

"Well, is there any way by which one can find out what is in these executive orders when they are issued?"

"I think it would be rather difficult," the attorney candidly admitted, "but it is possible to get certified copies of the executive orders and codes from the NRA."[9]

In response to another question, Stephens estimated that several hundred codes and executive orders of this type had been issued. The judges were shocked by the extent and slipshod method of this executive lawmaking. Hughes decided to write the opinion himself. He found the root of the trouble in Section 9 (c) of the National Industrial Recovery Act. Congress had not laid down a policy to aid the states in controlling oil production or to regulate the flow of oil in interstate commerce. It had merely given the President "unlimited authority to determine the policy and to lay down the prohibition, or not to lay it down, as he may see fit." [10] And disobedience to his order had been made a crime punishable by fine and imprisonment.

From the beginning of the government, the Chief Justice said, Congress had conferred upon executive officers the power to make regulations to carry out the law. In every case the court had upheld such regulations, while recognizing that there were limits to the delegation of power that could not be transcended. "We think," he added, "that Section 9 (c) goes beyond those limits." It was no answer to insist that "deleterious consequences follow the transportation of 'hot oil.'" Even to meet recognized evils Congress could not "abdicate, or transfer to others, the essential legislative functions with which it is vested." To permit the delegation of such "unfettered discretion" to the President would be to invest him with "an uncontrolled legislative power."

9 *Washington Post*, Dec. 11, 1934.
10 *Panama Refining Co.* v. *Ryan*, 293 U.S. 388.

"Yes Sir," Brandeis wrote on the proof sheets when Hughes circulated the opinion. "Complete and even the layman can understand." Sutherland commented: "Clear, convincing and written with careful discrimination." Only Cardozo dissented, arguing that a sufficient standard to guide the President could be found in the Act.

The "hot-oil" decision was a severe jolt to the Administration. Now it was apparent that several New Deal statutes were in jeopardy. Tension gripped the country as hearings on the gold-clauses cases began the very next day after the "hot-oil" decision had come down. "The whole American economy was haled before the Supreme Court." [11] Under the Act of May 12, 1933, the President had reduced the gold value of the dollar by 40.94 per cent. The policy had been a failure so far as raising prices and stimulating business were concerned, but it had brought the dollar more nearly into line with devalued foreign currencies. The country had accepted the "59-cent dollar" and had been making contracts and settlements on that basis for about a year. Economists foresaw unimaginable chaos if the devaluation Act should be upset.

Two principal issues were argued before the court. The first was the validity of the gold clause in private contracts. For many years lawyers had been writing into bonds, mortgages, and contracts a standard clause to the effect that the principal and interest should be payable only in gold coin of the same weight and fineness as the dollar in circulation when the contract was entered into. Gold obligations of this sort outstanding in the United States probably amounted to a hundred billion dollars. Since Congress had forced the surrender of all gold to the Treasury, the holder of a railroad bond calling for an interest payment of $22.50 in gold dollars demanded $38.10 in the new devalued currency. To recognize such demands would vastly enrich the creditor class and plunge debtors into ruin.

The other issue involved the gold clause in the government's own obligations. John M. Perry contended that, in the absence of gold, the government should pay him $16,931.25 in devalued currency on a $10,000 Liberty Bond. The court seemed to have the alternative of increasing the public debt by about 60 per cent or of acknowledging congressional power to repudiate at any time the solemn bond of the United States. The Chief Justice bore down heavily on counsel in this case. "Here we have a bond issued by the United States Government . . . in time of war," he said, ". . . a bond which the Government promised to pay in a certain kind of money. Where do you find any power under the Constitution to alter that bond, or power of Congress to change that promise?" [12] The Assistant Solicitor General could only point lamely to the power of Congress to fix the value of money.

[11] Robert H. Jackson, *The Struggle for Judicial Supremacy* (New York, Knopf, 1941), p. 101. Copyright, 1941, by Robert H. Jackson.
[12] *New York Times*, Jan. 11, 1935.

While the Justices mulled over their momentous problem, tension became so acute that they ordered the clerk to announce at the end of each successive week that no decision in the gold-clause cases would be forthcoming the following Monday. President Roosevelt was so worried over the potential disaster of a decision holding the government to its promise to redeem its bonds in gold that he wrote a radio speech announcing his refusal to enforce such a ruling.[13] It was to be delivered, of course, only if the decision went against the government. The court knew nothing of it. On February 8, 1935, when the Justices dined at the White House "on the President's gold plates," the unmentionable gold cases and the secret repudiation speech must have haunted the table like Banquo's ghost.

The Chief worked the problem out in his own mind before he took the cases to conference. The gold clause in private contracts gave him no trouble. Back in 1911 his opinion in the McGuire case had made it clear that governmental powers could not be nullified by private contracts.[14] Now it was only a question of applying this principle to the gold-clause contracts. His conclusion was clear and forceful:

Contracts, however express, cannot fetter the constitutional authority of the Congress. Contracts may create rights of property, but when contracts deal with a subject matter which lies within the control of the Congress, they have a congenital infirmity. Parties cannot remove their transactions from the reach of dominant constitutional power by making contracts about them.[15]

The Perry case was more difficult. Hughes was deeply perturbed by the spectacle of the great United States repudiating its word. The terms of the bond were explicit. While there was no question about the power of Congress to regulate the value of money, the promise to pay bonds in gold rather than currency was apparently intended to assure investors that they would not suffer loss through any depreciation of the currency. There was a clear distinction between asserting the dominance of this power over private contracts and using it to alter the government's own engagements. The Chief Justice feared that failure on the part of the Supreme Court to recognize the binding character of these promises might have a serious effect on the public attitude toward government bonds in the future.[16]

". . . The binding quality of the promise of the United States is of the essence of the credit which is so pledged," he said. "Having this power to authorize the issue of definite obligations for the payment of money borrowed,

[13] Arthur Krock in *New York Times,* Jan. 26, 1947.
[14] *Chicago B. & Q. Ry. Co.* v. *McGuire,* 219 U.S. 549; see also *Philadelphia B. & W. Ry. Co.* v. *Schubert,* 224 U.S. 603
[15] *Norman* v. *B. & O. R.R.,* 294 U.S. 240.
[16] Author's interview with CEH, April 30, 1946.

the Congress has not been vested with authority to alter or destroy those obligations." [17]

But Hughes' sense of responsibility would not let him stop there. To permit every owner of a $10,000 bond to collect $16,931.25 would constitute "unjustified enrichment" and place an appalling burden upon the government. The bondholder had not shown, or even attempted to show, that in relation to buying power he had sustained any loss whatever. Having suffered no loss because of the government's unconstitutional act, he could claim no damages.

It was an ingenious solution reminiscent of Marshall's *Marbury* v. *Madison*. While rebuking the political branches for their breach of faith, it gave them a victory that they would have to accept in order to save the government from financial catastrophe. In this respect it was a typically Hughesian performance. For while he was deeply concerned with the maintenance of integrity and constitutional principles, he also had a passion to make government succeed. This decision alone should be sufficient to dispose of any idea that he was actuated by hostility toward Roosevelt or the New Deal.

Seven members of the court agreed with the Chief that repudiation of the gold clause in government bonds was unconstitutional. Stone insisted that it was not necessary to pass upon the constitutional issue, but he concurred in the result. The four conservatives dissented from the result, contending that the bondholder should be allowed to take his pound of flesh. In the two other cases—those involving the gold clause in private contracts and the status of gold certificates [18]—Hughes won by a single vote. McReynolds blurted out one of the most acid dissents since Harlan's outburst in the Standard Oil case. The policy upheld meant "repudiations," he exclaimed, "spoliation of citizens . . . legal and moral chaos."

At first Hughes had contemplated assignment of the opinions to Stone. He changed his mind and wrote them himself when it became apparent that Stone would partly dissent in one case. It was obvious that all three opinions should be written by the same judge. Brandeis, Roberts, and Cardozo stood solidly with the Chief throughout. "The three opinions are clear and forceful," Brandeis wrote on the proof sheets. "You have said all that should be said in support of our view." Cardozo told the Chief that he was "100 per cent right" in saying that repudiation of the gold clause in government bonds was unconstitutional.[19]

The dominant feeling through the country was one of profound relief. "America thanks God for a man of independent opinion," one jubilant citizen telegraphed. "In history the name of Hughes will be greater than that of Marshall." [20] Although confused over the details of the decisions, the people

[17] *Perry* v. *U.S.*, 294 U.S. 330.   [18] *Nortz* v. *U.S.*, 294 U.S. 317.
[19] CEH's Notes, 1930–1941, p. 14.   [20] Hughes' papers, Supreme Court.

felt that sound judgment had prevailed on one of the most important issues ever to come before any court. "The Constitution has been stretched, perhaps," said the *San Francisco Chronicle,* "but not beyond its limit of elasticity." [21]

At the National Theater the night after the decision came down, the Chief Justice and Mrs. Hughes laughed heartily as Gilbert's and Sullivan's two Gondoliers decided that they should occupy the throne jointly so that "the validity of their acts" would not be questioned. Returning to the theater of reality, Hughes smiled whimsically as a newsboy shrieked at him, "All about the gold decision!"

During the next few months official Washington breathed easier. The Administration's margin of victory was narrow, but the court had demonstrated that a majority of its members were examining New Deal statutes with open minds. In several cases that could be decided on other grounds the court refused to pass on the constitutionality of congressional acts. May, 1935, however, brought an upset of the Act providing a compulsory retirement and pension system for railway employees. A majority of five, with Roberts as spokesman, concluded that the Act denied due process of law "by taking the property of one and bestowing it upon another." [22]

Hughes wrote a stiff dissent and was joined by Brandeis, Stone, and Cardozo. While admitting that there were defects in the Act, he struck powerfully at the majority argument that it was not a regulation of interstate transportation:

What sound distinction, from a constitutional standpoint, is there between compelling reasonable compensation for those injured without fault of the employer and requiring a fair allowance for those who practically give their lives to the service and are incapacitated by the wear and tear of time, the attrition of the years? I perceive no constitutional ground upon which the one can be upheld and the other condemned. . . . The fundamental consideration which supports this type of legislation is that industry should take care of its human wastage, whether that is due to accident or age.

The power committed to Congress to govern interstate commerce does not require that its government should be wise, much less that it should be perfect. The power implies a broad discretion and thus permits a wide range even of mistakes.

Meanwhile the Administration had been searching for a favorable case by which to test the validity of the NRA. By early 1935 the grandiose experiment was breaking down. Employers were rebelling, little business was complaining that the "Blue Eagle" meant monopoly, and consumers were disgruntled by higher prices. With suits multiplying, the NRA had to hasten a test in the Supreme Court or risk collapse of its enforcement program. A case involving

[21] Feb. 19, 1935.   [22] *R.R. Retirement Board* v. *Alton R.R. Co.,* 295 U.S. 330.

the Lumber Code was chosen for the test,[23] but after it had advanced to the Supreme Court the more responsible lawyers in the Department of Justice discovered that some of the facile minds of the "brain trust" had tricked the lower court. To avoid resting a test on this slippery ground, the Solicitor General had the case dismissed.

About the same time a poultry dealer from Brooklyn asked the Supreme Court to review a Court of Appeals decision upholding the "Live Poultry Code," and the department found itself obliged to defend the NRA at one of its most vulnerable points. The arguments in the case high-lighted the petty local transactions that the NRA was attempting to control. The Schechter brothers had been convicted of selling an "unfit chicken" to a butcher, of permitting the "selection of individual chickens" from their coops, and of selling to unlicensed dealers. These trivial "offenses" had about as much effect on interstate commerce as a mosquito on a herd of elephants.

The Chief Justice presented the case to conference in his usual thorough and precise manner. Every judge agreed that the NRA was beyond the pale, and the importance of the case dictated that the Chief himself should write the opinion. He met the arguments of the government one by one. "Extraordinary conditions may call for extraordinary remedies," he conceded. "But . . . extraordinary conditions do not create or enlarge constitutional power." Officials exercising the limited powers of the national government "are not at liberty to transcend the imposed limits because they believe that more or different power is necessary." [24]

To the argument that the NRA was a cooperative effort among those engaged in trade and industry, he replied that it was also a coercive exercise of the lawmaking power. Violations of the codes were punishable as crimes. Obviously the NRA had to be treated as an exercise of governmental power. As such, it had two fatal weaknesses. It involved a surrender of lawmaking power to trade associations and the President, and it reached out to control local activities that had no real bearing upon interstate commerce.

As he had done in the "hot-oil" case, Hughes elaborated the difference between Congress laying down a policy, with provision for administrative details to be filled in, and turning over the lawmaking power to some other agency. "The Recovery Act," he said, "supplies no standards for any trade, industry or activity. . . . Instead of prescribing rules of conduct, it authorizes the making of codes to prescribe them." Of course, the codes had to have the approval of the President, and if he did not like a code drawn up by industry and labor he could discard it and substitute one of his own. But this only meant that the President had acquired the lion's share of the arbitrary lawmaking power that Congress had given away. "Such a delegation of legislative

[23] *U.S.* v. *Belcher*, 294 U.S. 736.   [24] *Schechter* v. *U.S.*, 295 U.S. 495.

power is unknown to our law," Hughes said, "and is utterly inconsistent with the constitutional prerogatives and duties of Congress."

Turning to the second fatal defect, he noted that the "Live Poultry Code" was not concerned with the transportation of poultry into New York or even with the sales of commission men to the Schechters. All the Schechters' business was wholly within the state. No "flow of commerce" into and out of the state was involved. The real question was whether the Schechters' local business "affected" interstate commerce so as to bring them within the scope of federal regulation.

It is often assumed that Hughes took a narrow view of the commerce clause in this case. The reverse is true. "The power of Congress," he said, "extends not only to the regulation of transactions which are part of interstate commerce, but to the protection of that commerce from injury. It matters not that the injury may be due to the conduct of those engaged in intrastate operations." It is the "effect upon interstate commerce," not "the source of the injury," he quoted from previous opinions, which is "the criterion of congressional power." To show the broad scope of this federal power, he went back to his own opinion in the *Shreveport Case,* in which the court had upheld federal control of local railroad rates when that was necessary to protect interstate commerce from unjust discrimination. Only a few months before the Schechter decision the court had also held that a conspiracy of market men, wholesalers, and a labor union to monopolize the poultry business in the New York metropolitan area was a violation of the Sherman Act because it obstructed interstate commerce.[25] Hughes strongly reiterated the doctrine behind these decisions in his NRA opinion. But in those cases the injury done to interstate commerce was direct and immediate. He searched in vain for any impact on interstate commerce from the Schechters' chicken coops. If the test case had involved a big interstate industry, NRA would still have gone down, but only on grounds of unconstitutional delegation of power.

The court did insist on maintaining a distinction between direct and indirect effects of local activities on interstate commerce. Hughes regarded the distinction as fundamental. Otherwise, he said, "there would be virtually no limit to the federal power and for all practical purposes we should have a completely centralized government." He also recognized the great difficulty of drawing the line between direct and indirect effects on interstate commerce and observed that the line may shift from decade to decade, but that did not obviate the necessity of drawing it from case to case for the sake of preserving our federal system.

Justice Cardozo wrote a concurring opinion to indicate why he was now

[25] *Local 167* v. *U.S.,* 291 U.S. 293.

going along with the court after dissenting in the "hot-oil" case. "This is delegation running riot," he declared. "No such plenitude of power is susceptible of transfer." Both Hughes and Cardozo emphasized the lack of federal power to regulate wages and hours in the Schechter establishment. But each confined his remarks strictly to wages and hours in a local business having no repercussions across state lines. There was no suggestion, as some critics have assumed, that Congress could not regulate wages, hours, and industrial relations in big enterprises operating across state lines. Nor were intrastate industries placed beyond the reach of Congress if their working conditions had a direct impact upon interstate commerce. In simple fairness to the court these opinions must be read in the light of the facts about the Schechter brothers' business.

Stone joined in the Cardozo opinion because he had disagreed with Cardozo in the "hot-oil" case and did not wish to give the impression of pulling away from his close friend. The unanimity of the court stands out starkly from the comments scribbled on Hughes' proof sheets. Brandeis' barb may be a little shocking to those who have thought of him primarily as a New Dealer. "Yes," he wrote. "This is clear and strong—and marches to the inevitable doom. It seems to me ready for delivery on Monday—and I hope that will be possible." Van Devanter commented, "Nothing essential is omitted and nothing said goes beyond what is appropriate." Sutherland responded with obvious delight: "You make the thing so clear that it is a marvel that anyone should think otherwise. I am glad to concur in so fine an opinion."

The knell for the NRA was accompanied by two other unanimous opinions —one striking down the Frazier-Lemke Act for relief of farm debtors and the other rebuking the President for his removal of William E. Humphrey from the Federal Trade Commission. Brandeis administered the *coup de grâce* to the recklessly drafted Frazier-Lemke Act.[26] All the brethren agreed that it authorized an unconstitutional taking of private property for a public purpose, without just compensation.

In the Humphrey case [27] the court said, through Justice Sutherland, that the Federal Trade Commission was an independent, nonpartisan body of experts charged with quasi-judicial duties. Unlike the postmaster whom the Taft court had held removable by the President, an FTC member could be ousted only for the causes specified by Congress, and F. D. R. had frankly admitted forcing the commissioner out because their minds ran in different channels. Humphrey was dead by the time the case was decided, but the decision came as a severe blow to the President's concept of his powers.

These three unanimous decisions made Monday, May 27, 1935, the black-

[26] *Louisville Joint Stock Land Bank* v. *Radford*, 295 U.S. 555.
[27] *Humphrey's Executor* v. *U.S.*, 295 U.S. 602.

est day in the history of the New Deal. The Chief Justice had raised a question as to whether three such jolts should be inflicted on the Administration in a single day.[28] Brandeis had replied that he could see no objection. Later he declared that the momentous session on May 27 was "the most important day in the history of the court and the most beneficent." [29]

When the news reached the White House, the first question the President asked was, "Where was Brandeis?"

"With the majority," replied one of his legal advisers.

"Where was Cardozo? Where was Stone?" he queried.

"They too were with the majority." [30]

For the moment the President seemed to find solace in the suggestion of his adviser that the court had relieved him of a political white elephant. He could not have been unaware of the fact that the NRA was breaking down of its own weight. But F. D. R. had invested much pride in this experiment. "History," he had grandiloquently predicted upon signing the bill, "probably will record the National Industrial Recovery Act as the most important and far-reaching legislation ever enacted by the American Congress." [31] His sense of personal injury quickened as the "palace guard" flocked in to bewail the audacity of the court. Four days later his anger boiled over in a press conference, and he accused the court of taking the country back to a "horse-and-buggy" definition of interstate commerce.

Speaking for an hour and a half, seriously, vigorously, and sometimes with biting satire, the President said that the destruction of the NRA was the most important Supreme Court ruling since the Dred Scott case precipitated the Civil War. The court had stripped the Federal Government of its power to deal with social and economic problems, he asserted, and the people would have to meet the issue thus raised. Ignoring the utterly local nature of the "sick-chicken" case, he assumed that the court would block any future federal control over the national economy.

Outside the Administration circle there were few mourners at the NRA funeral. Some experienced lawyers in the President's own following realized, moreover, that the court had merely done its judicial duty. General Hugh Johnson, former head of the NRA, later insisted that the Administration had brought defeat upon itself by "putting up to the Court the supernal absurdity that Kosher chicken killing of one gallinaceous bird in Brooklyn affected interstate commerce." [32] That feeling was sufficiently widespread at the time to bring an avalanche of criticism upon the President for his assault upon the

[28] Author's interview with CEH, April 30, 1947.
[29] Alpheus T. Mason, *Brandeis* (New York, Viking, 1946), p. 620.
[30] Confidential source No. 1.
[31] *The Public Papers and Addresses of Franklin D. Roosevelt*, II, 246.
[32] General Johnson's radio address, April 13, 1937.

court. If the President was then thinking of legislation to subdue the judges, he got a negative response from the country.

In the next two years the clash between the Administration and the Supreme Court moved toward a historic climax. Unshaken by the scolding from the White House, the court continued to wipe off the books acts for which it could find no constitutional footing. The next in line was a provision of the Home Owners Loan Act of 1933 authorizing the conversion of state savings and loan associations into federal ones in violation of state law. Justice Cardozo, speaking for the court, said it was an unconstitutional invasion of powers reserved to the states by the Tenth Amendment.[33]

Probably the most troublesome case the court had to deal with involved the validity of the Agricultural Adjustment Act. For the first time the government had undertaken to regulate farm production. Under this Act the Secretary of Agriculture estimated the amount of each basic crop that could be sold at specified prices and the number of acres required to grow the desired volume. Acreage allotments were then parceled out to each farmer, and if he reduced his planting accordingly he was entitled to benefit payments financed largely by taxes on the processing of the commodities. The case that reached the Supreme Court in 1936 was a suit by Butler *et al.*, receivers for the Hoosac Mills Corporation, to prevent collection of this tax.[34]

Hughes' analysis of the case led him back to an opinion on the general welfare clause that he had prepared for a private client in 1919. His research at that time had convinced him that Hamilton and Story had been right in contending that the Constitution gives Congress power to tax and spend for "the general welfare" beyond the scope of its enumerated powers. Madison had been wrong in trying to confine the taxing and spending power to the relatively narrow scope of the purposes mentioned in the Constitution. Hughes' notable achievement in the Butler case was in bringing the entire court to acceptance, for the first time, of the broad Hamiltonian thesis. He always felt that this was the most "significant and important ruling in the Butler case." [35]

For the majority, however, this liberal view of the spending power did not give the AAA a clean bill of health. It undoubtedly meant that Congress was free to make benefit payments to farmers. But the AAA was also controlling farm production. Was the government free to levy taxes for this purpose, without relating its action to any federal regulatory power?

Once more the court was confronted by an inept statute. Any alert constitutional lawyer should have known that the taxing power was not a secure foundation on which to rest a sweeping regulatory law. In 1922 the Taft

[33] *Hopkins F.S.L. Association* v. *Cleary*, 296 U.S. 315.
[34] *U.S.* v. *Butler*, 297 U.S. 1.   [35] CEH, Notes, 1930–1941, p. 27.

court, with both Holmes and Brandeis concurring, and only Clarke dissenting, had ruled that Congress could not outlaw child labor by means of the taxing power.[36] On the same day the court had unanimously rejected an Act using the taxing power to control trading in grain futures on the Chicago Board of Trade.[37] Taft had taken pains to point out that the end sought could probably be accomplished under the commerce power, and a similar Act based on the commerce clause had then been passed and sustained. Yet Congress had set up the AAA under its taxing power in reckless defiance or ignorance of this pertinent history. It was blandly attempting to make a revenue power do the duty of a regulatory power, thus controlling local activities "irrespective of any relation to interstate commerce."

This experiment could be upheld under the Hamilton-Story-Hughes concept of the spending power only if the acreage controls were deemed to be voluntary. That is where the split came. A majority of six Justices concluded that the Act was coercive. Stone and Cardozo, believing that the purchase of compliance was not coercion, stood strongly for upholding the Act. Brandeis had not made up his mind when the vote was taken in conference and said that he would let the Chief Justice know later how his vote was to be recorded.[38] Ultimately he joined the dissenters.

Gossip has the Chief Justice denouncing his brethren for this decision and then changing his vote to avoid another five-to-four split. One story was to the effect that newspaper men standing in the corridor heard him shout above a tumult in the conference room, "Gentlemen! You are not only ruining this country, you are ruining this court." The Chief wrote his son that this gem of journalistic quackery was "manifestly absurd." [39] No newspaper men were in the corridor. If they had been, they could not have overheard the discussion in conference. At no time in his judicial career, moreover, did Hughes indulge in any such foolish emotional outburst. The rumor of Hughes changing his vote is equally void of substance. While he was zealous in safeguarding the prestige of the court, his profound sense of integrity never permitted him to alter his judgment in a case before the court for the sake of creating a better impression.

Roberts wrote the majority opinion, concluding that the processing tax was only a device for the unconstitutional regulation of farm production. While he stated the broad Hamiltonian doctrine as to the taxing and spending power, he limited its effectiveness in this case by saying the Tenth Amendment reserving the ungranted powers to the states was a bar to the type of taxing and spending that Congress had undertaken. This was because the majority regarded the benefit payments as coercive.

[36] 259 U.S. 20.
[37] 259 U.S. 44.
[38] Confidential source No. 2.
[39] CEH to his son, Feb. 22, 1937.

Stone's dissent was unusually bitter and this almost cost him the vote of Justice Brandeis. Accusing the majority of taking a stand "that must lead to absurd consequences," Stone declared: "Courts are not the only agency of government that must be assumed to have capacity to govern." His brethren of the majority felt that his words were unduly theatrical because of the narrowness of the difference between the two groups. Stone himself recognized that "the power to tax and spend" could "not be used to coerce action left to state control." [40] Likewise he acknowledged that the penalty taxes of the Bankhead Act of 1934 for the restriction of cotton acreage were "coercive," but drew a distinction between these and the AAA's benefit payment plan. The strong inference is that if the minority had thought the AAA controls to be coercive the court would have been unanimous. But Stone's view of the voluntary nature of the benefit payments has prevailed. Subsequent thinking has put the majority in the wrong on this point, and few commentators have taken the trouble to note how narrow the point really is.

While the casualties were heavy, the court also continued to sustain many Acts of Congress. It upheld the Trading With the Enemy Act,[41] the National Bankruptcy Act,[42] the Silver Purchase Act,[43] the Ashurst-Sumners Act prohibiting the shipment of prison-made goods in interstate commerce,[44] and the Chaco Arms Embargo Act. In the latter case Sutherland wrote a scholarly opinion confirming the broad sweep of the President's power in international affairs. In this field, "with its important, complicated, delicate and manifest problems," the court asserted, "the President alone has the power to speak or listen as the representative of the nation." [45]

Hughes wrote the opinion upholding the authority of Congress to build and operate the Wilson Dam in the Tennessee River.[46] The war and commerce powers gave ample authority for the project, he said, and the sale of power generated at the dam was an orderly disposition of government property under authorization from Congress. Since the broad-gauge program of the Tennessee Valley Authority was not involved in the case, the court expressed no opinion as to its validity.

Before taking its summer recess, however, the court struck down two more congressional Acts. A five-to-four decision, with McReynolds writing for the majority, sent the Municipal Bankruptcy Act of 1934 into the discard as an invasion of state sovereignty.[47] Hughes joined Cardozo, Brandeis, and Stone in a strong dissent, refusing to look upon voluntary petitions to which the state

---

[40] 297 U.S. 87.   [41] 292 U.S. 449.
[42] *Kuehner* v. *Irving Trust Co.*, 299 U.S. 445.
[43] *U.S.* v. *Hudson*, 299 U.S. 498.
[44] *Kentucky Whip & Collar Co.* v. *Illinois Central R.R. Co.*, 299 U.S. 334.
[45] *U.S.* v. *Curtiss-Wright Export Co.*, 299 U.S. 304.
[46] *Ashwander* v. *TVA*, 297 U.S. 288.
[47] *Ashton* v. *Cameron Co. Water Dist.*, 298 U.S. 513.

itself gave assent as impairing any state's rights. More important was the three-way split within the court which left the Guffey Act a shambles.

The Guffey Act had been passed in 1935 to give the bituminous coal industry a new code after the invalidation of NRA and to sound out the Supreme Court once more as to how far federal regulation of distressed industry might go. The President had been advised that the bill was unconstitutional. But this had not cooled his sponsorship of it. He had sent a message to the hesitant subcommittee in charge of the bill saying: "An opportunity should be given to the industry to attempt to work out some of its major problems. I hope your committee will not permit doubts as to constitutionality, however reasonable, to block the suggested legislation."

When a test case reached the supreme bench, a majority of five rejected the Guffey Act with a flat declaration that the evils it was designed to correct "are all local evils over which the Federal Government has no legislative control." [48] Justice Sutherland's opinion spread on the record so narrow a view of the commerce clause that the President's "horse-and-buggy" tag seemed belatedly fitting. Not content to upset the controls over wages, hours, and working conditions, the court said that the price-fixing provisions would also have to go as part of the general scheme, although Congress had specifically made the two sections separable. Dissenting vigorously, Cardozo, Brandeis, and Stone defended the price-fixing provisions as applied to interstate sales and to local sales "where interstate prices are directly or intimately affected." They thought it was not necessary to consider the labor provisions.

Both wings of the court had broken away from the middle ground the Chief Justice had offered them. So he wrote a separate opinion speaking only for himself. He was in accord with the majority in saying that the heavy tax designed to force every coal producer to adhere to the code was not a real tax but a penalty; it could be imposed only so far as the commerce power extended. Mining is not itself commerce, he declared, but he again emphasized that Congress could protect interstate commerce from injury from any source and "provide for the peaceful settlement of disputes which threaten it." As Congress had ample authority to regulate the prices of coal sold in interstate commerce and to prohibit unfair methods of competition, he insisted that the inoffensive price-fixing section of the Act should be permitted to stand. The labor provisions he regarded as invalid chiefly because of the broad delegation of legislative power, without standards or limitations, and the arrangement under which one group of producers and employees could impose rules governing hours and wages on other groups not parties to the agreement.

A week later, as previously recounted, the court's revolt against innova-

[48] *Carter* v. *Carter Coal Co.*, 298 U.S. 238.

tion reached its climax in the Tipaldo case invalidating the New York mini-mum-wage law for women. Having blocked an orderly evolution of federal power in the name of states' rights, the majority suddenly turned and clamped the states themselves in the irons of standpattism. A rumble of discontent swept through the land. Many who had previously been reluctant to criticize the court now chorused angry protests. For the court had created a political vacuum into which no government was supposed to enter regardless of how serious economic and social conditions might become.

Hughes was deeply troubled. In three important cases within two weeks the court had repudiated his leadership. That in itself was a minor matter, but the Chief Justice was convinced, as his ringing dissent in the Tipaldo case showed, that the court was inflicting fresh wounds upon itself. Rumors of Administration plans to pack the court were beginning to circulate. An epidemic of proposals to curb the court's powers broke out on Capitol Hill. Everywhere the prestige of the judiciary was sinking.

The extremes to which the majority had gone in a few cases tended to cast a shadow over all the careful work the court had done to bring the New Deal into line with the Constitution. Most of its decisions overturning hastily drafted emergency laws were sound. No court could have accepted all the undigested and ill-founded legislation of that period without abdicating its constitutional function. We must remember also that, of the twelve decisions upsetting New Deal statutes, six were unanimous, and in two others the vote was eight to one.[49] When Hughes, Brandeis, Stone, Roberts, and Cardozo stood shoulder to shoulder and carried the more conservative Justices with them, it would be absurd to say that they were acting on caprice or illiberal bias. But in a few cases this liberal-moderate combination had broken up and left the court really vulnerable to criticism.

Its three errors that seemed to give some color of excuse for action against the court were the Tipaldo and Carter Coal decisions in both of which Hughes had dissented, and the AAA decision in which he had stood with the major-ity. In other words, the substantial counts against the court would have been reduced to one if the brethren had followed the Chief's leadership. And in those circumstances the court-packing venture might have been avoided.

In Hughes' mind there was no contest between the court and the New Deal. He had gone straight down the line of judicial duty, giving sanction to Acts that squared with the Constitution, as he understood it, and setting aside those that did not. Sometimes he was represented as shuttling erratically between liberal and conservative doctrines, but this was only because of the foolish notions that he was voting for or against the New Deal and that every-thing the Roosevelt Administration sponsored was liberal. The consistency of

[49] Senate Report 711, 75th Congress, 1st session, pp. 18, 45.

his struggle is inescapable if judged by his own objectives. Those objectives were to keep the law sensitive to the vibrant realities of his own day and at the same time preserve our constitutional system.

The tragedy of the situation, as this chapter in the court's history ends, is that Hughes seemed to be losing his fight in the squeeze between the judges who sought to petrify the law and the politicians who were determined to ride roughshod over the court if necessary to reach their goal.

Chapter 70

THE COURT-PACKING FIGHT

PRESIDENT ROOSEVELT watched the trend of the Supreme Court's decisions with mounting anger. He felt that the court was disregarding the national will and thwarting the national interest. As his recovery measures continued to go down, the President discussed with the Attorney General four possible remedies for "the court problem": a constitutional amendment enlarging federal powers, a statute limiting the court's jurisdiction, a law requiring more than a majority vote to nullify an Act of Congress, and enlargement of the court's membership. The President was not willing to wait for a constitutional amendment and did not think it was necessary. Although each of the other schemes had grave defects, "new blood" on the bench seemed to offer some hope of a solution. He ordered Attorney General Cummings to continue his research in this field.

Adding to the President's irritation was a feeling that the court had snubbed him. At the beginning of a new term it is customary for the Chief Justice to notify the White House that the court is in session and for the President to ask the Justices to call on him. In 1936 no such call was made. Two years later Roosevelt told Harry Hopkins that he had returned to Washington from a campaign tour to be present for the annual court visit and that no telephone call had come from the court. "After waiting three days," according to Hopkins' notes recorded by Robert E. Sherwood, "he had Marvin McIntyre get in touch with Justice Stone's secretary to find out what was going on. McIntyre was informed that 'There will be no visit to the White House this year.' "[1]

Obviously the President thought the court was nursing a grievance. But the ascertainable facts do not bear out his story. Actually the President was in Hyde Park on Monday, October 5, the day on which the court opened its new term.[2] He returned to Washington on Tuesday, but the court was then immersed in the work of disposing of its summertime accumulation of petitions for certiorari. Where McIntyre got his information is a mystery, for neither

[1] *Roosevelt and Hopkins* (New York, Harper, 1948), p. 94. Copyright, 1948, by Robert E. Sherwood.
[2] *Washington Post*, Oct. 6, 1936.

Justice Stone's secretary nor his clerk had any call from the White House in connection with the incident.[3] Nor could any one in the Chief's office or among the personnel of the court itself remember such a call. The known facts strongly suggest that, in the three days the President spent in Washington between campaign trips, there was no mutually convenient time for the court to make its call.

No one who knew Charles Evans Hughes would accuse him of indulging in a petty discourtesy. As Chief Justice no less than as Secretary of State, he gave meticulous attention to protocol. The fact that differences had arisen between the court and the President would have stiffened his insistence on observing the amenities. Justice Roberts and many others affiliated with the court are certain that "no snub was intended." [4] The President's resentment on this score appears to have been conjured out of thin air.

The decision to go ahead with a court bill was taken only after Roosevelt had won a whopping victory in the 1936 election. In his campaign speeches there had been no word about subduing the Supreme Court. On the contrary, his platform had pledged the Administration to meet the economic and social problems of the day "through legislation within the Constitution," or, if that should prove impracticable, to seek a "clarifying amendment." Some Republican orators had hinted that, if reelected, Roosevelt might pack the Supreme Court, but this line of campaigning had brought incensed denials from his supporters. "A more ridiculous, absurd, and unjust criticism of a President was never made," cried Senator Ashurst, the Democratic chairman of the Judiciary Committee.[5] Court-packing, he said, was a "prelude to tyranny."

But once the election was over, the President felt that he had a new mandate from the people—that if the court stood in his way the people would support him in brushing it aside. On his trip to South America in November, 1936, he took along two huge volumes of Department of Justice proposals to deal with the court, but found none of them satisfactory. Cummings then came up with the idea of naming new judges to supplant or replace the aged men on the bench. Recalling that Justice McReynolds, when he had been Attorney General in 1913, had recommended the appointment of substitutes for judges who failed to retire at the age authorized by law, Cummings felt sure that he had hit upon the right approach.[6] Even though McReynolds had exempted Supreme Court Justices from his proposal, the temptation to turn his own device against him seemed irresistible. The scheme got a warm reception at the White House, and the Attorney General, carrying his secret like a wise

---

[3] Gertrude Jenkins (the secretary) to author, March 25, 1950; Harold Leventhal (the clerk) in conversation with author, March 15, 1950.

[4] Justice Roberts to the author, March 21, 1950.

[5] Merlo J. Pusey, *The Supreme Court Crisis* (New York, Macmillan, 1937), p. 67.

[6] Alsop and Catledge, *The 168 Days* (New York, Doubleday, 1937), pp. 34–36. Copyright, 1937, by Joseph Alsop and Turner Catledge.

old owl, spent several tense weeks filling in details and giving the whole plan a veneer of judicial reform.

Meanwhile the President assured Congress in his annual message that the New Deal would go forward in spite of the court. On the evening of February 3, 1937, the President and Mrs. Roosevelt gave their dinner for the judiciary with eighty guests present, including all members of the court except Brandeis and Stone. Still treasuring his secret, the President was unusually gay; he was enjoying "one of those ironical little moments" [7] of which he was so fond. Two days later he sent his bombshell to Capitol Hill.

The bill was first disclosed to a small group of incredulous Cabinet members and congressional leaders on the morning of February 5. The President talked briefly without asking for advice, then hastened away to break the news in "the most jubilant press conference he ever had."

His drastic measure was represented as being a step to relieve the courts of congestion and avoid injustice. "Even at the present time," he said, "the Supreme Court is laboring under a heavy burden." Noting the large number of petitions for review denied in the previous year, he inferred that the court was keeping its calendar clear only by sloughing off its responsibilities. The general picture he drew was one of judges of "lowered mental and physical vigor" unable to meet the demands of a modern, progressive judicial system. This set the stage for his appeal for a "persistent infusion of new blood" into the judiciary. The only hint of his real purpose lay in his suggestion that if this bill were passed more fundamental changes in the powers of the courts or in the Constitution could be avoided.

The bill provided for a maximum of fifty additional judges. It called for a proctor to investigate the needs of the courts and aid the Chief Justice in dispatching what were later called "flying squadrons" of judges to district and circuit courts with congested calendars. But all this was sugar-coating. The central provision gave the President authority to appoint a sort of coadjutor for every federal judge who had been on the bench for ten years and who had not resigned within six months after reaching the age of seventy. In effect this meant that the President could enlarge the Supreme Court from nine to fifteen Justices.

Almost instantly the bill was stripped of the swaddling clothes of reform in which Roosevelt and Cummings had so diligently wrapped it. Congress was rent by the naked issue of packing the Supreme Court. Legislators who thought the end justified the means hailed the bill as a master stroke, and some of the Democratic wheelhorses hastened to endorse it to prove their party loyalty. But the constitutionalists of both parties acted as if the bottom were about to fall out of the American system. The first flush of anger and surprise gave

[7] *Ibid.*, p. 64.

By Eugene Elderman in the *Washington Post*, February 6, 1937.

TO FURNISH THE SUPREME COURT PRACTICAL ASSISTANCE

way to fear gnawing deep in the bowels of democracy, for it was generally assumed that the President's sweeping victory had given him the power to make his will effective. "Why," exclaimed Senator Glass in voicing his opposition, "if the President asked Congress to commit suicide tomorrow they'd do it."

Across the country came a rumble of protest. First it was the press. Then it was the press and radio echoing civic, patriotic, fraternal, religious, professional, and political organizations. The conscience of America had been deeply stirred. Indignation fed upon the deceptive nature of the President's message. The leaders of powerful groups in the President's following were also disgruntled because he had taken them for granted. Neither the Cabinet, nor congressional chieftains, nor party bigwigs, nor labor, nor farm leaders had been consulted.

As the conflict gained new intensity, the Supreme Court was the calmest spot in the Washington vortex. News of the bill reached Chief Justice Hughes while he was presiding in the courtroom. Always alert for information of interest to the court, the marshal, Thomas E. Waggaman, had secured copies of the President's message and bill and immediately distributed them to the Justices on the bench. Whatever inner excitement they may have felt, the judges maintained a stoic silence. Even in the seclusion of their offices and conference room, there was very little discussion of the bill.[8]

Without exception, however, the Justices were hostile to the scheme. Brandeis, the oldest member of the court and therefore presumably the chief target of the clamor for "new blood," was deeply wounded. Roberts, the youngest Justice who would not have been personally affected by the bill, nevertheless decided to resign if it were passed. Hughes, who was seventy-four, was determined to ride out the storm regardless of what might happen. "If they want me to preside over a convention," he said, "I can do it."[9] Under no circumstances would the court go down to humiliation and loss of confidence if he could prevent it.

President Roosevelt soothed the growing fears of his lieutenants by repeating a sort of standard refrain: "The people are with me, I know it." But in the office of the Chief Justice one got a very different impression. Thousands of letters and telegrams addressed to the court were almost unanimous in their opposition to the bill. Business men, professors, great lawyers, organizations of every description, and plain citizens of both parties gave vent to their wrath: "It makes my blood boil. . . . Every citizen resents this insult to the court. . . . Please do not allow the President to change this great court." Many letters "begged" the Chief Justice not to resign. "More power to you. . . . God bless you gentlemen and spare you to save our highest

[8] Author's interview with CEH, Nov. 19, 1945.   [9] Confidential source No. 2.

court. . . ." [10] If there had been any doubt as to the standing of the court with the people, the flood of mail that went both to the court and to Congress quickly removed it.

After four weeks of mounting criticism the President recognized the necessity of making a gloves-off fight. In his address to the Democratic victory dinner on March 4, he openly accused the court of usurping power and of vetoing his program. Five days later he went to the people with a "fireside chat" full of appealing sentiment, plausible arguments, and deep indignation toward the court. He accused the Justices of acting as a "superlegislature" and took out of context, with torturing effect, Governor Hughes' impromptu remark: "We are under a Constitution, but the Constitution is what the judges say it is."

"We have, therefore," the President concluded, "reached the point as a Nation where we must take action to save the Constitution from the Court and the Court from itself." [11] The implication was unmistakable—the President, with the aid of his advisers, was a better judge of what the Constitution means than was the Supreme Court.

Meanwhile the opposition had been effectively organized. The first meeting of Democratic legislators hostile to the bill had been held at the home of Senator Millard E. Tydings. Among those present were Senators Wheeler, Byrd, Copeland, George, Burke, King, and Van Nuys. A few days later a group of Democratic and Republican Senators lunched together and selected Wheeler as their leader, the Republicans agreeing to remain discreetly in the background.

As hearings on the bill got under way on March 10 before the Senate Committee on the Judiciary, the opposition concluded that its first task was to dispel the myth of a senile court unable to keep abreast of its work. For this purpose an authoritative statement from the court itself was sought. The Chief Justice gives us the following account of his negotiations with members of the committee:

As the opponents of the bill were about to present their case, Senators Wheeler, King and Austin called upon me—I think it was on Thursday, March 18th, 1937— and asked me to appear before the Committee. I was entirely willing to do this for the purpose of giving the facts as to the work of the Court. Even in appearing for such a purpose, however, I thought it inadvisable, in view of the delicacy of the situation, that I should appear alone. It seemed to me that at least one other member of the Court should accompany me,—preferably Justice Brandeis—because of his standing as a Democrat and his reputation as a liberal judge.

I so informed the Committee. But when I consulted Justice Brandeis I found that he was strongly opposed to my appearing—or to any Justice appearing—before the

---

[10] Hughes papers, Supreme Court.
[11] Senate Report 711, 75th Congress, 1st session, p. 41.

Committee. I stated the desire of the Committee to have the facts as to the state of the work of the Court and suggested that I might, in response to a request, write a letter for that purpose. With that suggestion Justice Brandeis fully agreed. I found that Justice Van Devanter took the same view.

Accordingly, I telephoned to Senator King and to Senator Wheeler on the morning of Friday, March 19, 1937, that I had found that there was a very strong feeling that the Court should not come into the controversy in any way, and that it was better that I should not appear; but that if the Committee desired particular information on any matters relating to the actual work of the Court, I should be glad to answer in writing giving the facts.

Later—on Saturday, as I recall it—Senator Wheeler, who I understood had seen Justice Brandeis in the interval, called on me and asked me to write such a letter. He said that the Committee desired this letter so that it could be used on Monday morning at the opening of the hearing on behalf of the opponents of the bill. This gave me very limited time but I proceeded at once to assemble the necessary data, and on Sunday, March 21st, the letter was completed. I at once took it to Justice Brandeis and to Justice Van Devanter, and each went over it carefully and approved it.[12]

Wheeler called at the Hughes home for the letter late Sunday afternoon. "The baby is born," said the Chief Justice with a broad smile as he put the letter into Wheeler's hand. In the brief chat that followed Hughes said that he had had all the honor that he could expect from the American people and that he was not worried about the impact of the bill upon himself or upon his brethren. "But if this bill should pass," he declared, "it would destroy the court as an institution." [13]

There was a precedent for Hughes' proposal that he and Brandeis testify before the committee. In 1935 they and Justice Van Devanter had gone before the same committee to oppose Senator Black's bill providing for immediate appeals to the Supreme Court from lower court orders restraining compliance with federal laws. While he rigorously eschewed any discussion of politics or policy-making, the Chief Justice felt that, if requested, he should give Congress any information about the work of the court that might save it from legislating under a misapprehension. It was only Brandeis' vehement opposition that prevented the Chief from going personally before the committee.

The next time the judges met, Hughes told them he had hoped to consult with each of them about the letter but had found it impossible because of the short time allowed him for its preparation; he hoped they all approved his action.[14] Several said they did, and Hughes thought everyone acquiesced. Actually, however, Stone was merely concealing his irritation. While he never

[12] CEH, Notes, 1930–1941, pp. 20–21. A memorandum of the March 19 conversation with the senators is in Mr. Hughes' private papers.
[13] Author's interview with Burton K. Wheeler, April 4, 1950.
[14] CEH, Notes, 1930–1941, p. 21.

uttered a critical word about the letter in the presence of the Chief, he let other members of the court know that he resented Hughes' failure to consult the entire court. Considering the delicacy of the issue, Hughes' action with the approval of only two of his eight colleagues was certainly a tactical error.

Wheeler released the Chief's letter in dramatic fashion in his opening statement for the opposition. The letter itself was cool, judicial, and factual:

> The Supreme Court is fully abreast of its work. When we rose on March 15 (for the present recess) we had heard argument in cases in which certiorari had been granted only 4 weeks before—February 15. . . . There is no congestion of cases upon our calendar.
>
> This gratifying condition has obtained for several years. We have been able for several terms to adjourn after disposing of all cases which are ready to be heard.

Hughes then went into details as to how the court works, completely undermining Roosevelt's insinuations that full justice had not been done because so large a percentage of the petitions for certiorari had been denied. The ends of justice were met, he pointed out, when a litigant dissatisfied with the verdict of a district court had an opportunity to carry his case to the Court of Appeals. "If further review is to be had by the Supreme Court," he said, "it must be because of the public interest in the questions involved. . . . I think it is the view of the members of the Court that if any error is made in dealing with these applications it is on the side of liberality." His conclusion was:

> An increase in the number of Justices of the Supreme Court, apart from any question of policy, which I do not discuss, would not promote the efficiency of the Court. It is believed that it would impair that efficiency so long as the Court acts as a unit. There would be more judges to hear, more judges to confer, more judges to discuss, more judges to be convinced and to decide. The present number of Justices is thought to be large enough so far as the prompt, adequate, and efficient conduct of the work of the Court is concerned. As I have said, I do not speak of any other considerations in view of the appropriate attitude of the Court in relation to questions of policy.[15]

With equal ease, he disposed of the suggestion that an enlarged court might hear cases in divisions. "A large proportion of the cases we hear are important," he wrote, "and a decision by a part of the Court would be unsatisfactory." Besides, the Constitution authorized "one Supreme Court" not two or more Supreme Courts or two or more units functioning as separate courts.

In spite of its dispassionate tone, the letter blasted the court bill with bombshell effect. Its sincere recital of facts stood out in damning contrast to the transparent pretense of the President's message. Its restraint threw the

[15] Committee Report (see note 11), pp. 36–39.

dignity of the court into the balance against the bombastic charges in the President's recent speeches. "Others may speak for weeks or months," Henry L. Stoddard wired the Chief, "but you have closed the debate." [16]

One week later the judges seemed to give another disconcerting jerk to the rug on which the court-packers were standing. Shortly before Christmas, 1936, the court had voted four to four, in the West Coast Hotel case, to uphold the Washington minimum-wage law and overrule its six-month-old decision in the Tipaldo case. Roberts had abandoned the standpatters and voted with Hughes, Brandeis, and Cardozo to sustain the Act. This meant that the Washington minimum-wage law would stand, for it had previously won the sanction of the highest court in that state. It meant also that Hughes would have a majority behind his broad interpretation of the state police powers as soon as Stone, who was ill, could return to the bench. To avoid a four-to-four decision on so important an issue, the case had been held temporarily. Stone had returned about February 1, 1937, and a majority of five overturned both the Tipaldo decision and *Adkins* v. *Children's Hospital.*[17] Before the opinions could be written and handed down, however, the court found itself under threat of being packed.

Hughes had been overjoyed by his success in swinging the court back into line with the Blaisdell and Nebbia cases. When Roberts, in a private chat, had divulged his intention of voting to sustain the Washington law, the Chief had almost hugged him. But now it was obvious that this triumph of liberal thinking *within* the court would be interpreted as a reversal under pressure. The court had no official spokesmen or ghost writers. Its conference proceedings were always kept secret. Hughes held back his opinion for a short time, to avoid the impression of an immediate response to the court-packing plan.[18] But that did not change the inevitable.

The story of how the court corrected itself in this case has never before been told. Hughes felt justified in disclosing the confidential details in his Biographical Notes "in defense of the Court's integrity." His most pointed comment was: "The President's proposal had not the slightest effect on our decision." [19]

On the same day that the Chief Justice dramatically reversed his court on the minimum-wage issue, three other favorable opinions came down. One of these upheld the National Firearms Act,[20] another the new Frazier-Lemke Act [21] recast to meet the court's objections, and a third the collective bargaining requirements of the Railway Labor Act as applied to shop employees.[22] The jubilant foes of the court bill dubbed the day (March 29, 1937) White

[16] Hughes papers, Supreme Court.   [17] CEH, Notes, 1930–1941, p. 31.
[18] Author's interview with CEH, May 7, 1947.   [19] Chapter XXIII, p. 31.
[20] *Sonzinsky* v. *U.S.,* 300 U.S. 506.   [21] *Wright* v. *Vinton,* 300 U.S. 440.
[22] *Virginian Ry.* v. *Federation,* 300 U.S. 515.

Monday in contrast to Black Monday when the NRA had been deflated. The court was said to be on the march. Some sponsors of the court bill regarded this performance as a Machiavellian plot to defeat the President's bill. Actually, however, a badly divided court had merely corrected one of its own mistakes and rendered independent judgment upon three acts involving no serious abuse of power.

Now foes of the court bill began to pray for a favorable decision on the National Labor Relations Act. Every day the fight to pack the court was losing momentum, although the President was still determined to force a showdown. The fate of the NLRB might be the decisive factor. Lawyers, legislators, and officials as well as curious spectators jammed the courtroom on April 12 expecting to see the court seal its doom or, possibly, rise to its salvation. They were not disappointed. After a few moments of preliminary business the Chief Justice began to deliver the court's judgment in *National Labor Relations Board* v. *Jones and Laughlin Steel Corporation.*[23] He read it magnificently, without a trace of histrionics or pomposity, yet with such a tone of authority that the law itself might have been speaking. Faces flushed and heartbeats quickened as his listeners realized that he was weaving a mantle of constitutionality around the NLRB.

The board had ordered Jones and Laughlin to reinstate ten employees dismissed for union activity, and the Circuit Court of Appeals had refused to enforce the order on the ground that it lay beyond the range of federal power. Hughes took note of the little empire that the company operated—its iron and steel plants in Pennsylvania, its mines in Michigan and Minnesota, its limestone properties in West Virginia, its steamships on the Great Lakes, its railroads, and its nineteen sprawling subsidiaries. Here was no Schechter chicken business but an interstate octopus. Congress had a right to protect interstate commerce from labor disturbances in such vast enterprises clearly beyond the reach of state power.

It was not necessary, he said, to relate the business of Jones and Laughlin to the "stream of commerce" cases.

The congressional authority to protect interstate commerce from burdens and obstructions is not limited to transactions which can be deemed to be an essential part of a "flow" of interstate or foreign commerce. Burdens and obstructions may be due to injurious action springing from other sources. The fundamental principle is that the power to regulate commerce is the power to enact "all appropriate legislation" for "its protection and advancement." . . .

It is thus apparent that the fact that the employees here concerned were engaged in production is not determinative. The question remains as to the effect upon interstate commerce of the labor practice involved.

[23] 301 U.S. 1.

In the Schechter case the court had found the effect to be so remote as to be beyond federal power. But repercussions from industrial strife in the Jones and Laughlin empire would be immediate and might be catastrophic. Hughes continued:

We are asked to shut our eyes to the plainest facts of our national life and to deal with the question of direct and indirect effects in an intellectual vacuum. . . . When industries organize themselves on a national scale, making their relation to interstate commerce the dominant factor in their activities, how can it be maintained that their industrial labor relations constitute a forbidden field into which Congress may not enter when it is necessary to protect interstate commerce from the paralyzing consequences of industrial war? . . .

Instead of being beyond the pale, we think that it presents in a most striking way the close and intimate relation which a manufacturing industry may have to interstate commerce and we have no doubt that Congress had constitutional authority to safeguard the right of respondent's employees to self-organization and freedom in the choice of representatives for collective bargaining.

Accompanying the Jones and Laughlin opinion were two other cases in which the Chief Justice found the Labor Relations Act applicable to a trailer company [24] and a men's clothing manufacturer [25] because of the interstate character of their businesses. With the basic principle of protecting commerce from labor disturbances established, it was evident that the court would apply it wherever the repercussions from labor strife upon interstate business might be substantial.

"Admirably done!" was Brandeis' comment. "Yes, sir," wrote Cardozo, "a magnificent opinion!" McReynolds, Van Devanter, Sutherland, and Butler dissented, writing a sort of "swan song of a dying philosophy." But even with a slender majority of one it was a momentous victory for liberal interpretation of the basic law. The legislators fighting to save the court from being packed were ecstatic, and lukewarm supporters of the bill fell away in droves.

"We did it," [26] chortled the President. At the same time he looked upon the decision as only a token victory that made it all the more necessary to press on with the fight for a court that would "cooperate." A five-to-four majority was not enough. With Tommy the Cork (Thomas G. Corcoran, counsel to the RFC) turning the heat on the opposition and with judicial appointments held up in states where the Senators were not "going along," [27] the President was still confident and refused to countenance talk of a compromise.

On May 18 the Judiciary Committee rejected the bill. A few days later the Supreme Court removed the last vestige of excuse for enlarging its membership by upholding the Social Security Acts. Both opinions, one giving

[24] *NLRB* v. *Fruehauf Trailer Co.*, 301 U.S. 49.
[25] *NLRB* v. *Friedman-Harry Marks Clothing Co.*, 301 U.S. 58.
[26] James A. Farley in *Collier's*, vol. 119, p. 11, June 21, 1947.   [27] *Id.*

a clean bill of health to the tax supporting unemployment insurance [28] and the other to the old-age benefit plan,[29] were based squarely upon the broad concept of the spending power for which Hughes had won the court's approval in the AAA case. In writing the opinions Justice Cardozo specifically cited *United States* v. *Butler* as having settled the right of Congress to spend money in aid of the "general welfare." Since the federal unemployment compensation law did not operate directly upon the citizen but made it possible for each state to set up its own unemployment insurance system, the question of coercion, which had troubled the majority so much in the AAA case, was not present. The old-age benefit plan seemed to fall clearly into the pattern that the court had outlined in the AAA opinion. There were only two dissents in this case.

Only one other step was needed to complete the liquidation of the court-packing scheme. During his four years in office President Roosevelt had had no opportunity to name a Supreme Court Justice even though six of the men on the high bench were over seventy. From the White House it looked as if the old men were clinging to their posts in order to prevent Roosevelt from naming their successors. In an effort to refute this assumption and to enable the Administration to give up its court bill with a minimum loss of face, Justice Van Devanter notified the President on May 18 of his intention to retire in June.

The ironical fact is that both Van Devanter and Sutherland had wanted to retire before 1937.[30] Butler and McReynolds had tried to dissuade them, but Van Devanter at seventy-eight was eager to lay down his burden, and Sutherland, with his high blood pressure, could keep abreast of his work only by writing most of his opinions in bed. They had clung to their posts chiefly because of the unfairness of Congress to Justice Holmes.[31] After Holmes had resigned, relying on a congressional pledge to continue the salaries of judges over seventy stepping down after ten years of service, Congress had reduced his compensation. The Constitution afforded no protection, for it forbade diminution of judges' pay only "during their continuance in office." Supreme Court Justices did not then have the privilege of retirement (as distinguished from resignation) which was accorded to the judges of the lower courts. The result was that Justices who otherwise would have retired remained on the bench.

The Administration had gone ahead with the court-packing bill without offering the aged Justices an opportunity to retire with continuance of their salaries assured. It was only after the court fight had been launched that the

---

[28] *Steward Machine Co.* v. *Davis*, 301 U.S. 548.
[29] *Helvering* v. *Davis*, 301 U.S. 619.
[30] Author's interview with CEH, May 28, 1947.
[31] CEH, Notes, 1930–1941, p. 16.

opposition rushed through a retirement bill in the hope of thwarting the more drastic measure. Senator Borah then impressed upon his close friend Van Devanter the great service he could render the cause by stepping down at that time. The Chief Justice had nothing whatever to do with it.[32]

At the White House, however, this conciliatory gesture turned to gall and wormwood. Long before the court fight had begun the President had promised the first vacancy on the supreme bench to Senator Joseph T. Robinson, the majority leader who was now fighting to get the court bill through the Senate. The pledge was well known among Robinson's colleagues, and as soon as the Van Devanter resignation was announced they swarmed into the Senate to congratulate him.[33] But Robinson was a conservative Arkansas politician of sixty-five. To single him out for the first vacancy on the court while the President was clamoring for younger and more liberal judges, would turn the court fight into a roaring farce. To disregard the pledge would produce an explosion in the Senate. Now it seemed imperative to create places for several liberal Justices to balance the inescapable Robinson appointment.

While the President was wrestling with this dilemma, Senator King presented the Judiciary Committee's historic "Adverse Report." It was a devastating attack. The committee recommended that the bill be rejected "as a needless, futile, and utterly dangerous abandonment of constitutional principle." Its ultimate operation, said the report, "would be to make the Constitution what the executive or legislative branches of the Government choose to say it is— an interpretation to be changed with each change of administration."

"It is a measure which should be so emphatically rejected that its parallel will never again be presented to the free representatives of the free people of America." [34]

With the fight still going on, the court's summer recess became the signal for a new blast from the White House. The President said that the court had cleared its docket only by ordering reargued six cases that had already been argued. The judges were going off for a four-month vacation, he complained, leaving undetermined cases of vital concern to the PWA, the TVA, and the SEC.

Actually the court had disposed of every case that had been ready for hearing. Rearguments had been ordered in four cases partly because the government, although it had vital interests in the cases, had not been represented in the first argument. The court had also agreed to hear two cases involving the right of the government to finance municipal power plants; but these cases

---

[32] Author's interview with CEH, May 28, 1947.
[33] Alsop and Catledge, *op. cit.*, pp. 210ff.
[34] Senate Report 711, 75th Congress, 1st session, p. 23.

had not been ready for argument when the court adjourned, and the government had made no request for a summer hearing.[35] The President's criticism was significant only as a measure of his irritation with the court.

Throughout the fight the Chief Justice had maintained a complete silence, except for his letter to Senator Wheeler. In May he declined an invitation to speak on Constitution Day, feeling that he could not attempt "to deal adequately at this time with such an important subject." But when he visited Amherst College on June 19 to attend the graduation of his grandson, Henry Stuart Hughes, fighting blood was coursing through his veins.

Stuart was really the lion of the occasion, being president of his class, the class orator, and the recipient of the highest award for "excellence in culture and faithfulness as man and scholar." Grandfather Hughes beamed with pride. When it came his turn to speak, at the Amherst alumni luncheon, he was the antithesis of an old man doddering in conservatism. ". . . we know nothing of age," he declared exuberantly, "but what we have read in Cicero. We come to you with youthful hearts, with spiritual arteries not yet hardened. To have the zest of youth and the memories of years is one of the most precious of the blessings of life."

Without mentioning the court bill or its sponsors, he proceeded to drive home a lesson in public morals which could not have been more pointed if it had been part of the Senate debate:

Nor is it fitting that I should discuss contemporary political questions. But there are fundamental needs which, I think, require emphasis at a time when the institutions of democracy are threatened by an authoritarian philosophy. . . .

We shall always have crusaders. I should be swift to recognize our indebtedness to crusaders who have aroused a lethargic public in a war upon abuses. But crusaders may have more fervor than wisdom, and extreme demands may create an intolerable civil strife. Where shall we look for the balanced judgment, the sane appraisements and the reasonable methods by which civilized society may attain its purposes without surrendering the democratic principle to a regime of force? . . .

I put first the passion for truth. Of course I do not refer to a mere philosophical aspiration. I mean the mental habit of thoroughness, the emotional drive of the will to know one's subject with precision, a mental habit which does not detract from but rather promotes alertness and vigor. I put that mental habit in contrast with a mere search for arguments to triumph in a controversy. I contrast it with the cultivation of facility, to quote Justice Holmes again, in "dodging difficulty and responsibility with a rhetorical phrase." I contrast it with contentment with showy superficialities, with the easy flippancy of cynical criticism, with the ambition to be plausible enough to "sell" something. . . .

The tolerant spirit is as important as the crusading ardor. It is so easy to be unfair and vindictive. Ruthlessness in trampling upon the rights of individuals in the exercise of the brute strength of the majority, if unchecked, will inevitably lead to

[35] CEH to Prof. Douglas Johnson, June 10, 1937.

By S. J. Ray in the *Kansas City Star*.

REGARDLESS OF HOW THAT THIRD HORSE PULLS, HE'S
CERTAINLY NIMBLE-FOOTED!

the entire overthrow of democratic processes and the substitution of the tyranny of force. Democratic society can never have the complete efficiency of a machine dominated by a single will. But it carries the banner of freedom and safeguards the priceless aspirations of the human spirit. Between liberty and progress there can be no lasting conflict,—for progress, if true, must be that of a community in which men enjoy the essentials of freedom in the exercise of their highest capacities and are not the mere puppets of the State.

Two days later Hughes addressed an alumni meeting at the Brown University commencement where Charles Evans Hughes 3d received his A.B. degree and gave one of the student orations and Charles Evans Hughes, Jr., received an honorary LL.D. Once more the Chief lashed out in general terms against the rise of totalitarianism in Europe and the attempt at judicial coercion in America:

We still proclaim the old ideals of liberty but we cannot voice them without anxiety in our hearts. The question is no longer one of establishing democratic institutions but of preserving them. . . . The question is not one of the adequate power of government, designed to keep clear the highways of honest endeavor, but how that power shall be used. . . .
The arch enemies of society are those who know better but by indirection, misstatement, understatement and slander, seek to accomplish their concealed purposes or to gain profit of some sort by misleading the public. The antidote for these poisons must be found in the sincere and courageous efforts of those who would preserve their cherished freedom by a wise and responsible use of it. Freedom of expression gives the essential democratic opportunity, but self-restraint is the essential civic discipline.

While the Chief Justice and Mrs. Hughes began a delightful summer at Jasper Park, Alberta, the Senate debated the court bill in Washington's July heat. By this time all prospect of enacting the original measure had disappeared. The debate was on a face-saving substitute, but, as the principle of court-packing was still at stake, the fight was waged with bitterness and tenacity. Eager to claim a place on the supreme bench as his reward, Senator Robinson was still trying to rally the Administration forces with an outward show of almost fierce determination. But his heart had never been in it. Secretly he had kept in touch with the opposition, sending word to Senator Wheeler whenever a supporter or an opponent of the court bill seemed to be wavering.[36] Sick and worried, Robinson succumbed to a heart attack alone in his room the night of July 13, and the fight was over. No one else had a chance of leading the shattered Administration ranks to victory.

After Robinson's funeral Vice President Garner, who had demonstrated his contempt for court-packing by going home to Texas in the midst of the struggle,

[36] Author's interview with Mr. Wheeler, April 14, 1950.

returned to the capital and negotiated the President's surrender to the jubilant Wheeler-Burke-King-O'Mahoney junta in the Senate. On July 22 the bill was finally recommitted to the Judiciary Committee, which is the Senate's way of administering euthanasia to its progeny that is unfit to live.

"Glory be to God!" exclaimed Hiram Johnson, and the country seemed to respond with a fervent, "Amen."

Chapter 71

TRIUMPH OF RESTRAINT

CONGRESS and the Supreme Court had won an incredible victory over President Roosevelt. The President's ablest lieutenant in the fight, Robert H. Jackson, has said that Hughes' letter to Senator Wheeler "did more than any one thing to turn the tide in the Court struggle." [1] Harold L. Ickes, Secretary of the Interior, put it this way: "The whole world knows that, while at first it appeared that the President would be strong enough to carry his reform through Congress, he was outmaneuvered in the end, largely by Chief Justice Charles Evans Hughes." [2] However one looks at it, Hughes' unwavering courage and cool restraint contributed powerfully to saving the Supreme Court from the most formidable attack ever launched against its independence.

The unsettled questions are how the Chief Justice achieved his victory and what price he paid. The prevalent belief seems to be that the court saved itself from being packed by reversing its opinions. "A switch in time saved nine," the flippant say. As the supposed planner and director of this supposed strategic retreat, Hughes is variously accused of resorting to Mephistophelean methods and praised for "judicial statesmanship"—sometimes with the insinuation that he trimmed his principles and browbeat his brethren to save the court as an institution.

In the introduction to his state papers published in 1941, Roosevelt took it for granted that the court had yielded to pressure. For two decades, he asserted, the Supreme Court "had been successfully thwarting the common will of the overwhelming majority of the American people." But after the "definite turning point" in 1937 the kind of government the people wanted was permitted to function. "For that reason," he boasted, "I regard the effort initiated by the message on the Federal Judiciary of February 5, 1937, and the immediate results of it, as among the most important domestic achievements of my first two terms in office." [3]

Certainly F. D. R. is right in saying that 1937 marks the beginning of a new era of harmony between Congress and the Supreme Court. The extreme conservatives on the court did not thereafter muster a majority on any vital issue involving the exercise of federal power. It is equally true, however, that the

[1] *New York Times,* June 24, 1943.   [2] *Saturday Evening Post,* July 3, 1948.
[3] *Collier's,* Sept. 13, 1941, p. 11.

extreme New Dealers did not thereafter regain control of the lawmaking branch. Was the court subdued by the White House, or was Congress subdued by the court?

The great about-face of the Chief Justice is supposed to have come in the Jones and Laughlin case. His opinion is superficially said to be a reversal of what he had written in the NRA and Carter Coal cases. Some shift in emphasis is undeniably apparent, but it may be traced entirely to the vast differences between the situations with which the court was dealing. In the NRA case the court found that the commerce power did not reach into the Schechters' chicken coop, and Hughes employed every legitimate argument to buttress that conclusion. In the NLRB case it was clear that the Jones and Laughlin empire could be reached through the commerce power, and he naturally emphasized that fact. This is the universal practice of judges. Once a decision has been made, they properly support it with the strongest arguments at their command.

The important point is that the same basic principle underlies all three of these opinions.[4] In each instance Hughes insisted that Congress may use the commerce power to regulate activities that are not in themselves interstate commerce if they directly affect that commerce. All three opinions drew the distinction between direct and indirect effects upon interstate commerce. Indeed, these principles had taken firm root in Hughes' mind during his first year on the bench, and he held fast to them before and after the court-packing venture.

This fact is widely recognized by judges and lawyers. Looking back at those early opinions, Attorney General (later Justice) Jackson said that "Hughes' vigorous championship of federal power under the commerce clause is reminiscent of Marshall." [5] Francis Biddle, soon to be Attorney General, also saw that Hughes was treading in his post-1937 opinions a new segment of the same path he had trod as Associate Justice. Chief Justice Stone spoke of Hughes upholding "the constitutional validity of the National Labor Relations Act, upon principles which twenty-four years before he had stated with clarity and precision in the *Minnesota Rate Cases*." [6] Speaking later of the vast reserve of federal power that Hughes had opened up in the *Minnesota Rate Cases* and the *Shreveport Case,* Stone said, "It is evident that when Congress, many years afterward, began to exercise that power on a large scale, in order to accomplish desired social and economic reforms within the states, *it was a legislative and not a judicial revolution which was being staged . . .*" [7] (italics supplied).

One must remember, too, that in the Texas and New Orleans case of 1930 Hughes had given strong underpinning to a congressional act protecting the right of railroad employees to bargain collectively. This opinion plus the

[4] F. D. G. Ribble in *Columbia Law Review*, November, 1941, p. 1199.
[5] *American Bar Association Journal*, July, 1941, p. 410.   [6] *Id.,* p. 408.
[7] Address to Association of the Bar of the City of New York, March 16, 1946.

doctrine he had laid down in the *Minnesota Rate Cases* and the NRA case pointed unmistakably to *NLRB* v. *Jones and Laughlin*. The Chief Justice himself insisted that there was no change in his concept of governmental power in this sphere between the writing of these opinions,[8] and the record bears him out.

Nor did Hughes high-pressure his brethren. While he presented the NLRB case before the conference with vigor and thoroughness, this was his usual practice. Rumors that he assumed the role of schoolmaster and that he issued dire warnings to his fellow judges are pure fiction. Equally unfounded are the reports that he pleaded with Justice Roberts to save the NLRB,[9] although he was delighted to have Roberts' concurrence. Undue pressure on the part of the Chief Justice was scarcely less abhorrent to him than undue pressure from the President. Hughes gave reason its full sway, but threats and appeals to the emotions were as completely absent from the conferences during the period of the court fight as they had been before.

"Nor can it be supposed," Hughes wrote in his Notes, "that the President's proposal had any effect upon the views of Justices Brandeis, Stone and Cardozo in relation to the National Labor Relations Act. And as to Justice Roberts, I feel that I am able to say with definiteness that his view in favor of these decisions of the Court would have been the same if the President's bill had never been proposed. The Court acted with complete independence." [10]

Sweeping changes had indeed taken place, but they were largely in the character of legislation going up to the court. The New Deal laws of the early thirties had been drawn, as we have seen, with almost no regard for their constitutionality. In the National Industrial Recovery Act, Congress had attempted to sweep under control of the President *all* industry in virtually all phases of its activity, regardless of whether this activity had any substantial effect on interstate commerce. Likewise the Guffey Act had cut loose from any interstate-commerce yardstick of federal power, asserting control over "every" coal producer as if a sweeping new general welfare clause had been written into the Constitution. It was this loose assertion of unlimited federal power that caused most of the New Deal reverses in 1935 and 1936. After the NRA and the AAA went down, greater care was exercised in the drafting of bills. The young lawyers writing the Administration's proposed laws tardily discovered that the commerce clause was the proper measure of the Federal Government's regulatory power and that there were some limits to the reach of even the commerce clause. The Hughes court was not again asked to pass on a measure comparable to the NRA or even the AAA.

When the statutes invalidated by the court were reenacted with regard for

---

[8] Author's interviews with CEH, Nov. 19, 1945, and Dec. 3, 1946.
[9] *Id.*   [10] Chapter XXIII, p. 33.

constitutional limitations, they were invariably sustained. In March, 1937, the court had given sanction to the revised Frazier-Lemke Act. In 1938 Hughes wrote the opinion upholding an amended version of the Municipal Bankruptcy Act.[11] Congress passed a new Bituminous Coal Act in 1937, correcting various provisions of the Guffey Act and leaving out the invalid labor provisions, and it was upheld in *Sunshine Coal Company* v. *Adkins*.[12] Pointing to these changes the court observed, through Justice Douglas: "There is nothing in the *Carter* case which stands in the way. The majority of the Court in that case did not pass on the price-fixing features of the earlier act. The Chief Justice and Mr. Justice Cardozo in separate minority opinions expressed the view that the price-fixing features of the earlier Act were constitutional. We rest on their conclusions for sustaining the present Act."

Taking the hint contained in the AAA decision, Congress based its new agricultural programs on the commerce clause, and they were sustained. In 1939 the Chief Justice spoke for the court in rejecting a challenge to the Tobacco Inspection Act.[13] Going back to the *Shreveport Case,* he said that the commingling of intrastate and interstate transactions in the tobacco markets did not restrict the overriding federal power. "It is the essence of the plenary power conferred," the Chief concluded, "that Congress may exercise its discretion in the use of that power. Congress may choose the commodities and places to which its regulation shall apply. . . ." A few months later the court gave an accolade to the new Agricultural Adjustment Act, which imposed its controls upon basic farm crops at the "throat" where the produce entered interstate commerce.[14] Justice Roberts wrote the opinion, as if to imply that the first AAA would have survived its test in 1936 if the commerce clause had been used as the measure of federal regulatory power.

Finally, in 1941, the court upheld the Fair Labor Standards Act[15] and overthrew *Hammer* v. *Dagenhart,*[16] in which the White court had upset the Federal Child Labor Act in 1918. Here again, however, a significant step toward that end had been taken before the court fight. On January 4, 1937, Hughes had delivered a unanimous opinion upholding the Ashurst-Sumners Act with the effect of forbidding the movement of convict-made goods across state lines in violation of state law.[17] Without overruling the 1918 decision, Hughes asserted that Congress was not estopped from exercising its power because convict-made horse collars were useful and harmless articles. He seemed to recognize also that Congress could prevent the interstate shipment of such goods irrespective of state consent. Only one more stroke was needed to cut off the limb on which *Hammer* v. *Dagenhart* rested. That strike came in

[11] *U.S.* v. *Bekins,* 304 U.S. 27.   [12] 310 U.S. 381, 396, 397.
[13] *Currin* v. *Wallace,* 306 U.S. 1.   [14] *Mulford* v. *Smith,* 307 U.S. 38.
[15] *U.S.* v. *Darby,* 312 U.S. 100.   [16] 247 U.S. 251.
[17] *Kentucky Whip & Collar Co.* v. *Illinois Central R.R. Co.,* 299 U.S. 334.

United States v. *Darby* with Stone writing for a unanimous court. The opinion was a sweeping recognition of congressional power to control the national market for the sake of protecting the public health, morals, or welfare.

The Hughes court did not, however, abandon the distinction between what is national and what is local. It merely recognized that the evolution of our economy had lengthened the reach of the commerce power. In a closely integrated economy interstate commerce was more sensitive to the impact of local interferences. Hughes again expounded his view in *Santa Cruz Fruit Packing Co.* v. *Labor Board*,[18] in which the court sustained the application of the National Labor Relations Act to a fruit canning and shipping company:

. . . injurious action burdening and obstructing interstate trade in manufactured articles may spring from labor disputes irrespective of the origin of the materials used in the manufacturing process. . . . It is also clear that where federal control is sought to be exercised over activities which separately considered are intrastate, it must appear that there is a close and substantial relation to interstate commerce in order to justify the federal intervention for its protection. However difficult in application, this principle is essential to the maintenance of our constitutional system. The subject of federal power is still "commerce," and not all commerce but commerce with foreign nations and among the several States. The expansion of enterprise has vastly increased the interests of interstate commerce but the constitutional differentiation still obtains. . . .

To express this essential distinction, "direct" has been contrasted with "indirect," and what is "remote" or "distant" with what is "close and substantial." Whatever terminology is used, the criterion is necessarily one of degree and must be so defined. This does not satisfy those who seek for mathematical or rigid formulas. But such formulas are not provided by the great concepts of the Constitution such as "interstate commerce," "due process," "equal protection." In maintaining the balance of the constitutional grants and limitations, it is inevitable that we should define their application in the gradual process of inclusion and exclusion.

What we have in the whole range of Hughes' opinions is a gradual unfolding of the vast scope of the commerce power. The fact that he used a checkrein when this great power was pushed beyond what seemed to him its constitutional limitations is an indication of commendable independence on the bench.

Along with his liberal concept of the commerce clause went a profound distrust of using the taxing power, or any other nonregulatory power, as a means of controlling local activities in the states. National controls resting on the commerce power were consistent with our federal system. National controls imposed through the taxing power knew no bounds. This vital distinction is often overlooked, as when Professor Swisher speaks of the Hughes court abandoning the Tenth Amendment as a check upon the expansion of federal power between the AAA decision in 1936 and the *United States* v. *Darby* in 1941.[19]

[18] 303 U.S. 453.
[19] Carl Brent Swisher, *The Growth of Constitutional Power in the United States*, pp. 34f.

In the AAA case the Tenth Amendment was invoked to arrest what the majority believed to be a misuse of the taxing and spending power to regulate local activities. The Fair Labor Standards Act upheld in the Darby case rested on the commerce power. Obviously the Tenth Amendment would not bar any legitimate use of the commerce power given to Congress specifically for regulatory purposes.

Both the written record and confidential testimony from the Justices who sat with Hughes through the conferences from 1937 to 1941 are utterly barren of evidence that he trimmed his principles, reversed his judgment, or high-pressured his brethren. It does appear that the travail through which the court passed in 1937 consolidated his leadership. During the next few years it was more distinctly a Hughes court than it had been before. But to assume, as some have done, that it became a "Roosevelt court" is grossly to distort the facts. F. D. R. had sought the delegation of power "running riot" as well as overriding federal controls that threatened to absorb the police powers of the states. What he got from the Hughes court was recognition of a broadened but still limited sweep of the commerce power, with delegation held in check and some semblance of balance retained in the federal system.

Undoubtedly several factors contributed to the temporary cut-off of decisions holding Acts of Congress to be unconstitutional. "New blood" on the bench soon minimized the influence of the old conservative wing. The changed temper of American democracy may have subconsciously influenced the thinking of some judges. But no other factor seems to be as important as the changes in the character of the legislation passed—the self-reversal on the part of Congress. Especially after it had saved the court from being packed, Congress was eager to avoid passing legislation that the court would have to invalidate.

What has been widely proclaimed as the self-reversal of the court narrows down, therefore, to the West Coast Hotel case, decided before the court-packing threat was made, and a few other cases in which it is assumed that, had they been decided before the court fight, Justice Roberts would have voted with the four ultraconservatives. Such speculation is futile. The one thing certain is that there was no sudden shift from conservative to liberal thinking on Roberts' part. Before 1937 he was on the liberal side of the court in the Blaisdell, Nebbia, West Coast Hotel, and gold-clause cases. Since there was no extreme stretching of federal power between 1937 and 1941, his acceptance of the federal legislation coming before the court in this period can be reconciled with his former record without reflecting upon his courage or his integrity.

Certainly there was no modification in the rock-ribbed conservatism of Butler and McReynolds. As for Hughes, Brandeis, Stone, and Cardozo, they had stood together in eight of the twelve New Deal cases and a majority of them were in full or partial accord in three others. To assume that all of them shuffled their principles in response to a threat against the court is an irresponsible surmise unrelated to any demonstrable facts. The constitutional doctrines on which these men agreed became the guiding principles both of Congress and of the Supreme Court in 1937 and the years immediately following.

What the record does show is a steadiness and moderation on Hughes' part both in passing judgment on New Deal legislation and in resisting the assault on the court. Under great stress he drove straight ahead without losing his nerve, his balance, or his high sense of integrity—without permitting himself to be drawn into a maelstrom of vindictiveness. His combination of restraint, courage, and tenacity to principle in piloting the court through its dark days is perhaps the best measure of the man in the high office of Chief Justice.

Chapter 72

CULMINATION

WHEN the Supreme Court assembled for its October term in 1937, it had a new member for the first time in five years. To succeed Justice Van Devanter the President had nominated Senator Hugo L. Black of Alabama, a fiery New Dealer and a stalwart fighter for the court-packing bill. It is said that Black was chosen primarily because he would be unacceptable to those who had beaten the court bill but would have to be confirmed nevertheless because he was a Senator.[1]

The Senate had voted confirmation amid muffled rumors that Black was or had been a member of the Ku Klux Klan. Later the press had dug up unmistakable evidence that Black had joined the Klan in 1926 when he ran for the Senate, and indignant protests against seating him in the court were heard through the rest of the summer. Returning from a tour of Europe, the new Justice admitted his former membership in the Klan while repudiating all that the Klan stood for. The episode thus ended on a note no less sardonic than the court fight itself.

When Black took his seat, however, Hughes greeted him with all the courtesy and cordiality that could have been bestowed upon the most distinguished jurist in the land.[2] Black was now a duly confirmed member of the court. That settled the matter so far as Hughes was concerned. In their subsequent relations there was not the slightest show of antagonism on the part of the Chief Justice because Black had voted against his confirmation in 1930 and worked to pack the court. Some of the Justices complained that the new member lacked judicial craftsmanship,[3] but not Hughes. While at first he assigned relatively minor cases to Black, that was the custom with all new members. In the conference Black had free rein to speak his mind. At no time did the Chief rebuff him or cut off expression of the views that went into his numerous lone dissents. Black thus came to have a high regard for Hughes' fairness, his intellect, and skill as a presiding officer, and a real affection for him as an individual.[4]

The Chief made a special point of giving Black opportunities to demonstrate

[1] Alsop and Catledge, *The 168 Days*, p. 299.
[2] Author's interview with Justice Black, Feb. 2, 1950.
[3] Marquis Childs in *Harper's*, May, 1938, pp. 587ff.
[4] Author's interview with Justice Black, Feb. 2, 1950.

that no taint of klanism influenced his thinking. When *Chambers* v. *Florida* [5] came up on petition for certiorari, Black voted against taking it. [6] There were plenty of other votes for hearing it because of the evidence that a group of Negroes had been forced to confess by third-degree methods. Hughes had almost scorched the earth of Mississippi a few years earlier for a similar third-degree conviction. After the Florida case had been heard on its merits and all the judges accepted the Chief's recommendation that the verdict be reversed, he assigned the opinion to Black. The latter wrote a strong denunciation of the third degree, and *Chambers* v. *Florida* has become one of his best known opinions.

Vacancies came fast after 1937. Justice Sutherland had decided to step down as soon as the Retirement Act was passed, but he waited until Van Devanter's seat had been filled to avoid creating two vacancies at the same time. He was succeeded by the able, steady, but unspectacular Solicitor General, Stanley F. Reed. The court was saddened in July, 1938, by the death of Justice Cardozo—the friend whom Hughes described as "a beautiful spirit, an extraordinary combination of grace and power." In his place President Roosevelt chose Professor Felix Frankfurter of Harvard Law School. During the years that remained to the Chief, the dynamic and scholarly jurist from Harvard was to become one of his most devoted friends. Indicative of their relationship is the following comment by Frankfurter after they had worked together about a year:

No outside student of the work of the Court could be unaware of the intrinsic authority with which you have exercised your chief justiceship. But only one who has been privileged to sit under you as chief can possibly appreciate the sweep and impact of [the] resources and fruitful tradition and creative energy with which you lead the Court. Of your complete dedication to its functions in our national life it would be almost humorously impertinent to speak. [7]

Justice Brandeis was the fourth member of the "old court" to go. After suffering a heart attack at the age of eighty-three, "the master of both microscope and telescope" whose advice "weighed a ton," divested himself of his judicial burden in February, 1939, and was succeeded by William O. Douglas.

Up to 1939 Hughes' zest remained unabated. In nine years he had not missed a single session of the court or the conference, or indeed a single hour of the work of the court. His enjoyment of life was still keen, as indicated by the frequent trips he took with Mrs. Hughes to Europe and to various favorite spots in Canada and the United States. With astonishing ease, he could put

[5] 309 U.S. 227.　　　[6] Confidential source No. 3.
[7] Frankfurter to CEH, Feb. 24, 1940.

aside the dignity of the Chief Justiceship for a pun, a joke, or a story. On one of their jaunts in New England he and Mrs. Hughes decided to drop in unannounced at Beverly Farms, the summer home of Justice Holmes, then in retirement. Earlier in the year Holmes had asked them to visit him, and Hughes had said it would be impossible. But their plans had changed, and Hughes seized the opportunity to surprise his old friend. Holmes himself came to the door wearing a quizzical smile.

"Well, Mr. Justice," Hughes began, with a grin playing around the ends of his mouth, "your invitation was so enticing that we just couldn't resist it. We changed our plans, and here we are."

Holmes put his thumb to his nose and waggled his fingers—his favorite gesture—then extended his usual salty welcome.

In the family circle Hughes continued to be an incorrigible tease. He seemed never to tire of bantering Mrs. Hughes on how young she looked. "Everyone says," he would tell her, " 'I didn't know the Chief Justice had married a second time.' "

In the presence of the family one day he said, "Your mother will live to be an old, old lady, and she'll be saying to you, 'Children, I can't quite remember what he looked like.' "

"Don't you dare say that!" Mrs. Hughes exclaimed, pulling his whiskers and laughing in spite of her exasperation. But the nature of her response assured repetition of his persiflage as soon as another favorable occasion arose.

The relationship between the Chief Justice and his bride of half a century was still that of a boy and girl in love. She was the object of his deep and unwavering adoration, and in return she almost worshiped her hero. Nothing was too good for him. Ever aware of his intellectual powers, she brought to him the serenity, the love, and understanding that alone made possible his sustained concentration upon public affairs.

On the Chief's seventieth birthday Mrs. Hughes had given him a memorable party attended by the Hughes children and grandchildren and a few other guests, including President and Mrs. Hoover, General Pershing, Justice Cardozo, former Undersecretary of State William Phillips, and Mrs. Hennen Jennings, a neighbor. The Hughesian custom of exchanging verses or notes of greeting on birthdays and other anniversaries persisted. Typical of the verses penned only for her eyes is the following:

> Intent upon "opinions" terse,
> I have no time or skill for verse.
> How can I hope to meet your pleasure
> In vain attempt to write in measure!
> Enough—that hard judicial lives
> Are made serene by charming wives.

April 11th. 1937.

2223 R STREET, N.W.
WASHINGTON, D.C.

My dearest and my gallant
"old soldier" -

How can I be
grateful enough on this - your
75th birthday - that we are
together, that we are well
and sound of mind and,
above all, that our love has
grown deeper and truer with
the years?

With these blessings we
can bear anything, even "the
slings and arrows" of an

outrageous Court plan; and
let us face the future some-
thing as follows.
"Then, whatsoever wind doth blow.
My heart is glad to have it so.
And blow it East or blow it West,
The wind that blows, that wind is best."

Devotedly

Wifie

Here is the beginning of a little
"Poets Corner"!

On one of their "days" Mrs. Hughes wrote a sentiment-laden rhyme beginning:

> Darling, I am growing old!
> More "silver threads" than can be told,
> But dearer far you are today
> Than any words of mine can say.

Hughes did not see it exactly that way. When they celebrated her seventy-second birthday that same year at the Plaza Hotel in New York, he attached to the present he gave her this warmhearted note:

> How can it be true
> That she's seventy-two!
> So slim and so trim
> With so graceful a carriage
> I see her still as I saw her when
> We clasped our hands in marriage.

From your old lover—May it be the happiest of birthdays.

Antoinette Carter Hughes returned the compliment when her husband reached the venerable age of seventy-five:

My dearest and my gallant "old soldier"—

How can I be grateful enough on this—your 75th birthday—that we are together, that we are well and sound of mind and, above all, that our love has grown deeper and truer with the years?

With these blessings we can bear anything, even "the slings and arrows" of an outrageous Court plan; and let us face the future something as follows:

> "Then, whatsoever wind doth blow,
> My heart is glad to have it so.
> And blow it East or blow it West,
> The wind that blows, that wind is best."

Devotedly,

Wifie.

On their wedding anniversary in 1937—the year of the court-packing plan —the supposedly austere Chief Justice penned these sentimental lines:

To my Dearest—to whose care and love, unfailing watchfulness and encouragement, I owe everything—health, peace of mind, the most congenial companionship, and the unbroken happiness of forty-nine years. How could the evening of life be more glorious! How can I express the love that feeds upon the years!

The following year, on December 5, they celebrated their golden wedding anniversary. Their fifty years together had brought no disillusionment but only

Dec. 5 - 1937

To my Dearest — to whose
care and love, unfailing
watchfulness and encouragement, I owe everything —
health, peace of mind, the
most congenial companionship,
and the unbroken happiness
of forty-nine years — How
could the evening of life be
more glorious! How can
I express the love that
feeds upon the years!

December 5, 1938

Dearest,—

That was a stout young tree — the tree of our love, and each year — in storm and sunshine it has grown in beauty and strength; — and under its spreading branches we have found rest and peace. —

It is a magic tree, which has never known blight and it has the perennial freshness of the evergreen with the sturdiness

of the oak. — Its roots have
run deep into the soil of our
common interests and our
unity of spirit has been its
never failing vital force. —

Fifty years are all
too short for such happiness. —
All I have I owe to you.
If I could have my
dearest wish, it would be
that I should live with
you forever. —
                        G

deeper understanding and exaltation of marital love. It cannot be doubted that Hughes laid greater store upon his sustained romance than upon all the official honors that had come to him. The depth of his emotion and the ripening of his appreciation are beautifully caught up in the note that he wrote to his wife:

DEAREST,

That was a stout young tree—the tree of our love, and each year—in storm and sunshine—it has grown in beauty and strength, and under its spreading branches we have found rest and peace.

It is a magic tree, which has never known blight and it has the perennial fresh-ness of the evergreen with the sturdiness of the oak. Its roots have run deep into the soil of our common interests and our unity of spirit has been its never failing vital force.

Fifty years are all too short for such happiness. All I have I owe to you. If I could have my dearest wish, it would be that I should live with you forever.

C.

In spite of his health, happiness, and success, Hughes was determined not to overstay his time on the bench. Within his family he had arranged for a secret ballot (the result of which would be communicated to him) if any one of his children felt that he was slipping into senility. No one had thought of raising such a question. In late February, 1939, however, his iron constitution began to waver, and it appeared that he might be the next to leave the court.

Hughes had agreed to address a joint session of the Senate and House of Representatives on March 4—the sesquicentennial of the meeting of the first Congress. About a week before the celebration, as he sat at the big table in the conference room after all the brethren had left, a gray-green pallor spread over his face. Wiping his hand across his brow, he acknowledged to Cropley, the court's faithful clerk, that he was ill. Cropley helped him to a couch. The Chief closed his eyes and looked as if he were about to expire.

"Cropley, where are you?" he called as the clerk moved toward the door with the intention of seeking a doctor.[8] He would not let Cropley leave the room. After a while he felt better, sat up, cautioned Cropley not to mention the incident, and then went home, refusing to let Cropley accompany him because some question might be raised as to the reason for it.

Feeling very weak, the Chief continued his work. On the day of the celebra-tion the Justices and their wives gathered in the old Supreme Court chamber in the Capitol, Mrs. Hughes looking worried. Seeing Cropley's anxious expres-sion, the Chief whispered, "I'm all right." They went on to the House chamber, which was crowded by members of Congress, ambassadors, chieftains of the Army and Navy, the Cabinet, and other dignitaries. Hughes took his seat with a feeling of terrible weakness pulling him down. The Speaker of the House and the president pro tempore of the Senate delivered their orations. At last

[8] Author's interview with Mr. Cropley, Jan. 18, 1950.

Senator Barkley, the majority leader, was introducing the Chief Justice of the United States. Hughes wondered if he could get to the rostrum.[9] Summoning all his reserve, he managed to walk the short distance without swaying and began to speak with something less than his usual gusto. Using no notes, he nevertheless spoke with precision and a Lincolnesque sense of dedication to his task:

The most significant fact in connection with this anniversary is that after 150 years, notwithstanding expansion of territory, enormous increase in population and profound economic changes, despite direct attack and subversive influences, there is every indication that the vastly preponderant sentiment of the American people is that our form of government shall be preserved.

We come from our distinct departments of governmental activity to testify to our unity of aim in maintaining that form of government in accordance with our common pledge. We are here not as masters, but as servants, not to glory in power, but to attest our loyalty to the commands and restrictions laid down by our sovereign, the people of the United States, in whose name and by whose will we exercise our brief authority. If as such representatives we have, as Benjamin Franklin said—"no more durable preeminence than the different grains in an hour glass"—we serve our hour by unremitting devotion to the principles which have given our Government both stability and capacity for orderly progress in a world of turmoil and revolutionary upheavals.

. . . If we owe to the wisdom and restraint of the fathers a system of government which has thus far stood the test, we all recognize that it is only by wisdom and restraint in our own day that we can make that system last. If today we find ground for confidence that our institutions which have made for liberty and strength will be maintained, it will not be due to abundance of physical resources or to productive capacity, but because these are at the command of a people who still cherish the principles which underlie our system and because of the general appreciation of what is essentially sound in our governmental structure.

Aside from intensity of his words, it was evident that the Chief was speaking under a great strain. His appraisal of our constitutional heritage was punctuated by several pauses. Once his voice faltered, and for a moment it appeared that he might not go on. Then came another wave of strength, and his voice built up to a dramatic conclusion:

I am happy to be here as the representative of the tribunal which is charged with the duty of maintaining, through the decision of controversies, these constitutional guarantees. We are a separate but not an independent arm of government. You, not we, have the purse and the sword. You, not we, determine the establishment and the jurisdiction of the lower Federal courts and the bounds of the appellate jurisdiction of the Supreme Court. . . .

But in the great enterprise of making democracy workable we are all partners. One member of our body politic cannot say to another—"I have no need of thee." We work in successful cooperation by being true, each department to its own

[9] CEH, Notes, 1930–1941, p. 46.

function, and all to the spirit which pervades our institutions—exalting the processes of reason, seeking through the very limitations of power the promotion of the wise use of power, and finding the ultimate security of life, liberty, and the pursuit of happiness, and the promise of continued stability and a rational progress, in the good sense of the American people.

Sick though he was, Hughes had compressed into a few ringing paragraphs his philosophy of the wise use of public power—a philosophy that is pregnant with meaning for the modern world. The concluding speaker was the President, but the occasion had already found its zenith in the words of the Chief Justice. He was overwhelmed with compliments both oral and written: ". . . your wonderful address . . . splendid . . . brilliant . . . gave me a thrill . . . a godsend . . . profoundest admiration . . . It was the most perfect piece of oratory I have ever had the pleasure to hear." [10] With the ceremony over, however, Hughes' chief interest was neither the glowing acclaim of his friends nor his own physical condition but the Saturday conference which the ceremony had disrupted.

"Well, come on, brethren," he said. "We have work to do."

"Oh, Chief Justice," Roberts remonstrated. "You have done enough today. Let the conference wait until next week." [11] Several other Justices joined in the protest, but Hughes was adamant. The conference had never been postponed since he had presided over it. It could not be postponed now. All afternoon until six o'clock he sat at the head of the table analyzing cases and directing the discussion. Then he made his assignments for the writing of opinions. That evening he and Mrs. Hughes gave one of their large dinners. When it was all over, the Chief went to bed feeling that the lifeblood had been drained out of him.

On Monday, Hughes called in his physician and learned that he had a bleeding duodenal ulcer and had sustained a serious loss of blood. For the next several weeks he was confined to his bed. Rest and diet soon cleared up the internal bleeding, and by April 11, his birthday, he was able to go for a walk again. Soon he was back on the bench. As the term closed about June 1, the Chief thought he detected a recurrence of internal bleeding symptoms, and his doctor put him to bed on a water diet for two days, but the subsequent exploration showed no serious trouble.

Justice Butler, looking the picture of health, dropped in at the Hughes home just before leaving on his vacation. "We'll never see the Chief again," was his gloomy prediction. He was right, but it was because of his own death in November of that year. After a summer of comparative rest the Chief Justice was in fine fettle once more. When he and Mrs. Hughes celebrated their wed-

[10] Hughes papers, Supreme Court.
[11] Author's interview with Justice Roberts, May 21, 1946.

ding anniversary on December 5, he was especially mindful of how she had nursed him back to health. His note to her said:

DEAREST—

The past year has had its difficulties—unusual because of physical troubles—but my dependence and your care have made my love more tender and more strong— if that be possible. Here's to the 52nd—my darling,—the best gift of life.

With the selection of Attorney General Frank Murphy to succeed Butler, the supreme bench had a majority of Roosevelt appointees. Hughes remained unquestionably the dominant figure in the court, but he found himself more frequently in the minority in controversial cases. Still there were numerous amenities. On February 1, 1940, the court celebrated its own sesquicentennial. The Chief would not agree to an elaborate ceremony, but he responded to commemorative remarks by Attorney General Jackson and Charles A. Beardsley, president of the American Bar Association. "Democracy is a most hopeful way of life," he said, "but its promise of liberty and of human better- ment will be but idle words save as the ideals of justice, not only between man and man, but between government and citizen, are held supreme." Thanks in no small measure to his own efforts, he could proudly say that the court still stood, after 150 years, "as an embodiment of the ideal of the independence of the judicial function." [12]

"Not your greatest predecessor," commented Justice Frankfurter, "could have bettered what you said and how you said it." [13]

Later in the month all the brethren joined in saluting him and Mrs. Hughes on his tenth anniversary as Chief Justice. "We all look forward with joy," their message read, "to the continuance for years to come, of the association which means much to each of us." From his retirement Brandeis wrote, "You have, as Chief Justice, given to the Court ten great years." [14] Brandeis was telling his friends that in all his long experience Hughes was the best Chief Justice he had ever known.[15]

The war against Hitlerism in Europe had taken the spotlight off the Supreme Court and all other domestic concerns. As 1940 wore on, interest was divided between the clash of arms abroad and the clash of words at home, where another contest for the Presidency was in progress. Roosevelt was making his bid for a third term against a formidable challenge by Wendell Willkie. In spite of the President's assault upon the court, Hughes remained scrupulously aloof from the struggle. His attitude remained unchanged when, on October 17, he received a frantic appeal from Herbert Hoover. "I am about to make a sugges- tion that may impress you as fantastic," the former President wrote. "I would

[12] U.S. Reports, 309, pp. XIIff.   [13] Frankfurter to CEH, Feb. 1, 1940.
[14] CEH's private papers.   [15] Author's interviews with Justice Roberts and others.

not do it if I did not believe that the whole future of the American people hangs upon the decision of this election." [16] His "fantastic suggestion" was that Hughes resign the Chief Justiceship "with a declaration to the country of the complete necessity for a change in Administration."

Hughes did not reply in writing, but he told Lawrence Richey, who had delivered the letter, that such a gesture would be futile for the simple reason that there would promptly be another Chief Justice; the prestige of the office would not follow him in such a venture.[17] In any event, the Chief declined to think seriously of ending his career on the bench with a little partisan sputter.

Before and after the election he maintained pleasant relations with the President. When King George and Queen Elizabeth visited Washington in June, 1939, the Chief was undergoing his two-day physical exploration and could not attend the state dinner. Learning this, the President personally called Mrs. Hughes on the telephone, expressed his regrets, and said in his usual gay manner that he hoped she would come and that he was going to seat her next the King. And this he did.[18]

On January 20, 1941, Hughes administered the oath of office to Roosevelt for the third time. Some weeks later, as the two men sat on a sofa in the White House library after the judicial dinner, the inaugural ceremony came into the conversation, and Hughes confessed to the President, "I had an impish desire to break the solemnity of the occasion by remarking, 'Franklin, don't you think this is getting to be a trifle monotonous!' " [19]

Hughes' seventy-ninth birthday, April 11, 1941, was an occasion for almost a barrage of congratulations and good-will messages. One of them read:

DEAR CHIEF:
My affectionate regards & best wishes on your Birthday. You are not a day older—mentally or physically than I am—just 59!
As ever yours,
FRANKLIN D. ROOSEVELT

The Chief Justice replied the next day:

DEAR MR. PRESIDENT:
Your extraordinary appraisal of my youth has almost turned my head. While I am old enough to know better, I am young enough to like it.

It is most kind of you in the midst of your heavy responsibilities to send me such a generous and encouraging greeting. I heartily reciprocate your good wishes.
Very sincerely yours,
CHARLES E. HUGHES [20]

Several notes from the newer members of the court attest the cordial relations that prevailed. "It is comforting," wrote Justice Murphy, "to find you on

---

[16] Herbert Hoover to CEH, Oct. 17, 1940.
[17] Author's interview with CEH, June 4, 1946.   [18] CEH, Notes, 1930–1941, p. 33.
[19] Id., p. 34.   [20] Mr. Hughes' private papers.

your birthday at the very zenith of your matchless intellectual and physical powers." Justice Reed commented: "You have come to be the symbol of the Court and one in which all of us take great pride. It is a great satisfaction to work in your team." Justice Frankfurter sounded a note that ran through many of the felicitations: "May you long be spared, in your superb vigor, for your country and your colleagues." [21]

Actually, of course, Hughes was far beyond the zenith of his powers, and he knew it. While he was still in good health and had not missed a day of work, except for the two occasions in the spring of 1939, he found the maintenance of sustained effort over long hours increasingly difficult. If he remained on the bench, he would have to slow down. As he had criticized judges for hanging on after they were unable to bring full vigor to their tasks,[22] he concluded early in 1941 that the time was approaching when he should follow his own advice. It is a mark of his greatness that he could apply an objective judgment to himself, even when it meant extinction of his power. No other Chief Justice has laid down the reins in good health since John Jay resigned in 1795 to become Governor of New York.

When he first decided to quit, Hughes was strongly inclined to resign outright and not claim the benefits of retirement. Having a fortune of about $1,200,000, he did not need the retirement allowance that Congress had made available. On full consideration, however, he concluded, as had Justice Brandeis, whose fortune was much larger, that a resignation would set an undesirable precedent—that in the interests of the court the policy of the Retirement Act should be maintained.[23] Accordingly, he wrote a brief note announcing his retirement, to take effect on July 1, 1941, and sent it to the White House just before he ascended the bench for the last time to preside over the final session of the term.

The message was telephoned to the President at Poughkeepsie, New York, and he wrote the following reply in longhand:

I am deeply distressed by your letter of June second telling me of your retirement on July first from active service as Chief Justice of the United States. This comes to me, as I know it will to the whole Nation, as a great shock for all of us had counted on your continuing your splendid service for many years to come. My every inclination is to beg you to remain; but my deep concern for your health and strength must be paramount. I shall hope to see you this coming week in Washington.[24]

Returning to the capital, F. D. R. invited the Chief to lunch at the Executive Offices to discuss the choice of his successor. Ever conscious of the value of experience on the bench, Hughes strongly recommended Stone,[25] who was then

[21] Id. [22] The Supreme Court of the United States, pp. 74–77.
[23] CEH, Notes, 1930–1941, p. 18. [24] Washington Evening Star, June 3, 1941.
[25] CEH, Notes, 1930–1941, p. 47.

senior Associate Justice. The President talked favorably of Stone and of Attorney General Jackson. Hughes thought well of Jackson, but he felt that Stone's record gave him first claim upon the honor. At Hughes' suggestion the President also consulted Justice Frankfurter, a close friend of Jackson, who urged the appointment of Stone, a Republican, in the interest of national unity in meeting the international crisis then gripping the country. Roosevelt responded in fine spirit, and Stone took the oath of office two days after Hughes' retirement became effective. The appointment is indicative of how far the President had retreated from his court-packing days in spite of his continued efforts to justify the course he had pursued in 1937. For Stone had voted to upset the NRA and five other New Deal Acts. He had stood with Hughes in the New Deal cases, excepting *United States* v. *Butler,* one point in the gold-clause decisions, and partial disagreement in the Carter Coal case.

One of Chief Justice Stone's first acts was to write his predecessor a humble note:

When I reflect upon the fact that I have taken it [the oath of office] as your successor and upon the great service which you have rendered as Chief Justice, to the country and the Court, I bow my head in humility and pray that I may in some moderate degree prove worthy to be your successor.[26]

Hughes' retirement unloosed an avalanche of commendation. The formal letter from the court signed by all the brethren was heavy with conventional encomiums. Most of the Justices wrote warmer personal notes: Justice Black, "I would be untrue to my own impulses if I should fail at this time to tell you that as a result of our association I entertain for you a genuine personal affection." Justice Douglas, "Your generosity, kindliness and forbearance meant much to me. Your professional performance . . . was a real inspiration." Justice Frankfurter wrote to Mrs. Hughes, ". . . there can be no doubt that his name will be among the ultimate few who have served this country as the voice of law."

A host of distinguished friends seemed to vie for the honor of paying the most glowing compliment. Hoover wrote, "You have given the most distinguished service to America that she has had in your generation." William Allen White commented, "I wanted you to know how proud I am to have lived in the generation with you." From Henry L. Stimson came, ". . . you have stood as one of the great pillars of integrity and morality in public life"; from Secretary Ickes, "You have been a great Chief Justice and a great citizen and no man could ask more of life"; from William Hard, "You have surpassed them all [the public men he had reported] in the number and variety of your exploits"; from Senator Wagner, "Every phase of this great transitional era

[26] Stone to CEH, July 3, 1941.

By Leo Joseph Roche, *Buffalo Courier-Express*, June 7, 1941.

THAT'S THE QUESTION

By Harold Talburt, Scripps-Howard Newspapers, June, 1941.

"WE'VE COME A LONG WAY TOGETHER!"

bears the mark of your labors"; [27] from Attorney General Jackson, "The bar ranks Chief Justice Hughes in a class with John Marshall"; from Judge Learned Hand, "The Court will look back to him as one of its great figures"; from Chief Justice Lawrence Groner of the United States Court of Appeals, "When shall we look upon his like again? . . . I have heard from the lips of the judges who served with him that all regard him as the ablest Chief Justice in the history of the Court."

Some of the men who served under him were even less restrained in their praise. "God must have gotten his formulas mixed," said Thomas E. Waggaman, marshal of the court, "for he gave the Chief more intellect than any mortal was supposed to have." Cropley, the clerk, brought his veneration to a climax by saying that the Chief's "criticism left you richer than another man's praise." The press was equally laudatory. Hughes had made himself the "symbol of the integrity," "the very embodiment of justice," the exemplar of "equal justice under law," "the judge *par excellence* with no tag line to his integrity." The widespread similarity of the comment is indicative of the impact of his career upon the public mind.

Any appraisal of Hughes' eleven years as Chief Justice must recognize at least four outstanding facets of his work. His enhancement of efficiency within the courts would alone give distinction to a lesser figure. One eminent jurist regards the Act setting up the Administrative Office of the United States Courts —largely Hughes' handiwork—as "the most important legislation affecting the federal judiciary to be passed since the Judiciary Act of 1789." [28] This will be a lasting monument.

His mastery in presiding over the court and the conference of the Justices has probably never been equaled. An indefinable quality in his makeup kept the deliberations on a plane of high-mindedness and inspired those about him to put forth their best efforts. "Everyone who came into contact with him," as Justice Roberts has said, "was charmed by his personality," [29] and Hughes took full advantage of this fact to make his standards prevail.

Among his positive contributions to the law, the firm establishment of the four freedoms of the First Amendment as guarantees to the citizen against state action is an achievement of the first order. In the field of civil liberties his record is more consistent than that of Holmes; and Hughes, instead of becoming another great dissenter for freedom, succeeded in making most of his opinions the law of the land. In expounding the commerce clause his influence was perhaps even more profound. Chief Justice Marshall had given the commerce clause its initial standing as a great instrument of national power. Hughes adapted it to the necessities of our modern industrial economy.

[27] CEH's private papers.   [28] Judge John J. Parker to CEH, June 5, 1941.
[29] Address to New York bar, Dec. 12, 1948.

Finally, of course, he was helmsman of the judiciary at a time when it had to be saved from executive domination as well as from ossified thinking. The nice balance that he maintained between sagacity and courage, determination and restraint, stands out in contrast to previous clashes between the President and the Chief Justice. When Jefferson attempted to remake the Supreme Court by impeaching Federalist judges, Chief Justice Marshall's courage sagged and he suggested that Congress reverse court opinions that it deemed unsound—an utter retreat from the great principle he had established in *Marbury* v. *Madison*.[30] In the Civil War period, following the tragic Dred Scott decision, Chief Justice Taney hurt the court by taking an openly hostile attitude toward the Lincoln Administration. Hughes judiciously avoided both precedents. As to the court's function and the constitutional doctrines he believed to be sound, he held steadfastly to his convictions. But he adroitly refused to get into a feud with the White House. His defense of the court without rancor and his treatment of the law as a progressive, living organism are among the finest fruits of our judicial tradition.

Here was the "meekness with power" that Hughes had once eulogized before a Baptist Sunday-school gathering. His leadership of the court through this troublesome period was essentially a triumph of character. It will occasion no surprise if, in the history of our constitutional system, Hughes' name is written beside Marshall's in the same relationship that Lincoln holds to Washington.

[30] Albert J. Beveridge, *The Life of John Marshall* (Boston, Houghton Mifflin, 1916), II, 177. Copyright, 1916, by Albert J. Beveridge.

Chapter 73

THE LITTLE FINISHING CANTER

RETIREMENT meant complete withdrawal from the life Hughes had known for nearly four decades. We get the key to his attitude from an incident that happened a year and a half before he left the bench. At Butler's funeral members of the court were seated as a body, with the two retired Justices at the end of the line. McReynolds thought it was improper to have the older retired members placed as if they were junior to the most junior active Justice. Roberts agreed and at a subsequent conference suggested to the Chief that on ceremonial occasions the retired brethren should have their old places in the line. Hughes sharply objected. "If I retire," he said, "there will not be two Chief Justices." [1]

It was not easy for Hughes to keep himself completely out of the limelight. At first he spent much of his time declining invitations. The American Bar Association asked him to be its guest of honor at Indianapolis in September, 1941, and President Roosevelt urged him to accept and discuss the Nazi peril in Europe. "As you know," he wrote, "it is a task of the utmost difficulty to make people realize what the effect of a German victory would be, and I know of nothing more effective than a speech broadcast by you." [2] Hughes had already declined the invitation. To the President he replied: "I feel that the time has come when I should be excused from preparing addresses and be spared the fatigue of public performance. I must leave to others the effort to inform, clarify and persuade." [3]

Three different bar associations in New York wished to give dinners in his honor. Then former Attorney General Mitchell came to Washington and urged him to consent to one dinner in which all the New York bar associations would join. Columbia University tried to induce him to deliver a series of lectures as the first Cardozo professor of jurisprudence. But in no instance would he budge from the quiet little world into which he had settled down with his family. The idea of going to a public function merely to hear himself lauded to the skies was repugnant. And he was so determined to do nothing that would in any way detract from the prestige of his successor that he even declined invitations to Sunday dinner from old friends on the court.

---

[1] Author's interview with Justice Roberts, May 21, 1946.
[2] F. D. R. to CEH, Aug. 25, 1941.   [3] CEH to F. D. R., Aug. 30, 1941.

Those who tried to lure him into political activity found him even less receptive. Being still a member of the court, at least in theory, he felt that it was up to him to set a precedent for exemplary conduct in retirement. There was also the fact that he felt like an antediluvian. When he had been in harness, he had spoken with authority and conviction. Now he feared that whatever he might say would be mere words, and mere words to put in the newspapers were not worth his lifeblood.

Silent he might be, but he was not forgotten. His eightieth birthday, April 11, 1942, brought a fresh outpouring of good wishes from the press and many friends, including President Roosevelt. "Is there a more enviable American?" asked the *New York Times*. To one of his former colleagues Hughes replied:

In my safe octogenarian harbor I welcome the friendly greetings from the staunch ships that are sailing the open sea. My pride is that I was once with them, and their messages to one who can no longer ride the waves outside are doubly precious. My best wishes for good voyages.[4]

As he took Mrs. Hughes for a walk in the sunshine, an old friend crossed the street to wish him many happy returns. Hughes replied, with a good-natured smile, that he had similarly greeted Root on his eightieth birthday, and Root had expressed precisely what he (Hughes) now felt: "I'm as good as I ever was—one hour a day." [5] Hughes himself gave a party at the Plaza Hotel in New York in celebration, as he put it, of "my 80th and Teddy's 14th"— referring to his grandson, Theodore Hughes Waddell. "Do not be disturbed," he wrote to his daughter, Mrs. Waddell. "I am giving this celebration (wifie and I are one)—a dinner to my children and such of my grandchildren as can come. No *presents* desired—just *presence*."

Hughes' role was now that of the proud father and grandfather. It was the second and third generations that were "sailing the open sea." His pride was magnified as three of his grandsons won distinction in the war. Lieutenant Charles Evans Hughes, 3d, fought through the battles of the Pacific on a destroyer in Admiral Halsey's fleet. Lieutenant Colonel Henry Stuart Hughes and Lieutenant Richard Hughes Waddell served in Europe, the former doing field research for the Office of Strategic Services.

There was one significant exception to Hughes' aloofness to public affairs. In April, 1944, Secretary of State Cordell Hull sought his advice, as a former Secretary of State, on the creation of an international organization to keep the peace. First, Myron C. Taylor called at Hughes' home, as a representative of Secretary Hull, asked his cooperation, and left him copies of a tentative draft of the United Nations Charter. The Chief said that, loath though he was to

[4] CEH to Justice Frankfurter, April 13, 1942.
[5] Author's interview with Sir Willmott Lewis, Oct. 24, 1949.

be drawn into any controversy, he would do his duty as a citizen. A few days later Secretary Hull spent an hour and a half at the Hughes home going over the problem in detail.

Hull stressed his desire to avoid Wilson's mistake in shaping the Covenant of the League of Nations. Accordingly, he had asked members of the Senate, including Republicans, to go over the project with him. It was to be kept on a strictly nonpartisan basis. Hull also said that he was trying to keep away from the idea of a world government. Hughes fully agreed, saying that Russia would not for a moment enter any superstate and certainly our Senate would not. In response to the Secretary's request, Hughes said that he would give his advice freely if he could be protected against being drawn into controversy over any of the questions presented.[6]

The Chief said there could be no effective international plan to keep the peace unless the United States, Great Britain, and Russia were prepared to work together. Hull, who had recently returned from Moscow, thought Russia would come along if the other powers were patient. While Hughes accepted the basic premise of the charter—that the Big Four, including China, would have to be in accord to apply force—he suggested a more liberal representation of the smaller powers on the Executive (Security) Council. The tentative plan called for four permanent members of the Council and four others elected annually. "As long as the great powers control the decision as to the use of force," Hughes urged, "there would not seem to be any harm in enlarging the number of smaller powers which would be in a position to be consulted and give their views." [7] Remembering the Washington Conference, he also put in a special word for France. The French were very sensitive, he said, and always wanted to be recognized in any international set-up. France was not at that time included as one of the permanent members of the Council.

Hughes objected to the sweeping nature of the provision then forbidding any member of the Council to vote in the decision of any dispute involving itself. If Russia should get into a squabble with Poland, he said, she would not be willing to stand aside and have it settled by the United States and Great Britain. As to the use of force, Hughes felt that it could be successfully employed against any new aggressions by Germany or Japan and to arrest any trouble among the smaller powers. But it would be futile, he agreed, to look to the use of force against Russia, Britain, or the United States, for that would mean another world war, which the organization was designed to prevent.

On May 5 the discussion was resumed in a conference attended by Taylor, John W. Davis, Nathan L. Miller (former Governor of New York), and Hughes at the latter's residence. The following day the Chief sent Taylor a memorandum suggesting seven specific changes in the proposed charter. The

[6] Memorandum of interview in Hughes Papers.   [7] *Id.*

most important of these was his suggestion that the membership of the Council be increased from eight to eleven. If France insisted on becoming a permanent member, that would leave six members to be chosen by the Assembly. This suggestion became a part of the charter. Hughes thought the office of "President of the General organization" should be eliminated as being merely ornamental and a potential cause of strife. This too was accepted. He suggested that protective policies such as the Monroe Doctrine should be more specifically recognized; that justiciable disputes should go to the World Court rather than to the Council, unless the parties agreed to ask the Council for a "just and equitable settlement"; that in disputes growing out of internal issues, such as immigration, the Council be limited to inquiry, conciliation, and other means short of compulsion. He advised against a provision for withdrawal because it might weaken the organization, while recognizing that any great power wishing to leave would have its way in any case.

When Hull called on Hughes a second time, on May 7, he was troubled by the question of whether the President could order American military forces into action at the request of the Council, without the approval of Congress. Senator Vandenberg and others had raised that query. Hughes said that a strong President would not hesitate to use the force at his command, if he saw fit, without waiting for Congress to act; that he would be able to say that he was acting in accord with the treaty.

The next day Taylor asked the Chief to explore this problem further, and he replied that he "could not undertake to give any opinion on constitutional questions." Nevertheless, he offered his advice in discussing with Taylor the practical situations that would probably arise. "Our Presidents have used our armed forces repeatedly," Hughes pointed out, "without authorization by Congress, when they thought the interests of the country required it." [8] He assumed that the American representative on the Council would act under direction of the Secretary of State and the President. Any provision requiring the approval of Congress before these officials could back up the Council with armed force, he concluded, would be regarded as emasculating the treaty. He thought the plan might well go forward on the assumption that, with armed forces at his disposal, the President would use them at the request of the Council to carry out our international obligations.

Secretary Hull expressed his gratefulness for Hughes' "extremely helpful comments," [9] and the latter had the satisfaction of seeing a number of his suggestions come to fruition in the United Nations Charter adopted at San Francisco in 1945. He thought the charter "stood as a beacon in a darkened world." But he had no illusions about the efficacy of mere organization. "Structure of any sort, and any defined method," he wrote to the president of

[8] Memorandum of interview, May 11, 1944.   [9] Hull to CEH, May 25, 1944.

the American Society of International Law, "will bring nothing but disillusion unless they are infused by good will and permeated by a spirit of reasonableness which alone makes possible the effective use of any form of organization that may be devised."[10]

His work on the United Nations organization was only an interlude. For the most part he and Mrs. Hughes lived for each other. Conscious of the fact that his long absorption in public affairs had deprived them of many happy hours together, he now lavished most of his attention upon her. When she was confined to Johns Hopkins Hospital for two operations in 1941, he motored to Baltimore every day to see her. His daughter, Mrs. Waddell, cautioned him not to wear himself out making so many trips.

"Don't you worry," he replied. "How *could* I get tired going to see my best girl!"

They spent happy days together in Jasper Park, in Arizona, at Skytop, and other favorite spots. In Washington they lived in delightful seclusion, with Hughes tending to his correspondence, working on his Biographical Notes, reading the newspapers, and dipping into history, philosophy, and biography. "If a person is philosophical or has intellectual interests," he said, "old age is a very agreeable time." [11]

Both were well and happy as they celebrated their fifty-fifth wedding anniversary on December 5, 1943, and Hughes penned his customary note with the ardor of a young lover:

DEAREST—How precious are these years! Each one draws us closer together as in loving companionship we review the long past with its wonderful experiences and manifold blessings. *You are all in all to me.*

As she reached the venerable age of eighty on September 14, 1944, he was still courting her with devotion that knew no bounds, as indicated by this birthday note written at the Plaza Hotel:

> Happy Birthday to my best beloved!
> We "climbed the hill together"
> And, now that we are going down
>   on the other side, we find the
>   slope gentle and beautiful!
> And so we go hand in hand—
>   in the eighties!
>   Your "steady company"
>   C

But these days were numbered. At Skytop in the summer of 1945 Mrs. Hughes had a fainting spell from vascular spasms, and Hughes learned from

[10] CEH to Frederic R. Coudert, read to ASIL, April 25, 1946.
[11] New York *Herald Tribune,* April 15, 1943.

her doctor that the end of their blissful union was not far off. She was looking frail and worn when they went to the Waddells' home in New York for dinner in honor of her eighty-first birthday. The next night she collapsed on the bathroom floor of their hotel and was taken to the hospital in an ambulance. When she seemed well enough a few weeks later, Hughes took her home to Washington and watched over her as her strength ebbed away. Every day he wrote the details of her condition to one of his children. At times she seemed to improve but would then suddenly collapse again. In late October she had difficulty in feeding herself and in speaking.

As her condition worsened, Hughes went by car to lonely Hains Point to take his walks so that he would not meet friends and have to talk about her illness. On November 26, 1945, he wrote to his daughter in New York:

Do not worry about me. I am taking good care of myself and am as well as can be expected in these sad circumstances. I am sustained by the thought of the beautiful life I have had with Mother and by the constant manifestations of your devotion and that of Charlie and Elizabeth. Was ever a husband and father so blessed!

On the Hugheses' fifty-seventh wedding anniversary, December 5, Dr. B. W. Leonard, the family physician, noted a sharp deterioration in her condition and said the end was approaching. Still, Hughes was reluctant to have the children come. During the day he wrote to Mrs. Waddell:

He [the doctor] knows our plans to have you come down and my reluctance to ask you to come before it is necessary. It would be a miserable business to have you just sitting around here waiting for Mother to pass. Dr. Leonard says that about the best estimate that can be made now is that it is a matter of four or five days and possibly less.

Today is our 57th Wedding Anniversary! I am trying to fix my thought upon our long and beautiful companionship, a perfect union with a radiant spirit.

So much love,

FATHER

As he was eating breakfast alone the next morning, the nurse came in and said that Mrs. Hughes was dying. He rushed upstairs and saw that she was unconscious. A wave of hysteria swept over him. Almost running to the telephone, he called his daughter in New York. "Catherine! Catherine!" he shouted. His voice was broken—hysterical sounds akin to laughter alternating with sobs. "Mother is sinking rapidly," he managed to say. "Come as fast as you can." "Father!" she called to him, "Father! . . ." But he was too choked with emotion to reply.

When his storm had subsided, he calmly telephoned his daughter again and apologized for having lost control of himself. His son and both daughters hastened to his side, and Mrs. Hughes died peacefully at eight o'clock that night, December 6, 1945. The Chief was now in full control of his emotions and insisted on taking command of the arrangements. It was he who called the press and handed to reporters a brief biographical statement about her.

The body was taken to New York for a private funeral and interment in Woodlawn Cemetery. At the departure from Washington the funeral party found Union Station jammed with postwar travelers, but as the solemn procession made its way through the diplomatic entrance a hush fell upon the milling crowd. The people instinctively cleared a path; the men removed their hats; and everyone stood silent, many with bowed heads, while the casket was wheeled to the train and Hughes followed, haggard and completely oblivious to his surroundings. It was a touching tribute.

The Pennsylvania Railroad won the Chief's gratitude by providing a special funeral car and another special car for him and his children. As the casket was placed in this beautiful setting, he murmured, "Fit for a queen, and she was a queen!"

After the family was settled on the train, Hughes felt a temporary lifting of his grief and told the children the story of his courtship—a story never to go beyond the bosom of the family. At times he laughed and seemed almost gay. Then a deep gloom once more settled upon him. Not long after the funeral was over he was back in Washington. His son and daughters had tried to convince him on the night of Mrs. Hughes' death that he should give up his home and move to New York where he would be close to them—and away from the memories that would haunt him. While he had agreed at the time, the next morning he had changed his mind and said he would continue to live in the old home. It was too late to start a new life.

There was some comfort in the deluge of tributes to Mrs. Hughes. Everyone seemed to love her. William Phillips, who had been close to the Hugheses as Undersecretary of State, expressed what was in many hearts: "We can never think of you separately, for together you stand, and will always stand, for all that is finest and noblest in this world."

But the old home was a shell of loneliness. The servants were there to satisfy every whim. Mischler, his faithful secretary, was there. Old friends dropped in to cheer the Chief. His children became frequent visitors, and the author of these volumes claimed many hours of the great man's time. During intervals of this sort he was able, after a few months, to laugh, joke, and forget himself in reminiscences. But the gaping void of her absence always engulfed him again as soon as he was alone. Sometimes he grew impatient over his own longevity and wished that "the little finishing canter," as Holmes had called it, might end more abruptly. There was nothing left for him now. His chief dread was that he might become helpless, as Cardozo had.

There was no self-pity in his attitude, and he made a conscious effort to avoid being morbid. "You can always make yourself think of something else," he would say. In addition to this deliberate shifting of his thoughts to cheerful things, he kept reminding himself of how generously fortune had smiled upon him. "I have everything to be thankful for," he would say. But no philosophizing could overcome his loneliness or fill the void her absence left.

The living room of the R Street home became a shrine to Mrs. Hughes. Everything in the room was kept precisely as she had left it. The next night after her death he went to the dictionary to look up a word and almost sat in the chair that Mrs. Hughes had invariably occupied in the evening when she was reading or writing letters; but a sudden impulse checked his motion and he did not sit. "I can hardly bear to look at that chair," he said to the children. "But I know that the time will come when I'll get great comfort out of it."

Mrs. Waddell came to Washington to be with her father on the first anniversary of her mother's death. On December 5, the anniversary of his marriage, he was in a gay mood and talked all day about his courtship and his wedding trip, about the bright red bathrobe his bride had worn on that occasion and his own blue one, about their travels and happy times together. The next day he was immersed in gloom. "Do you know what day it is today?" he asked his daughter as evening approached. "Yes, Father," she answered, "I have been aware all day of what day it is."

After dinner he tried to read a newspaper, then impatiently turned on the radio. Nervous and agitated, he kept looking at the clock. He went to his room and a few minutes later was back again. It was not until eight o'clock, the hour of her passing, that his mood changed. Then quick as a flash he said, "Have you read Davenport's *East Side, West Side*? I think I should like to read some of it aloud and discuss it with you." At ten o'clock he was relaxed and ready for sleep.

For a change of scene after his wife's death Hughes spent his winters in Florida and his summers on Cape Cod. On the Cape he shared a cottage with his daughter, Mrs. Gossett, and her children. His chauffeur, Clarence Lucas, was always close by, and drives through the countryside were a favorite diversion. Being very fond of Lucas, the Chief made certain that pleasant accommodations could be provided for the chauffeur and his wife before deciding to spend his summer at the Cape. On some of his drives he insisted that Mrs. Lucas should accompany her husband in the front seat and took pleasure in showing her the sights.

At the Wianno Club cottage quiet hours of reading on a cool porch and a more intimate acquaintance with "Tibby" also lifted his spirits. Tibby was a lively, charming, and intelligent young lady of five—his granddaughter, whose real name is Elizabeth Evans Gossett. Finding that she had a way with her grandfather, she soon had him taking her for walks, playing games, and singing to her "The Golden Slippers," "In the North Sea Lived a Whale," and other favorites. Tibby claimed so much of his interest that he sometimes labeled his letters from the Cape as "reports from Tibbyland." On July 16, 1947, he wrote to Mrs. Waddell from this retreat:

I am living in luxurious ease—never felt better. I never tire of sitting on our porch—with the view of the "neighboring ocean"—and the drives are charming.

Tibby is a constant delight, with her never ending—"Tell me a story about the bears." And I put my old and weary brain to the test of imaginative feats. We are great pals!

One evening during the second summer at the Cape, Grandpa Hughes substituted for a baby-sitter, and Tibby saw no reason to respond to his efforts to get her to bed at the accustomed hour.

"I'm the Chief Justice now," she declared with feminine finality, "and I'm not going to bed."

"I'm sorry, young lady," her astonished grandfather retorted, "but I'm still the Chief Justice and you are going to bed."

She finally went.

On another occasion Mrs. Gossett returned to the cottage to find the retired Chief Justice draped in bath towels and Tibby kneeling reverentially by his side.

"Sh-h-h-h-h!" he whispered, raising his finger to his lips, "I'm a nun."

Before returning to Washington from Cape Cod, Hughes made a practice of stopping for a few weeks at the Plaza Hotel in New York. Here his children frequently dropped in to enjoy a quiet dinner with him in his room. He didn't care to go to the hotel dining room. "You know I am quite shy," he explained, "and don't like a lot of attention."

Florida claimed his interest from January to March each year. Members of his family visited him at Ormond Beach, and he spent pleasant hours reminiscing with Owen D. Young, whose Washington Oaks cottage was only twenty-five miles away. Hughes' moods were as variable as the winds. Returning from Florida by motor with Mrs. Waddell, he was exuberant the first day and (after a restless night) despondent the next. All day long he said little, and that evening in Wilmington, North Carolina, they subsisted on string beans and shredded wheat in a cafeteria because the hotel dining room had been taken over by service men. Mrs. Waddell was worried, tossed most of the night, and awoke with a cold the next morning. But her father was feeling gay. "I slept like a top," he said, slapping her on the knee. "I'm ashamed of feeling so young." He laughed heartily, sang off key, told stories, and recited Shakespeare, Goethe, and Schiller mile after mile.

His sense of humor was still keen. One day when he and Justice Frankfurter were talking about aged men not knowing when to quit, the Chief remarked that he had taken no chance of remaining too long on the bench.

"But you can't claim any credit for knowing when to quit," Frankfurter put in, "because God gave you a sense of humor."

"Sh-h-h-h-h!" Hughes replied, finger on lips. "I'm not supposed to have a sense of humor."

Sometimes he even reverted to bits of nonsense. When a crank wrote him a letter asking for a lock of his "silvery hair to put in a gold case," he sent it on to his daughter with this note:

> DEAR CATHERINE:
>> Well, here is a true friend.
>> He wants a lock of my hair.
>> But I am sorry to say
>> I have none I can spare.
>> So much love,
>>> FATHER.

In Washington during both his spring and fall sojourns he gave an enormous amount of time, over a period of two and a half years, to answering the author's questions. He would sit in the governor's chair, with myself across the desk, and respond to any and every sort of query, talking so fast that he would need frequently to wipe his beard with his handkerchief. His mind was not only clear but amazingly sharp. His memory—stretching over fourscore years —was encyclopedic. At no point in his career was it possible to bring to light any hidden regrets, for he had never been consumed by ambition. Never had he sought an office, except to campaign after nominations without effort on his part. "It is better to take what comes," he would say. "Poor Harding would have been happier if ambition had not driven him beyond his depth." Hughes clung to his thesis that in order to be fit to wield power a man must be ready to relinquish it at any time. Even where failure had attended his efforts, he could truthfully say, "I did the best I could." His conscience was clear; his soul free.

One more brief moment in the limelight remained to him. In April, 1946, death suddenly beckoned to Chief Justice Stone, and after the funeral President Truman called Hughes on the telephone and asked if he might come to see him. Hughes replied that, if the President wished to see him, he would come to the White House. Within an hour he was there, and after greetings had been exchanged the President remarked that he wished Hughes himself were available for the Chief Justiceship. While the Chief interpreted this as only a friendly gesture, and while he said nothing at that time about the interview, except to his son, *Time* published his picture and said flatly that Truman had asked him to head the court once more.

Hughes went over the President's list of possible nominees and spoke highly of some of the judges on it. Then he volunteered an account of his conference with President Roosevelt when Stone had been named Chief Justice in 1941. F. D. R. had questioned him about both Stone and Robert H. Jackson. Hughes had spoken very well of both, preferring Stone because of his long experience. He had come away with the distinct impression that if Stone were not chosen the mantle would fall on Jackson. As Jackson had since proved his capacity and independence as an Associate Justice, Hughes recommended him to Truman as the best available choice.[12] The President, too, was reported to be favorable to Jackson at that time, but there were threats of resignations from the court if Jackson should be chosen, and the appointment went to Secretary of the Treasury Fred M. Vinson. When Jackson, who was in Nuremberg as United States prosecutor in the war crimes trials, learned of this knifing from two of his brethren, he issued a sizzling statement that made the feud within the court front-page news throughout the land. It was a pointed illustration of how morale on the high bench had sagged since Hughes' retirement. Some months before this Justice Roberts had resigned in a state of indignation and written to the Chief:

To work under you was the greatest experience and the greatest satisfaction of my life. When you left the Court, the whole picture changed. For me it could never be the same.[13]

On April 11, 1947, Hughes attained the ripe age of eighty-five. "The only reason I have lived so long," he said, "is because I have never been absorbed in the past. Instead of brooding over disappointments, I have pushed what is done out of my mind and gone on to new activities."

As he sat in his room at the Plaza the telephone rang and a voice asked, "Is this Chief Justice Hughes?" Before he could answer there was a clatter on the wire and the connection was broken. A few minutes later the same voice asked the same question and was followed by the same sort of clatter. When the telephone rang a third time, he seized it irritably, prepared to cope with a practical joker taking advantage of the telephone strike. But this time a pleasant voice said, "This is Harry Truman," and there followed a warm birthday greeting from the President.

That evening Hughes was the guest at a family dinner given by his son.

[12] The details of Mr. Hughes' recommendation to the President were given to me in a confidential interview on May 29, 1947. Subsequently, Mr. Hughes looked over my notes of the interview and penciled in some corrections. He made no mention whatever of Secretary Vinson coming into his discussion with the President. When I took the matter up with the White House three years later, however, President Truman disputed my report that Mr. Hughes had recommended Justice Jackson and gave me a memorandum saying that Mr. Hughes had finally wound up his conversation by saying that, in his opinion, Secretary Vinson would be the best man for the Chief Justiceship.
[13] Roberts to CEH, July 16, 1945.

While he had "as wonderful a time as an old man can have," he could not help reflecting that he would never again see all his offspring together.

Early in January, 1948, he suffered a recurrence of his bleeding duodenal ulcer. Not until February 16 was he able to make his annual trip to Florida. In the interval he had lost twelve pounds and looked haggard and worn. In Florida he was very weak, and near the end of his stay he could scarcely walk to the dining room. Dr. Leonard had prescribed digitalis to stimulate the Chief's sluggish heart, but it nauseated him and left him only the choice between weakness from poor circulation and weakness from an upset digestive system. As soon as he arrived home in April he was put to bed with two nurses in attendance.

Most of his talk now was about his trips to Europe as a young man, his college days, and his grandfather's farm, although he continued to read the newspapers and magazines and the *Congressional Record*. His deepest thinking was of God and the hereafter. One night he told Mrs. Waddell that he felt he could demonstrate to his own satisfaction that there is a spiritual force operating in the world above the power and doings of men. She begged him to go on. He said he was too tired to make the explanation that night, but they would talk about it some other time. She never succeeded in getting him onto the subject again.

For every small favor his thanks were profuse. "So many people," he exclaimed one day, "to take care of an old relic. But the old relic," he added, "will not be bothersome much longer." Then, with an obvious effort at cheerfulness, he waved his hand to his daughter, wagging his fingers and smiling as he had done when she was a child. Soon he was singing. "How long since you last saw *The Pirates of Penzance*?" he asked. As if to make up for any neglect of Gilbert and Sullivan, he recited dialogue from their enchanting light operas until he was ready to sleep.

Hughes was well aware that the end was approaching. He talked frequently of death in a half-joking manner. It was always, "When I have turned up my toes . . ." By way of avoiding self-pity he would say, "I've been the luckiest man in the world. I've had everything. I've drunk the wine of life to the bottom of the glass. Now only the dregs are left."

But he would not sit around and wait for the Inevitable Intruder. Feeling weary and irritable in Washington, he decided to make the trip to Cape Cod in spite of his weakness. Dr. Leonard asked him if he really thought he was strong enough to go. "I have more reserve strength than you think," he replied. His nurse refused to accompany him alone, and Dr. Leonard took the same train without letting the Chief know about it. He was furious when he found out. There was no need for "babying" him in that fashion.

At the cottage near the Wianno Club, where he once more joined the Gossett family, Hughes seemed to experience a renewal of strength. But it was of short duration. When an attack of uremic poisoning and congestive heart failure struck him, he sank fast. The doctors put him in an oxygen tent, and Mrs. Gossett called her sister and brother. By the time they arrived he seemed a little better, and they were afraid that if they went in to see him he would know that the hour was at hand. Finally, Mrs. Gossett told him that she had called her sister and brother the day before when he had been so ill.

"They shouldn't have come," he said.

"Don't you want to see them?" she asked.

"You bet I do," he replied.

In his last hours, however, he said he would rather be alone. They waited on the porch outside his room. In the afternoon he lapsed into a coma; he did not suffer. His period of helplessness had been cut short. Fully prepared for the great adventure, he drew his last breath at 9:15 P.M. on August 27, 1948,

By Clifford Berryman in the *Washington Sunday Star*, August 29, 1948.

EPITAPH FOR A GREAT AMERICAN

as unpretentiously as he had drawn his first eighty-six years and four and a half months before. He had often remarked that it is almost impossible to come into or go out of this world gracefully, but such gracefulness as there can be in death he attained.

A wave of sadness went out over the nation. Pointing to Hughes' career as a "superb example of a life dedicated to reason and justice in human affairs," President Truman issued a proclamation ordering flags flown at half-mast until after the funeral service. Governor Dewey did the same in New York. Everywhere men realized that one of the great minds of the century had come to rest. To those who knew him best it was as if a towering peak had suddenly disappeared from the horizon.

The funeral was held in Riverside Church in New York. More than 1600 officials, judges, lawyers, former associates, and personal friends filled the church. The service was brief and simple but full of dignity and profound emotion. The Reverend Dr. Fosdick spoke feelingly of "strong nails that hold the world together" and of "forget-me-nots in the Alps"—the little human incidents among the towering peaks of achievement. As Hughes was laid to rest beside his wife in beautiful Woodlawn Cemetery, eulogies filled the press and dropped from many tongues. Great men searched for words to describe "so magnificent a mind, so elevated a character." But Hughes himself had penned the lines that seemed most appropriate:

The most beautiful and the rarest thing in the world is a complete human life, unmarred, unified by intelligent purpose and uninterrupted accomplishment, blessed by great talent employed in the worthiest activities, with a deserved fame never dimmed and always growing.

His words had been spoken in tribute to Holmes, but they are a true reflection of his own career. On the strength of his own industry, character, and intellect he had touched the superlative. The sum of what he took from life is dwarfed only by the almost unfathomable total of what he gave in return.

Appendix I

DAVID CHARLES HUGHES

WE FIRST hear of Hugh Hughes, who hailed from Carnarvonshire, North Wales, when he joined the famous "farm and labour colony" at Trevecca, established prior to 1769 by Howell Harris, the fiery apostle of the Methodist Revival. When Harris' evangelical efforts were interrupted in 1751 by a breakdown in health, he decided "to sell all I have . . . and build an Alms House and School House and employ as many as I could of the followers." [1] Every member of the "Family" thus assembled at Trevecca was required to cast all personal possessions into the common purse and to submit to strict discipline, including three religious services a day, the first at five o'clock in the morning. Sixty trades were followed within the "Family," and so long as Howell Harris lived this "marvellous experiment, . . . a reformatory and monastery all in one," enjoyed "a strange success." [2]

In this stern spiritual environment Hugh Hughes courted and married Jane Owen in 1773. The eldest of their three children, Nathan Hughes, who was baptized February 9, 1780, was to become Charles Evans Hughes' grandfather. Nathan was apprenticed to the printing trade at Trevecca. Being "naturally gifted" and having "literary tastes," according to the records of the colony, he wrote and printed in Wales a short biography of Howell Harris. Sometime before 1828 he married Jane Evans from the Vale of Clivyd in North Wales, who contributed to her famous grandson his middle name. The couple moved to Tredegar in Monmouthshire, England, where he engaged in business and became a schoolmaster. It was at Tredegar that David Charles Hughes was born to them on June 24, 1832, the youngest of six children. [3]

Information as to the life of young David Charles before he migrated to the United States is meager. His father, Nathan Hughes, died at the age of about sixty-five when the lad was in his thirteenth year. His elder brother Samuel had not survived young manhood. The family consisted, then, of Jabez, John Richard, Jane, and Eliza Hughes in addition to their mother and young David Charles. The latter acquired a great respect for his brother Jabez, who was a man of wide reading, intellectual ability, independence of character, and kindly disposition. His brother John Richard was in the process of becoming an eminent preacher of the Calvinistic Methodist denomination. Having been brought up in a religious atmosphere and being fond of public speaking, young David Charles also had his eye on the ministry, but first he became a printer. He worked at his trade at Merthyr Tydvil and for a time was employed on the staff of the *Hereford Times*. [4] What schooling he had is not known, but "he was very studious and read widely, devoting himself

---

[1] Script, "The Hughes Family," sent to Charles E. Hughes by his cousin, Reverend Howell Harris Hughes.
[2] *Ibid.*   [3] CEH, Notes, pp. 3–4.
[4] *South Wales News* (Cardiff), Nov. 7, 1916.

chiefly to history and biography." In speaking of his efforts at self-improvement, he often quoted from Bailey's *Festus:*

> I know what study is: it is to toil
> Hard, through the hours of the sad midnight watch,
>
>   ·   ·   ·   ·   ·
>
> Wring a slight sleep out of the couch, and see
> The self-same moon which lit us to our rest,
> Her place scarce changed perceptibly in Heaven,
> Now light us to renewal of our toils.[5]

Apparently his first opportunity to preach came in 1854–1855 when he was licensed for that purpose and put on the Wesleyan Hereford Circuit. Then a new idea took firm root in his mind. He happened to read the story of another printer who had left his home and succeeded in making a name for himself in that new and thriving land called America. It was Benjamin Franklin's *Autobiography.* Young Hughes was deeply impressed. He had no friends in the United States, not even an acquaintance. Nor was there any opening or particular prospect that lured him. Yet he decided to leave his native land and become an American.

It may well be that the prospect of having to wait some time for a permanent assignment in England or Wales influenced his decision. One of the letters he carried with him to the New World said that he would have offered himself to the English Conference but was afraid that he would have to wait longer than was convenient in view of the number of applicants. Other reasons for his going, however, seem to predominate. Benjamin Roberts, superintendent of the Swansea Circuit, gave the young Welsh preacher a letter of recommendation which stated that "had this good brother offered himself to the full work of the Ministry in his native country, he would undoubtedly have been accepted and stationed on a circuit as soon as an opening should occur." But he thought it to be "his providential call to cross the Atlantic with a view to offer himself to the full work of the Ministry in the Methodist Episcopal Church of America." [6]

Underlying this desire to preach in America was a no less positive wish to be an American. David Charles Hughes was a republican by conviction; having gained an affection for the United States from the books he had read in the little print shops of England and Wales, he longed to identify himself with that challenging land across the sea. The fact that he intended to remain a preacher suggests that he sought neither fame nor fortune, but the idea of sharing the life and the experiences of a free people in a republic of their own making was alluring to him.

His family took a sharply differing view. Jane Hughes, his sister, who married Edward Jones, a colliery agent at Abertillery, Monmouthshire, a man of importance in that community, had only angry resentment for what she regarded as her brother's rash undertaking. With a woman of her dominating personality leading the family's opposition to his venture, David Charles must have spent some very uncomfortable days before his departure. But he held to his resolution and sailed for New York on the *Jacob A. Westervelt*, arriving on September 20, 1855, at the age of twenty-three.

[5] CEH, Notes, p. 7.   [6] *Ibid.,* p. 8.

Appendix II

MARY CATHERINE CONNELLY

THE CONNELLYS are an old American family. Tradition handed down to successive generations says that they came from the province of Ulster (northern Ireland) to Ulster County, New York. "Michel Connolly" (the name is variously spelled) appears as one of the freeholders of Kingston who signed the "Agreement to Maintain Constitutional Rights," on July 1, 1775.[1] This same Michael Connelly, or a son by that name, was an officer in the Revolutionary War. He served with General Clinton, commander of the Revolutionary forces in New York [2] and later Governor of New York and Vice President of the United States. On July 11, 1777, General Clinton recommended his devoted follower to General Washington for a commission in the Continental Army. "The Bearer Mr. Connolly," he wrote, "is the Person I formerly mentioned to your Excellency as a supernumerary Officer, I having given a Warrant to him as a 1st Lieutenant after the 4 Companies officered by me were compleat." [3]

Among Michael Connelly's eight children was William Connelly, who was born in 1769 and lived until 1835. A printed obituary found in his Bible handed down through the Hughes family says that he was a physician of repute at Saugerties, about twelve miles from Kingston, and a Baptist minister. He married Lydia Merihew, who was of English descent. Their son, William Connelly, Jr., born in Shandaken, Ulster County, in 1807, became the grandfather of Charles E. Hughes. The younger William Connelly did not follow his father's profession, but made his start as a contractor and builder. Soon after his marriage to Margaret Ann Terpenning on July 11, 1829, he contracted to build some tanneries in the wilds of Delaware County. It was there among the beautiful hills near Margaretville—then still unspoiled—that Mary Catherine Connelly was born on November 22, 1830.

Her maternal ancestors were chiefly Dutch. The line has been traced back to Barent Burhans, a weaver, and his wife Elizabeth who had moved into Holland from Wesel, Germany, near the Dutch frontier, and were married at Deventer in 1593.[4] Apparently they were of "Holland extraction." Across the street from the Burhans home lived an ancestor of Justice Willis Van Devanter.[5] More than three hundred years later a descendant from each of those homes found time between the writing of opinions for the Supreme Court of the United States to speculate as to whether their ancestors hobnobbed together and chatted over their schnapps about the virtues of the remarkable new plant being imported from Virginia—"quite unable to imagine the part their remote descendants would be called upon to play in the marvelous new world." [6] One of Barent's and Elizabeth's three children was

---

[1] Schoonmaker, *History of Kingston*, 1888, pp. 517–518.
[2] *Public Papers of George Clinton as First Governor of New York* (published by the State, 1899), I, 566.
[3] *Id.*, II, 102, 103.
[4] Burhan's Genealogy, pp. 3, 4.
[5] Van Devanter to CEH, Nov. 2, 1935.
[6] CEH, Notes, p. 12*a*.

Jacob Burhans, who came to America as a soldier in the Netherlands service on the *Esopus* and settled at Wiltwyck (Kingston, New York) about 1660. The following year he was appointed "Collector" by the Honorable Lord Petrus Stuyvesant, and in 1666 he was elected and confirmed Schepen (justice-magistrate) of the court at Wiltwyck. Jacob's son, Jan Burhans, arrived in America in 1663 on the *Bonte Koe* (Spotted Cow). A decade later he was magistrate for the town of Swaenburgh and in 1693 he became magistrate of the Town Court at Kingston.

Mary Connelly was in the seventh generation from Jan Burhans. The line was Dutch, save for the infusion of German when Deborah Ostrander, great-granddaughter of Jan Burhans, married Leonard Krows. Leonard was born in Kingston, but his father, John Krows, was from Germany. Both fought in the Revolutionary War as soldiers in the First Regiment of Ulster County.[7] Leonard, who had enlisted when he was only sixteen, was wounded and received a pension.[8] His eldest daughter Mariah married Tjerck Vilie Terpenning (Tjerck's father, Henricus Terpenning, had also fought in the Revolution and received a commission from General Washington) and they were the parents of Margaret Ann Terpenning, who married William Connelly, Jr.

To William and Margaret Connelly their Old World connections seemed very remote. Yet they brought up their children in the traditions of thrift and self-reliance characteristic of Mrs. Connelly's Dutch ancestors. Mary Catherine, the eldest, became a little mother to her brothers and sister. Her brother, Henry Cantine Connelly, was her best loved companion. Later he became a successful man of business, first at New Salem and then at Kingston. Succeeding to his father's business at Eddyville, he greatly extended its operations and his firm (Connelly & Shaffer) at one time owned extensive slate quarries. His reputation for integrity and sound judgment took him to the State Senate in 1874–1875 and again in 1886–1887. The dignity of his manner and appearance in his full suit of black broadcloth made a lasting impression on his nephew, Charlie Hughes.[9] Mary Connelly's only sister, Cathalina, who was fourteen years younger than she, became Mrs. Alfred Van Nostrand of Kingston. Her younger brother, Carey Simpson Connelly, became active in Ulster County politics and for many years was employed in the Customs House in New York City.

[7] *New York in the Revolution* (published by the State, 1904), pp. 189, 206, 403.
[8] CEH, Notes, p. 12*b*.   [9] *Ibid.*, p. 17.

INDEX